Also in the Variorum Collected Studies Series:

CHARLES M. de la RONCIERE
Religion paysanne et religion urbaine en Toscane (c.1280-c.1450)

ROGER E. REYNOLS
Law and Liturgy in the Latin Church, 5th-12th Centuries

ROSAMOND McKITTERICK
Books, Scribes and Learning in the Frankish Kingdoms, 6th-9th Centuries

CYRILLE VOGEL
En rémission des péchés
Recherches sur les systèmes pénitentiels dans l'Eglise latine (IIe-XIIIe siècles)

PAUL FREEDMAN
Church, Law and Society in Catalonia, 900-1500

CHARLES W. JONES
Bede, the Schools and the Computus

RICHARD E. SULLIVAN
Christian Missionary Activity in the Early Middle Ages

JACQUES DUBOIS
Aspects de la vie monastique en France au Moyen Age

HARRY A. MISKIMIN
Cash, Credit and Crisis in Europe, 1300-1600

YVES DOSSAT
Évolution de la France méridionale, 1249-1328

KATHERINE FISCHER DREW
Law and Society in Early Medieval Europe

ROBERT-HENRI BAUTIER
Sur l'histoire économique de la France médiévale

ROBERT HENRI-BAUTIER
Recherches dur l'histoire de la France médiévale

ELIZABETH A.R. BROWN
Politics and Institutions in Capetian France

COLLECTED STUDIES SERIES

Society, Law, and Trade in Medieval Montpellier

Professor Kathryn L. Reyerson

Kathryn L. Reyerson

Society, Law, and Trade in Medieval Montpellier

VARIORUM
1995

Published by VARIORUM
Ashgate Publishing Limited
Gower House, Croft Road,
Aldershot, Hampshire GU11 3HR
Great Britain

Ashgate Publishing Company
Old Post Road,
Brookfield, Vermont 05036
USA

ISBN 0-86078-460-6

British Library CIP Data
Reyerson, Kathryn
Society, Law and Trade in Medieval Montpellier.
(Variorum Collected Studies Series; CS475)
I. Title. II. Series.
944. 8402

US Library of Congress CIP Data
Reyerson, Kathryn.
Society, Law and Trade in Medieval Montpellier / Kathryn Reyerson.
p. cm. -- (Collected Studies Series; CS475)
Includes bibliographical references.
ISBN 0-86078-460-6 (alk. paper)
1. Montpellier (France)--History. 2. France--History--Medieval period, 987-1515. 3. Montpellier (France)--Social conditions. 4. Montpellier (France) Commerce--History.
I. Title. II. Series: Collected Studies; CS475.
DC801.M81R49 1995
944' . 84--dc20 94-29911
CIP

The paper used in this publication meets the minimum requirements of the American National Standard for Information Sciences – Permanence of Paper for Printed Library Materials, ANSI Z39.48-1984. ∞ ™

Printed by Galliard (Printers) Ltd
Great Yarmouth, Norfolk, Great Britain

COLLECTED STUDIES SERIES CS475

CONTENTS

This volume contains x + 308 pages

PREFACE

My research into the history of medieval Montpellier spans twenty-five years. I was inspired in my early work by the late Robert S. Lopez, Stephan G. Kuttner, André Gouron, Danièle Neirinck and Guy Romestan. My debt to each one of them looms large. The twelve articles reproduced here represent themes of continuing scholarly interest to me. Although the southern French town of Montpellier has enjoyed significant research emphasis from the early works of the nineteenth-century historian Alexandre Germain and the early twentieth-century historians Louise Guiraud and Louis J. Thomas and more recently, in the works of the late Jean Combes, the complexities of urban life in a town as large as Montpellier are such that much more remains to be written.

Montpellier was in the twelfth through the fourteenth centuries first a divided lordship under the Guilhem family and the bishop of Maguelone; the lay lordship became a possession of the kings of Aragon in 1204. At the death of Jacme I of Aragon and Majorca in 1276, Montpellier passed to the cadet branch of the family. The king of France purchased the episcopal quarter of Montpellier from the bishop of Maguelone in 1293 and the lay lordship from Jacme III of Majorca in 1349.

In the Middle Ages Montpellier was among the main urban centers on the Mediterranean between Genoa and Barcelona. The town had a diverse population with numerous agricultural workers and significant representation in local and international commerce and finance. The University of Montpellier attracted students from all over southern Europe specializing in medicine and law.

Society, Law, and Trade in Medieval Montpellier explores the social, economic, and legal dimensions of life in this Lower Languedocian town in the late Middle Ages. Montpellier was a magnet for in-migrants from all over southern France and from Spain and Italy. This town of 30,000 to 40,000 people was the site of much commercial activity in local, regional, and international trade. An active market in rural real estate and urban housing characterized the period 1293–1348, as did a full investment agenda in real property rights. Women of Montpellier invested heavily in urban real estate.

The urban economic infrastructure was sustained by apprenticeship training in trades and commercial occupations which prepared the transition to new generations and offered a form of old-age security to the generation in power. Young women as well as men were participants in apprenticeship, though in a narrowly defined sex-specific sphere, the food and textile trades. Young women passed from the control of their fathers to that of their masters under apprenticeship.

Trade was the basis of the urban economy as Montpellier fulfilled its role of *entrepôt* and intermediary between the Mediterranean world and northern Europe. Studies in this volume examine the silk trade, the cloth trade, and the grain trade. Specific study of women's participation in a wide spectrum of business activities reveals sedentary investments in long-distance trade and in local trade. Of foreign immigrant communities active in Montpellier, the Lucchese stand out because of their frequent role as mintmasters of the French royal mint of nearby Sommières, which was transferred to Montpellier and as a result of the impact of products of the Lucchese silk industry on Montpellier trade.

The active market in Montpellier occasioned the need for supervision of economic activities, a responsibility assumed by the consular administration. A celebrated case of saffron fraud illustrates the complexities of the urban juridical environment with French royal courts, Majorcan courts, and the episcopal court of Maguelone. Criminality brought the court systems into conflict over the issue of asylum in local religious establishments. The civil courts claimed increasing influence of jurisdiction over the old concept of religious asylum.

Usury was another legal issue of significance in this economically dynamic town. Again the situation was complicated by the differing positions of canon law and the church, of the communal charter of 1204, and of the kings of France and Aragon-Majorca. Montpellier merchants occasionally ran afoul of French attempts to exploit the financial position of the Jews and the Italians by accusing them of usury and confiscating their credits. Overall however, the ecclesiastical prohibition of usury seems to have had little effect in practice on the trade and finance of Montpellier.

The Black Death dealt a tremendous blow to the population of Montpellier, but in terms of religious orientation, significant changes can be noted in testamentary behavior before 1348. The early fourteenth century saw an upsurge in loyalty to the Franciscans whose house became an overwhelming burial choice for Montpelliérains. These religious enthusiasms were only reinforced by the crisis of the plague.

I wish to acknowledge the assistance over the years of the archivists of the Archives Municipales de Montpellier and the Archives Départementales de l'Hérault. Thanks are also due to the University of Minnesota for support of my research. These essays exploit the extraordinarily rich archival resources of Montpellier – charters and notarial registers – of the period before 1350. Some of the many facets of the medieval past of Montpellier are revealed in this examination of its society and economy in the pre-plague era.

KATHRYN L. REYERSON

Minneapolis
May, 1994

PUBLISHER'S NOTE

The articles in this volume, as in all others in the Collected Studies Series, have not been given a new, continuous pagination. In order to avoid confusion, and to facilitate their use where these same studies have been referred to elsewhere, the original pagination has been maintained wherever possible.

Each article has been given a Roman number in order of appearance, as listed in the Contents. This number is repeated on each page and quoted in the index entries.

ACKNOWLEDGEMENTS

Grateful acknowledgement is made to the following publishers, societies and journals for their permission to reprint the articles included in this volume: the Regents of the University of California (I); the Committee for Medieval Studies at the University of British Columbia (II); JAI Press Inc., Greenwich, Conn. (III); The American Society of Church History, Chicago, Ill. (IV); Duke University Press, Durham, N.C. (V); *The Journal of Medieval History* (VI); A Giuffrè Editore SpA, Milan (VII); Indiana University Press, Bloomington, Ind. (VIII); Istituto Storico Lucchese, Lucca (IX); the *Journal of European Economic History* (X); Editions Edouard Privat SA, Toulouse (XI); the Société Archéologique de Montpellier (XII).

I

PATTERNS OF POPULATION ATTRACTION AND MOBILITY: THE CASE OF MONTPELLIER, 1293–1348

In his recent work, *Medieval Regions and Their Cities,* J. C. Russell noted the rapid growth of the town of Montpellier to dominance over the region of Lower Languedoc from its first appearance in the documents at the end of the tenth century to the early fourteenth century.[1] By 1300 the town had reached its peak medieval population of between 30,000 and 40,000 inhabitants.[2] This remarkable expansion has given rise to considerable speculation concerning its origins. In general, demographic studies have shown that the population growth of a settlement could owe its explanation to biological, economic, geographic and other factors.[3] Some, such as

[1] J. C. Russell, *Medieval Regions and Their Cities* (Newton Abbot 1972) 161. I am indebted to Danièle Neirinck, formerly Conservateur aux Archives départementales de l'Hérault, Montpellier, and now Directeur des Archives de l'Aude, Carcassonne, for her guidance concerning the use of apprenticeship and work contracts and her advice in medieval demography. I am also grateful to R. S. Lopez for his reading of an earlier draft of this study and for his suggestions. I appreciate the advice of Josiah C. Russell upon his reading of the manuscript, as I do that of Russell B. Adams of the Department of Geography of the University of Minnesota. I thank the Inter-Library Loan Division of Wilson Library, University of Minnesota, for assistance in obtaining necessary works.

* [2] There exist no documents before the *compoix* of the fifteenth century to permit population estimates. J. C. Russell, "L'Évolution démographique de Montpellier au moyen âge," *Annales du Midi* 74 (1962) 345-360, made a somewhat exaggerated estimate of 40,000 for the population of Montpellier in the medieval period. With the considerations of surface area and type of habitation common in the town, a top figure might be 40,000, but 30,000 may well be more accurate. Jean Baumel, *Histoire d'une seigneurie du Midi de la France* 1: *Naissance de Montpellier (985-1213)* (Montpellier 1969) 224-230, made an estimate of the peak twelfth-century population from an analysis of tax lists in the seigneurial cartulary of Montpellier, the *Liber instrumentorum memorialium.* His study yielded a figure of between 6,000 and 7,500. He then counted an additional 2,000 for the outlying rural settlements attached to Montpellier. Using the figure of 9,000 for the twelfth-century population, expansion to 30,000 by the fourteenth century would seem plausible.

[3] The most useful reference in historical demography remains R. Mols, *Introduction à la démographie historique des villes d'Europe du XIVe au XVIIIe siècle*, 3 vols. (Louvain 1955). See also Gideon Sjoberg, *The Preindustrial City, Past and Present* (New York 1960). As more information concerning medieval demography becomes available, it is increasingly difficult to generalize about the urban demographic profile; each urban situation was unique. As far as demographic models go, Montpellier resembles Toulouse in some respects. See Philippe Wolff, *Commerces et marchands de Toulouse* (Paris 1954) 67ff. Using Wolff's method with data drawn from extant wills, I have calculated that there were fewer than two children, on the average, per household in Montpellier in the period 1293-1348. Wolff's findings were comparable.

*** p. 257, note 2, line 1, read: There exist no documents before the *compoix* of the late fourteenth and fifteenth centuries to permit population...**

the biological factor of fertility, are difficult to measure in any pre-modern era; yet demographic studies in the Middle Ages, hampered though they are by a lack of adequate statistics, remain feasible. The following examination of the attraction of population is an effort to explore one potential growth mechanism in the demographic history of Montpellier.

The attraction of Montpellier as an urban center and the movements of local population have been described in general terms by Charles Higounet and J. C. Russell.[4] Using the surname data of consular lists in the twelfth and thirteenth centuries, Higounet determined a region of attraction extending in length from Roquemaure on the Rhone River to the corridor of Aquitaine in western France, with a maximum of density of attraction along the road through the Narbonnaise between Béziers and Nîmes. To this area he added Spanish relations revealed by a probable Aragonese colony in Montpellier, Provençal ties and an Italian colony.[5] He signaled the close connections between the Quercy region of central France and Montpellier which additional studies by Jean Combes and Jean Lartigaut have amply confirmed.[6] Finally, Higounet placed emphasis on the immediate region of Montpellier as a source of population for the town.[7] J. C. Russell, using the geographical concepts of regionalism and rank-size arrangements, defined the region over which Montpellier was the dominant urban center as the area stretching from Nice in the east to Carcassonne in the southwest and Perpignan in the south.[8] The northern boundary of this field of dominance cut through central France south of Le Puy and Valence. The geographic fields of attraction, identified by both historians, encompass many of the same territories which were indisputably the major sources of newcomers to Montpellier. They fail, however, to reveal details of the mechanisms and patterns of attraction of population. It is my purpose in this study to examine population movement in the period 1293-1348 from which notarial records are first preserved.[9] By way of back-

[4] Charles Higounet, "Mouvements de population dans le Midi de la France du XIe au XVe siècle, d'après les noms de personne et de lieu," *Annales: Economies, sociétés, civilisations* 8 (1953) 1-24, and Russell (n. 1 above).

[5] *Ibid.* 12. The problems of methodology are numerous in the study of medieval population movements. A recent article by Benjamin Kedar, "Toponymic Surnames as Evidence of Origin: Some Medieval Views," *Viator* 4 (1973) 123-129, summarized the traditional positions of debate. On the Spanish colony, see Higounet 8-9.

[6] Higounet 19, on the Quercy migration. See also J. Lartigaut, "Témoignages sur la dépopulation du Quercy au XIVe siècle," *Annales du Midi* 84 (1972) 5-15 and J. Combes, "Une famille de négociants quercynols à Montpellier et à Marseille au XIIIe siècle," *Bulletin de la Fédération historique du Languedoc Méditerranéen et du Roussillon* (Perpignan 1953, Saint-Gilles 1954), offprint.

[7] Higounet (n. 4 above) 12: "On y trouve [in the consular lists] les noms des villages des environs immédiats: Lattes, Juvignan, Orques, Prades."

[8] Russell (n. 1 above) 162, table.

[9] Collections of notarial registers of the Archives départementales de l'Hérault, série II E 95/368 – II E 95/377, spanning the years 1327-1348, were consulted. Also examined were registers of the Archives municipales de Montpellier, série II, 1, 2, 3, the first of which begins in 1293. After 1348 there is a lacuna of more than a decade before registers of the 1360s are extant. The abbreviations A. M. Montp. (Archives municipales) and A. D. Hérault (Archives départementales) will be used hereafter in the notes.

ground two related issues will be treated briefly: the periodization of the expansion of Montpellier and the problem of emigration.

J. C. Russell conjectured that the dominance of Montpellier was due to the decline of Marseilles which he attributed to the latter's reduction by Genoa.[10] However, the long series of treaties between Marseilles and Genoa in the twelfth and thirteenth centuries never resulted in the destruction of Marseilles, although the Genoese, as evidenced in other diplomatic endeavors, desired that end.[11] The decadence of Marseilles seems rather to have been the result of its conquest by Charles of Anjou in 1262 and the subsequent subordination of Marseillais interests to Angevin political designs.[12]

While the decline of Marseilles may have contributed to the rise of Montpellier, a conjuncture of circumstances favoring this emergence makes unlikely the isolation of any one conclusively explanatory clue to development. The reasons for the town's growth have yet to be satisfactorily illuminated. Montpellier was never a Mediterranean port, but its site on firm ground at several kilometers from the sea made it secure and accessible.[13] For coastal commerce, Montpellier was able to use the small Languedocian ports, especially Lattes. From the late thirteenth century the newly constructed port of Aigues-Mortes served as an outlet for Montpellier in the Levant trade.[14] The proximity of these ports created a propitious context for commercial expansion.

A tentative explanation for the development of Montpellier in an international commercial role lies in the influence of Genoese and Pisan commercial designs on southern French towns as a whole in the twelfth century and in the failure of those ambitions at the end of the century. Montpellier first fell under Genoese control during the urban revolt of 1141-1143. The local seigneur, Guilhem VI, was able to quell this uprising thanks to the assistance of the count of Barcelona and the Genoese.[15] The Pisans also participated in the rescue enterprise.[16] In recompense for

[10] Russell (n. 1 above) 161.

[11] Régine Pernoud, *Histoire du commerce de Marseille* 1: *Le Moyen Age jusqu'en 1291* (Paris 1949) 181-209. See also André Dupont, *Les relations commerciales entre les cités maritimes de Languedoc et les cités méditerranéennes d'Espagne et d'Italie du Xe au XIIIe siècle* (Nîmes 1942) 119.

[12] Pernoud 346-360 and Edouard Baratier, *Histoire du commerce de Marseille* 2 (Paris 1951) 207-219.

[13] For a discussion of Montpellier's geography, see studies by Gaston Galtier, "Les conditions géographiques de Montpellier," in *Mélanges géographiques offerts à Philippe Arbos* (Clermont-Ferrand 1953) 237-246, and "Le vignoble et le vin dans le Languedoc oriental de la fin du XIe siècle à la Guerre de Cent Ans," in *Études médiévales offertes à M. le doyen Fliche de l'Institut* (Montpellier 1952).

[14] On the history of Aigues-Mortes, see for example, Jean Combes, "Origine et passé d'Aigues-Mortes," *Revue d'histoire économique et sociale* 50 (1972) 304-326.

[15] Alexandre Germain, *Histoire du commerce de Montpellier* (Montpellier 1861) 1.93-94. See also Dupont (n. 11 above) 74-75.

[16] *La chronique romane: Le Petit Thalamus de Montpellier*, ed. F. Pégat, E. Thomas and Desmazes (Montpellier 1840) 329: entry for 1141 mentions only the count of Barcelona and the Genoese, but galleys under the command of a Pisan took part in the rescue. See Dupont (n. 11 above) 75.

this aid, Guilhem VI granted certain commercial advantages to the Genoese and the Pisans: exemption from taxation, *fondachi* at Montpellier, protection for their representatives and support against the count of Toulouse.[17] Guilhem VI, who was not unaware of the positive influence of Italian commercial activity in his lands, provided leverage for the bargaining position of Montpellier through these favors to both dynamic Italian towns. The rivalry of Genoa and Pisa was already legendary by 1143, and the possibility of playing one master off against the other would facilitate for Montpellier the emancipation of its international commerce.

The Genoese made harsher exactions of Montpellier in a treaty which dates from about 1150.[18] The most telling regulation was the prohibition for Montpelliérains to sail eastward beyond Genoa, thus eliminating the possibility of trade with the Levant.[19] However inhibiting this obligation seemed, the interaction between Genoa and Montpellier ultimately served the latter well. In the west, the most decisive event for southern French history in the second half of the twelfth century was the defeat of the political ambitions of the house of Toulouse for the creation of a southern French and Catalan empire. The Genoese were collaborators in 1174 with their traditional enemies of Toulouse in this grand design which would have resulted in a Genoese commercial monopoly.[20] From 1182 the difficulties of the Italians in Byzantium and the conquests of Saladin directed Genoese and Pisan energies away from southern France.[21] The collapse of commercial monopoly and the renewal of problems in the Near East left Montpellier and its counterparts free to profit from the trading patterns already established by the Italian commercial giants.

Montpellier embarked upon independent diplomatic ventures in the Levant, profiting from the crusaders' need for support.[22] Montpelliérains frequented Genoese markets in the late twelfth century.[23] While pursuing their Levantine and Italian activities, they broadened their commercial efforts geographically. In 1222 and 1229 they obtained approval and protection from the count of Champagne for their presence in his lands and their establishment at the fairs.[24] In 1246 it was a Montpelliérain who was chosen captain of the southern French merchants in Champagne.[25]

[17] Dupont 75.

[18] The reasons for dating the treaty in 1150 are resumed by Dupont 78 n. 1.

[19] *Ibid.* 79. Additional privileges granted to the Genoese included tax exemption, renunciation of shipwreck rights by Guilhem VI, and his promise to refuse protection to all except pilgrimage ships coming from the high seas which the Genoese sought to control.

[20] Pernoud (n. 11 above) 186. Peace in 1176 between the house of Aragon and that of Toulouse readjusted the balance of power.

[21] Dupont (n. 11 above) 119.

[22] Germain (n. 15 above) 2.1-24.

[23] See, for example, M. Chiaudano and M. Moresco, eds., *Il cartolare di Giovanni Scriba,* 2 vols. (Turin 1935) passim, and M. Chiaudano, ed., *Oberto Scriba de Mercato (1186)* (Turin 1940) passim.

[24] F. Bourquelot, *Étude sur les foires de Champagne* (Paris 1865) 1.155, and R.-H. Bautier, "Les foires de Champagne: Recherches sur une évolution historique," *Recueils de la Société Jean Bodin* 5: *La foire* (Brussels 1953) 121.

[25] Germain (n. 15 above) 1.201, no. 14; 202, nos. 15 and 16.

The progress of commercial activity began for Montpellier in the second half of the twelfth century, and these succeeding milestones only chart the directions of growth of a commercial network linking Montpellier with Champagne and the Levant.

As an international commercial center Montpellier presents a desirable urban context in which to study population movement. Already in the 1160s the cosmopolitan atmosphere of the town caught the eye of that seasoned world traveler, Benjamin of Tudela, who wrote:

> You meet here with Christian and Mahometan merchants from all parts: from Algarve [Portugal], Lombardy, the Roman Empire [Byzantium], Egypt, Palestine, Greece, France, Spain and England. People of all tongues meet here, chiefly in consequence of the traffic of the Genoese and Pisans.[26]

Montpellier was a typical Mediterranean town in the Middle Ages in that it had a heterogeneous population with numerous agricultural workers as well as local and international merchants and artisans. The presence of a renowned university added legal specialists and doctors of medicine to the urban elite.[27] An unusual feature of the urban environment by medieval standards was the absence of an indigenous cloth industry and its accompanying proletariat.[28] Only the cloth-dyeing trade was present. The reputation of Montpellier was based upon commerce, finance and the prominence of its university.

By the second half of the thirteenth century Montpellier was the major urban center on the Mediterranean coast between Genoa and Barcelona. However, its prosperity was to be short-lived. A mixture of commercial and agricultural crises climaxed by the devastation of the Black Death in 1348 and recurrent visitations of the plague thereafter led to a downward demographic and economic trend in the later Middle Ages, broken only by the brief interlude of Jacques Coeur's Mediterranean commercial empire in the 1440s.[29]

The mid-fourteenth century also marked a political watershed for Montpellier. Although located in an area of French domination which dated from 1229, Montpellier had been first an Aragonese and then a Majorcan enclave in French territory.[30] In 1349 Philip VI purchased the remaining Majorcan quarter of the town from James III.[31] Before this event relative political isolation had left the operations of

[26] Manuel Komroff, *Contemporaries of Marco Polo* (New York 1928) 254.

[27] On the university, see M. Boriès, "Les origines de l'Université de Montpellier," *Les universités du Languedoc au XIIIe siècle,* Cahiers de Fanjeaux 5 (Toulouse 1970) 92-107.

[28] The remaining notarial registers of 1293-1348 (see n. 9 above) carry no mention of local fullers or weavers, a lacuna pointing to this conclusion. Dyers are present in the notarial acts.

[29] On Jacques Coeur, see Louise Guiraud, *Recherches et conclusions nouvelles sur le prétendu rôle de Jacques Coeur* (Paris 1900).

[30] On the purchase of Montpellier, see Louis J. Thomas, "Montpellier entre la France et l'Aragon pendant la première moitié du XIVe siècle," in *Monspeliensia* 1 (1928-1929) 1-56. For general background on the history of Montpellier, the classic work of A. Germain, *Histoire de la commune de Montpellier,* 3 vols. (Montpellier 1851) may be consulted.

[31] Thomas (n. 30 above). Names of famous figures will be given in English. All other names have been left in the original spelling of the documents.

the Montpellier marketplace independent of serious exterior intervention. French pressure, which had increased steadily since the purchase of the episcopal quarter of the town by Philip IV in 1293, enjoyed free rein after 1349.[32] The most celebrated witness of change in Montpellier in the later fourteenth century was the poet Petrarch who had been a law student in the town in 1316-1320. In his old age he noted with regret the negative results for the former Majorcan citadel of its incorporation into the French kingdom.[33] From both economic and political considerations the present study of population movement will be limited to the period before 1350 which coincided with the expansive phase of Montpellier demography.

* * *

The discovery of the destinations of Montpellier emigrants is a far more difficult process than is the study of population attraction. Although the resulting patterns are more anecdotal than systematic, it is nonetheless useful to attempt a reconstruction of tentative trends in emigration as the natural complement of an examination of attraction. Within the region defined by Charles Higounet there were reciprocal population movements. In the twelfth century Montpelliérains, under the leadership of lords of the Guilhem family, participated in the Spanish Reconquista.[34] Higounet has cited probable emigrants from Montpellier among numerous southern French natives in residence at towns such as Saragossa and Huesca.[35] The 1204 communal charter of Montpellier elaborated on a seigneurial provision of 1190 authorizing emigration. It was stated that the men of Montpellier could, at any time, sell all their goods and, taking the proceeds, go wherever they chose without obstacle.[36] The lord

[32] A. Lecoy de la Marche, *Les relations de la France avec les royaumes de Majorque (Iles Baléares, Roussillon, Montpellier, etc.)* 2 (Paris 1892) 311ff.

[33] Francesco Petrarca, *Opera omnia,* ed. H. Petri (Basel 1554), *Rerum senilium lib.* 10 "De mutatione temporum," 960: "Et quanquam de maioribus possem, ut memoria tamen tua, nostrae astipuletur assertioni, de his quae simul ambo vidimus, cupidius tecum loquor, inde igitur simul quoque, nam quid divisim magna aetatis partis gessimus, vicina iam pubertate ad Montem Pessulanum, florentissimum tunc oppidum, iurisque ad studium delati, aliud ibi quadriennium exegimus, cuius tunc potestas, penes maiores Balearice regem erat, exiguum praeter loci angulum, Francorum regi subditum, qui ut semper praepotentium importuna vicinia est, brevi totius oppidi dominium ad se traxit, quae nam vero tunc ibi quoque tranquillitas? quae pax? quae divitiae mercatorum? quae scholarium turbat? quae copia magistrorum? quanta ibi nunc horum omnium penuria, publicarumque et privatarum rerum, quanta mutatio, et nos scimus, et cives qui utrumque viderunt tempus sentiunt." Petrarch's stay in Montpellier was described by his biographer, Jerome Squarzafico of Alexandria, in *Cartulaire de l'Université de Montpellier, 1181-1400* 1 (Montpellier 1890) 703, app. 4. Petrarch died in 1374. See also André Gouron, *L'Histoire de l'université des droits de Montpellier,* exposition catalogue (Montpellier 1963) 6.

[34] For a treatment of the Guilhem family's activities, see Archibald R. Lewis, "The Guilhem of Montpellier: A Sociological Appraisal," *Viator* 2 (1971) 159-169.

[35] Higounet (n. 4 above) 4-5.

[36] *Petit Thalamus* (n. 16 above) 8, art. 12, an. 1204: "Homines Montispessulani, quotiescumque voluerint, universa bona sua vendere, et pretium secum deferre possunt, et abire quocumque voluerint sine impedimento. Dominus vero debet eis et rebus suis et familie sue ducatum prestare per totam terram suam, et per totum posse suum. Et omnia que vendere illi voluerint in quibus dominus habebit laudimium, debet ipse dominus vel ejus bajulus sine contrarietate laudare, salvo sibi suo consilio."

of Montpellier owed them safe-conduct in his lands for their persons, those of their family and their goods.

The current of Spanish emigration from Montpellier continued in the thirteenth century with some variation of destination. Emigration to the Balearic Islands and Valencia was then prominent. The inhabitants of Montpellier who had participated under their king James I in the conquest of these lands in the years 1229-1233 were rewarded with one hundred houses in the town of Palma and with considerable urban real estate in Valencia.[37] Although some trace of real estate holdings of Montpelliérains in Majorca can still be found in the fourteenth century, there is little evidence of active cooperation between descendants of the colonists of Majorca and residents of Montpellier.[38] Acts of piracy, such as that perpetrated in 1333 by Petrus de Tornamira, a Majorcan sea captain, against merchants of Montpellier, hindered the normal flow of commerce between Montpellier and Majorca.[39] The merchants of Majorca were organized in an *universitas de Majorca* with sindics to defend them in Montpellier against reprisals ordered by the king of France.[40]

Emigrants from Montpellier appeared in Metz at the end of the thirteenth century. E. Perrin noted them in lists of induction of bourgeois into the municipality, a gesture indicative of their stature.[41] In Italy students from Montpellier in attendance in considerable numbers at the law school of Bologna in the 1260s may have been only temporary expatriots.[42] Their financial activities and their role in the scholarly book trade between Italy and France have been discussed by S. Stelling-Michaud.[43] More sustained emigration can be noted in records of the English court from the

[37] On the conquests of Majorca and Valencia, see Charles de Tourtoulon, *Études sur la maison de Barcelone, Jacme Ier le Conquérant, roi d'Aragon, comte de Barcelone, seigneur de Montpellier, d'après les chroniques et les documents inédits* (Montpellier 1863) 1.245ff.; Lecoy de la Marche (n. 26 above) 1.41ff., 75-78 and 382ff.; R. I. Burns, *The Crusader Kingdom of Valencia* (Cambridge, Mass. 1967) 2.419.

[38] Regarding real estate, I am indebted to Francisco Sevillano Colon, archivist of the Archivo historico of Mallorca, who kindly communicated the following reference to me during a visit in 1971. See Archivo historico de Mallorca, Archivos privados, Lletres reals 1, fol. 55.

In 1303 James II, king of Majorca, advised his lieutenant in Montpellier of the debts of Guillelmus Nigre of Montpellier and his wife Ricarez with regard to the Majorcan Bertrandus Morge. Ricarez had received real estate in Majorca as part of her dowry. Nigre, according to Morge, had neglected these lands in favor of his properties in Montpellier. Hence, in an assessment for debt against the property of Nigre, Morge insisted that the Montpellier properties, presumably more valuable, be considered. This incident illustrates that there were property remnants in Majorca from the thirteenth-century implantation of Montpelliérains, but that, at least in this case, there was little attempt to maintain them on the part of descendants.

[39] A. D. Hérault, II E 95/369, fol. 18v.

[40] For reprisals, see Arch. hist. Mallorca, Arch. priv., Lletres comunes 1, fol. 37v, and Lletres comunes 7, fol. 86v.

[41] E. Perrin, "Le droit de bourgeoisie et l'immigration rurale à Metz au XIIIe siècle," *Annuaire de la Société d'histoire et d'archéologie de la Lorraine* 30 (1921) 576.

[42] *Cartularium Studii Bononiensis: Documenti per la storia della università de Bologna dalle origine fino al secolo XV,* 13 vols. (Imola 1907; Bologna 1913-1936) passim.

[43] S. Stelling-Michaud, "Le transport international des manuscrits juridiques bolonais entre 1265-1320," in *Mélanges d'histoire économique et social en hommage au professeur Antony Babel* 1 (Geneva 1963) 95-127.

mid-thirteenth century to the 1320s. Montpelliérains served in various official capacities in England: as sergeants and purveyors of the wardrobe; as royal clerks and attorneys; as wine confectioners and spice suppliers.[44]

Emigration of Montpelliérains to Avignon in the fourteenth century was stimulated by the installation of the papal court, a focus of spiritual and commercial attraction for the south of France as a whole.[45] Philippus de Crusolis, damoiseau and squire of the pope, was the most prominent Montpellier merchant involved in supplying the papal court and may well have been a temporary if not a permanent emigrant. In the years 1318-1322 Crusolis provided the court with such luxuries as cloves, several varieties of ginger, pepper, "basket sugar," cinnamon, "sugar of Babylon," anise and marzipan.[46] In the entourage of Pope John XXII were to be found masters of medicine from Montpellier, Johannes de Tornamira and Johannes Jacobi, as well as other former Montpellier professors.[47]

The above examples cannot offset the impression conveyed by the limited local evidence that the late thirteenth and fourteenth centuries witnessed a decline in emigration. Departures in the earlier centuries, particularly to Spain, had been more numerous. In the later era, marriage alliances between foreign merchants and daughters of local bourgeois and mercantile families were rarely recorded.[48] The notarial acts contain only isolated examples of emigration for commercial purposes. Thus, Petrus de Calvo, merchant of Montpellier, inhabited Valencia in the 1330s and 1340s, supplying silks to the Valencian market and saffron to Montpellier.[49] Guillelmus de

[44] See the multiple volumes of the *Calendar of Patent Rolls* and the *Calendar of Liberate Rolls* for examples. Specific citations can be found in K. L. Reyerson, "Commerce and Society in Montpellier: 1250-1350," Ph.D. diss. (Yale University 1974) 1.136-139 and 2.67-68. See also Roger Dion, *Histoire de la vigne et du vin en France des origines au XIXe siècle* (Paris 1959) 313ff.

Only one Englishman, a transient, can be identified conclusively in the remaining Montpellier notaries. See A. D. Hérault, II E 95/368, fol. 10v, an. 1327. Hostilities leading to the Hundred Years War may have curbed relations between Montpellier and England. See Edouard Perroy, *The Hundred Years War* (New York 1965) 34-59, for the events leading to war.

[45] See, for example, Petrus de Gaiani, *aurifaber* (goldsmith) of Montpellier, inhabitant of Avignon: A. D. Hérault, II E 95/372, fol. 33. and Dulsolina Daure of Montpellier, inhabitant of Avignon: II E 95/372, fol. 50v. On the papal court, see Y. Renouard, *La papauté à Avignon* (Paris 1954) and G. Mollat, *Les papes d'Avignon (1305-1378)* (Paris 1912). Bernard Guillemain, "Les Français du Midi à la cour pontificale d'Avignon," *Annales du Midi* 74 (1962) 33 n. 12, cited sixteen curialists from the diocese of Maguelone in records of the papal chamber. The registers kept for tax purposes under John XXII and Innocent VI in the matter of lodgings at Avignon reveal twenty inhabitants whose place of origin was either Montpellier, Nîmes, Narbonne or their surrounding areas.

[46] K. H. Schäfer, *Die Ausgaben der apostolischen Kammer unter Johann XXII, nebst der Jahresbilanzen von 1316-1378* (Paderborn 1911) passim.

[47] B. Guillemain, *La cour pontificale d'Avignon (1309-1376): Étude d'une société* (Paris 1966) 377-379. See also Mollat (n. 45 above) 43.

[48] It is possible that in such cases the foreign merchant took up residence in Montpellier. The term *foreign* is used in this study to refer to persons of nonlocal origin.

[49] I am indebted to Guy Romestan of the Faculté des lettres et des sciences humaines of Montpellier for the following references to Valencian archival documents: Archivo del Reino de Valencia, Protocolos, nos. 2801 and 2880. See also A. D. Hérault, II E 95/370, fol. 48, and II E 95/374, act no. 312. The latter register was not foliated when I consulted it.

Cabanis, installed at Chalon-sur-Saône, furnished merchants of his Montpellier family with Burgundian wool in the 1340s.[50] In general, however, merchants of Montpellier became more sedentary as the focus of commerce narrowed amidst fourteenth-century crisis.

* * *

In contrast to the phenomenon of emigration, population attraction continued to be an important feature of the demography of Montpellier in the first half of the fourteenth century. From an early date Montpellier had been receptive to newcomers. The communal charter of 1204 specified that the foreigner who married in Montpellier and decided to establish residency would be exempt for a year and a day from the three military services required of urban inhabitants.[51] It further stated that if a foreigner who owed homage to someone for any benefice should come to reside in Montpellier, he would thenceforth be free of that homage, provided that he returned the benefice to his lord.[52] The only profession subject to a residency requirement in Montpellier was the dyeing trade. The town was especially renowned for its scarlet dyeing process. The charter of 1204 reiterated a regulation of 1181 which held that it was forbidden for a foreigner to engage in the cloth dyeing trade.[53] By the same regulation, the retail trade in cloth was closed to all foreigners except peddlers.

Statutes of 1226 revised the dyeing prohibition to permit the occupation to be assumed by a foreigner after five years' residence, or after two years' stay and marriage to a woman of Montpellier.[54] An oath of loyalty to the lord of the town – then the king of Aragon – to the town consuls and to the keepers of the town walls was also required.[55] In 1251 a further modification of rules stipulated that two years' residence and a fortune of 300 pounds of Melgueil with the promise of a ten-year stay in the town would allow a newcomer to exercise the dyeing trade, provided that he obtained the authorizations of the town consuls and of the council and guardians of the trade.[56] By the mid-thirteenth century the requirements for entry into the prestigious dyeing trade had diminished considerably.

[50] A. D. Hérault, II E 95/370, fol. 129, and II E 95/372, fol. 154. The Cabanis' activities can be studied in II E 95/374, passim.

[51] *Petit Thalamus* (n. 16 above) 42, art. 94, an. 1204: "Extraneus homo qui in villa Montispessulani ducet uxorem et ibi remanebit, liber sit per annum et diem de cavalcada et host et gacha."

[52] *Ibid.* 48, art. 106: "Si quis extraneus pro quolibet honore homo alterius fuerit, et in Montepessulano venerit pro statga, deinde liber est ab eo hominio, dumtamen honorem pro quo fuerit homo domino desemparet."

[53] *Ibid.* 48, art. 110: "Nullus extraneus homo aliquos pannos laneos in Montepessulano tingere potest in grana vel in aliquo colore: nec quis extraneus pannos aliquos in hac villa vendere debet ad tallium, nisi eos quos ad collum portaverit per villam." For the 1181 regulation, see *ibid.* 137.

[54] *Ibid.* 138, an. 1226.

[55] Sample oaths are given, *ibid.* 245-312.

[56] *Ibid.* 138-139, an. 1251.

Although a precise description of the size and nature of the population of Montpellier must remain a subject of speculation, it is possible to study the geographic origins of newcomers and some of the avenues of entrance into the business community. By the late thirteenth century the use of surnames was almost universal in the remaining notarial documents of Montpellier.[57] As a rule individuals were identified by first and last names, profession or social status and geographic origin, even when they were natives of Montpellier. In the case of residents of non-local origin, a designation such as "Bernardus Fabri of Cajarc, merchant, inhabitant of Montpellier" was employed.[58] Since the use of a placename as a surname might by the fourteenth century refer to the origin of an ancestor of a current Montpellier inhabitant rather than to a recent arrival, I have chosen to regard as newcomers only those individuals clearly designated as in the "Bernardus Fabri" example.

Ideally it would have been useful to distinguish between the potentially transient inhabitants of Montpellier such as university students, foreign merchants, workers and apprentices who might be in residence for several months or a period of years, and those who made the town their permanent home. In practice such distinctions proved impossible. In the case of apprenticeship and work contracts, which were the most valuable sources of information on the attraction of population, there was no proof that the contractants became lifetime or long-term residents.[59] Nonetheless, the establishment of origins and economic vocations of the nonlocal labor force provides one type of insight into the dynamics of attraction of Montpellier as an urban center. The findings of these contracts can be supplemented with additional data on newcomers drawn from the pre-1350 notarial registers.

For the years 1293-1348, two hundred eight contracts of work and apprenticeship are extant, sixty-seven of which involve newcomers.[60] Geographic patterns of attraction of nonlocal labor emerge from an analysis of this material. Approximately half of the nonlocal apprentices and workers (thirty-three) were natives of the towns and villages within a radius of fifty kilometers of Montpellier. Table 1 gives the number of contracts within a specific radius of distance and their frequency of distribution.

A correlation exists between distance and vocation in the thirty-three cases of

[57] See R. S. Lopez, "Concerning Surnames and Places of Origin," *Medievalia et humanistica* 8 (1954) 10, for a discussion of chronology. Higounet (n. 4 above) 10 suggests that the use of surnames was widespread by the twelfth century. By the late thirteenth century there is some certainty of surname use.

[58] See n. 114 below.

[59] Wolff (n. 3 above) 80 stated that his most coherent sources of documentation on migration to Toulouse were the apprenticeship and work contracts, of which he had a rich mine of some 1,150 acts. Although the same sources are not as abundant for Montpellier, they have proved to be the most useful type of document for the study of attraction of population.

[60] I have encountered the same problems of distinguishing in these contracts between beginner apprentices and journeymen that Wolff did (n. 3 above) 432-436. Terms referring to a learning experience, such as *disciplina,* were at times associated with terms such as *opera* which may imply that the apprentice was already productive. Three categories of contracts, pure apprenticeship, an intermediate stage involving work, and work contracts were chosen. The contracts were distributed in the following fashion:

TABLE 1

Distance (in kilometers)	*Numbers of Apprentices and Workers*	*% of Nonlocal*	% of Total
0–10	2	2.9	1
10–20	5	7.5	2.4
20–30	7	10.4	3.4
30–40	10	14.9	4.8
40–50	9	13.4	4.3
50–100	16	23.9	7.7
100–200	7	10.4	3.4
200–300	9	13.4	4.3
300+	2	2.9	1

% approximations to the nearest tenth

geographic origin within a fifty-kilometer radius. Newcomers were concentrated in the food trades, artisanal occupations and menial work, as opposed to the major retail, commercial, financial and professional vocations which forged the international reputation of Montpellier, as Table 2 shows.[61] Artisans were almost equally represented in both categories of distance, a fact suggesting their relative mobility.

			Apprenticeship		*Intermediate*		*Work*		*Total*
Notary	*Year*	*Other*	*Local*	*Nonlocal*	*Local*	*Nonlocal*	*Local*	*Nonlocal*	*Contracts*
A.M. II, 1	1293-94		3	4			1		8
A.D. II E 95/368	1327-28	2	27	5	6	1	15	4	60
A.D. II E 95/369	1333		7	8			4	1	20
A.D. II E 95/373	1333		1				1		2
A.D. II E 95/370	1336		9	2	1	1	1		14
A.D. II E 95/374	1337-42		2	1		1	1	1	6
A.D. II E 95/375	1339-40	1	1	2			4	1	9
A.D. II E 95/371	1342	1	15	7	4	1	4	2	34
A.M. II 3	1342-43						1		1
A.D. II E 95/372	1343-44	4	9	10			2	1	26
A.D. II E 95/376	1343-46						1		1
A.D. II E 95/377	1347-48	2	3	8		1	8	5	27

A.D. = A. D. Hérault — Total Contracts: 208
A.M. = A.M. Montp. — Total Nonlocal: 67

[61] Categories of Table 2: Food: bakers, butchers. Artisans: ironmongers, blacksmiths, barbers, innkeepers, cordmakers, beltmakers, coffermakers, shoemakers, silversmiths, wood merchants, tailors, knifemakers, silver-cloth workers, silk-cloth workers. Retail/Wholesale: apothecaries, mercers, drapers, linen merchants, pepperers, furriers. Commerce/Finance: changers, merchants. Artists: painters. Menial work: domestic work, physical labor (hauling, etc.). Others: business representatives, teachers, resellers, old clothes dealers, two unidentified. All distances mentioned in this study refer to approximate road distance.

TABLE 2
Vocation of Nonlocal Apprentices and Workers

Distance	*Food Trades*	*Artisans*	*Retail Wholesale*	*Commerce Finance*	*Artists*	*Menial Work*	*Others*
0–50	5	11	4	3	2	5	4
50+	2	9	12	5	1		4

In those cases where members of prestigious occupations came from distances of less than fifty kilometers, they were generally natives of towns of some importance. Saint-Thibéry, the site of a Languedocian fair, was the origin of a changer and a linen merchant.[62] Lunel, about thirty kilometers distant with a commercial and financial reputation which was the legacy of its former Jewish population, was the home of another apprentice changer and a furrier, as well as a shoemaker.[63] While the merchant from Saint-Guilhem-le-Désert and the furrier from Sauve were natives of less commercially distinguished centers, these towns were respectively sites of an important monastery and of a baronial jurisdiction. Only Viols-le-Fort, home of another linen merchant, was a rurally oriented settlement.[64]

Noteworthy is the cluster of origins within a radius of thirty to one hundred kilometers of Montpellier. The preponderance of newcomers from this area were natives of the semi-mountainous region north of Montpellier. Map 1 illustrates geographically the concentration of attraction.[65] The major roads sketched on Map 1 were supplemented by many secondary routes linking towns of minor importance. In contrast with the straight-line Roman road system which ran between major urban centers, the medieval road network consisted of a web of such routes. Access from

[62] A. D. Hérault, II E 95/374, act no. 309, and II E 95/372, fol. 11v. On the Languedocian fairs, see J. Combes, "Les foires en Languedoc au moyen âge," *Annales: Économies, sociétés, civilisations* 13 (1958) 231-259.

[63] A. D. Hérault, II E 95/371 fol. 124; II E 95/372, fols. 46v and 85. On Lunel, see T. Millerot, *Histoire de la ville de Lunel depuis son origine jusqu'en 1789* (Montpellier 1879).

[64] Sauve: A. D. Hérault, II E 95/368, 26 September 1327. St-Guilhem-le-Désert: II E 95/369, fol. 110. Viols-le-Fort: II E 95/374, act no. 238. Viols-le-Fort is about twenty kilometers northwest of Montpellier.

[65] For background on medieval road systems, see R.-H. Bautier, "Recherches sur les routes de l'Europe médiévale, 1: De Paris et des foires de Champagne à la Méditerranée par le Massif Central," *Bulletin philologique et historique* 1960 (1961) 99-143; R. S. Lopez, "The Evolution of Land Transport in the Middle Ages," *Past and Present* (1956) 17-29; J. Combes, "Transports terrestres à travers la France centrale à la fin du XIVe siècle et au commencement du XVe siècle," *Bulletin de la Fédération historique du Languedoc-Roussillon, XXIXe congrès* (Mende 1955) 3-7; Y. Renouard, "Les voies de communication entre pays de la Méditerranée et pays de l'Atlantique," in *Mélanges Louis Halphen* (Paris 1951) 587-594; Thérèse Sclafert, "Problèmes d'histoire routière: Les routes du Dauphiné et de la Provence sous l'influence du séjour des papes d'Avignon," *Annales d'histoire économique et sociale* 1 (1929) 183-192.

The two maps of this article were drawn initially by Marie-Madeleine Campère Julia, archiviste-paléographe, and produced in final form by the Cartography Laboratory of the Department of Geography, University of Minnesota. The road network which I have sketched in was inspired, in particular, by the maps and research of Bautier and Sclafert in the above articles. On the question of distances of travel in the Middle Ages, see Bautier 102-103.

Map 1: GEOGRAPHICAL ORIGIN OF APPRENTICES AND WORKERS

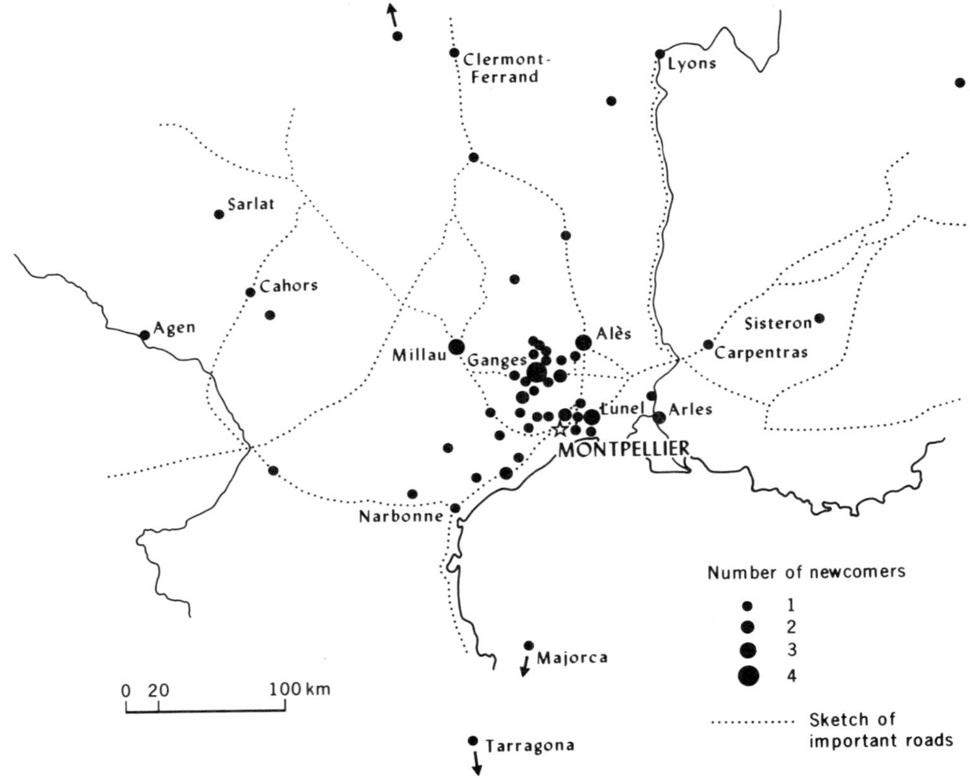

the area framed by the triangle of the towns of Millau, Alès and Ganges was facilitated by the existence of important long-distance overland trade leading along the same routes from the Mediterranean gateway of Montpellier to the Champagne fairs and to Paris.

The contracts of nonlocal workers and apprentices represent approximately 32.3 percent of the 208 extant. Of these, approximately 15.9 percent refer to newcomers from the region within a fifty-kilometer radius of Montpellier. The remaining nonlocal recruits had more distant geographic origins as Table 1 shows. The findings of Philippe Wolff in his study of Toulouse displayed a different pattern of attraction from the hinterland. Wolff found that only twenty-seven percent of the apprentices in Toulouse from the mid-fourteenth to the mid-fifteenth century were natives, while another seventeen percent came from the immediate neighborhood around Toulouse.[66] The above evidence for Montpellier indicates that almost seventy percent of apprentices and workers were natives of the town while about sixteen percent came from a fifty-kilometer radius. The different configurations of the business communities in the two towns may account to some extent for the varying patterns of population attraction. In Toulouse the cloth industry, absent in Montpellier, recruited large numbers of apprentices from the hinterland. Several additional levels of explanation should also be examined in the case of Montpellier.

J. C. Russell calculated that the population density in the countryside was relatively low, about 12.1 persons per square kilometer in the region of Montpellier, without an inclusion of the ten largest cities.[67] The region of Toulouse, without the ten largest cities, yielded an average density of about 24.2 persons per square kilometer, twice as dense as the region of Montpellier.[68] Russell suggested that the cities of the region of dominance of Montpellier received little support in population from the rural area and were dependent on commerce and industry for attraction. Lack of crowding in the countryside may be one factor of explanation for the relatively few apprentices and workers drawn from the immediate hinterland. Other elements in the experience of Montpellier may also be significant in explaining its pattern of population attraction.

The political history of Montpellier may explain to some extent the seemingly small influx of labor from nearby areas. The twelfth-century seigneurs of Montpellier, the Guilhem family, held little land outside the town, and indeed, little land within it.[69] During the consular period from 1204 on, when the overlordship of

[66] However, Wolff (n. 3 above) 79ff. found distinctions of zones of attraction according to the trade considered. Thus 68% of the weavers in Toulouse came from the town itself and another 18% from the neighboring villages, whereas in the spice merchants' and apothecaries' occupations only 17% of the recruits came from Toulouse, 23% from the neighborhood and 60% from farther away.

[67] Russell (n. 1 above) 166.

[68] *Ibid.* 159.

[69] See Martine Dépinay, "Étude du cartulaire des Guilhem: Un aspect des seigneurs de Montpellier, l'extension territorial de la seigneurie des origines à la mort de Guilhem VIII," thèse de maîtrise (Montpellier, Faculté des lettres 1971).

Montpellier was first Aragonese and then Majorcan, the town exercised little political dominion over the small towns of the surrounding area.[70] From the extant land transactions of 1293-1348 there is some evidence of urban inhabitants investing in rural holdings, but the geographic expanse of these lands does not seem to have been great.[71] When combined, the above factors suggest that the town did not have a *contado* in the Italian sense. However, it would be unwise to make too much of the political divorce of Montpellier from the neighboring region in the context of this study, since it is not certain that the political barriers of the area presented any obstacles to the movement of population.

Another level of explanation for the seeming lack of local in-migration to Montpellier lies in the limitations inherent in notarial evidence. Much of the hiring in medieval Montpellier in unskilled occupations was undoubtedly conducted without the use of a formal contract passed before a notary, and will inevitably escape analysis.[72] The inheritance of skills from father to son and from mother to daughter needed no legally binding contract. The first steps in nearby rural in-migration may well lie beyond the possibilities of detection. It is very likely that a large number of the agricultural workers in Montpellier, estimated in 1239 at between 6000 and 7000 persons, were really in-migrants from the immediate countryside.[73] This group may have been renewed by a constant stream of newcomers from the hinterland. From an agricultural orientation, these newcomers may have moved up the urban social ladder, filling first the humbler occupations until they finally entered the network of apprenticeship contracts. Such a process may have taken several generations.

This hypothesis of gradual upward social mobility of rural in-migrants is consistent with the previous findings that, in the thirty-three cases from a radius of fifty kilometers or less from Montpellier, those trades and professions which did receive apprentices and workers were comparatively humble. As indicated earlier, it was in this area that newcomers to the food trades and artisanal occupations originated, as opposed to the major retail, commercial, financial and professional vocations which forged the international reputation of the town.

It was also from within this radius that most of the female apprentices came.[74] Thirty of the 208 contracts involved female apprentices and workers, fourteen of whom were foreigners. They were concentrated in the food trades, in needle work and in precious metal work. They might be apprenticed to the wives of tradesmen to

[70] The beginnings of the French *sénéchaussées* are treated in Dom Claude Devic et Dom Joseph Vaissette, *Histoire générale de Languedoc,* 14 vols. (Toulouse 1872-1904) 6.464-465. See also Robert Michel, *L'Administration royale dans la sénéchaussée de Beaucaire au temps de saint Louis* (Paris 1910). In the consular period, Lattes was controlled by Montpellier.

[71] Inhabitants invested substantially in vineyards near the town. Some families such as the Cabanis were building concentrated holdings at villages like Prades-le-Lez, about ten kilometers from Montpellier.

[72] This hiring may have been done on a daily basis in the town square.

[73] Émile Bonnet, "Les séjours à Montpellier de Jacme le Conquérant roi d'Aragon," *Mémoires de la Société archéologique de Montpellier,* ser. 2, 9 (1927) 176-177.

[74] An exception to this generalization is found in A. D. Hérault, II E 95/372, fol. 145v.

learn the spinning of gold or the making of silver cups.[75] The baker's trade provides the most telling illustration of the above geographic phenomenon: of the six female bakers' apprentices, five came from within the fifty-kilometer radius; one from Saint-Jean-de-Buèges, one from Ganges and three from the diocese of Nîmes.[76] The sixth came from the diocese of Saint-Flour in the Massif Central.[77]

In comparison with the geographic profile of the more modest urban occupations, the pattern of recruitment varied distinctly for the prestigious trades of commerce and finance. These trades employed men exclusively. Over one-half of all nonlocal contracts of apprenticeship and work involved newcomers from regions at a distance greater than fifty kilometers from Montpellier, most of whom were attracted to mercantile and financial professions. These same occupations drew few recruits from within the fifty-kilometer radius.

Money changers, apothecaries, pepperers, merchants and drapers drew apprentices to Montpellier from considerable distances. The three areas providing the greatest numbers of newcomers were the region of central France including the Lot River district, the Massif Central and the Cévennes Mountains, a wide area crisscrossed with routes leading to Champagne and Paris; a second region, the Rhone River valley, with its communications to Champagne and its gateway eastward to Italy; and finally, the third source of immigrants, the Corbières area around Narbonne, the town whose merchants were the major partners of merchants of Montpellier in the Levant trade of the thirteenth and fourteenth centuries.[78] Narbonne lay on the road from Montpellier to Spain.

Six of the fifteen extant changers' contracts involved nonlocal recruits. Apprentice money changers debarked from Saint-Thibéry, Lunel, Arles, Lyons, Cahors and Tarragona.[79] The changers were the cornerstone of the financial elite in Montpellier, and the reputation of the town in financial affairs was international. The areas of recruitment for this trade were hardly unexpected. In addition to Saint-Thibéry, Arles and Lyons on the Rhone River were important commercial centers in their own right.[80] There were well established currents of financial exchange radiating from

[75] For example, A. D. Hérault, II E 95/369, fol. 38; II E 95/371, fol. 38v; and II E 95/377, fol. 277.

[76] A. D. Hérault, II E 95/377, fols. 11v, 37, 227v, 262; II E 95/375, fol. 122.

[77] A. D. Hérault, II E 95/377, fol. 250v. It should be noted that no correlation could be established between the age of the apprentices and the distance of recruitment. Few contracts in fact actually cited the age of the apprentice. No male apprentice under fourteen years of age was noted, nor were there female apprentices under twelve. There was some distinction in length of contract between local and nonlocal apprentices, but no correlation regarding distance of displacement or type of profession existed. The average length of apprenticeship involving local girls where no work was included was 4.3 years, for nonlocal girls, 5.3 years. For local boys average length was 3.3 years, for nonlocal, 6 years.

[78] On the medieval road system, see n. 65 above.

[79] A. M. Montp., II 1, fol. 36; A. D. Hérault, II E 95/371, fols. 63, 90, 124; II E 95/372, fols. 11v, 53v.

[80] Bautier describes two routes connecting north and south (n. 65 above) 111ff. The Rhone valley route, involving travel partly on water, partly on land, lay for the most part outside French territory. The Regordane ran entirely within France from Montpellier or Nîmes to Alès and

Montpellier in the direction of Paris, Champagne, Italy and Spain. The presence of an apprentice changer from Tarragona is testimony to the financial dynamism of Montpellier. Little need be added concerning the renowned financial center of Cahors and its ties to Montpellier.[81]

The apothecaries, pepperers, merchants and drapers drew apprentices from as far afield as the changers. Four out of five apothecary contracts concerned newcomers from the diocese of Albi and from the towns of Sarlat, Sisteron and Carpentras.[82] Men from Alès, Beaucaire and Narbonne came to Montpellier to study the pepperer's trade, apprentice drapers arrived from a small town near Cahors and from Alès, while merchant apprentices were natives of Millau and Saint-Guilhem-le-Désert.[83]

The cloth trade of Montpellier had evolved considerably since its appearance in the twelfth century. A variety of French and Flemish high-quality wool cloths, as well as the newer products of the local Languedocian cloth industry, were exported by Montpelliérains to ports in the western Mediterranean basin and to the Levant.[84] The active cloth trade of the fourteenth century undoubtedly stimulated an interest in these activities on the part of outsiders, in this case, men of the interior regions of France. Maritime trade in general, and especially the Levant trade out of the port of Aigues-Mortes, made the vocation of merchant a popular one in Montpellier.

The attraction of would-be pepperers and apothecaries can also be explained by the longtime reputation of Montpellier in these fields.[85] From the twelfth century and probably earlier, the town had been the site of medical instruction.[86] Medieval medicine was closely related to the practices of apothecaries and pepperers; inspiration for the concoction of special elixirs and alcohols flowed freely here. Moreover, Montpellier was an important port of entry for Levantine goods and the access to spices and herbs of Eastern origin was greatly facilitated.

The apprentices to all the above trades came from towns of considerable importance or from areas near such towns. Carpentras and Sisteron were located near the papal court at Avignon. They were part of an extended Rhone valley region. Alès and Beaucaire were centers of French royal domination, while Albi and Sarlat on the western edges of the Massif Central were points of transit on commercial routes between the Mediterranean and the Atlantic.[87] Millau also lay on an overland route linking Montpellier with northern France. Narbonne was a logical source of interested apprentices. In the case of all of the nonlocal recruits, there were well-

north across the Cévennes to Le Puy, Brioude, Issoire, Clermont and beyond. See notes 62 and 63 above on St-Thibéry and Lunel.

[81] On relations between Montpellier and Cahors, see Combes (n. 6 above).

[82] A. M. Montp., II 1, fol. 25 (bis) v; A. D. Hérault, II E 95/370, fol. 73v; II E 95/371, fol. 140; II E 95/372, fol. 9v.

[83] A. D. Hérault, II E 95/368, 12 Sept. 1327; II E 95/369, fol. 80; II E 95/372, fol. 100v; II E 95/370, fol. 73; II E 95/371, fol. 14; II E 95/375, fol. 78; II E 95/369, fols. 72v, 110.

[84] On the Languedocian cloth industry, see Guy Romestan, "Draperie roussillonnaise et draperie languedocienne dans la première moitié du XIVe siècle," *Bulletin de la Fédération historique du Languedoc-Roussillon* (Perpignan 1969) 31-60.

[85] Dion (n. 44 above) 316ff.

[86] Boriès (n. 27 above), and Germain 3 (n. 30 above) on the medical school.

[87] Renouard (n. 65 above). See Map 1.

established transportation or commercial networks in which their regions of origin and Montpellier were included.

Of these towns, Narbonne stands out as the one with which merchants of Montpellier had the closest contacts in the period 1293-1348. Many natives of Narbonne were residents of Montpellier during that period.[88] In addition to apprentices, Narbonnais frequented the university of Montpellier for professional training.[89] The relatively short distance of about one hundred kilometers which separated Montpellier from Narbonne undoubtedly favored mutual ties, but distance alone is not a sufficient explanation. Fruitful and longtime cooperation in Mediterranean trade is probably the key to the close rapport.

Southwest of Narbonne, on an axis leading to Catalonia and beyond, the strong current of population attraction which Higounet signaled was somewhat attenuated by the fourteenth century.[90] Spaniards and Roussillonnais often used Montpellier as a place of repayment in financial exchanges, but not as a site of establishment of commercial contracts.[91] Majorcan and Minorcan merchants frequented Montpellier in much the same fashion, as transients rather than as immigrants.[92] A few merchants of Perpignan held property in Montpellier, but there is no indication that they were actual residents.[93] Portuguese students were drawn to Montpellier by the reputation of its university.[94] An occasional Spanish immigrant such as a merchant from Huesca, a beltmaker from Majorca or the apprentice changer from Tarragona can be cited.[95] It would seem, however, that the traditional movements of population between Languedoc and Spain had fallen off by the fourteenth century. The severance of political ties with Aragon which occurred at the division of the kingdom of James I in 1276, and the passage of Montpellier and Roussillon to the younger Majorcan branch of the ruling family, may have contributed to a decline in Spanish contacts.[96]

In contrast, a continuous source of numerous newcomers to Montpellier in the fourteenth century was the central mountainous region of France which had traditionally poured forth its overflow population towards the Mediterranean coast of Lower Languedoc and Provence, with another thrust towards Aquitaine and Tou-

[88] For example, A. D. Hérault, II E 95/368, fols. 25, 55v; II E 95/377, fol. 178v; II E 95/369, fols. 4v, 61v, 64v, 81v, 98; II E 95/371, fol. 97v.

[89] See A. Gouron, "Enseignement du droit, légistes et canonistes dans le Midi de la France à la fin du XIIIe et au début du XIVe siècle," *Recueil de mémoires et travaux de la Société d'histoire du droit et des institutions des anciens pays de droit écrit* 5 (1966) passim, for details about natives of Narbonne at the Montpellier Law School.

[90] Higounet (n. 4 above) 12 limited most of his remarks regarding Montpellier to the twelfth and thirteenth centuries.

[91] A. M. Montp., II 1, fol. 4v. Examples could be multiplied.

[92] A. D. Hérault, II E 95/368, fol. 11v, a case in point.

[93] A. M. Montp. II 2, fol. 121.

[94] See Joaquim Verissimo Serrão, *Les Portugais à l'université de Montpellier (XIIe – XVIIe siècles)* (Paris 1971).

[95] A. D. Hérault, II E 95/372, fols. 43v, 51, 65, 71: immigrant from Huesca; II E 95/371, fol. 90: apprentice from Tarragona.

[96] See Tourtoulon (n. 37 above) for general background.

louse.[97] Mercantile families such as the Conchis and the Crusolis had branches in the mountainous Lot River region as well as in Marseilles and Montpellier.[98] The notarial registers recorded newcomers from Cajarc, Figeac and Cahors, engaging in money changing and long-distance commerce from a base in Montpellier.[99] For example, Jacobus Gimelli, changer of Figeac, residing in Montpellier, made several loans to Montpelliérains and worked closely with changers of Montpellier such as Bernardus de Sancto Johanne.[100] Bernardus Fabri of Cajarc is representative of the successful newcomer in Montpellier. He appeared for the first time in the documents in 1294.[101] At an earlier date he had married the daughter of Guillelmus de Putheo, Sr., bourgeois of Montpellier. In 1302 Fabri was associated in his father-in-law's draper business along with his brother-in-law.[102] In 1301 his son, Guiraudus Fabri, merchant, married Beatrix de Sancto Michaele, daughter of the late pepperer Bartholomeus. Bernardus emancipated his son on this occasion, giving him several houses outside the walls of Montpellier as well as a drapery shop and 1,000 pounds of Melgueil in cash.[103] It would seem that Bernardus had accumulated a considerable fortune through his drapery trade and through skillful marriage alliances with the commercial elite in Montpellier. Nothing is known of Fabri's origins, outside of his place of birth, but his business success and the integration of his family into Montpellier society suggest that the town was receptive to newcomers and that social mobility was possible.

Natives of the Massif Central region were also drawn to Montpellier by the attraction of international trade. They were frequently traveling partners of Montpellier merchants in the Levant trade.[104] In 1339 Jacobus Roncia of Aurillac, resident in Montpellier, took 428 pounds *petits tournois* invested in French wool cloth to Cyprus for the Montpelliérain, Jacobus de Magalassio.[105] Gibbertus Jireu, pepperer

[97] See Lartigaut (n. 6 above). E. Bonnet (n. 73 above) 3-4 quoted the thirteenth-century chronicler Ramon Muntaner who complained about the "gens de Cahors, de Figeac, de Saint-Antonin," who found Montpellier to their liking, stayed and supported the king of France against the king of Aragon. Muntaner estimated their presence in Montpellier at thirty or forty houses within the town.

[98] Combes (n. 6 above) has made a study of these families.

[99] Six immigrants from Figeac, three from Cahors and two from Cajarc were, according to the remaining evidence, actively involved in business affairs. See A. D. Hérault, II E 95/372, fols. 12, 13v, 61, 63, 63v, 96, 97, 97v; II E 95/375, fols. 102, 122, 123v; II E 95/372, fols. 3v, 13; II E 95/377, fols. 5, 10, 101v, 280v; A. M. Montp., II 1, fol. 77; II 2, fols. 10, 20, 79, 120v.

[100] A. D. Hérault, II E 95/377, fols. 10, 101v, 281, 298; II E 95/372, fol. 19v.

[101] A. M. Montp. II 1, fol. 77.

[102] A. M. Montp. II 2, fol. 120v.

[103] A. M. Montp., II 2, fol. 10. Father and son established a *societas* of 850 pounds, 550 pounds of which represented part of the dowry of Beatrix. See fol. 11v. See also fol. 79, for the receipt of the 850 pounds acknowledged by Guiraudus; the sum included several small loans plus the price due for a horse. A daughter of Bernardus Fabri was the wife of Guillelmus Gauberti of Béziers, master in medicine. In 1301 she bought a house with oven and accessories in the quarter of Castelmoton in Montpellier for 200 pounds. See fol. 20 of the same register.

[104] See, for example, Guillelmus de Sudre, draper, native of Monfaucon near Cahors: A. D. Hérault, II E 95/371, fols. 13r-v, 14. Sudre traveled for the drapers of Montpellier, Guillelmus Bertholomei and Andreas Tilholi, in the Levant.

[105] A. D. Hérault, II E 95/375, fol. 76v.

of Aurillac and inhabitant of Montpellier, invested in the spice trade of Montpellier in 1339 along with other local pepperers.[106] These examples could be multiplied. Newcomers from Millau also participated in the Levant trade, and one merchant apprentice hailed from this town, as noted above.[107] Additional evidence of attraction from small towns of the Massif Central such as Vabre or Saint-Affrique can be detected in the wills and marriages of the years 1293-1348. Marriages, for example, were recorded between Montpelliérains and inhabitants from the dioceses of Rodez, Saint-Flour, Mende, Lodève and Alès, as Map 2 illustrates.[108]

Limited population attraction from the extended Rhone valley region existed in the fourteenth century. In addition to the apprentices from Carpentras and Sisteron, several newcomers from Avignon and Lyons were recorded.[109] Details about their activities are scanty, but some seem to have been involved in the overland trade between Montpellier and Burgundy. Linen and wool from this region were in demand on the Montpellier markets.

On occasion, notarial acts furnish isolated information about Italians living in Montpellier. Italian political exiles who flooded much of Europe in the late thirteenth and fourteenth centuries made their impact on the town.[110] Lucchese exiles in particular became permanent inhabitants, making a contribution to financial and commercial circles and to the intellectual community. Tuscan artists immigrated to Montpellier in the same period, and Piedmontese also came in considerable numbers to settle in the Languedocian town.

Exiles par excellence, Lucchese immigrants concentrated their activities in money lending to private individuals and to local consulates, in the cloth trade and in the administration of real estate. Raynunchius Arnulphini and Barca Esbarre were engaged in finance as was Chinchinus de Advogatis.[111] Arnulphini also had dealings in the cloth trade.[112] Bonacruce Bossi lent money to the consuls of Cournonterral, a small town to the west of Montpellier, while Pelegrinus Bosse managed the property

[106] A. D. Hérault, II E 95/375, fol. 57.

[107] A. D. Hérault, II E 95/369, fol. 72r-v. The merchant of Millau, Petrus Selanh, apprenticed himself to the Montpelliérain, Petrus Guersi, for a trip to Cyprus in 1333. In 1339 Pontius Pinharelli of Montpellier hired Guillelmus Riperie of Millau to travel with him to Cyprus with French cloths to sell. See II E 95/375, fol. 78.

[108] A. D. Hérault, II E 95/368, fol. 125; II E 95/375, fols. 24, 34, 54v, 91v; II E 95/377, fol. 4v. I am indebted to Marie-Madeleine Campère Julia, archiviste – paléographe, for the initial form of this map of marriages involving foreigners, drawn from the over 130 marriage contracts preserved in the notarial registers before 1350 and from two other local collections, the *Grand chartrier* and the *fonds de la Commune clôture.* See *Archives de la ville de Montpellier: Inventaires et documents* 1 (Montpellier 1895) and 12 (Montpellier 1974).

[109] Among those designated as inhabitants from Avignon were Stephanus Genesii, Marita Clara, Dulsolina Argenterii, Raymundus Gaiani. See A. D. Hérault, II E 95/371, fol. 148; II E 95/372, fols. 42, 162; II E 95/375, fol. 97; II E 95/377, fol. 25. Peter Yvernalis, merchant of Lyons, was also an inhabitant of Montpellier. See II E 95/372, fol. 162.

[110] See F. de Roover, "Lucchese Silks," *Ciba Review* 40-80 (1950) 2902-2931.

[111] A. D. Hérault, II E 95/370, fols. 27, 49, 125. See also D. Neirinck, "Répertoire des Archives communales de Cournonterral," manuscript inventory of A. D. Hérault (1969), entry AA 14.

[112] A. D. Hérault, II E 95/370, fol. 79v.

Map 2: IMMIGRATION ACCORDING TO MARRIAGE CONTRACTS

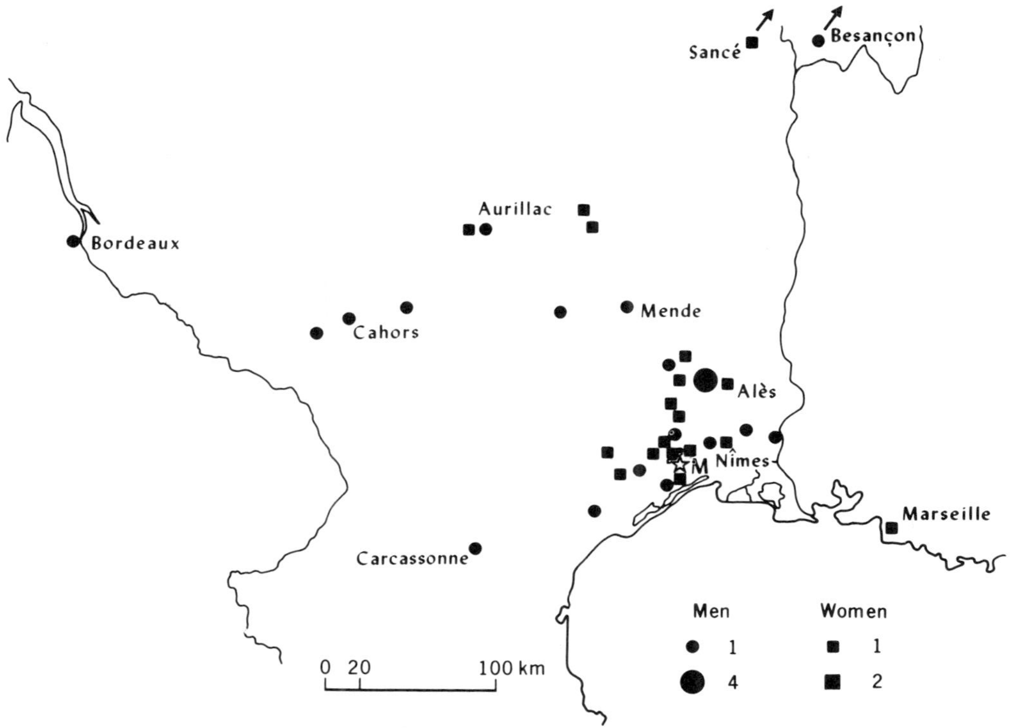

I

of a local nobleman and other inhabitants.[113] A notary of Lucca, Guido Malagallie, was also a resident of Montpellier.[114] The political troubles of Lucca encouraged emigration in the early fourteenth century, and the Lucchese in Montpellier were part of a larger community scattered throughout France.[115]

Tuscan painters established in Montpellier in the 1340s received commissions for works of art from regional and local religious establishments and from private individuals.[116] Their school drew apprentices from as far away as Agen.[117] Immigrant artists from Florence, Prato and Siena were in contact with the artistic community in Avignon and occasionally cooperated on works with Italian painters based there.[118]

Merchants from the Piedmont were present in Montpellier in the 1330s and 1340s. The prototype of these immigrants was the merchant, Boninus de Meldeo, who was actively engaged in the cloth and grain trades with a loan business on the side.[119] Ardussonis Mutonis, an immigrant from Chieri, who attained the status of bourgeois of Montpellier, was a specialist in finance and in real estate investments.[120]

There were also Pisan and Genoese merchants resident in Montpellier in the years 1293-1348. Sicilian documents mention the activities of several Genoese inhabitants of Montpellier in the grain trade of the 1340s.[121] Johannes Boni Amici of Pisa, inhabitant of Montpellier, formed an association of six years' duration with two Montpellier pepperers.[122] The scattered remaining evidence suggests, however, that the twelfth-century *fondachi* of the Genoese and the Pisans in Montpellier had long since disappeared. The Italian community, which was probably sizable in 1278 when Philip III of France ordered Italians to change their residence from Montpellier to Nîmes, may well have diminished after that time.[123] Nonetheless, in the fourteenth century, immigrants from Tuscany, Lombardy and Piedmont restored the Italian influx to a relatively high level.

Outside the realms of commerce and finance, the university of Montpellier acted as a magnet for foreigners from all over Europe. Raised to the rank of *studium*

[113] A. D. Hérault, II E 95/377, fol. 74; II E 95/375, fols. 6v, 22v, 81, 98, 108. See also Neirinck (n. 111 above) AA 13.

[114] A. D. Hérault, II E 95/369, fol. 107.

[115] De Roover (n. 110 above).

[116] See, for example, A. D. Hérault, II E 95/377, fols. 12, 31, 77, 111v, 226v. Artists included Donatus and Daneus Johannes, natives of Florence, Franciscus Bernardi, native of Prato, Michael Minhani of Siena. On artists in Montpellier, see J. Renouvier and Ad. Richard, "Des maîtres de pierre et des autres artistes gothiques de Montpellier," *Mémoires de la Société archéologique de Montpellier* 2 (1850) 135-350.

[117] A. D. Hérault, II E 95/377, fol. 80. See also fols. 28 and 226v.

[118] A. D. Hérault, II E 95/377, fols. 12, 31.

[119] For example, A. D. Hérault, II E 95/370, fols. 11v, 92v, 93v, 107v; II E 95/368, fols. 16, 24, 39, 41r-v, 44r-v, 47r-v, 82, 138v; II E 95/369, fols. 29v, 32, 82v.

[120] A. D. Hérault, II E 95/375, fols. 21v, 46, 48v, 93; II E 95/370, fols. 16v, 70; II E 95/372, fols. 115v, 160v.

[121] See H. Bresc, "Marchands de Narbonne et du Midi en Sicile (1300-1460)," *Bulletin de la Fédération historique du Languedoc-Roussillon* (Montpellier 1973) 94.

[122] A. D. Hérault, II E 95/370, fol. 112.

[123] Germain (n. 30 above) 1.288-289.

generale in 1289 with three faculties, law, medicine and the arts, the schools of Montpellier had had from the twelfth century an international reputation.[124] A list of twenty-nine doctorates in civil and canon law awarded in 1341 provides a cross-section of geographic origins of students of the law faculty.[125] Students were present from Coimbre, Urgel and Perpignan. Candidates also hailed from the dioceses of Vabre and Rodez to the north of Montpellier. Links with this central French region and the law school had been cemented by the presence on the faculty of the renowned civil law jurist, Petrus Jacobi of Aurillac, in the early fourteenth century.[126] The Rhone valley and Provence provided candidates from Sisteron, Carpentras, Orange, Vaison, Saint-Paul-les-Trois-Châteaux, Saint-Jean-de-Maurienne and Nice. From farther afield came Guillelmus Grimoardi, monk of Cluny, the future Urban V.[127] There was even a student from Osnabrück in the province of Hanover.[128] The region of Montpellier was naturally represented among the doctorates of 1341. Two monks of Aniane were recipients.[129] There was one student from the nearby small town of Poussan, but Bernardus de Tornamira of Montpellier was the only native present in the class of 1341.[130] The specialization of the doctorate as the summit of university training explains the displacement of foreigners from great distances and the relative scarceness of local candidates.[131] The university attraction reached a somewhat wider geographic area than did the recruitment to urban professions in commerce and finance, but there was considerable duplication in regions such as central France and the Rhone valley.

* * *

[124] On the University of Montpellier, see H. Rashdall, *The Universities of Europe in the Middle Ages* (Oxford 1895) 2.111-136. Most of Germain's lengthy bibliography on the university is indicated in Rashdall. See also Gouron (nn. 33 and 89 above), and Boriès (n. 27 above).

[125] A. D. Hérault, série G, 1244, Jean de Sala, Montpellier, "Réception de docteurs en théologie, droit canon et droit civil." The following geographic details were drawn from this list of receptions.

[126] On Petrus Jacobi, see R. Grand, "Un jurisconsulte du XIVe siècle, Pierre Jacobi, auteur de la *Practica aurea*," *Bibliothèque de l'École des chartes* 79 (1918) 68-101, and P. Fournier, "Pierre Jame d'Aurillac, jurisconsulte," *Histoire littéraire de la France* 36 (Paris 1929) 481-521.

[127] A. D. Hérault, série G, 1244, fol. 56. Urban V became a patron of the law school during his papacy.

[128] *Ibid.* fol. 57v.

[129] *Ibid.* fols. 17, 44v.

[130] *Ibid.* fol. 1r-v.

[131] In finishing this survey of population groups within Montpellier, a word of explanation is necessary for the omission of any information concerning the Jews. Many Jews were mentioned in A. M. Montp., II.1 and 2, covering the periods 1293-1294 and 1301-1302 respectively. Thereafter, there were no references in the local notaries. R. W. Emery, *The Jews of Perpignan* (New York 1959), made frequent references to the Jews of Montpellier. See in particular 131-133, app. 3. For additional treatment of the Jews of Montpellier, see Reyerson (n. 44 above), esp. 1.46-48, 154 and chap. 4. Studies of the history of the Jews of Montpellier include E. Azémar, *Étude sur les Israélites de Montpellier au Moyen-Age* (Nîmes 1924) and several older studies by Salomon Kahn in the *Revue des études juives*. The Jews of Montpellier undoubtedly felt repercussions and probably direct effects of the French banishments of 1306 and 1311. Because their trace is lost for the most part in the first half of the fourteenth century, I have chosen not to treat of them here.

The foregoing detailed, although admittedly fragmentary, view of population movements in fourteenth-century Montpellier can be most fruitfully compared with the findings of Philippe Wolff in his study of Toulouse. Wolff noted from his research in apprenticeship and work contracts that almost every region of France was represented among the origins of newcomers to Toulouse.[132] In contrast, the zones of attraction of Montpellier, as the foregoing discussion illustrates, represented a more concentrated region: apprentices and workers came primarily from the southern half of modern France.[133] The differences in apprenticeship recruitment from the two towns and their surrounding regions have already been explored.[134]

There were similarities between the experiences of Toulouse and Montpellier in the trends of long-distance attraction for prestigious occupations such as those of apothecary, spice merchant and pepperer. For Montpellier, money changing and overseas commerce exerted a long-distance pull, and students came from even farther afield to attend the law school. In Montpellier, as in Toulouse, it has been possible to isolate several major areas of attraction: the Rhone valley with an extension into Italy, the Massif Central and central France, and Narbonne in the Corbières. For Toulouse, regions such as the Rouergue and the Béarnaise provided considerable population.[135]

Comparisons between Montpellier and Italian towns provide more contrasts than similarities. It has been suggested above that Montpellier did not have a hinterland in the sense of the Italian *contado.* There is little indication of neighboring landowners migrating to Montpellier to participate in trade and finance.[136] The connections between town and countryside were more tenuous in the case of Montpellier than in a town such as Padua for which J. K. Hyde described detailed relations between town and country, or for Florence according to the studies of J. Plesner and G. Brucker for the thirteenth and fourteenth centuries.[137]

In northern Europe patterns of attraction of population also provide sharp contrasts with the Montpellier experience. According to J. Lestoquoy, northern towns such as Dome-en-Périgord, Arras, Vézelay, Brussels, towns of the Mâconnais region and even Metz, had a basic radius of attraction of between twenty and thirty kilom-

[132] Wolff (n. 3 above) 79ff.

[133] The geographic zone of attraction shown in the marriage contracts of Montpellier is somewhat broader. See Map 2.

[134] See n. 66 above.

[135] Wolff (n. 3 above) 80-81.

[136] An exception might be made for the seigneur of Lunel, Raimundus Gaucelini, who obtained rights of bourgeoisie in Montpellier in 1251 in return for his renunciation of certain tolls. See Germain (n. 15 above) 1.218-219, act. 22.

[137] J. K. Hyde, *Padua in the Age of Dante* (New York 1966) 34ff. and 50ff. "By the mid-thirteenth century, the landowning nobility were firmly rooted in the city" (50). See also Johan Plesner, *L'Émigration de la campagne à la ville libre de Florence au XIIIe siècle* (Copenhagen 1934). Gene Brucker, *Florentine Politics and Society* (Princeton 1962) 41, described the immigration of the *gente nuova* from the *contado* to the city in the fourteenth century. See also W. Bowsky, "Impact of the Black Death upon Sienese Government and Society," *Speculum* 39 (1964) 7, for details of an influx of newcomers to Siena from somewhat farther afield in 1328.

eters.[138] In the case of Metz, J. Schneider maintained that most attraction was concentrated within a radius of twenty kilometers although E. Perrin in his examination of admission lists for the bourgeoisie in Metz noted no local centers of intense in-migration and, in fact, evoked a broad but scattered geographic scope of attraction for the upper echelons of society, which included Montpellier itself.[139] As a general rule, however, northern towns present a narrower zone of attraction than do Montpellier and Toulouse.

The evidence for Montpellier has revealed a pattern of attraction which coincided closely with the commercial and financial network of which it was a part. Geographic origins of newcomers have been traced to the multiple road system crossing the Cévennes and the Massif Central leading to Champagne and Paris. Areas of attraction also reflected the trading links between Montpellier and the Atlantic regions of France, and the close commercial partnership between Montpellier and Narbonne. By the fourteenth century the earlier important Spanish ties were diminishing in the face of increasing French influence, but commercial contacts remained and accounted for some population movement. Italy, due more to the internal chaos of its major towns than to the draw of Montpellier, was a source of considerable immigration.

Within a fifty-kilometer radius of Montpellier there were few towns of importance. Newcomers from this area joined food trades and artisanal occupations within Montpellier. The patterns of recruitment to commercial, financial and university vocations revealed a connection between the importance of the urban center of origin of nonlocal apprentices, the distance of their displacement and the prestige of the professions themselves. Information flowed freely among the cosmopolitan commercial, financial and university circles of southern France with easy movement from one major urban center to another. University and business vocations often existed within the same family. So in 1342, Arnaudus de Alba Fortis of Cahors, acting with the advice of his uncle, a bachelor of laws, apprenticed himself to a Montpellier changer.[140] The Crusolis, Conchis and Tornamira families show the same breadth of geographic situation and vocation. Circles of acquaintance and family ties reinforced one another, accentuating the centripetal effect of Montpellier. Because of its international reputation and its Mediterranean location, Montpellier was a strong magnet for the ambitious intellectual, merchant, and financier.

[138] J. Lestoquoy, "Les villes et la population urbaine (L'exemple d'Arras)," *Cahiers de civilisation médiévale* 1 (1958) 55-62.

[139] See the discussion of Jean Schneider, *La ville de Metz aux XIIIe et XIVe siècles* (Nancy 1950), in Lestoquoy 61. See also Perrin (n. 41 above).

[140] A. D. Hérault, II E 95/371, fol. 63.

II

LAND, HOUSES AND REAL ESTATE INVESTMENT IN MONTPELLIER: A STUDY OF THE NOTARIAL PROPERTY TRANSACTIONS, 1293-1348

Throughout the Middle Ages land was the main source of wealth and status in Europe. In spite of the rapid development of towns in the twelfth and thirteenth centuries, agriculture remained the livelihood of the vast majority of the population. In the south Languedoc town of Montpellier, a center of commerce and finance with an important university, a mid-thirteenth-century chronicler counted 6,000 agricultural workers.[1] Montpellier attained a population of between 30,000 and 40,000 inhabitants by the early fourteenth century.[2] Allowing for literary exaggeration, the link with the land remains inescapable.

Whatever the political situation of a particular region, all medieval towns enjoyed economic exchanges with the surrounding countryside. Rural areas were sources of food and raw materials. They furnished in-migrants to the towns. The countryside might provide a market for urban goods. By the late thirteenth century the close interrelationship of town and country led to the penetration of urban credit practices into the rural world.[3] Urban inhabitants began to buy rural lands, adding them to their possessions in urban real estate.

Property holding arrangements were complex, and there was ample variety in local forms. This examination of property relations in Montpellier and its immediate region, based on transactions in the earliest extant notarial registers of 1293-1348, seeks to contribute a further case study to the body of local and regional studies.[4] For this era of demographic apogee before the arrival of the Black Death, over eight hundred contracts concerning real estate have survived.[5] These acts provide a rich source of information on specific contractual arrangements and on the range of inhabitants who possessed real property, data all the more valuable in the absence of fiscal inventories of property which date from the end of the fourteenth century in Montpellier.[6] What follows is not an agricultural history or a history of urban/rural relations, but rather a social and financial history of notarial property transactions.

While notarial registers were not the exclusive depositories of property transactions—individual charters and cartularies being the other main sources—the notaries served as registries of public deeds recording legal proof of contractual arrangements.[7] The activities of selling, leasing and renting real property and rights related to it have been traced in detail. Buyers and sellers, lessors and lessees have been tabulated in an effort to reveal what, if any, differences existed in the patterns of real estate holding among various urban social groups. The investment strategies of inhabitants in the acquisition of rural lands and in the housing market activity in Montpellier form further areas of inquiry. Changes in average values of land and house transactions have been graphed. I have made an effort to determine the return on various types of real estate investment. The role of credit in real estate operations is a continuous theme of this study. In addition to sales contracts and recognitions of debt for the cost of houses and lands, Montpelliérains currently employed rentals, long-term leases, sharecropping and land exchanges with infrequent use of provisional sales and annuities. Further, they sold the revenues, fruits and use of houses, shops and lands. The appendix of this study provides examples of seven commonly-found property transactions.

The structure of landholding as it appeared in the notarial acts of Montpellier comprised a complexity of property rights, extending from full ownership to multiple subdivisions of interest in real estate. The many-tiered framework of property rights offered numerous possibilities for the operation of credit and the derivation of profit.

The region and the town of Montpellier contained allodial lands and houses which may be seen within the framework of the Roman concept of full ownership. In allodial ownership neither homage nor *census* payment nor dues of any kind were owed to a third party.[8] No restrictions regarding disposition of the property encumbered such holdings, either with regard to succession or to living alienations through gift or sale. The owner of an allod could, in fact, grant out the land in fief or lease it in *census* tenure.[9]

Ownership could be divided into abstract rights of property and concrete rights of use.[10] Allodial ownership comprised at the outset both *dominium directum*, the abstract rights of eminent domain, and *dominium utile*, possession of rights of use. In many land transactions of Montpellier, the owner of abstract rights was not the possessor of the property. Eminent domain endowed the owner with certain specific rights: receipt of an annual *census* fee; the right to seize the tenure in the case of failure of payment; the right of approval of sale or transfer which resulted in monetary compensation (*directum, consilium, laudimium*). In contrast, rights of use conferred upon the owner the possibilities of exploiting a holding as he saw fit, or making transformations and of selling or transferring the property as long as the appropriate payments of *census* and *laudimium* were made to the owner of rights of eminent domain.[11] The owner of use was without certain honorific prerogatives in the property and, in theory, was not authorized to create a subsidiary tenure.[12]

The landholding situation just described evolved with the rediscovery of Roman law terminology in the south of France in the High Middle Ages. In the centuries following the fall of Rome in the West, written contracts of all kinds declined in number. The written law tradition of the former Roman areas of the south of France experienced a nadir in the tenth century.[13] A revival of Roman law techniques began slowly in the late eleventh century. In the tenth through the twelfth centuries in the region of Montpellier there was a lumping of terms in acts regarding the transfer of property.[14] Legal distinctions among terms such as *venditio, traditio, cessio, derelictio, guirpetio* were blurred. By the date of the appearance of the municipal *consuetudines* of Montpellier in 1204, the confusions in terminology had subsided. The sale appeared in 1204 as a formal or real contract concluded by a hand shake or *by part* or full payment of the purchase price, or by the transfer of the thing purchased, evidence thus of the credit sales contract.[15]

Several features of the real estate contract (*venditio*), the most common property transaction of the notarial registers, are worthy of note.[16] Beginning with the clause of sale using the verb *vendere* in the appropriate person and number, the seller affirmed the final and perpetual character of the sale by stating that it applied for him and for successors and heirs. The seller also made an explicit statement of good faith. In appropriate cases, the approval of the titulary of rights of eminent domain was acknowledged with a statement of the annual *census* or *usaticum* owed. Later in the act or in a separate act the titulary might confirm the sale and acknowledge the receipt of an approval fee, generally ten per cent of the sales price. The property was then described and its geographical location situated according to contiguous holdings. Rarely was the surface area of a parcel given, a regrettable omission given the resulting impossibility of comparative cost analysis. The seller acknowledged having received the purchase price, or the earnest money (*arrhae*) in a credit sale, *in bona pecunia numerata.*[17] Details about the schedule of payments of the remainder of the purchase price were included in credit sales. A series of Roman law renunciations and further guarantees on the seller's part assured the buyer's property rights.[18] Down payment sales followed by recognitions of debt were characteristic of some by not all of the credit transactions in real estate, involving both lands and houses.[19]

This study begins with an analysis of land sales for which the greatest number of transactions survive. An examination of house sales follows. A lengthy third section, entitled "Real Estate Revenues," explores the multitude of ways in which Montpelliérains managed real property for profit. Reflections on property holding in Montpellier and in other parts of medieval Europe form the conclusions of this work.

LAND SALES

The impact of Montpellier on its surrounding region was limited by the unique political situation of the town as an enclave of Majorcan political allegiance in French territory.[20] Sites of French royal administration lay close by at Nimes, fifty kilometers to the northeast and at Béziers, sixty kilometers to the southwest. Sommières, site of a French mint, lay only thirty kilometers to the northeast. At about twenty kilometers to the north, near Pic Saint Loup, stood a French royal château and a fortress of the bishop of Maguelone. Aigues-Mortes, the Mediterranean port founded by Saint Louis and the main outlet for shipping from Montpellier to the eastern Mediterranean, lay twenty-six kilometers to the east.[21] Circumscribed by these French coordinates, the hinterland of Montpellier extended, at best, to a radius of twenty to thirty kilometers from the town (125,600 hectares to 282,600 hectares). It was within this area that rural real estate transactions were concentrated. Map I illustrates this extent of rural territory.

To the north of Montpellier in the *garrigue,* land was generally dry and infertile.[22] There were attempts throughout the medieval period to bring isolated areas under cultivation, but these met with varying success. Sheep and goats were raised in this region and were led north to summer pasturage in the Cévennes. Livestock from the region of the Montagne Noire around Saint-Pons joined *garrigue* animals for winter grazing on the salt marshes along the coastal plain from Montpellier to Sête.[23]

In the area around Montpellier grape vines were the most important component of local agriculture in the Middle Ages, as today, though olive trees and cereals were also cultivated. The vineyard is favored by Montpellier's climate which is typically Mediterranean with long dry summers and mild winters.[24] While vineyards were cultivated on the hills and in sandy marshlands, grain was grown on the richest lands on the plain. The overall dryness of the climate prevented a spring planting of cereals. The biennal rotation system of antiquity—winter wheat alternating with fallow—was commonly in use. With the growth of its population in years of poor harvest in the late thirteenth and early fourteenth centuries, Montpellier had to rely on grain imports.[25]

* * *

Land transactions of the notarial registers involved meadows, fields and vineyards with the occasional mention of other holdings such as salt marshes.[26] Two hundred sixty-two sales of agricultural lands survive in the notarial registers. The sellers and buyers of these contracts will be differentiated according to social group in the tables which follow.[27] Inhabitants employed both cash and credit methods of purchase with their relative use reflecting the particular resources and financial strategies of Montpelliérains from different walks of life.

Table 1 gives the distributions of sellers and buyers in all of the land sales of the Montpellier registers. Table 2 provides the breakdown according to social and occupational group of the participants in credit sales of land, including sales with a down payment and credit for the balance, as well as full credit sales. Fifty-three or approximately twenty per cent of the sales involved some extension of credit. Ten of the land sales were full credit contracts.[28]

Sellers in the general pool of land transactions were drawn, as Table 1 shows, from a broad spectrum of the population. Land was an asset which might be sold to generate cash capital. Sale of land might reflect the difficult economic straits of the seller; it might also indicate a decision to alter investments, to place capital elsewhere.[29] The notarial contracts do not reveal the motivations behind land sales.

The largest group selling land was comprised of women.[30] Table 3 gives the social background of wives, widows and single women who sold land. They were most heavily concentrated among agricultural workers. As Table 1 shows, male agricultural workers and foreigners, primarily villagers of the region of Montpellier, were also prominent among land sellers, as were artisans and members of the service trades, each of these three categories having approximately fifteen per cent of the sales. The active involvement of artisans and members of the service trades in land purchases as well as sales suggests the possible interpretation of land speculation.[31]

If the sellers of land in the overall pool of participants (Table 1) are compared with the group of credit sellers (Table 2), several distinctions can be noted. Merchants, changers and moneyers, women and members of the artisan and service groups were more heavily represented in the whole pool of sellers than in the group of credit sellers. Members of the food trades had a similar percentage of participation in both

TABLE 1

SALES OF LAND (262)*

	Sellers		Buyers	
	No. of Acts	% Total Acts	No. of Acts	% Total Acts
Merchants	26	9.9	26	9.9
Changers/Moneyers	2	0.8	13	5.0
Retail/Wholesale	26	9.9	25	9.5
Nobles/Burgenses	2	0.8	4	1.5
Professions/Education			5	1.9
Jews				
Royal Administration	1	0.4	1	0.4
Ecclesiastics	6	2.3	3	1.1
Women	57	21.8	28	10.7
Artisans/Service	40	15.3	61	23.3
Food Trades	5	1.9	16	6.1
Agriculture	41	15.6	32	12.2
Foreigners	41	15.6	41	15.6
Unidentified				
Local	2	0.8		
Other	13	5.0	7	2.7

*Data for this table and all of the following tables in this article have been drawn from the Montpellier notarial evidence of 1293-1348.

TABLE 2

CREDIT SALES OF LAND (53)

	Sellers			Buyers		
	No. of Acts	% Total Credit Sales	Credit Sales as % of All Sales	No. of Acts	% Total Credit Sales	Credit Sales as % of All Sales
Merchants	4	7.5	1.5	2	3.8	0.8
Changers/Moneyers						
Retail/Wholesale	7	13.2	2.7	2	3.8	0.8
Nobles/Burgenses	2	3.8	0.8	1	1.9	0.4
Professions/ Education						
Jews						
Royal Administration	1	1.9	0.4	1	1.9	0.4
Ecclesiastics	3	5.7	1.1	1	1.9	0.4
Women	5	9.4	1.9	6	11.3	2.3
Artisans/Service	7	13.2	2.7	22	41.5	8.4
Food Trades	1	1.9	0.4	2	3.8	0.8
Agriculture	10	18.9	3.8	7	13.2	2.7
Foreigners	12	22.6	4.6	8	15.1	3.1
Unidentified Local Other	1	1.9	0.4	1	1.9	0.4

TABLE 3

WOMEN AS BUYERS AND SELLERS IN LAND SALES
SOCIAL BACKGROUND

	Land Sellers	Land Buyers
Merchants	5	1
Changers/Moneyers	4	3
Retail/Wholesale	7	3
Nobles/*Burgenses*		
Professions/Education	4	
Jews		
Royal Administration		
Ecclesiastics	1	
Artisans/Service	7	3
Food/Trades	1	1
Agriculture	18	2
Foreigners	2	7
Unidentified		
Local	4	5
Other	3	3
TOTALS	56	28

groups. The remaining social categories recorded a greater percentage of participation among the credit sellers. Among this last group, agricultural workers and regional villagers showed the most frequent extension of credit in land sales. Several interpretations can be offered for the willingness of agricultural workers and regional villagers to extend credit in these circumstances. They may not have been pressed to obtain cash in return for their land; or, on the contrary, they may have been sufficiently anxious to sell to accept a down payment in cash immediately, and the balance on credit. A third possibility was again land speculation. The extension of credit on the seller's part widened the field of potential buyers and thereby increased the likelihood of sale. Given the worsening conditions of the rural economy in the fourteenth century, the latter two explanations seem more plausible.[32]

TABLE 4

VINEYARD SALE TRANSACTIONS (151)

	Sellers		Buyers	
	No. of Acts	% Total Vineyard Sales	No. of Acts	% Total Vineyard Sales
Merchants	19	12.6	10	6.6
Changers/Moneyers			11	7.3
Retail/Wholesale	22	14.7	15	9.9
Nobles/Burgenses	2	1.3	1	1.0
Professions/Education	1	1.0	3	2.0
Jews				
Royal Administration				
Ecclesiastics	4	2.6	3	2.0
Women	29	19.2	16	10.6
Artisans/Service	34	22.5	51	33.8
Food Trades	2	1.3	7	4.6
Agriculture	21	13.9	19	12.6
Foreigners	10	6.6	11	7.3
Unidentified				
Local	2	1.3		
Other	5	3.3	4	2.6

A comparison of Table 1 (buyers) with Table 2 (credit buyers) highlights the use of credit in land purchases by artisans and service trades and to a lesser degree, by agricultural workers and villagers. Merchants and financiers, on the contrary, tended to buy (and sell) for cash, no doubt because they had greater liquidity. Members of the artisan and service trades, as well as agricultural workers and villagers, bought on credit with greater regularity than they sold on credit probably because they had less ready cash. With the exception of the Jews, members of every level of society in Montpellier were engaged in land transactions, revealing the involvement of urban inhabitants in landholding in the immediate countryside.[33]

Of the lands purchased, vineyards accounted for one hundred fifty-one of the two hundred sixty-two sales or approximately fifty-eight per cent of the total. As in Toulouse, suburban Montpellier and the immediate region contained numerous vineyards.[34] They were already mentioned in twelfth-century episcopal, seigneurial and monastic cartularies of the region.[35]

Table 4 shows the distribution of buyers and sellers of vineyards in the notarial sales transactions. Artisans and members of the service trades were acquiring vineyards in greater numbers than any other social group. They purchased 33.8 per cent of the vineyards noted. Women concentrated their purchases of land in vineyards; sixteen of their total of twenty-eight land purchases were in vineyards. Over half (nineteen of thirty-two) of the purchases of lands by agricultural workers were in vineyards. Merchants, changers and moneyers, members of retail/wholesale trades and regional villagers were also recorded in multiple purchases of vineyards. Indeed, in the period under study all classes of self-respecting urban inhabitants of southern France placed considerable importance in the possession of his or her own vineyard and wine cellar.[36] Buying and selling to acquire vineyards producing high yields and good quality grapes may account for some of the turnover in land.

Grapes were a cash crop of significance in the Montpellier hinterland. The region of Montpellier today draws an important part of its revenues from its wine, characterized by rather mediocre quality and light alcoholic count, which is the beverage of wide-spread current consumption. The pre-eminent role of wine among medieval beverages hardly needs to be recalled here. In the south of France, wine was consumed by every social class. It is well known that people in the Middle Ages drank the new wine; they lacked modern methods of wine preservation.[37] As soon as the grapes were harvested, they had to be trampled for their juice. Wine production was *artisanal* in nature; most vineyard owners probably made their own wine.

The remaining notarial registers of Montpellier provide little information about the sale of wine and no details of its vintage. Nevertheless, the skills of Montpelliérains in the processing of unusual wines formed part of the town's reputation abroad in the thirteenth century. It has been suggested that the existence of a medical school and the perfection of medieval apothecary science in Montpellier led to the production of special wines, seasoned with various spices. English documents mention a certain Robert of Montpellier who was sent before Christmas of

1251 to York to prepare *giroflé* (*garhilfilatum*), a wine seasoned with cloves, and claret as he was accustomed to do in the past.[38]

Wine of Montpellier appeared on the table of the king of France at the beginning of the thirteenth century.[39] The reputation of local wine also reached the papal court in Avignon which was itself situated in a region of wine production. Papal accounts recorded purchases of wine of Melgueil and Castelnau along with wine of Lunel, Saint-Gilles and Nimes.[40] These prestigious outlets for wine of the region of Montpellier prove the existence of an export trade in wine the details of which escape analysis in the notarial registers.[41] They suggest the potential profit in vineyards producing wine grapes. The production of table grapes might also be a function of viticulture.

In most sales of vineyards and of grapes the geographical location of the vineyard was sufficient to characterize the quality of the grapes and hence of the wine. There were clearly geographical locations more prized than others, yielding a better-quality wine grape. The quality of the vineyard yield undoubtably varied according to growing conditions, the fertility of the land and its appropriateness for the vine, the type and quality of the vine, the exposure to sunshine, and other factors, incalculable from the notarial evidence. Without dimensions of vineyards in the sale contracts, little comparative analysis is possible. However, if one can judge by the frequency with which inhabitants of Montpellier bought vineyards in the territory of Montaubérou, lying just to the east of Montpellier, it must be considered the most favored area of grape production in the years 1293–1348. Pérols and Soriech to the southeast came next in local renown. The great variety of vineyards cited in the vineyard sales and grape sales suggests just how widespread this cultivation was in the Montpellier hinterland.[42] Prices for grapes varied in the years 1327–1343 from 5 *s.* to 15 *s.* per *saumata,* the highest price being quoted for grapes from the terrains of Montaubérou.[43]

What did the vineyard represent for Montpellier and its region? Frequently, the sale of grapes or wine was the only source of financial resources or credit for a humble tradesman or cultivator because grapes were the only surplus production he could rely upon. The acts mentioning wine were sporadic, but they show that inhabitants employed the barrel of wine as a sort of unity of barter. One sold wine in order to pay one's debts or to finance one's trade. In 1301 a goldsmith and his wife owed 16 *l.* to another goldsmith. A decision of the *bayle's* court on October 5, 1301, just following the grape harvest, ordered the couple to sell the three barrels of wine in their cellar in partial payment of their debt.[44] For the well-to-do artisan or member of the service trades, purchase of vineyards with an eye to the sale of grapes or the production of wine represented an attractive investment option promising a cash return. For those without family ties to the long-distance luxury trade, commerical investment, albeit it of great potential profit, required high capitalization and may have seemed a larger risk. The greater use of credit by artisans and members of the service trades may reflect not only fewer cash reserves than those of the merchant classes but also the nature of viticulture. Viticulture is cost-intensive in the beginning, for newly planted vines or a replanted vineyard did not reach full productivity for a few years. Since viticulture was a long-term investment with initial cost outlays, inhabitants with fewer cash reserves may have preferred credit purchases of the lands themselves to retain sufficient operating capital.

For the region of Montpellier it is impossible to draw conclusions regarding the extent of arable lands, or indeed, about the propor-

TABLE 5

PERCENTAGE OF VINEYARDS IN LAND SALES

Notarial Register	Year	Lands Total	Vineyards Total	Percentage
A.M. II 1	1293-94	11	10	90.9
A.M. II 2	1301-02	9	5	55.6
A.D.E 95/368	1327-28	41	24	58.5
A.D.E 95/369	1333	20	11	55.0
A.D.E 95/373	1333	7	2	28.6
A.D.E 95/370	1336	30	12	40.0
A.D.E 95/374	1337-42	13	4	30.8
A.D.E 95/375	1339-40	20	14	70.0
A.D.E 95/371	1342	32	27	84.4
A.M. II 3	1342-43	5	1	20.0
A.D.E 95/372	1343-44	21	12	57.1
A.D.E 95/376	1346			
A.D.E 95/377	1347-48	53	29	54.7
TOTALS		262	151	

tion of vineyards in the land economy. However, the notarial transactions suggest that concentration of investments in vineyards was high in 1293–1294, a period of relatively good harvests and general economic prosperity, when ten of the eleven sales involved vineyards. Table 5 shows that the second quarter of the fourteenth century, a less propitious period, witnessed a drop in vineyard investments to about fifty per cent of land purchases, the remaining purchases being in arable land for the most part. The need to cultivate more land in grain was understandable in years of documentably poor harvest such as 1333.[45]

The cost of investment in land and the use of credit in land acquisition deserve further exploration in spite of the limitations of the evidence. The predilection of merchants and financiers to buy land for cash may reflect a desire to avoid the higher cost involved in credit. That credit prices were higher, however, can only be surmised. Few documents quote exact prices, precise size and location of lands, and few specify circumstances that would affect the value of parcels, such as proximity to water sources, exposure to sun, quality of the soil, and, in the case of vineyards, qualities of the wine to be obtained there. Nor is it always clear whether the sale price included an increment because of the level of *census* to be paid to a third party. These often unknown factors, of course, will have to be kept in mind in the tentative calculation of the movement of prices sketched in Graph 1.[46]

It has not been possible to establish price series for land values given the omissions in the notarial contracts cited above. However, the average value of land transactions in years of surviving evidence does admit of analysis.[47] The average price of land transactions recorded annually declined from a peak at the beginning of the fourteenth century to a level rarely surpassing a third of the earlier average transaction level at the mid century. Land prices in general spanned a wide range: from a high of 273 *l.t.* in 1301 to a low of .36 *l.t.* in 1348.[48] The data of 1301–1302 come from the second surviving notarial register in which, as Table 5 shows, there were only nine land sales, most of which were high in price. The 273 *l.t.* price was paid for two vineyards at Morinhac in the *decimaria* of Montaubérou, mentioned above as a source of quality grapes.

If credit transactions alone are considered, the range of land prices was from a high of 82.5 *l.t.* in 1347 to the same low of .36 *l.t.* Each year for which evidence remains there was considerable variation of values in both credit and cash transactions. Comparison of the overall average value of credit transactions yields a figure of 17.3 *l.t.* per sale in

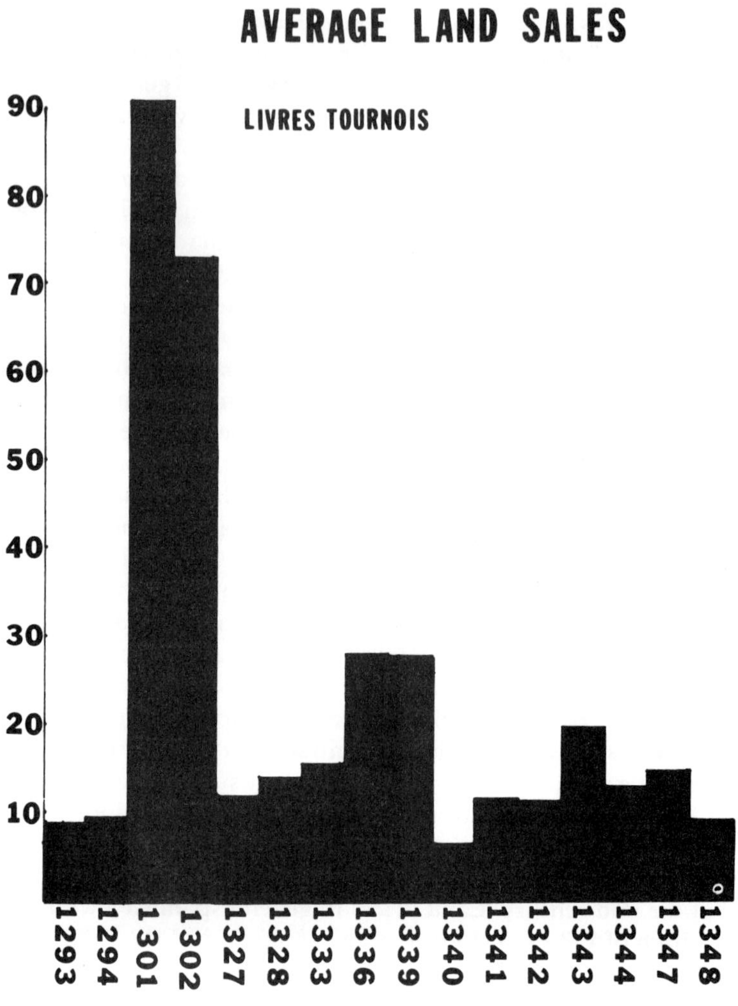

GRAPH I

contrast to 22.8 *l.t.* for the total pool of sales, credit and cash. The data are not sufficiently reliable to permit a conclusive interpretation.[49] It may have been that the poorer credit buyers were priced out of the market for the choicer or larger parcels of land. The financial resources of the artisan and service trades and of agricultural workers and villagers, all active in the land market, were not the equal of merchants, financiers and retail/wholesalers.

In credit transactions the need for large cash outlays was reduced. The down payment in a credit sale of land might, in fact, represent only a fraction of the total price of sale. The lowest figures for the down payments noted amounted to approximately 23 per cent of the sale price.[50] However, down payments could go as high as 86 per cent of the price of sale.[51] About 50 per cent down payment was a common figure.[52] Almost 20 per cent (10 of 53) of the credit sales contracts can be identified as full credit transactions with future arrangments to pay. The terms of payment in down payment sales and full credit sales ranged from "on demand" agreements, *de die in diem*, to schedules of payments which were spread over several years.[53] Most contracts stipulated repayment on the date of a religious feast after a period of from three to nine months. Major religious festivals were chosen as terms of payment.[54] In contrast to the concentration of repayments of loans at specific times of the year, terms in land sales were scattered throughout the calendar year.[55] The evident variety of arrangements for payment may have enabled artisans, members of the service trades, agricultural workers and villagers to participate more fully in the acquisition of real estate.

* * *

In summary, the salient features of the agricultural land market in Montpellier can be briefly rehearsed. The preeminent interest in vineyard acquisition among Montpelliérains of all social groups and, in particular, among artisans and members of the service trades stands out among possible conclusions. Agricultural workers and regional villagers were also active in the vineyard market. While grapes were a cash crop, grain production was an essential rural occupation, and Montpellier, with its substantial population, was a large client. Thus, sales of arable land figure in land transactions providing access to food supplies and additional sources of income.

The land market in Montpellier showed the use of credit in a minority of transactions, approximately 20 per cent. The ratio of credit to cash may have been smaller, in fact, since some cash sales could have escaped the notarial record. Given the medieval concern with land transfers, however, most land sales probably took some written form in the late Middle Ages.

Techniques of real estate acquisition varied according to social and occupational group in Montpellier. Merchants, financiers and retail/wholesalers dealt more frequently in cash than did artisans, agricultural workers and villagers who tended to buy land on credit and, to a lesser degree, to sell it on credit. The range in the size of down payments and in the terms of payment offered considerable flexibility for the credit buyer.

Price series for land transactions are elusive in the late Middle Ages and inexistent for Montpellier.[56] However, the general trend in land values would seem to be downward in concert with grain prices. In his study of medieval and renaissance Pistoia, David Herlihy noted a slight decline in land values from 1300–1350, at a time when commodity prices were also in decline.[57] In this respect, the Montpellier evidence of average values of land transactions reflects the general trend. The grain trade in Montpellier showed erratic overall behavior, affected by variation in annual harvests as well as by Mediterranean grain imports, and may account, in part, for the fluctuation in average land sales.[58] The importance of vineyards in the region of Montpellier may have supported the land market to some degree since wine was a product of greater elasticity of demand than grain.[59] Another hedge against falling grain prices lay in the conversion of lands to grazing pasture for sheep. Although sheep raising was a feature of the rural economy in the Montpellier hinterland, the notarial registers preserved no trace of such conversions.

The purchase of land was an investment choice in Montpellier as elsewhere in Europe in this period. By the late thirteenth century in Flanders, David Nicholas discerned a fluid land market representing new investment options for urban inhabitants of substance who were not always members of the traditional urban patriciate.[60] The latter declined to speculate in land. In Montpellier, well-to-do artisans and established peasants were more heavily involved in the real estate market in the vicinity of Montpellier than were the traditional moneyed groups of commerce and finance. For this "middle class," investment in vineyards, in particular, yielded a steady source of profit, more affordable and more reliable, in spite of the vicissitudes of climate, than investment in trade.

HOUSE SALES

Although purchases of rural land were the most numerous forms of real estate transactions which have been preserved in the notarial registers, they formed only a portion, albeit a substantial one, of the landed fortune of inhabitants of Montpellier.[61] Houses in town represented an important form of investment in real property. The extant urban real estate transactions dealt with houses and, to a lesser degree, shops in the town and its suburbs.

Certain historical and topographic features of Montpellier are worthy of note. The division of the town into two quarters can be documented from the eleventh century.[62] The seigneurial quarter, called Montpellier, was under the rule of the Guilhem family until 1204 when it passed under Aragonese control during an urban revolt which resulted in the establishment of a *consulat*.[63] In 1276 this quarter passed into Majorcan hands at the division of Aragonese lands among successors of Jacme I the Conqueror.[64] The quarter of Montpellier contained a more important concentration of population and business than did the episcopal quarter of the bishop of Maguelone, Montpelliéret, which was purchased in 1293 by Philip the Fair. The Commune Clôture fortifications, begun at the end of the twelfth century and completed during the

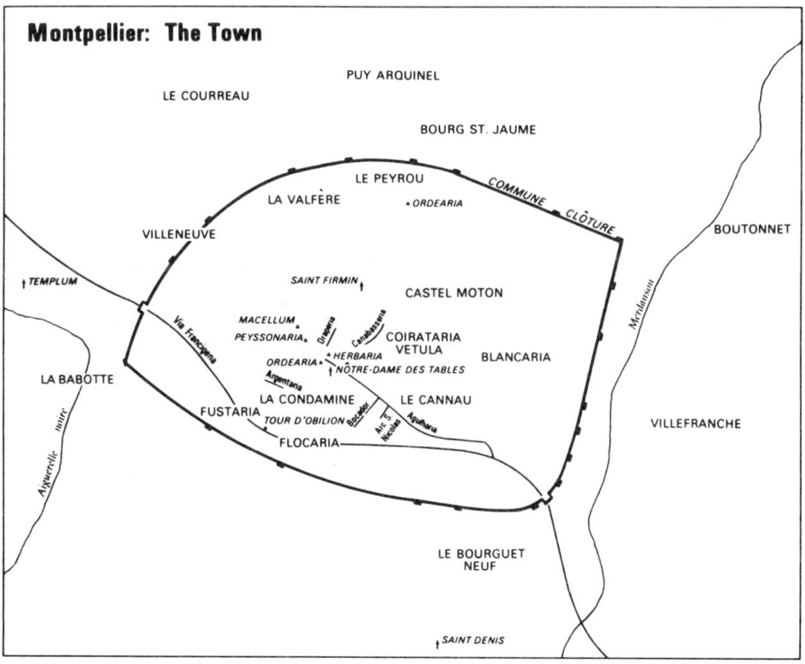

thirteenth century, enclosed in forty hectares portions of both Montpellier and Montpelliéret.[65] In the course of these centuries suburbs had grown up outside the walls. Of the 30,000 to 40,000 inhabitants in Montpellier in the period of this study, some possessed lands in both Montpellier and Montpelliéret. A complex interlace of politics and jurisdiction underlay business and property relations in the town of Montpellier. Map 2 provides a view of the town and its suburbs.

Few remains of architectural significance of the medieval period have survived in modern Montpellier. Once inside the fortifications of the Commune Clôture, the observer of medieval Montpellier would have been confronted with a maze of narrow streets, some carrying the names of occupations such as rue de l'Aiguillerie, rue de la Corraterie, rue de la Blanquerie. Neighborhoods partially or entirely enclosed by the Commune Clôture were also designated in some cases by

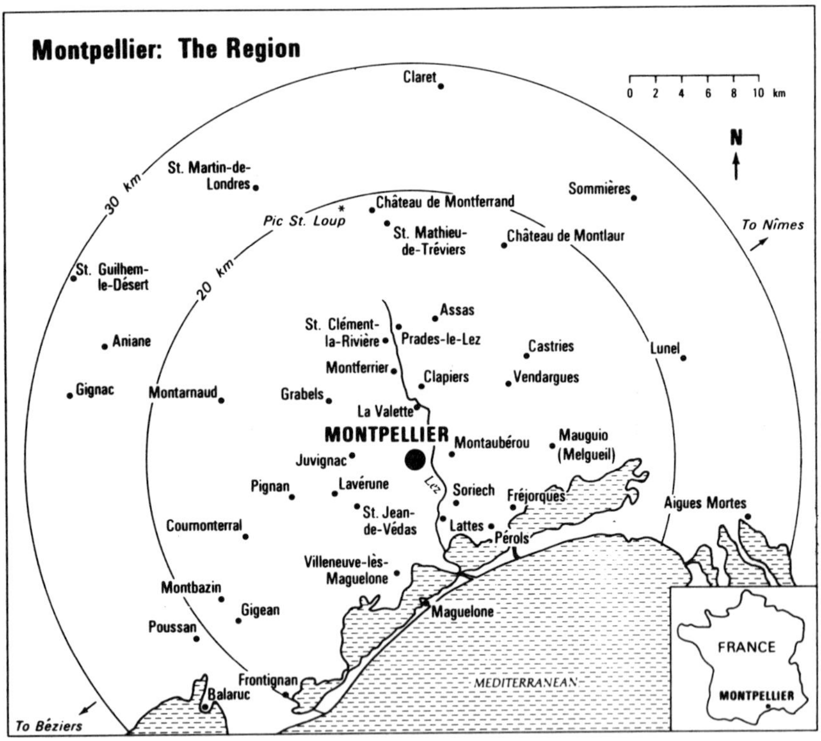

Montpellier: The Region

occupational name: the Blancaria and the Flocaria. The pilgrimage church of Nôtre-Dame-des-Tables, which lay in the southeastern corner of the fortifications not far from the Obilion gate, was the focus of the money changers' tables. The most important road crossing Montpellier was the via Francigena, the commercial road coming from Italy; it entered the Commune Clôture by the Nimes road and exited via the rue de la Saunerie and the road to Béziers to the west. Its path through Montpellier followed that of the Cami roumieu, the pilgrimage road from Saint Gilles in Provence to Santiago in Spain.[66] Greater or lesser proximity to sites of commercial importance or the major urban monuments such as churches and the seigneurial châteaux may have influenced the cost of urban housing. The size and architecture of the houses themselves must also have been factors in the sale price of houses.[67]

Little precise information remains regarding domestic architecture in Montpellier. In a recent article Jacques Peyron analyzed the few archeological traces of medieval houses that have survived.[68] He singled out several types of houses ranging from the little family house on a small parcel of land to the important urban dwelling with a vaulted first floor which served as a commercial warehouse. The extant notarial acts of Montpellier make only two distinctions in terminology regarding houses. The term *hospitium* was applied as a general rule to houses within the town. The *hospitium* usually had two stories, the first of which might have been a vaulted commercial entrepôt. The term *domus,* in contrast, was generally restricted in the remaining documents to simple, low structures in the suburbs or outlying rural districts. Even the small houses described by Peyron, to which he did not give a name, might accommodate a shop on the first or ground floor. Stories of *hospitia* might be sold or let separately. There is no indication in most of the notarial acts that the land on which a house sat was sold or held independently of the structure itself. Occasionally, however, an act specifically stated that an *hospitium* was sold "cum quadam domo seu subterranea et cum toto suo solo et cum omnibus soculis, solis, cameris, fundamentis, parietibus, tecto et edifficio. . . ."[69] Some houses were sold along with vineyards, orchards and wells. In a few cases, several houses were sold together. Four houses (*domus*) and a garden in a suburb of Montpellier behind the Temple of the Knights of St. John of Jerusalem were purchased in 1327 by a gardener.[70] Blocks of houses or *tenentia* were also recorded in the sales contracts.

* * *

The house sales contract, whether credit or cash, resembled the land transaction.[71] The house was situated topographically according to contiguous holdings of Montpellier inhabitants. Eighteen of the ninety-two extant house sales transactions were credit operations; the remaining were cash sales. The credit house sales reflect the same form of ambiguity of notarial practice in the use of down payment sales followed by recognitions of debt in some, but not all, of the credit transactions. Two of the remaining acts can be identified as full credit sales.[72]

Active sellers and buyers of houses in Montpellier were drawn from the retail/wholesale trades, from merchants and from Montpellier women (Table 6). These groups were also frequent house buyers along with artisans and members of the service trades. The breakdown by

TABLE 6

SALES OF HOUSES (92)

	Sellers		Buyers	
	No. of Acts	% Total Acts	No. of Acts	% Total Acts
Merchants	12	13.0	11	12.0
Changers/Moneyers	3	3.3	6	6.5
Retail/Wholesale	17	18.5	18	19.6
Nobles/Burgenses	3	3.3		
Professions/Education	4	4.3	6	6.5
Jews			4	4.3
Royal Administration	2	2.2	1	1.1
Ecclesiastics	2	2.2	2	2.2
Women	19	20.7	13	14.1
Artisans/Service	6	6.5	14	15.2
Food Trades	3	3.3	4	4.3
Agriculture	8	8.7	2	2.2
Foreigners	9	9.8	7	7.6
Unidentified				
Local	1	1.1	1	1.1
Other	3	3.3	3	3.3

TABLE 7

WOMEN AS BUYERS AND SELLERS IN HOUSE SALES
SOCIAL BACKGROUND

	House Sellers	House Buyers
Merchants	1	
Changers/Moneyers		1
Retail/Wholesale	5	1
Nobles/*Burgenses*		2
Professions/Education	1	1
Jews		
Royal Administration		
Ecclesiastics		1
Artisans/Service	6	1
Food Trades		1
Agriculture	2	2
Foreigners	3	2
Unidentified		
Local	1	
Other		1
TOTAL	19	13

social background of women engaged in the housing market, given in Table 7, reflects the breadth of participation of the population as a whole. Overall, only the Jews were absent from among total sellers (Table 1), although they bought houses.[73] Women represented the nobles and *burgenses* among buyers (Table 7). Table 8 shows the distribution of sellers and buyers in the eighteen credit sales which represent about 20 per cent of the total house sales. Worthy of note was the relatively high participation of artisans and members of the service trades as credit purchasers here in house transactions as they had been in land acquisition.

Houses purchased on credit would seem to be more expensive than cash purchases, but the number of contracts and the average differ-

TABLE 8

CREDIT SALES OF HOUSES (18)

	Sellers			Buyers		
	No. of Acts	% Total Credit Sales	Credit Sales as % of All Sales	No. of Acts	% Total Credit Sales	Credit Sales as % of All Sales
Merchants	2	11.1	2.2			
Changers/Moneyers	1	5.6	1.1	2	11.1	2.2
Retail/Wholesale	3	16.7	3.3	2	11.1	2.2
Nobles/<u>Burgenses</u>	1	5.6	1.1			
Professions/ Education	2	11.1	2.2	1	5.6	1.1
Jews						
Royal Administration						
Ecclesiastics						
Women	2	11.1	2.2	1	5.6	1.1
Artisans/Service	2	11.1	2.2	6	33.3	6.5
Food Trades				1	5.6	1.1
Agriculture	1	5.6	1.1	1	5.6	1.1
Foreigners	3	16.7	3.3	2	11.1	2.2
Unidentified						
Local	1	5.6	1.1	2	11.1	2.2
Other						

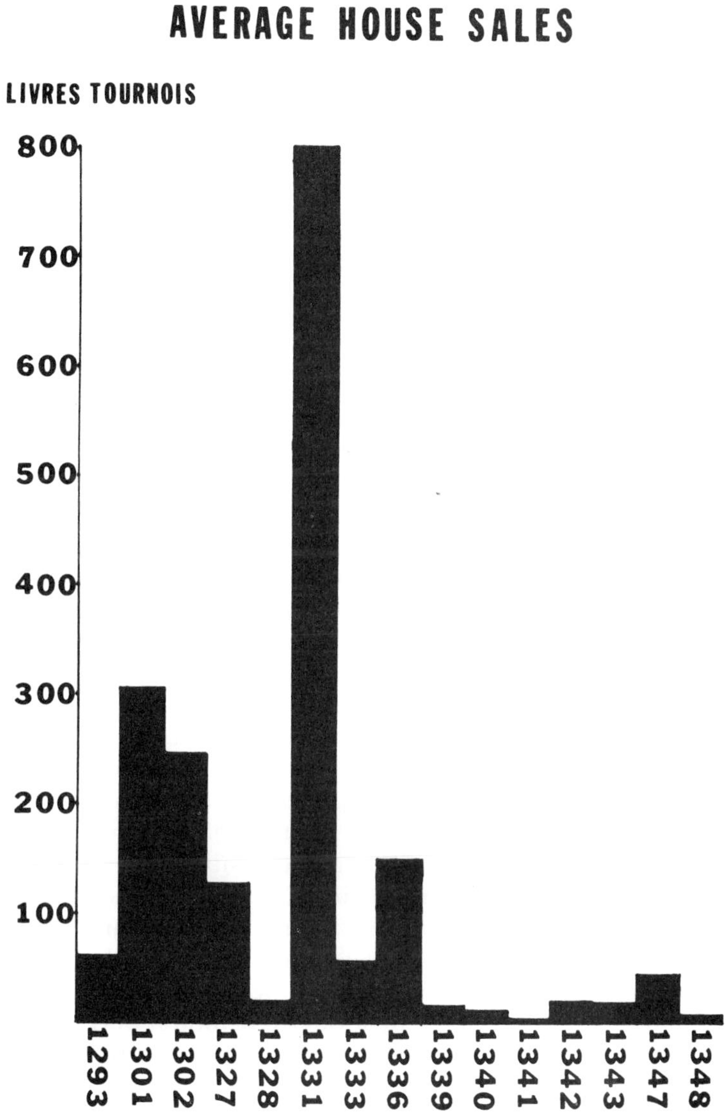
AVERAGE HOUSE SALES
LIVRES TOURNOIS
800
700
600
500
400
300
200
100
1293
1301
1302
1327
1328
1331
1333
1336
1339
1340
1341
1342
1343
1347
1348

GRAPH 2

ence in prices are too small to confirm this impression. The largest recorded sale price, concerning a group (*tenentia*) of houses, was charged on credit to a Montpellier draper in 1331.[74] Full payment had not yet been made two years later.[75] The amount of down payment varied widely in credit sales, from 10 per cent to 80 per cent; so did the terms of payment, whether "on demand," in several installments, or with a single deadline.[76]

Graph 2 gives the movement of average prices of houses per transaction.[77] With the exception of the year 1331 when the large credit sale above occurred, the overall trend in housing values was downward from the beginning to the mid-fourteenth century.

* * *

In conclusion, the patterns of market behavior visible in housing and land sales can be examined to illumine similarities and differences. When the rural land and urban housing markets are compared, several common phenomena emerge. In both, the use of credit in the acquisition of property was limited to about 20 per cent of all transactions. With the notable exception of houses in the year 1331, the average values of house sales show a more consistent downward trend from the late thirteenth to the mid-fourteenth century than do the fluctuating land values. In both land and house purchases, Montpelliérains took a conservative stance with regard to the use of credit. Even the credit transactions of the most frequent credit buyers, the artisans and members of the service trades, reflected only a modest percentage of total house and land purchases. Merchants, changers and members of the retail/wholesale trades preferred to use cash in real estate acquisition.

Several features further distinguish the activities of Montpellier social groups in the housing and land markets. Merchants, changers and members of the retail/wholesale trades participated at a higher percentage in the housing market than in the land market. In contrast, artisans, members of the service trades and agricultural workers bought and sold houses at lower percentages than lands. These three latter groups were more interested in investment in the countryside.

The predominance of cash in the real estate market contrasts sharply with the omnipresence of credit transactions in the commercial economy.[78] The hypothesis held by many economic historians of the fourteenth century that the medieval economy was starved for cash would bear reconsideration in light of the marked presence of cash in real estate transactions in Montpellier.[79] It may be that Montpelliérains directed available cash reserves at investment in real property, thus exacerbating coinage shortages, but that cash flowed freely in this sector of the local economy seems undeniable. However, if inhabitants poured cash into real estate, this tactic did not result necessarily in the immobilization of capital. The possibilities of exploitation of real property assets need further investigation in the following section.

REAL ESTATE REVENUES

Real estate holdings could provide urban investors with ready cash capital if they chose to sell their rural lands or houses. However, sale in cash or less frequently on credit was only one means of deriving a return from real estate investment. Many other possibilities for income production existed for the holders of rights over property. Abstract rights of eminent domain, unrelated to the productivity of a particular holding, could be alienated in perpetuity or until further sale or transfer, in return for a steady annual revenue. The use of lands or houses could be leased in perpetuity or sold for a limited period of time, in return for a lump sum or a yearly fee, or rented out for a limited period. The future fruits of real property could be sold for a specific term. Further credit techniques such as annuities and recovery sales (*ventes à rémeré*) have left traces in the Montpellier evidence. Some of these investments were speculative, i.e. tied to the productivity of real estate or to its resale value. Some were subject only to the risks of inflation and currency manipulation.

* * *

Owners of allodial real estate benefitted from a variety of means of exploiting their property. They could sell rights of use over property, permanently in the sale of *dominium utile* or for a limited period in the sale of usufruct. Allodial owners could also lease or rent real property. Allodial ownership, it will be recalled, included both *dominium directum*, the abstract rights of eminent domain, and *dominium utile*, possession or right of use. Owners of *dominium utile* could rent property out or sell rights over it for limited periods of time. Abstract rights of eminent domain over property entitled owners to yearly revenues and to approval fees for the sale or transfer of rights of use.

The prevalence of holdings of eminent domain can be compared with the frequency of allodial ownership in the house and land sales studied earlier. These sales provide a useful field of observation of the land holding situation in Montpellier. Table 9 provides the numbers of explicit mentions of rights of eminent domain held by a third party in house sales. The nineteen cases in which no reference to either allodial rights or eminent domain was recorded may conceal cases in which allodial ownership was the rule, yet the stated presence of rights of eminent domain in seventy-three of the ninety-two extant transactions suggests that much of the urban soil in Montpellier was subject to a regime of divided property rights: use (*dominium utile*) and eminent domain (*dominium directum*).

Those inhabitants in possession of rights of eminent domain in houses of Montpellier are listed in Table 10. As noted earlier, there was no indication in house sales contracts that the structures themselves were sold separately from the ground upon which they were located. In the first half of the fourteenth century the proprietors of eminent

TABLE 9

EMINENT DOMAIN AND ALODIAL RIGHTS IN HOUSE SALES

Notarial Register	Year	Total	Eminent Domain	Alodial Rights	No Record
A.M. II 1	1293-94	2	1		1
A.M. II 2	1301-02	11	9		3
A.D.E 95/368	1327-28	16	15		1
A.D.E 95/369	1333	7	6		1
A.D.E 95/373	1333	2	1		1
A.D.E 95/370	1336	8	7		1
A.D.E 95/374	1337-42				
A.D.E 95/375	1339-40	15	11		4
A.D.E 95/371	1342	6	4		2
A.M. II 3	1342-43	3	2		1
A.D.E 95/372	1343-44	12	10		2
A.D.E 95/376	1346				
A.D.E 95/377	1347-48	10	7		3
TOTALS		92	73		19

TABLE 10

POSSESSORS OF EMINENT DOMAIN IN HOUSE SALES*

	Number	% Total
King of Majorca	36	49.3
Burgenses	14	19.2
Ecclesiastical Institutions	8	11.0
Bishop of Maguelone	6	8.2
Domicelli	2	2.7
Merchants	2	2.7
Milites	1	1.4
Changers/Moneyers	1	1.4
Consuls	1	1.4
King of France	1	1.4
Unidentified	1	1.4
TOTAL	73	

*The social categories of Ecclesiastics and Nobles/*Burgenses* have been expanded to reflect the variety of participants. Categories have been added for the same reason.

domain belonged, in large measure, to the privileged social groups; the nobility, the ecclesiastical institutions, the bishop of Maguelone and the king of Majorca who was heir to the position of the former seigneurial family, the Guilhem, whose land holdings seem to have been concentrated within the town of Montpellier rather than in the surrounding countryside.[80] The urban nobility, comprised of *burgenses,* or titled bourgeois, the *domicelli,* holders of honorific title in the town and countryside, and the *milites,* the traditional urban nobility who had been members of the seigneurial entourage in the twelfth century, enjoyed prominence as possessors of eminent domain.[81] The presence of these groups within Montpellier can be dated from cartulary records of the early twelfth century.[82] The bishop of Maguelone, lord of the episcopal quarter of Montpelliéret until its sale to the king of France in 1293, retained some rights of eminent domain, as well as property, within the town.[83] Churches and monasteries of the town and the region enjoyed such rights. Compared with the holdings of the above groups, inhabitants from mercantile, financial and legal professions who dominated the trade of Montpellier and the university community were not frequently represented as owners of eminent domain in house sales. They had attained important urban status more recently than the urban nobility in the course of the thirteenth century.

Land sales, detailed in Table 11, reflect a heavy concentration of divided rights. Two hundred eleven of the extant two hundred sixty-two acts (80.5 per cent) noted the possession of rights of eminent domain in the hands of a third party. In nineteen cases specific mention was made of the allodial status of the land.[84] In thirty-two cases no specification of allodial rights or eminent domain was noted. Table 12, showing the distribution of owners of eminent domain in land reveals a somewhat different pattern than that observed in house sales. The urban

TABLE 11

EMINENT DOMAIN AND ALODIAL RIGHTS IN LAND SALES

Notarial Register	Year	Total	Eminent Domain	Alodial Rights	No Record
A.M. II 1	1293-94	11	9	2	
A.M. II 2	1301-02	9	7	2	
A.D.E 95/368	1327-28	41	37		4
A.D.E 95/369	1333	20	17	1	2
A.D.E 95/373	1333	7	4	1	2
A.D.E 95/370	1336	30	21	4	5
A.D.E 95/374	1337-42	13	6		7
A.D.E 95/375	1339-40	20	19		1
A.D.E 95/371	1342	32	28	4	
A.M. II 3	1342-43	5	5		
A.D.E 95/372	1343-44	21	14	2	5
A.D.E 95/376	1346				
A.D.E 95/377	1347-48	53	44	3	6
TOTALS		262	211	19	32

TABLE 12

POSSESSORS OF EMINENT DOMAIN IN LAND SALES*

	Number	% Total
Ecclesiastical Institutions	64	30.3
Burgenses	26	12.3
Bishop of Maguelone	22	10.4
Domicelli	19	9.0
Prévôt of Maguelone	18	8.5
Retail/Wholesale	17	8.1
Professions/Education	8	3.8
King of Majorca	7	3.3
Merchants	6	2.8
Foreign	6	2.8
Milites	5	2.4
Domini	4	1.9
Artisans/Service	4	1.9
Changers/Moneyers	2	0.9
Obriers	2	0.9
Agriculture	1	0.5
TOTAL	211	

*The social categories of Ecclesiastics and Nobles/Burgenses have been expanded to reflect the variety of participants. Categories have been added for the same reason.

nobility, ecclesiastical institutions, the bishop and the prévôt of Maguelone were the most frequently mentioned possessors of eminent domain in the countryside around Montpellier. These groups were the traditional owners of landed wealth in the Middle Ages; their landlord status is reflected in the distribution of these property rights of eminent domain. In rights of eminent domain over land, however, social categories representing the fourteenth-century population composition of

Montpellier were also recorded. The presence, in particular, of members of the retail/wholesale trades is indicative of broader distribution of these traditional rights in the countryside by the period under study. Investment by specialists of commerce in these property rights may signify a diversification of their assets, some, if not the majority of which, were probably directed to trade. The participation, in small numbers, of the artisan and service trades and of agricultural workers suggests just how widespread among the population eminent domain had become by the fourteenth century.

Rights of eminent domain could be turned into cash capital through sale. Yearly revenues were generated by the fees of recognition from the owners of rights of use. Approval fees in cases of transfer or sale provided occasional and unpredictable sources of income. There remain examples of the sale of rights of eminent domain by the older social groups to members of the mercantile trades. On July 17, 1336, a *miles* of Montpellier who was also the *dominus* of Poujols in the diocese of Nimes, sold to a Montpellier mercer the *consilium, laudimium* and all other rights over one-half of three houses in the rue de l'Argenterie, the *dominium utile* of which was held by third parties.[85] The yearly revenues amounted to 2 *d.t.*, payable at the feast of Saint Michael. The sale price for these properties was 25 *l.p.t.* A residual right of *consilium* was held by the king of Majorca; the document stated that the customary *census* (unspecified) was due him at the same feast. Appended to the act was an interlineated note recording the certification of sale for 50 *s.p.t.* by the *bayle* of the court of the king of Majorca in Montpellier.

This example contains several interesting features. First of all, rights of abstract ownership as opposed to possession over these houses were shared between at least two parties, the king of Majorca and the *miles*. Two approaches to the exploitation of property were possible for the owner of allodial rights, the alienation of rights of eminent domain or the alienation of rights of use. Paul-Louis Malausséna remarked in his study of Grasse that the first procedure was a means of generating credit; it resulted in a steady investment return on real property.[86] The above example suggests that the process could be carried even further and the rights of eminent domain themselves carved into several parts. The first right of refusal over sale or transfer of property could, for example, be sold separately from the *directum*, the rights to yearly revenues.[87] Division of rights produced the strata of prerogatives over the three houses of the above example.

In this example the annual return on rights of eminent domain was only a fraction of the price for which such rights could be sold in perpetuity. The 2 *d.t.* represented in fact less than one-tenth of one per cent of the sale approval (*laudimium*) of the alienation of *dominium utile*. The 50 *s.p.t.* paid the *bayle* on behalf of the king of Majorca amounted to ten per cent of the sale price, a level of profit consistent with approval fees in other sales.[88] The greater the turnover of property the more remunerative was the ownership of rights of eminent domain.

The possession of eminent domain by religious establishments and by ecclesiastical officials as a part of their prebends was noted above. Rights of eminent domain might also form the basis of income for chantries which were recorded in increasing numbers as the fourteenth century progressed.[89] Such rights could form part of the original endowment, or they could be acquired by the trustee as a means of steady, if generally modest, income. Thus, on July 4, 1342, a monk of Valemagne, a Cistercian monastery near Béziers, purchased for the chantry of his deceased brother, a flour merchant of Montpellier, rights of *directum, consilium* and *laudimium* over vineyards from a butcher of Montpellier for 219 *l.* current money (43.8 *l.* in money of 1330).[90] The annual return on this investment amounted to almost 5 *l.* or about a two-per cent return.

Rights of eminent domain might carry with them other prerogatives. On April 8, 1342, a priest sold a piece of land with a house and a well to a flour merchant of Montpellier for 35 *l.t.*[91] A merchant of Montpellier held the rights of eminent domain over this property. He had, however, on March 1, 1342, sold a right of first refusal over the property to a changer. The changer was able to intervene in the sale transaction and purchase the property from the flour merchant, invoking his right of approval. In principle there existed no *retrait lignager* in regard to the eminent domain of non-feudal property (*censives*), but, as P. Ourliac and J. de Malafosse have noted in their history of private law, the *Parlements* of Bordeaux and Toulouse permitted the lord to retain an inheritance which had been sold as long as he reimbursed the buyer for the purchase price and any other cost.[92] This example from Montpellier implies an extension of such a prerogative to the holder of rights of first approval. In the act in question, the changer made a down payment on the price of sale and drew up a recognition of debt in favor of the flour merchant, promising payment at Ascension and at the feast of Saint John. The right of recovery of property in a sale was explicitly called the *jus retinendi* in other acts.[93]

The rights of seizure of the *dominium utile* of property for nonpayment of *census* were also at times invoked. On October 2, 1343, a candlemaker came into conflict with the preceptor of the Hôpital de Nôtre-Dame de Montpellier, the possessor of direct domain over a field held by the candlemaker.[94] The latter resolved to cede the field to the hospital to be free of the eight *sestarii* of wheat which he owed in *census*. Some pressure must have been applied by the preceptor as the candlemaker received in the compromise three *sestarii* of wheat from him. No court intervention was cited.

In some cases the reason for conversion of rights of eminent domain into cash capital was given. Although the rate of return in a year without sale or transfer might bring only minimal profit, the inherent value of these rights could be realized in a time of need. On May 21, 1333, Maria, widow of the deceased merchant Petrus Lamberti, appeared before the vice-judges of the court of the king of Majorca, to seek the approval of the court for her sale of rights of eminent domain belonging to the estate of her dead husband.[95] The notarial record of this proceeding relates that she testified that her late husband had made a will, written by the Montpellier notary Guillelmus Nogareti, in which he, Petrus, had named his son Jacobus as his universal heir. Acting as *tutrix* of her son, Maria stated that there were no credits due or personal effects with which she could satisfy her late husband's debts to a Lombard, Antonius de Feria.[96] De Feria had threatened to institute legal proceedings to force liquidation of the goods of Petrus in order to obtain payment.[97] Maria proposed to sell rights of *consilia, laudimia* and *usatica,* in cash and kind over lands and vineyards, for a total price of 28 *l.* 10 *s.p.t.* She engaged the services of sworn brokers of Montpellier who declared, after the appropriate period of time, that if no other buyer appeared, the sale should be made to a grain merchant, Johannes Comitis, who had offered to pay the price which Maria sought. The court heard the details of the offer and then, having received assurances from Maria and from the brokers, declared the sale accomplished. Maria then proceeded to draw the contract of sale, with the approval of the testamentary executors of Petrus' will. Rights in cash and kind over eleven separate holdings were described; the properties were situated geographically and the possessors of rights of use were enumerated. The amount of revenue derived per holding varied from 6 *d.* to 3 *s.* in cash; cash and kind quotations consisted of revenues of three *eymine* of barley and 3 *oboles t.* The total yearly revenues from the sale of these rights came to 13 *s.t.* and six *eymine* of barley. If one *eymina* was worth 2 *s.* in an average year, the total income of all the above rights amounted to 25 *s.t.* which represented a rate of return of 4.4 per cent of the sale price.[98] To amortize the original investment, the purchaser would have needed to retain these revenues for twenty years under stable monetary and economic conditions. If the *dominium utile* of any of the properties changed hands, the payment of approval fees would have substantially increased the income of these rights.

A rate of between four and five per cent return on the original investment compares favorably with the rates of return from *rentes foncières* studied by Etienne Fournial for the Forez region, where the average was about 5 per cent.[99] Many yearly revenues on eminent domain in Montpellier and its region were substantially lower, as earlier examples have demonstrated. The term of amortization hypothesized above recalls that indicated by David Nicholas in his examination of the return on land rentals in Flanders by the later fourteenth century.[100] Nicholas suggested that landlordship had become less profitable then than it had been in the thirteenth and early fourteenth century. The remaining documents of Montpellier provide examples where the investment in rights of eminent domain proved only marginally profitable if yearly revenues at token levels of several *deniers* were considered.

However, exceptions to this low annual return can be noted. The chaplain of the monastery of Saint-Guilhem-le-Désert received 60 *s.t.* in fees of recognition from a field and a vineyard, worth only 8 *l.p.t.* in a sale made by a cultivator of Montpellier to a master mason.[101] Hence, the annual return represented 37.5 per cent of the original investment.

In another instance, one pound of pepper and 10 *l.t.* were due the prior of Saint-Pierre-de-Cluneset annually for his rights over a house and a well located in rue Pila Saint-Gély by which the via Francigena entered Montpellier from the northwest.[102] A leather worker sold the house to a grain merchant of Montpellier for 30 *l.p.t.* (worth 15 *l.p.t.* in the money of 1330). The annual return was thus 33.3 per cent. Such widely varying returns on investments in rights of eminent domain may reflect an era of changing real estate values.[103] The market value may have been depressed by the high *census* on the property.

Such widely varying returns on investments in eminent domain rights could have been the result of the specific circumstances surrounding their establishment. The rapid or infrequent turnover of properties might have affected the rate of yearly revenues. If an owner of allodial rights had alienated rights of eminent domain in the recent past, the rate of return on these rights may have been greater than the rates surviving from the twelfth century. Some revenues may have been in the hands of the same families for many years. Given the inflationary trends of the thirteenth and fourteenth centuries, such fixed fees could have come to represent only a fraction of the actual sale price.[104]

The owners of fixed rents, whether ecclesiastical institutions, clergy, nobility or members of the mercantile classes, suffered financial loss over time in the fourteenth century.[105] Although technically non-speculative in nature, such an investment was vulnerable to inflation and as a fixed revenue, was subject to the frequent currency manipulations of the period under study.[106] From the perspective of 1293–1348, ownership of rights of eminent domain was a conservative investment; in most cases purchase of such rights required a large capital outlay for proportionately low yearly returns. Other types of investment in rights over real property had developed as alternatives to the purchase of eminent domain in the fourteenth century.

For some inhabitants rights of eminent domain still provided a useful investment option. Rights over land which yielded an annual revenue were less speculative than ventures in commerce and finance and than purchases of houses and lands in the real estate market.[107] They provided the means of diversifying family investments which might otherwise have been directed at commercial activities. Rights of eminent domain furnished an automatic yield without the necessity of supervision or of additional investments of time, energy or resources. Revenues from eminent domain were not tied to the productivity of the particular holding, not dependent on the profits from leases or rentals of houses nor on the harvests from fields and vineyards. They could be held in perpetuity until a decision to sell or alienate them through gift or bequest was made. If sold, they generated cash capital for their sellers.

* * *

Many holders of allodial property did not participate in the direct exploitation of that property. The owner of allodial rights had the possibility of alienating rights of eminent domain, just noted. Another way of managing real estate possessions with some profit involved letting the properties out as tenures with the retention of annual *census* fees and payments for renewals of tenure on the occasion of sales or transfers through gift or inheritance. The creation of a tenure resulted in an initiation fee, as well, which could be prorated by the purchaser or scheduled for future payment.[108]

Particularly common in the south of France were grants of perpetual tenure in *emphyteusis* or *accapitum*.[109] There were no substantive distinctions in the Montpellier documents between these two tenures. John Pryor, in his study of the notarial acts of thirteenth-century Marseille, defined the contract of "*accaptum seu emphitheosis*" as an hereditary lease of land for a "fixed annual rent or *census*.."[110] The lessee could sell his tenure provided that he informed the lessor, who then had a first right of acquisition at the market price. In Montpellier the *census* or *usaticum* was generally calculated in cash, but on rare occasions an annual fee in kind has been noted.[111] If the property was sold, the lessor received a transfer fee. The original entrance fee for such a tenure could be considerable. In one grant of May 16, 1336, a merchant purchased a field, forest and vineyard for 210 *l.p.t.* from *domicelli* of the diocese of Maguelone to whom he then left the same property "*in acapitum seu emphiteosim*" for 180 *l.p.t.*[112] The nobles, perhaps in need of cash, found in this fashion a means of retaining their land albeit in tenure rather than in allodial ownership. The amount and quality of the land undoubtedly affected the cost of the tenure here and in other grants.[113] This type of lease was used for both houses in town and lands in the countryside. The surviving records are heavily weighted in favor of rural lands suitable for agricultural exploitation.

The differences between tenures in *accapitum* and *emphyteusis* on the one hand and the ownership of *dominium utile*, transferred in the sales contracts regarding lands and houses examined earlier, seem inexistent in those sales where annual dues and approval fees were included. The lessor in tenures of *accapitum* and *emphyteusis* retained annual dues and approval fees, relating to the rights of eminent domain (*dominium directum*). It is altogether possible that most tenures in Montpellier were by the fourteenth century holdings in *accapitum* and *emphyteusis*, the specific terminology of which was invoked only in new grants or in renewals or transfers of tenure but not in sales of *dominium utile* of properties held in this fashion.

The tenures of *accapitum* and *emphyteusis* have been distinguished by some legal historians from the *bail à cens* in that the former had nothing seigneurial about them.[114] In Montpellier as witnessed above, nobles could be lessees in *accapitum* and *emphyteusis*.[115] In Montpellier the distinction between these tenures and the *censive* is not apparent—even the annual dues were called *census* in the *accapitum/emphyteusis* documents—unless the historical development of tenures is considered.[116] Much of the urban soil of Montpellier in the twelfth century was held as censive tenure from the local lords, the Guilhem family. The fourteenth-century lord, distant successor to the Guilhem seigneurs, was the king of Majorca who held, as observed above, rights of eminent domain.[117] These may have been survivals of the twelfth-century situation. The Guilhem also enjoyed rights of *albergue* which was at its origin the repurchase or redemption of a right of hospitality.[118] A few survivals of this type of tenure were present in the fourteenth-century evidence, acknowledged by a small annual cash payment.[119] If the fate of the seigneurial *censive* cannot be traced in the notarial registers, the *accapitum/emphyteusis* has left, in contrast, a considerable record.

Table 13 provides the distribution of lessors and lessees in *accapitum* and *emphyteusis* contracts regarding lands and houses. Lessors were concentrated among the privileged groups of the town, the nobility, the clergy, merchants and members of the retail/wholesale business. A family whose interests lay in this type of exploitation of landed resources were the Conchis. In 1342, fourteen contracts of new and renewed tenures "ad acapithum seu in emphiteosim perpetuam" were granted by Johannes de Conchis, son of the *domicellus* Guillelmus de Conchis.[120] The family can be traced in Montpellier as early as the beginning of the thirteenth century.[121] Commercial successes of the thirteenth century had led to the accumulation of considerable landed fortune for the family. A total of thirty-seven *cartons* of land were granted out by Johannes to notaries, butchers, tailors, an exchange broker, a merchant, a woman of unidentified background, a stonemason, a *blanquerius*, a pepperer and two unidentified male inhabitants of Montpellier. Measures of barley were owed as yearly payments to Johannes de Conchis. Rights of initiation came to 25 *l.p.t.* of 1330 money.

Another member of the Conchis family, Raymundus alias Guillelmus de Conchis, *burgensis* of Montpellier, used his *accapitum/emphyteusis* holdings in 1347 and 1348 to generate capital by reducing the annual dues owed by the tenures. He made four adjustments of this nature, lowering the *usatica* to a fourth or a fifth of their earlier level, for a cash payment of 16.6 *l.p.t.* in all.[122] Such restructuring of tenure obligations provided real estate ownership with greater flexibility than might have been anticipated in a perpetual tenure. The negotiations which undoubtedly preceded these adjustments have not been preserved. This procedure is reminiscent of earlier commutations of servile work services in areas where serfdom existed. There was no

TABLE 13

ACCAPITUM/EMPHYTEUSIS TENURES OF LANDS AND HOUSES

	Lands-Lessors(120)		Lands-Lessees(120)		Houses-Lessors(8)		Houses-Lessees(8)	
	No. of Acts	% Total Acts	No. of Acts	% Total Acts	No. of Acts	% Total Acts	No. of Acts	% Total Acts
Merchants	25	20.8	7	5.8	2	25.0	2	25.0
Changers/Moneyers	3	2.5						
Retail/Wholesale	22	18.3	9	7.5				
Nobles/<u>Burgenses</u>	20	16.7	2	1.7	3	37.5		
Professions/ Education	3	2.5	3	2.5				
Jews								
Royal Administration								
Ecclesiastics	23	19.2	1	0.8	2	25.0		
Women	10	8.3	18	15.0	1	12.5	2	25.0
Artisans/Service	8	6.7	25	20.8			1	12.5
Food Trades			8	6.7			1	12.5
Agriculture	1	0.8	26	21.7			2	25.0
Foreigners	2	1.7	15	12.5				
Unidentified								
Local			3	2.5				
Other	3	2.5	3	2.5				

TABLE 14

SHARECROPPING ACTS (24)

	Lessors		Lessees	
	No. of Acts	% Total Acts	No. of Acts	% Total Acts
Merchants	3	12.5	1	4.2
Changers/Moneyers	2	8.3		
Retail/Wholesale	5	20.8	3	12.5
Nobles/*Burgenses*	1	4.2		
Professions/Education	1	4.2		
Jews				
Royal Administration				
Ecclesiastics				
Women	5	20.8		
Artisans/Service	2	8.3	5	20.8
Food Trades	1	4.2	2	8.3
Agriculture	4	16.7	10	41.7
Foreigners			1	4.2
Unidentified				
Local			2	8.3
Other				

servile overtone to the tenures of *accapitum* and *emphyteusis*, however.

To be expected was the participation of artisans and members of the service trades, agricultural workers and villagers as lessees in *accapitum* and *emphyteusis* tenure. However, also present in comparable percentages were merchants who held both lands and houses in tenure. Members of the retail/wholesale trades, professionals, clerics, women, members of the food trades and even members of the nobility were recorded as lessees of lands in *accapitum* and *emphyteusis*. By the fourteenth century it was common in the south of France for inhabitants of noble status to hold non-noble lands. From the standpoint of lessees, such tenures permitted possession of lands and houses for annual payments which were not onerous. Sale of these tenures by the lessees was possible. The new lessee was substituted for the old; the notarial acts preserve recognitions of tenure by the new holders, with approval fees for transfer or sale.[123]

The notarial registers are not the only repositories of leases of *accapitum* and *emphyteusis*. Records of the Commune Clôture defense organization contain concessions in *accapitum* of houses, towers, parts of the road bordering the interior of the ramparts and sections of the moat ditch outside the walls to individual inhabitants of Montpellier and to trade corporations such as the wood merchants.[124] The income derived from such grants supported the construction and maintenance of the town walls.

The trustees of religious establishments had recourse to this method of investment to generate operating income. For example, the consuls of Montpellier, acting on behalf of the hospital of Saint-Lazare, granted eleven land leases in *accapitum* and *emphyteusis* to artisans, agricultural workers, members of the food trades and to a silk merchant.[125] For private citizens and for institutions, these leases were a convenient technique of exploiting real estate assets. Because of their long-term nature, however, the lessor of the fourteenth century, like the owner of eminent domain, suffered from a potential decrease in the purchasing power of fixed annual revenues vulnerable to inflation and currency fluctuations. While revenues might be adjusted downward for a fee, it is unlikely that they could be adjusted upward.

* * *

Less permanent in duration than tenures in *accapitum* and *emphyteusis* were sharecropping contracts, grants of *meiaria*.[126] These lasted in general from four to six years.[127] This type of technique provided agricultural credit to the lessee. The lessor furnished the lessee with land in return for one-half of the harvest. Both lessor and lessee shared the risks associated with the vicissitudes of the growing season. Contracts of sharecropping carried various instructions regarding the planting, cultivation and harvesting of specific crops.[128] This form of exploitation of agricultural lands was common in the south of France, as P.-L. Malausséna has shown for Provence and Mireille Castaing-Sicard for Toulouse.[129]

Table 14 provides the distribution of participants in sharecropping contracts. The lessors were drawn from a variety of social groups, with the greatest concentration among members of the retail/-

wholesale trades (20.8 per cent) and women (20.8 per cent). Agricultural workers accounted for 16.7 per cent of the lessors. Among lessees, the largest number of participants were agricultural workers (41.7 per cent) as might have been expected. It is interesting to note, however, that inhabitants with commercial and artisan vocations entered into sharecropping contracts as lessees. There were few barriers to a diversification of occupational interests.

* * *

Rentals (*locatio*) were another temporary means of hiring the exploitation of agricultural lands. Houses in town might also be rented through the same type of contract (*locatio*).[130] The duration of rental contracts ran from several months to several years.[131] While rents were paid yearly in cash, payments might be staggered throughout the year.[132] Short-term concessions such as these permitted desirable financial flexibility, in that rents could be adjusted to economic changes at the end of each lease. In spite of this positive feature, extant land rental contracts were only a third as numerous as long-term leases of land in *accapitum* and *emphyteusis*. House rentals, on the contrary, were numerous.[133] Rentals of shops and tables have also been noted.

Table 15 shows the distribution of landlords and tenants in various rentals. Among the owners renting out rural lands, it is interesting to note the participation of agricultural workers at the same level as that of women and merchants.[134] While most of the lands mentioned in rental contracts were probably allodial, since the acts did not include allusions to owners of eminent domain, the practice of renting out *dominium utile* by owners has been recorded.[135] Tenants renting rural lands belonged in largest numbers to the agricultural workers, artisanal and service trades and retail/wholesale trades. Short-term possession of lands through rental may have accommodated the needs of these groups. In some cases the rental contract included instructions regarding the cultivation of the land, much as the sharecropping contracts had.[136] The costs of land rentals undoubtedly varied with the quality, quantity and location, much as the sale costs did. The remaining rental contracts fail, in most instances, to provide the dimensions of the lands involved; hence comparisons of rental fees were not feasible. No agricultural land rentals surpassed 10 *l.p.t.* in any one year; most were 5 *l.* or less. Since the sale costs of the lands were not provided, no estimation of the recovery cost of purchase through rental is possible.[137]

TABLE 15

RENTALS OF LANDS, HOUSES, TABLES AND SHOPS

	Lands-Landlords(41)		Lands-Tenants(41)		Houses-Landlords(153)		Houses-Tenants(153)		Tables and Shops-Landlords(31)		Tables and Shops-Tenants(31)	
	No. of Acts	% Total Acts	No. of Acts	% Total Acts	No. of Acts	% Total Acts	No. of Acts	% Total Acts	No. of Acts	% Total Acts	No. of Acts	% Total Acts
Merchants	7	17.1	2	4.9	39	25.5	11	7.2	4	12.9		
Changers/Moneyers	1	2.4			10	6.5	6	3.9	1	3.2	3	9.7
Retail/Wholesale	4	9.8	9	22.0	20	13.1	27	17.6	6	19.4	5	16.1
Nobles/_Burgenses_	1	2.4			8	5.2			2	6.5		
Professions/ Education	1	2.4			4	2.6	6	3.9				
Jews					2	1.3						
Royal Administration					1	0.7						
Ecclesiastics	6	14.6	2	4.9	2	1.3	5	3.3				
Women	7	17.1	2	4.9	27	17.6	21	13.7	10	32.3		
Artisans/Service	2	4.9	7	17.1	29	19.0	41	26.8	6	19.4	10	32.3
Food Trades			2	4.9	2	1.3	10	6.5			9	29.0
Agriculture	7	17.1	11	26.8	2	1.3	11	7.2			2	6.5
Foreigners	3	7.3	4	9.8	4	2.6	11	7.2			1	3.2
Unidentified												
Local			1	2.4			2	1.3				
Other	2	4.9	1	2.4	3	2.0	2	1.3	2	6.5	1	3.2

Landlords renting houses in town were broadly distributed with a prominent representation of merchants, retail/wholesalers, artisans, members of the service trades, and women. Among tenants of houses, artisans, the service trades and retail/wholesalers were the most numerous. The rental cost of some urban housing was quite high. In 1333, the widow of a silversmith rented a house and the "*fondaco* of Pisa" to an immigrant from Novara in the Piedmont.[138] Rental was for four years at 40 *l.p.t.* a year. The house and *fondaco* were situated in the Argentaria neighborhood in Montpellier. This district of Montpellier could command high rents from a foreign clientele. In 1328 the widow of a Montpellier merchant rented a house "in caput argentarie juxta plateam burgensium" to a Pisan tailor, who was also an immigrant, for four years at the equivalent of 7 *l.* 15 *s.p.t.* per year.[139] There were other prominent locations in town, including the neighborhood around Nôtre-Dame-des-Tables. Attempts to calculate the profitability of house rentals and the recovery of purchase costs encounter the same kinds of problems noted in regard to land rentals.

Rentals of the ground floor or second story of houses were recorded. Shops, tables and houses with workshops were also rented in town.[140] Tables in the meat markets, in the fish market, workshops in the Argentaria, in the Draperia and changers' tables near Nôtre-Dame-des-Tables were rented to members of the appropriate urban occupations. A table in the fish market rented in 1333 for 5 *l.* 5 *s.p.t.* for one year.[141] A butcher's table in the old meat market was rented at 7 *l.p.t.* per year for two years in 1333.[142] In 1339 a workshop in the Draperia rented for the equivalent of 6 *l.p.t.* per year for two years.[143] A changer's table fetched 3.4 *l.p.t.* a year for three years in 1342.[144]

* * *

Distinctions among participants in short-term rentals and those using long-term *accapitum* and *emphyteusis* leases are worthy of note. Artisans were more frequently noted as short-term lessors of houses and shops than as long-term lessors. Merchants showed a more consistent participation in both forms of leases. The nobles, however, were represented at higher percentages as lessors in the long-term than as lessors in short-term rentals. Women used short-term leases of houses, shops and lands more than long-term contracts, but the social background of women lessors, given in Table 16, showed use of both types of leases in moneyed categories; women of artisan and service and agricultural

TABLE 16

SOCIAL BACKGROUND OF WOMEN PROPERTY OWNERS: LESSORS

	Land Rents	House Rents	Share-Cropping	Land Accapitum Emphyteusis	Houses Accapitum Emphyteusis
Merchants		3		2	
Changers/Moneyers	1		1	2	
Retail/Wholesale			1	4	
Nobles/Burgenses	1	8	1	1	1
Professions/ Education	1	6	2	1	
Jews					
Royal Administration					
Ecclesiastics					
Artisans/Service	3	7			
Food Trades					
Agriculture	1				
Foreigners					
Unidentified					
Local		1			
Other		2			
TOTALS	7	27	5	10	1

background were found only in short-term rentals. Interpretation of women lessees (Table 17) is hampered by the failure of the notaries to identify their clients precisely.

In general, the artisans and members of the service trades may have been less willing and less able than other groups to support the long-term immobilization of capital in leases. Hence their predilection for the short-term as lessors. However, the greater number of house and shop rentals than of long-term leases of houses may account for the above disparities. Among lessees of houses, shops and lands there was a broader range of social and occupational participation than among lessors in both the long and the short-term.

TABLE 17

SOCIAL BACKGROUND OF WOMEN PROPERTY OWNERS: LESSEES

	Land Rents	House Rents	Share-Cropping	Land Accapitum Emphyteusis	Houses Accapitum Emphyteusis
Merchants		2		1	
Changers/Moneyers				1	
Retail/Wholesale		1		2	2
Nobles/*Burgenses*		1			
Professions/ Education					
Jews					
Royal Administration					
Ecclesiastics					
Artisans/Service		3		2	
Food Trades					
Agriculture	2			3	
Foreigners		3		5	
Unidentified					
Local		10		2	
Other		1		2	
TOTALS	2	21		18	2

* * *

The short-term rentals and long-term leases explained above were not the only means at the disposal of property owners in Montpellier for the exploitation of real estate. Revenues from property could be generated through the temporary sale of rights of use and of fruits. Sales of *ususfructus* carried with them the use of the property and the right to take its produce.[145] Sales (*venditio*) of *redditus* or *fructus* involved purchase of the control of the fruits or returns of the property without actual possession of it.[146] Sales of *ususfructus* differed from those of *dominium utile* in that the former was for a temporary period in return for a blanket sum or yearly payments. Notarial terminology at times combined the terms of *ususfructus, fructus* and *redditus* in sales of both use and fruits.[147] Objects of such sales of rights included lands, houses, shops, and mills.[148] Lengths of terms varied in general from two to six years.[149] In the case of farm lands, harvested grain, grapes or other agricultural produce constituted the fruits. If *ususfructus* were transferred, the lands were subject to the direct exploitation of the buyer.[150] They might also be sublet.[151] Further conditions might be included in the sales. For example, on January 7, 1344, a Montpelliérain sold the *ususfructus* of land to a local moneyer for five years for the equivalent of 15 *s.p.t.* (75 *s.* current money) as the total price.[152] The seller retained for himself the first two *setiers* of the grain harvest. If the *ususfructus* of a house or a shop were purchased, the locales might be occupied by the acquirer or be sublet. On September 28, 1342, two merchants sold a local changer the *ususfructus* of a house in the Castelmoton quarter of Montpellier for three years in return for the sum of 30 *l.* current money (6 *l.p.t.* in the money of 1330).[153] In another example of May 8, 1342, a merchant purchased the *ususfructus* of a *hoperatorium* and *solerium* in the pepperers' quarter from a local pepperer, for 35 *l.* per year (8.75 *l.* good money).[154]

The return on this type of investment for the purchaser must have varied considerably. The level of profit was not fixed in advance. Purchase of agricultural fruits from specific lands in periods of poor yields may have resulted in losses. The period of this study was an era of climatic changes and frequent bad harvests; there must have been risks involved in the investment in future yields.[155] Less speculation is obvious in the purchase of the *ususfructus* of houses and shops. In fact, it is difficult to distinguish such a purchase from a rental of such properties.[156] The two contracts were different in Roman law, of course, with the lessee by a *locatio* not considered to be the possessor of the property let.[157] Legal protection may have been at the origin of the contract choices by Montpellier inhabitants. Rentals were generally assigned annual payments; usufructs could stipulate payment in a lump sum. But even on these levels, the practical distinctions are not compelling, and notarial practice in fourteenth-century Montpellier displays a seemingly indiscriminate use of these contracts.

Buying and selling rights over lands and houses was a practice shared widely by the inhabitants of Montpellier, as Table 18 shows. Sales of rights, fruits and use of lands were also common among regional

TABLE 18

SALES OF RIGHTS, FRUITS, USE IN LANDS AND HOUSES

	Lands-Sellers(77)		Lands-Buyers(77)		Houses-Sellers(36)		Houses-Buyers(36)	
	No. of Acts	% Total Acts	No. of Acts	% Total Acts	No. of Acts	% Total Acts	No. of Acts	% Total Acts
Merchants	12	15.6	8	10.4	5	13.9	5	13.9
Changers/Moneyers			4	5.2	2	5.6	5	13.9
Retail/Wholesale	7	9.1	12	15.6	4	11.1	8	22.2
Nobles/Burgenses	3	3.9	1	1.3	4	11.1	2	5.6
Professions/ Education	2	2.6	1	1.3			1	2.8
Jews								
Royal Administration								
Ecclesiastics	4	5.2	1	1.3	1	2.8		
Women	12	15.6	8	10.4	5	13.9	1	2.8
Artisans/Service	3	3.9	11	14.3	5	13.9	7	19.4
Food Trades	4	5.2	1	1.3			1	2.8
Agriculture	9	11.7	19	24.7	4	11.1	2	5.6
Foreigners	19	24.7	11	14.3	5	13.9	3	8.3
Unidentified								
Local	1	1.3						
Other	1	1.3			1	2.8	1	2.8

TABLE 19

SOCIAL BACKGROUND OF WOMEN IN SALES OF RIGHTS

	Sellers Land Rights	Buyers Land Rights	Sellers House Rights	Buyers House Rights	Sellers Shop Rights
Merchants	3		1		
Changers/Moneyers			1		
Retail/Wholesale	3	2		1	
Nobles/Burgenses		1			1
Professions/Education	1				
Jews			1		
Royal Administration					
Ecclesiastics					
Artisans/Service	3	2			
Food Trades					
Agriculture		1			
Foreigners					
Unidentified					
Local		1			
Other	2	1	2		
TOTALS	12	8	5	1	1

TABLE 20

LAND EXCHANGES-PARTICIPANTS (25 Acts)

	No. of Participants	% Total Participants
Merchants	11	22.0
Changers/Moneyers	2	4.0
Retail/Wholesale	9	10.0
Nobles/Burgenses		
Professions/Education		
Jews		
Royal Administration		
Ecclesiastics		
Women	9	18.0
Artisans/Service	5	10.0
Food Trades	3	6.0
Agriculture	5	10.0
Foreigners	6	12.0
Unidentified		
Local		
Other		

villagers (foreigners, Table 18). Agricultural workers frequently took advantage of this means of obtaining land. Table 19 provides the social background of women involved as sellers and buyers in such contracts. Owners of the *dominium utile* of lands, houses, and on occasion, shops and tables, could exploit their investments in this fashion, just as they could rent their properties.[158] This type of short-term investment provided the buyer with the possibilities of access to houses and lands and the seller with the ability to change the conditions of sale with each new contract in order to account for inflation or currency manipulations over the short-term.

* * *

Records of the farming out of ecclesiastical revenues and of royal and municipal taxes were less frequent in the notarial registers than the sales of rights over houses, lands and shops. Ecclesiastical rents were farmed to laymen for collection in the region of Montpellier during the period of this study. For example, on June 26, 1343, a canon of the cathedral of Maguelone, who was also the prior of Saint-Hilaire-de-Sautreyrargues, acquitted a mercer of Montpellier and his *fidejussor* for 100 *l.* current money (the equivalent of 20 *l.* in 1330) for the first of two installments of rents due the priory in one year.[159] The basis of collection of these rents was not described in the acquittal. In another example of April 4, 1336, another canon of Maguelone, who was the prior of Pignan, acted on behalf of the prior of Nôtre-Dame-des-Tables to acquit a priest, a pepperer and a changer for the partial payment in 35 *l.t.* of the revenues of the latter church.[160]

Modest investments in tax farms can also be noted. Customs duties (*leuda*) for fishing in the *étang* (inland waterway) of Mauguio, taxes which belonged to the king of Majorca, were sold by two fishermen to a man of Mauguio for 5 *l.* good money each for one year.[161] The fishermen had assumed the responsibility of this tax farm for a longer period. The level of profits available to the purchaser of ecclesiastical rents or of royal taxes cannot be calculated from the remaining evidence.

* * *

Beyond sales of real property, grants of tenure, rentals and sales of rights, there were traces in the extent notarial acts of other credit and investment practices. Twenty-five exchanges (*causa cambii*) of vineyards, fields, gardens, houses and woods were recorded. Some of these holdings were allodial; some were merely possessions in *dominium utile*. In exchanges of real property (Table 20) participants simply traded one parcel of property for another, including in the transaction where appropriate an additional sum of cash to compensate for the lesser value of one of the possessions.[162] The most frequent participants in such exchanges were merchants and members of the retail/wholesale trades. Recognitions of debt for the additional sum owed might accompany the transactions; cash payments predominated, however. Any attempt to analyze the motivations underlying such transactions would be speculative. Better land or housing on the one hand, cash needs on the other are the most obvious, but proof of these rationales is lacking.

Some credit techniques of real estate which were common

throughout the south of France have left only a trace in the notarial registers of Montpellier. A case in point is the *vente à rémeré,* or provisional sale. In the *vente à rémeré,* sale of real property was provisional in that repurchase of the possession was possible during a set period of time if the sale price or debt were reimbursed. One example of the *vente à rémeré* was preserved in 1301.[163] On November 16 of that year, a draper sold to a merchant allodial property for 100 *l.p.t.* The merchant promised to return the land to the draper if the 100 *l.* were repaid to him within four years. Philippe Wolff and Etienne Fournial have noted frequent use of this type of credit device in Toulouse and the Forez respectively.[164]

In a study of real estate investments of the early fifteenth century in Montpellier, Jean Combes noted that the establishment of an annuity on real estate or property right revenues was rare in late medieval Montpellier.[165] In principle, such an annuity or *rente* was a perpetual grant, but it could be terminated generally if the holder so desired. At least one example of an annuity on gardens, a house and a well has been preserved in the notarial evidence of the first half of the fourteenth century. On November 29, 1336, Petrus Alamanni, a changer of Montpellier, bought from the wife of a merchant 63 *s.t.* "annuales seu pensionales in et supra quadam tenentia orti cum domibus et putheo" in a suburb of Montpellier outside the Blancaria gate. On May 9, 1343, Alamanni ceded these revenues to a *burgensis.*[166] The latter sold the revenues to another merchant for the equivalent of 17 *l.* in comparable money.[167] While Combes maintained that the establishment of an annuity on real property may have been the prerogative of the *"seigneurs fonciers"* and allodial owners, the above documents mentioned that the bishop of Maguelone held a right of *consilium* over the property for which 3 *s.t.* in *usaticum* were due at the Feast of Saint Michael.[168] The return on this annuity to its beneficiary represented 18.5 per cent of the sale price, a rate of return which compares favorably with the 20 per cent return which Combes identified. The *rente foncière* was present elsewhere in the south of France, in the Forez region, where E. Fournial discerned lower rates of return (about 5 per cent).[169]

* * *

The ways of generating revenues from real estate investments were many and varied in Montpellier. Rentals and the sale of temporary use and revenues from land presented proprietors with possibilities of adaption to a changing economic climate. Jean Combes maintained in an examination of fifteenth-century real estate investments that the acquisitions of revenues of a variety of kinds for limited periods were the most profitable forms of real estate investment, although also the most speculative in that the level of return on the investment was not fixed in advance.[170] The buyer of temporary revenues and/or use of property, if skillful in administration and fortunate in economic conditions and climate, undoubtedly derived profits from these rights. Long-term leases, though vulnerable to inflation and monetary devaluations, yielded a steady and administratively non-demanding return. The purchaser of allodial rights could make use of any and all of these techniques of exploitation through the alienation of eminent domain or of *dominium utile* and through the temporary sale of revenues and use. The owner of rights of eminent domain enjoyed remuneration which, while modest in annual returns, became more lucrative when transfers or sales of the corresponding *dominium utile* occurred. A combination of these techniques of real estate management provided the fortunate Montpellier inhabitant with a desirable mixture of profit and security.

CONCLUSIONS

The rural and agricultural world of the immediate region of Montpellier was an economic sphere in which cash predominated over credit, where the conservative and traditional values of land ownership came into play. The same propensities were present in the urban housing market in Montpellier. The real estate sector of the local economy stood thus in contrast to the commercial and financial sectors where credit transactions and risk-taking predominated.[171]

Withdrawal from business affairs does not seem to have characterized the Montpellier commercial elite to the degree that it did the *rentiers* of northern Europe. Even with the acquisition of bourgeois (*burgensis*) title in Montpellier, Montpelliérains would engage in commercial ventures. In this regard as in many others relating to the economic orientation of the town, Montpellier shared common features with Genoa which had had considerable influence on the former's early experience in Mediterranean trade in the twelfth century.[172] Although Montpelliérains of the merchant classes preserved a commitment over time to business, the accumulation of landed wealth was still an important aspect of their activities.

For the artisans and members of the service trades the profits of their labor were less ample, but the desire to buy land and houses was present all the same. Indeed, a wide spectrum of the urban population participated in real estate investment throughout the period 1293–1348. Artisans and members of the service trades made greater use of credit in real estate purchases than did other social and occupational groups in Montpellier. In contrast to these credit techniques merchants and retail/-wholesalers used cash more frequently than credit in the acquisition of real estate. While the notarial evidence does not permit a study of the overall fortune of urban inhabitants, the above difference in business practice is consistent with the conclusion that merchants and retail/-wholesalers invested the profits of commerce in cash real estate purchases.

Techniques of exploitation of land holdings also differed among the artisans and members of the service trade, on the one hand, and merchants and retail/wholesalers on the other. The latter two social and occupational groups employed both short and long-term leases to derive revenues from lands. Artisans and members of the service trades immobilized less capital in long-term arrangements, preferring short-term methods of exploitation. The amount of capital available to both sets of inhabitants may have governed the predilection for long or short-term leases. A third approach to real property, distinguished from both of the above, was the real estate exploitation by the urban nobility and the clergy. Their real property holdings were concentrated in long-term leases and rights of eminent domain. The merchant class of Montpellier was the pool from which new members of the urban nobility were drawn. That the techniques of merchants with regard to land should resemble is some cases those of the nobility is consistent with the social values of the period, values which endowed land-ownership with social and economic status.

The inhabitants of Montpellier made a conscious investment choice in acquiring real estate. Well-managed agricultural lands and urban housing could provide revenues which were secure, considerably less speculative than commerce, and not inconsequential. The returns on real estate investment have left some trace in the notarial registers. In many cases a yield of 5 per cent was probably the norm. Rights in real property where the yields were not fixed could, under favorable economic conditions, result in a larger return.

The fourteenth century experienced a vast expansion of the domain of credit with the result that interest rates went down to 5 to 10 per cent.[173] In Venice there was a fixed rate of 5 per cent on forced loans.[174] Even the investments from the profitable *commenda* contracts of maritime trade yielded no more than 9 per cent at times. For maritime trade the risks of seawreck, piracy and unpredictable market conditions weighed heavily on the commercial investment.[175] Profits could be enormous in propitious circumstances, but so could losses.

Real estate investment could produce a competitive rate of annual return. It also represented an important source of equity for inhabitants. Real estate holdings were potential reserves of capital which could be sold for cash in time of need. Credit techniques such as the annuity and the *vente à rémeré* offered alternatives to *venditio*. Real estate might be used as collateral in loans.[176] Property owners enjoyed many options and considerable flexibility of response to economic needs.

On the basis of the notarial registers it is impossible to determine what proportion of the fortune of Montpelliérains was invested in real property or the share of urban houses versus rural, agricultural lands among property investments. All social and occupational groups in Montpellier, with the exception of the Jews, were noted in land acquisition. All groups, with women representing the nobility, were listed as house buyers, and the nobles sold houses indicating their housing stock.

In her study of the *compoix*, fiscal inventories of the late fourteenth and fifteenth centuries in Montpellier, Anne Marin concluded that "The rural element is not dominant in Montpellier fortunes. Only the agricultural workers possess an essentially rural fortune, especially those living in the suburbs."[177] Most inhabitants' wealth lay in urban property and in personal property.[178] The activity of the real estate market in Montpellier in the years 1293-1348 would suggest that some changes may have occurred in the course of the fourteenth century. In the case of Toulouse, Philippe Wolff found that in 1335 rural lands predominated in the assets of 45 per cent of the fortunes of inhabitants of the Bourg of Toulouse.[179] He found considerable evolution by the end of the fourteenth century with the rural component of Toulousains' fortunes much less prominent and urban and personal property more predominent.[180] It may be that the same sort of evolution occurred in Montpellier. The watershed could have been at mid-century with the demographic catastrophe of the Black Death and the chaos created by marauding mercenary companies of the Hundred Years War in the 1350s.[181] Montpellier built a suburban fortification system in these years, enhancing the barriers between town and country.[182] Moreover, the inhabitants suffered psychological anguish over the threats of the mercenaries. On one occasion the municipal chronicle relates that inhabitants constructed a candle the length of the fortifications to enhance their spiritual protection in time of danger.[183] Events such as these and changing economic times could account for an evolution in the composition of urban fortune.

If Montpellier in 1293–1348 resembled Toulouse in the importance of rural landholding by urban inhabitants, this situation was sharply at variance with that of parts of northern France. Pierre Desportes in his study of Reims in the thirteenth and fourteenth centuries found that the bourgeois of Reims were, above all, urban property holders.[184] The differences in landholding patterns between northern and southern France would hardly surprise historians, but the situation is more complex. David Nicholas discovered considerable ties between town and countryside in Flanders with the emergence of an active market in rural real estate at the end of the thirteenth century.[185] Desportes explained the absence of rural assets by the low level of bourgeois involvement in feudal landholding arrangements. As he states, "the normal status of the large domain in northern France was still that of the fief, doted with seigneurial rights."[186] In Flanders, Nicholas found that the rate of fiefholding by bourgeois was on the increase at the mid-fourteenth century.[187] Bourgeois rural fortune in the north was related to the success of their penetration of the feudal landholding system. In southern France where the feudal system was never established in its classic form, there were many fewer barriers to the acquisition of rural lands.

The real estate economy responded in negative fashion to fourteenth-century economic crisis in Montpellier as elsewhere in Europe. Although the trends in the notarial evidence are not entirely uniform, in general, the average values of land and house sales experienced a downward progression over the period 1293–1348. Certainly by the mid-1330s this process was well underway in Montpellier. Through the mid-fourteenth century, however, the continued participation in real estate investment of a broad range of the urban population suggests that property acquisition was viewed as a valuable means of diversifying family fortune.

APPENDIX

Vineyard Sale

A.D. Hérault, II E 95, 368, f. 8r, J. Holanie

July 21, 1327.

Anno quo supra et die vicesima prima mensis julii, domino Karolo etc. Nos Petrus Pelegrini mercator Montispessulani et Maria coniuges, videlicet ego dicta Maria de voluntate, consilio, licentia et auctoritate et expresso assensu et concensu dicti Petri Pelegrini mariti mei presentis, quod ego dictus Petrus Pelegrini, maritus eiusdem Marie fateor esse (verum), nos ambo inquam dicti Petrus Pelegrini et Maria coniuges facti principales venditores rei infrascripte simul et quisque nostrum insolidum sine partis et persone excusatione pro nobis et omnibus iuris et facti successoribus et heredibus nostris bona fide etc. vendimus etc. Guillelme Laurone uxori condam Jacobi Lauroni mercerii Montispessulani licet absenti et tibi notario infrascripto tanquam publice persone stipulanti et recipienti pro Guillelma et suis ad omnes voluntates dicte Guillelme Laurone et suorum etc. cum consilio, tamen directo dominio et laudimio domini regis Maioricarum vel sui locumtenentis Montispessulani et suorum successorum in illis dumtaxat casibus in quibus juxta et secundum usum et consuetudinem Montispessulani sibi laudaminium [sic] dari debet et censu seu usatico duorum sestariorum ordei eidem et suis successoribus annis singulis solvendo in festo Sancti Petri de augusto et etiam cum consilio, tamen semper directo dominio et laudimio domini prioris ecclesie Sancti Ylarii de Sautrairanitis et suorum successorum et censu seu usatico sexdecim denariorum turonensium eidem domino priori et suis successoribus annis singulis solvendo in dicto festo Sancti Petri de augusto. Scilicet totam unam peciam vinee nostram que olim fuerunt due pecie terre cum omnibus introitibus, exitibus, aliisque pertinentiis et juribus suis situatam in decimaria dicte ecclesie Sancti Ylarii de Sautrairanitis in loco seu territorio vocato la Tineta que confrontatur cum possessione hospitalis Sancti Guillelmi de Montepessulano et cum possessione Bernardi Benameni et cum carrayrano per quem intratur ad dictam vineam et exitur de eadem. Pro hac autem venditione etc. confitemur nos a dicta Guillelma Laurona habuisse etc. nomine justi et legalis pretii quater viginti libras turonensium parvorum quodquidem pretium etc. de quo tenemus etc. et in predictis renunciamus etc. verum etc. Facimus etc. semper habere etc. et quare etc. omnes et singule persone etc. laudabunt etc. Aliud etc. Pro quibus etc. Et pro omni evictione etc. obligamus etc. omnia et singula bona et jura nostra et cuiuslibet nostrum insolidum presentia et futura. Sub viribus etc. sigilli etc. Non intendentes personas nostras pro predictis obligare sub viribus dicti sigilli, renunciamus etc. Promitimus et juramus etc. Actum in Montepessulano. Horum sunt testes: Firminus Pauli, Arnaudus Fabri, fusterii, Johannes Vilas, Georgius Stephani corraterii dicti loci et ego Johannes Holanie publicus notarius regis Montispessulani qui mandatus et requisitus hec in notam recepi.

Extractum est instrumentum.

Laudimium prioris Sancti Ylarii est inferius in XXVI folio ab isto et cum isto computando ad propositum signum.

() expansion of phrase

DOWNPAYMENT SALE—HOUSE

A.D. Hérault, II E 95/368, f. 97v, J. Holanie.

January 2, 1328.

Anno et die predictis. Ego Guillelmus Borcati de Monteferrario, nunc vero habitator Montispessulani, factus principalis venditor etc. vendo etc. vobis Guillelmo Gernayroti dicti loci de Monteferrario presenti etc. cum consilio tamen semper directo dominio et laudimio Bremundi, filii et heredis domini Eymos de Monteferrario, domicelli condam dicti loci de Monteferrario, et suorum successorum et censu seu usatico duorum denariorum et unius oboli turonensium eidem et suis successoribus annis singulis solvendo in festo Sancti Michaelis scilicet: totum unum hospitium meum cum omnibus fundamentis etc. situatum in Barrio de Monteferrario quod confrontatur cum hospitio Bernardi Raynaudi, et cum hospitio Raymundi Clementis, presbiteri, et cum hospitio Ermessendis Lhantrei et cum carreria publica.

Pro hac autem venditione etc. confiteor etc. me a vobis habuisse et nomine justi et legali pretii tresdecim libras et decem solidos turonensium parvorum. In quibus renuncio etc. Et quicquidem etc. Faciam etc. semper habere etc. Aliud promito reddere etc. Omne dampnum etc. Super quibus etc. Pro quibus etc. Et pro omni evictione etc. Obligo etc. me in personam et omnia bona mea presentia et futura. Sub viribus etc. sigilli etc. Promito et juro etc.

Actum in parte regia Montispessulani. Horum sunt testes: Jacobus Petri cultor, Bernardus Guntardi, cultor Montispessulani et Ego.

Extractum est instrumentum.

RECOGNITION OF DEBT—HOUSE SALE

A.D. Hérault, II E 95/368, f. 97v-98r, J. Holanie

January 2, 1328.
Anno et die predictis. Ego dictus Guillelmus Gernayroti etc. confiteor etc. me debere vobis dicto Guillelmo Borcati presenti etc. scilicet: octo libras turonensium parvorum restantes penes me ad solvendum vobis de dicto pretio dicti hospitii non obstante dicta confessione etc. Solvere promito etc. in proximo futuro festo Sancti Johanis Babtiste etc. Sub viribus etc. sigilli etc. et specialiter dictum hospitium etc. Promito et juro etc. Actum in parte regia Montispessulani. Horum sunt testes: dicti Jacobus Petri, Bernardus Guntardi et Ego etc.

Extractum est instrumentum.

RECOGNITION OF EMPHYTEUSIS TENURE OF LAND

A.D. Hérault, II E 95/374, f. 25v, G. Nogareti.

September 14, 1341.
Eadem die. Ego Guillelmus Gasqui, cultor Montispessulani, pro me et meis confiteor Jacobo de Cabanis, (mercatori) Montispessulani, absenti et tibi notario etc. me a dicto Jacobo tenere et velle et debere tenere in emphite (osim) sub eius directo dominio, consilio, laudimio, prelationis, comissionis, incurtionis, retentionis et laudandi jure (pro) usatico quadraginta quinque solidorum turonensium annuatim semper solvendo in festo Beati Petri de augusto (unam quan)dam peciam terre vineatis novem cartones terre in se continentem sitam in decimaria Beate Marie (de) Tabulis loco dicto A La Via Crosa, confrontatem ex una parte cum honore Jacobi (*) lii et ex alia parte cum honore Martini Verdierii carreria in medio et ex alia (parte cum) honore Martini Rodesii, fabri, et ex alia parte cum honore Petri Blaquissa et cum via publica, (Quo)d usaticum predictum dicto Jacobo vel suis solvere promito perpetuo quolibet anno in dicto festo sub obligatione (dicte) pecie terre et fructus et redditus ipsius et sub omni juris renunciatione etc. Hec acta fuerunt in Montepessulano (in hoperatorio) habitationis mei notarii infrascripti in testimonio Petri de Fano clerici de Subissio dyocesis Lodovensis, (Petri de) Albinhaço, clerici Montispessulani.

() expansions in mutilated sections of act
* mutilated section of act with expansion unknown

RENTAL OF STORIES OF TWO HOUSES

A.D. Hérault, II E 95/374, f. 33rR.

January 28, 1340.
Item, vicesima octava die mensis januarii.
Ego,Petrus de Albinhaco, clericus,procurator Jacobi de Cabanis, mercatoris Montispessulani, prout constat de procuratione mea publico instrumento inde in notam sumpto per Guillelmum Nogareti, notarium infrascriptum, sub anno predicto et vicesima nova die maii, nomine procuratorio predicto, loco et locationis titulo concedo vobis, Johanni Belleti, apothecario Montispessulani presenti, stipulanti et recipienti pro vobis et vestris, duos sotulos dicti Jacobi sitos, unum in carreria recta extra Portale Montispessulani, quod confrontatur cum hospitio domine Bastone et cum dogua, aliud vero est in dicta dogua quod confrontatur cum viridario dicti Jacobi et cum honore Gaucelmi de Casalias, cederii, videlicet de proximo festo Beate Marie de augusto ad quatuor annos continuos et completos, pro pensione cujuslibet anni sex librarum et decem solidorum turonensium dicto Jacobo vel suis solvendos per hec tempora videlicet: mediam in die carniprivii et aliam in festo Beate Marie de augusto, quolibet anno dicti temporis.
Et faciam habere etc. condirectum etc. Et pro majori etc. Aliud etc. Obligo etc. dictum Jacobum etc. et specialiter predictos sotulos ita etc. Renuncians etc. Fidem etc.
Et ego, dictus Johannes predicta recipiens, dictam pensionem quolibet anno dicti temporis vobis, dicto Petro, procuratorio nomine predicto, stipulanti et recipienti, promito persolvere dicto Jacobo vel suis, solutionibus predictis, una cum omnibus expensis etc. Obligo etc. Renuncio etc. Fidem etc.
Hec acta fuerunt in Montepessulano, in testimonio Bernardi Fornerii, Bernardi Majorini, clericorum habitatorum Montispessulani.

RENTAL OF A SHOP

A.D. Hérault, II E 95/368, f. 17v, J. Holanie

July 30, 1327.
Anno et die predictis. Nos Thomas de Londris, barberius Montispessulani, et Plazentina coniuges etc. locamus etc. vobis Guillelmo Genesii, pictori dicti loci, presenti etc. scilicet totam unam apothecam cuiusdam hospitii siti in Tribio Petro Montispessulani quod a Johanne de Pradis, canabasserio Montispessulani, tenemus et tenere debemus ad tempus

infrascriptum ex conducto. Que apotheca predicta confrontatur cum operatorio nostro dicti hospitii. Hanc autem locationem dicte apothece vobis ut supra stipulanti facimus a proximo festo Beate Marie de medio augusto in duos annos proximos, continuos et completos et pro pensione seu loquerio cuiuslibet anni dictorum duorum annorum sex librarum turonensium parvorum quas nobis debitis et solvetis anno quolibet dictorum duorum annorum per terminos et solutiones consuetos in villa Montispessulani scilicet medietatem in die carniprivi et aliam medietatem in festo Beate Marie de augusto etc. Et sic promitimus etc. Aliud etc. Pro quibus etc. obligamus etc. nos et omnia bona nostra presentia et futura. Renunciamus etc. Promitimus per fidem etc. Ego dictus Guillelmus Genesii predictam locationem etc. promito et convenio vobis dictis Thome de Londris et Plazentine, coniugibus presentibus, etc. quod pro dicto loquerio seu pensione apothece predicte ego dabo et solvam vobis seu vestris per terminos et solutiones superius et comprehensos scilicet medietatem etc. Pro quibus etc. Obligo etc. me et omnia bona mea presentia et futura. Renuncio etc. Promito per fidem etc. Actum in Montepessulano. Horum sunt testes: Bernardus Bouguieyras, fusterius Montispessulani, Johannes Duranti de Castro Novo prope Lanum et Ego etc.

SALE OF REDDITUS, USUSFRUCTUS ETC.

A.D. Hérault, II E 95/368, f. 33r, J. Holanie

August 20, 1327.
Anno et die predictis. Nos Arnaudus de Pena habitator de Latis et Esmeniardis coniuges etc. vendimus etc. vobis Petro Stephani de Frontiniano presenti etc. scilicet omnes et singulos redditus ususfructus, proventus, comoditatem, gausidas et eyssidas unius pecie vinee nostre site in decimaria Sancti Pauli de Frontiniano in loco seu territorio vocato Barnier confrontate cum possessione Raymunde Comte et cum possessione infantium den Cornon et cum possessione vestra et cum via publica. Hanc autem venditionem etc. vobis facimus ab instanti festo Sancti Michaelis in novem annos etc. Et pro precio universali totius dicti temporis centum solidorum turonensium quos a vobis habimus etc. Hoc acto inter me et vos et convento quod vos culturari faciatis dictam peciam vinee tribus operibus anno quolibet dictorum IX annorum vestris sumptibus scilicet fodendi, amputandi et magnitandi. Verum etc. Facimus etc. habere etc. pro quibus etc. Et pro omni evictione etc. Obligamus etc. nos et omnia bona nostra presentia et futura. Renunci-

amus etc. Promitimus et juramus etc. Et consequenter ego dictus Petrus Stephani etc. promito et convenio vobis dictis Arnaudo de Pena et Esmeniardi coniugibus presentibus etc. quod ego faciam culturari dictam peciam vinee dictis tribus operibus anno quolibet dictorum trium annorum meis sumptibus scilicet fodendi, amputandi et magnitandi. Pro quibus per me promissis etc. Et pro omni restitutione dampnorum etc. Super quibus credatur etc. Obligo etc. me et omnia bona mea presentia et futura. Renuncio etc. predictam etc. Promito per fidem etc. Actum in Montepessulano. Testes: Bertrandus Gaysseci, corraterius, Guillelmus Holanie junior, clericus Montispessulani et Ego etc.

Extractum est instrumentum pro
dicto Petro Stephani

NOTES

I would like to thank Robert S. Lopez, Bernard S. Bachrach and James D. Tracy for their comments on earlier versions of this study. I am grateful to the Inter-Library Loan Division of Wilson Library, University of Minnesota, for assistance in obtaining reference works. Thanks go to Carol Gersmehl and Reid Maier of the Cartography Laboratory of the University of Minnesota for the production of the maps.

1 As early as 1239, the Chronicle of Jacme I the Conqueror stated that there were between 6,000 and 7,000 agricultural workers in Montpellier. *v* E. Bonnet, "Les séjours à Montpellier de Jacques le Conquérant roi d'Aragon," *Mémoires de la société archéologique de Montpellier,* ser. 2, IX (Montpellier, 1927), 176-177.

2 On the problem of population size, *v* J.C. Russell, "L'Evolution démographique de Montpellier au Moyen Age," *Annales du Midi,* 74 (1962), 345-360. *v* also my comments in "Patterns of Population Attraction and Mobility: The Case of Montpellier, 1293-1348," *Viator,* 10 (1979), 257 n. 2.

3 Jacques Heers, *L'Occident aux XIVe et XVe siècles. Aspects économiques et sociaux* (Paris, 1970), 382-383 and Georges Duby, *L'Economie rurale et la vie des campagnes dans l'Occident médiéval,* II (Paris, 1962). pp. 631-634.

4 There exists no in-depth study of landholding and property law for the region of Montpellier in the Middle Ages. Such a study would have to begin with the cartulary materials of the early and high Middle Ages and trace the evolution of the system of property law through the notarial evidence of the late Middle Ages. For the purpose of the present study the examination of real estate investments will be limited to the notarial registers.

5 Thirteen notarial registers are extant in Montpellier before the Black Death of 1348. From 1348 to 1361 there is a lacuna in notarial evidence. Hence the mid-fourteenth century has been chosen as an end point for this study. The earliest register dates from 1293-1294. *v* Archives Municipales de Montpellier (hereafter abbreviated A.M.), II 1-3 and Archives Départementales de l'Hérault (abbreviated A.D.), II E 95/368-377. My dissertation, "Commerce and Society in Montpellier: 1250-1350," Diss. Yale University, 1974, II, pp. 115-123, provides a breakdown by category of all the extant notarial acts before 1349. There were 872 acts relating to real estate.

[6] A recent thesis of the Ecole des Chartes has dealt with the *compoix* of Montpellier. *v* Anne Catherine Marin, "Montpellier à la fin du moyen âge d'après les compoix (1380-1450)," Thèse, Ecole des Chartes, 1980.

[7] On notarial evidence, *v* David Herlihy, *Pisa in the Early Renaissance* (New Haven, 1958), pp. 1-20.

[8] On allodial ownership, *v* E. Chenon, *Etude sur l'histoire des alleux* (Paris, 1888). For general background on property law in the medieval period in France, P. Ourliac and J. de Malafosse, *Histoire du droit privé*, II: *Les biens*, 2nd ed. (Paris, 1971).

[9] The percentage of lands held in allodial ownership in the region of Montpellier still awaits determination, but studies elsewhere in the south of France have suggested that the Midi had a higher percentage of such holdings than did other regions of France. A very useful introduction to the history of real property is provided by Roger Aubenas, *Cours d'histoire du droit privé, Anciens pays de Droit Ecrit (XIIIe-XVIème siècle)*, IV: *Autour de la propriété foncière (Moyen âge et ancien régime)* (Aix-en-Provence, 1954-1961).

[10] A clear summary of the distinctions between *dominium directum* and *dominium utile* is provided by P. Ourliac and J. de Malafosse, (*v* n. 8), pp. 166-168. *v* also Edmondo Meynial, "Notes sur la formation de la théorie du domaine divisé (domaine direct et domaine utile) du XIIe au XIVe siècle dans les romanistes; Etude de dogmatique juridique," *Mélanges Fitting* (Montpellier, 1908), pp. 409-461. *v* also Adolf Berger, *Encyclopedic Dictionary of Roman Law, Transactions of the American Philosophical Society* (Philadelphia, 1953), pp. 441-442, on *dominium*.

[11] P. Ourliac and J. de Malafosse, pp. 167-168: "le preneur n'avait qu'un domaine utile et il ne pouvait prétendre à aucun droit honorifique sur le fonds, par example au droit de chasse."

[12] In fact, examples of subletting of *dominium utile* have been noted in the Montpellier documents, as will be evident in the section "Real Estate Revenues".

[13] André Gouron, "Les étapes de la pénétration du droit romain au XIIe siècle dans l'ancienne Septimanie," *Annales du Midi*, 69 (1957), 105.

[14] Edmondo Meynial, "De l'application du droit romain dans la région de Montpellier aux XIIe at XIIIe siècles," *Atti del Congresso internazionale di scienze storiche*, 9 (Rome, 1904), 147-169.

[15] Pierre Tisset, "Placentin et l'enseignement du droit à Montpellier. Droit romain et Coutume dans l'ancien pays de Septimanie," *Recueil de mémoires et travaux publiés par la société d'histoire du droit et des institutions des anciens pays de droit écrit* (abbreviated hereafter as *Recueil*), fasc. II (1951), p. 80. The italics are mine. The best editions of the *consuetudines* of Montpellier of 1204 and 1205 are found in A. Teulet, *Layettes du Trésor des Chartes*, I (Paris, 1863), pp. 255-266 and pp. 289-291. No notarial registers remain from this early period to permit a comparison of terminology between 1204 practices and the credit sales contracts in use at the end of the thirteenth century. *v* also Philippe Bouges who has made a study of the law of contracts in medieval Montpellier in his thesis, "La pratique contractuelle à Montpellier de la fin du XIIIe siècle à la fin du XVe," 2 v., Thèse d'Etat, Faculté de Droit et des Sciences Economiques—Université de Montpellier—1, 1972.

[16] An example of a vineyard sale can be found in the Appendix.

[17] The actual term *arrhae* was only infrequently noted in the extant notarial acts. An example can be found in A.D., II E 95 377, B. Egidii, f. 273r.

Notarial practice was not entirely uniform in this period. cf. Paul-Louis Malausséna, *La vie en Provence orientale aux XIVe et XVe siècles* (Paris, 1969), p. 48.

[18] On renunciations, *v* Peter Riesenberg, "Roman Law, Renunciations, and Business in the Twelfth and Thirteenth Centuries," *Essays in Medieval Life and Thought Presented in Honor of Austin P. Evans* (New York, 1955), pp. 207-225; and Edmondo Meynial, "Des renonciations au moyen âge et dans notre ancien droit," *Nouvelle revue de droit français et étranger, ser. 3, 24, (Paris, 1900), 108-142;* ser. 3, 25 (1901), 241-277.

[19] *v* the Appendix for examples of a downpayment house sale and subsequent recognition of debt.

[20] This situation dated from the French conquest of southern France as a result of the Albigensian Crusade and the Treaty of Meaux-Paris in 1229. Histories of the Albigensian Crusade and the Capetian conquest are numerous. The entire problem has been re-examined in detail by Michel Roquebert, *L'Epopée cathare. 1198-1212: L'Invasion* (Toulouse, 1970) and *L'Epopée cathare. 1213-1216—Muret ou la dépossession* (Toulouse, 1977). In English the studies of Walter L. Wakefield, *Heresy, Crusade and Inquisition in Southern France, 1100-1250* (London, 1974) and Joseph R. Strayer, *The Albigensian Crusade* (New York, 1971) are useful as background for this period. Also essential are the volumes VI, VII and VIII of Dom Devic and Dom Vaissete, *Histoire générale de Languedoc (*Toulouse-Privat, 1879) and Paul Dognon, *Les institutions politiques et administratives du pays de Languedoc du XIIe siècle aux guerres de religion* (Toulouse, 1895). The classic study of the political history of Montpellier remains that of Alexandre Germain, *Histoire de la commune de Montpellier,* 3 vol. (Montpellier, 1851).

[21] On Aigues-Mortes, *v* Jean Combes, "Origine et passé d'Aigues-Mortes," *Revue d'histoire économique et sociale,* 50 (1972), 304-326.

[22] For a discussion of regional geography, *v* Gaston Galtier, 'Les conditions géographiques de Montpellier," *Mélanges Philippe Arbos* (Clermont-Ferrand, 1953), pp. 237-246 and *Le vignoble du Languedoc méditerranéen et du Roussillon, Etude comparative d'un vignoble de masse,* 3 v. (Montpellier, 1960). *v* also R. Dugrand, "La garrigue montpelliéraine," *Bulletin de la société languedocienne de géographie* ser. 2, 34 (1963), pp. 3-266. Although the last two works focus on the modern period, they provide a useful geographical introduction to the region of Montpellier.

[23] Pasturage paths still exist today. Although their origin lies in the distant past, they were given a special judicial statute under the Intendants in the seventeenth century. *v* J.-B. Gèze, *Les drailles du Département de l'Hérault* (Montpellier, 1926), a publication of the Office Agricole Départemental de l'Hérault for a discussion of the location of the *drailles* or pasturage paths. *v* also a report by the Service Vicinal on the *drailles,* preserved in A.D., 2 S 39.

[24] For background on the effects of climate on the agriculture of Languedoc, *v* Emmanuel LeRoy Ladurie, *Les paysans de Languedoc,* I (Paris, 1966), especially pp. 17-19.

[25] *v* my dissertation, "Commerce and Society," I, pp. 212-224, on the grain trade.

[26] E.g., *v* Salt marsh: A.D., II E 95/370, J. Holanie, f. 95v; *garrigue:* II E 95/374, G. Nogareti, f. 15r; fish nets: II E 95/377, B. Egidii, f. 115r; *garrigue:* II E 95/374, G. Nogareti, f. 26v; stream: II E 95/374, G. Nogareti, f. 112r.

[27] The clientele of the extant notarial registers reflects the multiple urban identities of Montpellier as a commercial entrepot, a university center and the site of an active financial market in foreign exchange. The following social and occupational categories were developed on the basis of the identifications of clients made by the notaries:

MERCHANTS	CHANGERS MONEYERS	RETAIL WHOLESALE	NOBLES BURGENSES	PROFESSIONS EDUCATION	JEWS

ROYAL ADMIN.	ECCLESIASTICS	WOMEN	ARTISANS SERVICE	FOOD TRADES	AGRICULTURE	FOREIGNERS	UNIDENTIFIED	
							LOCAL	OTHER

These categories vary somewhat from those employed by Philippe Wolff in his study of the fiscal records of Toulouse, *Les "Estimes" toulousaines des XIVe et XVe siècles* (Toulouse, 1956) and by Louis Henry in an examination of the Ancien Régime, *Manuel de démographie historique* (Paris, 1967).

For this study of real property transactions, it seemed useful to separate the categories of merchants, on the one hand, and changers and moneyers on the other. Members of these two groups belonged to the specialized personnel of international commerce and finance. Participants in the wholesale and retail phases of trade have also been assigned a separate category. Included here are furriers, grain merchants, drapers, silk merchants, linen merchants, pepperers and apothecaries, among others. See the comments of Michael M. Postan, "Credit in Medieval Trade," *EcHR*, 1 (1928), 5, on the retail and wholesale trade; *v* also Robert L. Reynolds, "Origins of Modern Business Enterprise: Medieval Italy," *JEc Hist*, 12 (1952), 356-359.

The urban nobility was comprised of *milites*, the traditional urban nobles who in the twelfth century were seigneurial dependents, the *burgenses*, bourgeois holding a title from the town or from the king of France, and local and regional nobility generally termed *domicelli* in the documents. *v* my dissertation, "Commerce and Society," I, pp. 12-17; also Jean Combes, "Quelques remarques sur les bourgeois de Montpellier au moyen âge," *Recueil*, fasc. VII: *Mélanges Pierre Tisset* (Montpellier, 1970), pp. 93-132.

The university faculty, doctors, lawyers, jurists and paralegal personnel have been assigned a separate category of "Professions/Education." While the Jews of Montpellier left their greatest mark as specialists in loan credit, they appeared occasionally in property transactions. On the Jews of Montpellier, *v* R.W. Emery, *The Jews of Perpignan*, (New York, 1959), III, pp. 131-133. *v* also *Juifs et judaïsme de Languedoc, Cahiers de Fanjeaux*, 12 (Toulouse, 1977). Older studies include Salamon Kahn, *Etude sur les Israelites de Montpellier au moyen âge* (Nimes, 1924). Property transactions of officers of the royal administrations of the king of Majorca and the king of France in Montpellier have been examined separately as have those of the clergy. Under the heading of "Foreigners" are all individuals whom the notaries identified as inhabitants of localities outside Montpellier. As presented in my article, "Patterns of Population Attraction and Mobility," the markets of Montpellier attracted numerous foreign merchants from Italy and Spain and from regions of central and northern France as well as residents of the hinterland.

The category of "Artisans/Service" includes ironmongers, blacksmiths, barbers, innkeepers, brokers, transporters, cordmakers, beltmakers, coffermakers, shoemakers, precious metal workers, artists, wood merchants, tailors, knifemakers, silk cloth workers, silver cloth workers, raw wool bleachers, animal merchants and wine merchants, among others. Because of their importance in a large medieval town such as Montpellier, the food trades were isolated as a group. The agricultural population of the town was significant in number as suggested in the opening of this study. Within the category are cultivators, gardeners and fishermen. On the trade organizations of

Montpellier, *v* A. Gouron, *La réglementation des métiers en Languedoc au moyen âge* (Paris, 1958) and on the importance of the medieval food trades, *v* Philippe Wolff, "Les bouchers de Toulouse du XIIe au XVe siècle," *Annales du Midi*, 65 (1953), 375–395.

The activities of women in matters of property have been highlighted to reveal their economic participation. The social and occupational background of women has been further delineated in specific instances.

[28] Full credit land sales were found in A.M., II 1, J. Grimaudi, ff. 22v and 23v; A.D., II E 95/369, J. Holanie, ff. 47r, 59r, 65v and 85v; II E 95/371, J. Holanie, f. 34v; II E 95/372, J. Holanie, f. 118v; II E 95/377, B. Egidii, ff. 259v and 277r.

[29] For the west of France the study of the Bordelais by Robert Boutruche remains a classic examination of landholders in crisis: *Une société provinciale en lutte contre le régime féodal: l'alleu en Bordelais et en Bazadais du XIe au XVIIIe siècle (Paris, 1947).*

[30] David Herlihy, "Land, Family and Women in Continental Europe, 701-1200," *Traditio*, 18 (1962), 89–120, noted the comparatively high percentage of women landowners of southern France and Spain in the ninth through the eleventh centuries. Case studies for specific areas such as the region and town of Montpellier are needed to permit the refinement of his conclusions and the pursuit of the inquiry into the later Middle Ages.

At times, women were noted selling land in conjunction with their sons. *v* e.g., A.D., II E 95/369, J. Holanie, F. 93v; *v* also II E 95/368, J. Holanie, f. 80v: in which the widow of a cultivator and her son sold two *cartons* of land to a tailor.

[31] Compare the activity of urban residents in the land market of Flanders in David Nicholas, *Town and Countryside*, pp. 267–329. There exists no study of village artisan activity in the region of Montpellier in the medieval period. As G. Duby, *L'Economie rurale*, I, p. 261, noted, such work is necessary for the region of Languedoc.

[32] On fourteenth century crises, *v* Edouard Perroy, "A l'origine d'une économie contractée: les crises du XIVe siècle," *Annales ESC*, 4 (1949), 167–182; Marie-Josèphe Larenaudie, "Les famines en Languedoc au XIVe siècle," *Annales du Midi*, 64 (1952), 27–39; and Elisabeth Carpentier, "Autour de la peste noire: famines et épidémies dans l'histoire du XIVe siècle," *Annales ESC*, 17 (1962), 1062–1092.

[33] P. Wolff, *Les "Estimes"*, pp. 72–79, in his study of the tax documents of Toulouse of 1335, noted the heavy concentration of urban fortune in real estate and in particular in rural lands.

[34] P. Wolff, *Les "Estimes"*,, p. 66, noted that 58 per cent of the Toulousain *banlieu* contained vineyards.

[35] According to the *Cartulaire de Maguelone*, ed. J Rouquette and A. Villemagne, 5 vols, (Montpellier 1912–1925), vineyards were located, on the one hand, within a radius of a few kilometers of Montpellier at Montpelliéret, Boutonnet, Montaubérou, on the banks of the Merdanson and the Lez, at Saint-Jean-de-Védas, Lavérune, Juvignac and La Valette, and on the other hand, in pockets to the east of Montpellier at about fifteen kilometers distant in the territory of Mauguio and to the southwest at twenty to twenty-five kilometers distant at Gigean, Montbazin, Poussan and Balaruc. Notarial sales mention, in addition, the location of vineyards between Montpellier and the inland waterway leading to the sea, at sites such as Pérols, Fréjorgues and Soriech. *v* Map I. *v* also Gaston Galtier, "Le vignoble et le vin dans le Languedoc oriental de la fin du XIe siècle à la Guerre de Cent Ans," *Etudes médiévales offertes à M. le Doyen Fliche de l'Institut* (Montpellier, 1951), p. 9. For examples from the Montpellier documents, *v* A.D., II E 95/370, J. Holanie, f. 77r: Pérols; II E 95/377, B. Egidii, f. 21v: Soriech; II E 95/368, J. Holanie, f. 57v; Fréjorgues.

36 P. Malausséna, *La vie en Provence orientale*, pp. 75-76, commented of the inhabitants of Grasse, "Rares sont ceux qui ne possèdent pas au moins une 'vinea'."

37 For background on medieval wines, one can consult Roger Dion, *Histoire de la vigne et du vin en France des origines au XIXe siècle* (Paris, 1959). Also useful in Georges Duby, ed. *Histoire de la France rurale*, I (Paris, 1975), pp. 454-473. Medieval wine was of mediocre alcoholic content and could not be preserved over many years. On the spiced and perfumed wines of Montpellier production, *v* R. Dion, p. 315.

38 Roger Dion, *Histoire de la vigne*, pp. 316ff.

39 J. Viard, *Les Journeaux du trésor de Philippe IV le Bel* (Paris, 1940), pp. 621, 656.

40 K.H. Schafer, *Die Ausgaben des Apostolischen Kammer unter Johann XXII nebst der Jahresbilanzen von 1316-1375* (Paderborn, 1911), p. 160.

41 I have treated the grape trade in "Commerce and Society," I, pp. 232-240, and have examined the credit function in commodity products overall in my forthcoming book, "Business, Banking and Finance in Medieval Montpellier."

42 *v* my dissertation, "Commerce and Society," II, pp. 195-209, for a synopsis of grape transactions from the notarial registers.

43 A.D., II E 95/368, J. Holanie, f. 39v.

44 A.M., II 1, J. Grimaudi, f. 38v

45 The municipal chronicle, "La chronique romane" of *Le Petit Thalamus de Montpellier*, ed. F. Pégat, E. Thomas and Desmazes (Montpellier, 1840), 347, states that young men were weakened by a poor diet of raw herbs, and people were dying in the streets. No grain was to be had from Lombardy or Sicily because of a Genoese war, or for that matter from Catalonia.

46 The notarial contracts recorded the parish or *dîmerie* (*decimaria*) to which the land belonged and provided the contiguous owners with mention of a public road or stream when appropriate. Present knowledge of the medieval topography of the area of Montpellier is not sufficiently advanced to permit plotting of the manuscript evidence on actual maps. *v* G. Duby, ed., *La France rurale*, I, pp. 454ff on types of vines.

47 Because of the frequent currency fluctuations over the period 1293-1348, prices cannot be compared from one year to another without the establishment of a currency standard and the conversion of all prices to that standard. All sums used in the development of this graph and the graph for houses have been converted to the standard of good silver coins of April 1330. *Pied de monnaie* quotations from French mints permitted the determination of relative silver content in coins of other years and their fractional proportion of the 1330 standard. On problems relating to medieval coinage, *v* Harry A. Miskimin, *Money, Prices and Foreign Exchange in Fourteenth-Century France* (New Haven, London, 1963), especially Appendix D, pp. 158-169 and John Bell Henneman, *Royal Taxation in Fourteenth Century France* (Princeton, 1971), App. I, pp. 331-353.

48 Specific prices have been quoted in decimals of *livres tournois*, the money of account, and of *livres petits tournois*, real coins, rather than as denominations of *livres*, *sous* and *deniers*.

49 In sales where land dimensions were quoted, two systems of measurement, in *cartons* and in *séterées* were in use. A *carton* was approximately one *are* or 100 square meters; a *séterée* was the equivalent of 14.77 *ares*. In credit sales of *cartons* of land, prices per *carton* varied from .18 *l.t.* to 6.13 *l.t.* *v* A.D., II E 95/377, B. Egidii, f. 8r for the low figure; II E 95/370, J Holanie, f. 34v for the high figure.

In cash sales of *cartons* of land, the range was between 1 *l.t.* and 5 *l.t.* per *carton*: e.g., as the low, A.D., II E 95/368, J. Holanie, f. 80v; for the high, II E 95/370, J. Holanie, f. 91r.

If credit sales of *cartons* of vineyards are invoked, the range was between 2.6 *l.t.* and 6.8 *l.t.;* for cash sales of *cartons* of vineyards, prices per *carton* went from 1 *l.t.* to 8.1 *l.t.* For the credit low, A.D., II E 95/368, J. Holanie, f. 10r; for the credit high, II E 95/370, J. Holanie, f. 131r. For the cash low, II E 95/371, J. Holanie, f. 120v; for the high, II 95/371, J. Holanie, f. 80v. There were not sufficient measurements in *séterées* to allow similar comparisons. The uncontrolled factors regarding the value of lands sold, enumerated above, would render questionable any deductions from these figures even if a well-defined trend in prices were evident. cf. land measures in the studies of Etienne Fournial, *Les villes et l'économie d'échange en Forez auxXIIIe et XIVe siècles* (Paris, 1967). pp. xlvi-lii and Philippe Wolff, *Commerces et marchands de Toulouse* (ca. 1350-ca. 1450) (Paris, 1954), pp. xxvii-xxx.

50 A.M., II 1, J. Grimaudi, f. 46v.

51 A.D., II E 95/369, J. Holanie, f. 92v.

52 A.M., II 3, J. Laurentii, f. 90r.

53 For an example of "on demand" terms, *v* A.D., II E 95/368, J. Holanie, f. 68v. For a term of several years, II E 95/370, J. Holanie, f. 72r.

54 Common dates were All Saints, Christmas, Easter, Lent, Pentecost and Ascension and popular southern French saints' days such as the feasts of Saint Michel (September 29), Saint Gilles (September 1), Saint Hilaire (May 5), Saint Jean (June 25) and Saint Pierre (August).

55 *v* the chapter on loans in my forthcoming book, "Business, Banking and Finance."

56 B.H. Slicher van Bath, *The Agrarian History of Western Europe A.D. 500-1850* (London, 1963), pp. 105-106 and p. 138.

57 David Herlihy, *Medieval and Renaissance Pistoia. The Social History of an Italian Town* (New Haven, 1967), pp. 130-131.

58 *v* my dissertation, "Commerce and Society," I, pp. 212-224, for a history of the grain trade in Montpellier.

59 *v* Harry A. Miskimin, *The Economy of Early Renaissance Europe, 1300-1460* (reprint Cambridge, 1975), pp. 54-55 on wine. Toulousain wine prices provide an exception to the general rule of resilience.

60 David Nicholas, *Town and Countryside: Social, Economic, and Political Tensions in Fourteenth-Century Flanders* (Bruges, 1971), p. 274.

61 Compare the findings of P. Wolff, *Les "Estimes"*, p. 85. Pierre Desportes, *Reims et les Rémois au XIIIe et XIVe siècles* (Paris, 1979), pp. 254-256, found that the family house constituted a large share of the total family investments in real estate both urban and rural. A limited number of houses, five to ten perhaps, were owned by the wealthiest Rémois.

62 On the topography of Montpellier the best study remains that of Louise Guiraud, "Recherches topographiques sur Montpellier au moyen âge," *Mem. soc. arch. Mplr.* ser. 2, I (1899), 89-335.

63 On the origins of consular government in Montpellier, *v* Bernardin Gaillard, "Origines de la commune de Montpellier," *Bull. de l'Académie des sciences et lettres de Montpellier* (1914), and P. Laborderie-Boulous, "La viguerie de Montpellier au XIIe siècle," *Archives de la ville de Montpellier, Inventaires et documents,* IV (Montpellier, 1920), pp. v-xix.

64 On the political history of Montpellier in the thirteenth and fourteenth centuries, consult Charles de Tourtoulon, *Etudes sur la maison de Barcelone, Jacme Ier le Conquérant, roi d'Aragon, comte de Barcelone, seigneur de Montpellier, d'après les*

chroniques et les documents inédits, 2 vols. (Montpellier, 1863) and Louis J. Thomas, "Montpellier entre la France et l'Aragon pendant la première moitié du XIVe siècle," *Montpeliensia, Mémoires et documents relatifs à Montpellier et à la région montpelliéraine,* I, fasc. 1 (Montpellier, 1928-1929), pp. 1-56. A popularization of the political history was written recently by Jean Baumel, *Histoire d'une seigneurie du Midi de la France,* I: Naissance de Montpellier (985-1213) (Montpellier, 1969) and II: *Montpellier sous la seigneurie de Jacques le Conquérant et des rois de Majorque. Rattachement de Montpelliéret et de Montpellier à la France (1213-1349)* (Montpellier, 1971).

65 M. Vigié, "Des enceintes successives de la ville de Montpellier et de ses fortifications," *Bull. de la société languedocienne de géographie,* 21 (1899), 151 has given a conservative estimate of the length of the Commune Clôture at 1000 meters.

66 On the Cami roumieu *v* Jeanne Vielliard, *Le guide du pélérin de Saint-Jacques de Compostelle,* 3rd. ed., (Mâcon, 1963).

67 P. Wolff, *Les "Estimes,"* p. 56, found that there was a considerable range of prices for urban housing in Toulouse (from 3 *l.t.* to 1000 *l.t.*).

68 Jacques Peyron, "Montpellier médiéval, urbanisme et architecture," *Annales du Midi,* 91 (1979), 255-272. For the use of the term *hospitium v* Appendix. For a *domus v* A.D., II E 95/369, J. Holanie, f. 32r.

69 A.D., II E 95/370, J. Holanie, f. 61v.

70 A.D., II E 95/368, J. Holanie, f. 2v.

71 *v* Appendix.

72 Full credit house sales were found in II E 95/369, ff. 33r and 33v. An unpaid debt of 800 *l.* was mentioned on f. 91r.

73 A.M., II 2, J. Grimaudi, ff. 5v, 65v, 97r and 103r.

74 A.D., II E 95/369, J. Holanie, f. 91r. The houses in question were *domus.* A *tenentia* of houses would imply a block of structures. Graph 1 was developed as in n. 47 sup. Single entries are noted for 1293, 1331 and 1341.

75 In contrast, small credit transactions involving houses were also noted; a sale on partial credit for 6.5 *l.p.t.* in 1327 is a case in point, A.D., II E 95/368, J. Holanie, f. 51r.

The full credit house sales mentioned earlier fetched 17 *l.p.t.* in one instance, 20 *l.p.t.* in the other.

76 A.D., II E 95/369, J. Holanie, f. 118v for the high; II E 95/377, B. Egidii, f. 41r for the low.

For an "on demand" term see A.D., II E 95/368, J. Holanie, f. 136r; for a schedule of payments see II E 95/368, J. Holanie, f. 51r; for several months, II E 95/377, B. Egidii, f. 269r (December 20 to Lent).

77 The same caveats regarding interpretation of these values apply to houses as they did to lands. The overall average of credit sales was slightly higher at 92.4 *l.t.* than the average of all sales, 83.4 *l.t.* It may be that some advantage accrued to the cash buyer of houses. However, it would be pure speculation to argue that in a specific instance full cash payment for a house resulted in a lower price than if the sale had been made on credit.

78 The widespread use of credit in commerce is an issue explored in my forthcoming book, "Business, Banking and Finance."

79 There is scholarly disagreement regarding the supply of precious metals in western Europe. *v,* e.g., N.J. Mayhew, "Numismatic Evidence and Falling Prices in the Fourteenth Century," *EcHR,* 27 (1974), 1-15; John Munro, "Bullionism and the Bill of Exchange in England, 1272-1663: A Study in Monetary Management and Popular Prejudice," *The Dawn of Modern Banking* (New Haven and London, 1979), 169-239.

C.C. Patterson, "Silver Stocks and Losses in Ancient and Medieval Times," *EcHR*, 25 (1972), 205-233; Andrew M. Watson, "Back to Gold—and Silver," *EcHR* 20 (1967), 1-34. Harry A. Miskimin, *The Economy of Early Renaissance Europe*, p. 122, maintained that there was greater velocity of circulation of monetary stock in southern Europe than in northern Europe. *v* also J. Munro, 178, n. 22.

80 P. Wolff, ed. *Documents de l'histoire du Languedoc* (Toulouse, 1969), p. 97, provided a cartographic representation of the extent of the seigneury of the Guilhem in the twelfth century. The geographic expanse was never very great.

On the Guilhem family, *v* Abbé C. Guichard, "Les premiers Guilhems (Xe et XIe siècles)," *Revue historique du diocèse*, 6th year (Mende, n.d.) pp. 433 ff; Archibald R. Lewis, "The Guilhems of Montpellier: A Sociological Appraisal," *Viator*, 2 (1971), 159-169; and Martime Dépinay, "Un aspect de l'activité des seigneurs de Montpellier: l'extension territoriale de la seigneurie des origines à la mort de Guilhem VIII (985-1202), Thèse de Maîtrise, Faculté des Lettres et des Sciences Humaines de Montpellier, 1971. In 1347, the king of Majorca was still represented as a frequent possessor of eminent domain in Montpellier, two years before its purchase by Philip of Valois: e.g., when on December 20, 1347, the wife of a wood merchant purchased a house from a local *domicellus* for slightly over 8 *l.t.;* the equivalent of 5 *d.t.* were due annually at the Feast of Saint Michael to the king. (A.D., II E 95/377, B. Egidii, f. 269r.)

81 J. Combes, "Quelques remarques sur les bourgeois de Montpellier," pp. 93-132, on the urban elite.

82 *v* e.g., *LIM*, act CXXVII. *v* also Archibald R. Lewis, "The Development of Town Government in Twelfth-Century Montpellier," *Speculum*, 22 (1947), 51-57; "The Guilhems of Montpellier: A Sociological Appraisal," *Viator*, 2 (1971), 159-169; "Seigneurial Administration in Twelfth-Century Montpellier," *Speculum*, XXII (1947), 562-577.

83 On the bishopric of Maguelone the most recent treatment can be found in *Le diocése de Montpellier*, ed. Gérard Cholvy (Paris, 1976). *v* also Jean Rouquette, *Histoire du diocèse de Maguelone*, 2v (Montpellier 1921-1927) and Frédéric Fabrège, *Histoire de Maguelone, 2 v. (Montpellier 1921*-1927) and Frédéric Fabrège, *Histoire de Maguelone*, 3 v. (Paris, Montpellier, 1893-1911). The Fabrège work is somewhat dated.

84 For examples of sales *in franco alodio*, *v* A.M., II 1, J. Grimaudi, f. 4r: vineyard; A.D., II E 95/370, J. Holanie, f. 53r: field, vineyard and forest *in franco, libero et absoluto alodio;* II E 95/371, J. Holanie, f. 91v, 117r; II E 95/372, J. Holanie, 122r, 164r.

85 A.D., II E 95/370, J. Holanie, f. 84r. *v*, e.g. II E 95/371, J. Holanie, f. 66r and II E 95/377, B. Egidii, ff. 260v-261r.

86 P.-L. Malausséna, *La vie en Provence orientale, pp. 93*-94.

87 A.D., II E 95/377, B. Egidii, f. 284r.

88 This was also the finding of P. Bouges, "La pratique contractuelle à Montpellier," I, pp. 43-44. (*v* n. 15)

89 *v* my article, "Changes in Testamentary Practice at Montpellier on the Eve of the Black Death," *Church History*, 47 (1978), p. 260, n. 34.

90 A.D., II E 95/371, J. Holanie, f. 66r.

91 A.D., II E 95/371, J. Holanie, f. 25r.

92 P. Ourliac and J. de Malafosse, *Les biens*, p. 167.

93 A.D., II E 95/377, B. Egidii, f. 267r.

94 A.D., II E 95/372, J. Holanie f. 89r, loose page.

95 A.D. II E 95/369, J. Holanie, f. 40r.

[96] On the role of the *tutor*, *v* Louis de Charrin, *Les testaments de Montpellier au Moyen-Age* (Ambilly, 1961), p. 213. The lay courts had supervision over *tutores*.

[97] On *execution forcée*, legal procedure of seizure against the possessions of a debtor, *v* P. Ourliac and J. de Malafosse, *Les obligations*, p. 190.

[98] Price history for the medieval period in Montpellier is in need of future research. The *setier* was the most commonly recorded measure of grain (*sestarius*); it held 48.92 liters. Prices of barley were almost never noted. An *eymina* was about 12 litres.

[99] E. Fournial, *Les villes et l'économie d'échange en Forez*, p. 680.

[100] D. Nicholas, *Town and Countryside*, pp. 304–305.

[101] A.D. II E 95/369, J. Holanie, f. 47r.

[102] A.D. II E 95/368, J. Holanie, f. 137r.

[103] P.-L. Malausséna, *La vie en Provence orientale*, p. 95, discerned differences between practice in the thirteenth century on the one hand and the fourteenth and fifteenth centuries on the other.

[104] On inflation and price movements, there is no real consensis of opinion. cf. Harry A. Miskimin, *Money, Prices and Foreign Exchange*, pp. 53–82; B. H. Slicher Van Bath, *The Agrarian History of Western Europe, A.D. 500*–1850 (London, 1963) pp. 98–131; and Michael M. Postan, *Medieval Agriculture and General Problems of the Medieval Economy* (Cambridge, 1973).

[105] Problems were accentuated after the mid-fourteenth century. *v* Harry Miskimin, *The Economy of Early Renaissance Europe, 1300-1460* (Englewood Cliffs, N.J., 1969; Cambridge, 1975), pp. 51-57.

[106] *v* G. Duby, *L'Economie rurale*, II, pp. 496–497, on the means of defending against the depreciation of the fixed *census*.

[107] Weather was the largest variable. Inflation and currency manipulations were also of influence.

[108] E.g., A.D., II E 95/377, f. 253r. A wood merchant granted land in the parish of Pérols to an artist for 8 *l.* in *accapitum* (the equivalent of 2.7 *l.* in the money of April, 1330) in return for 5 *s.* current money (.08 *l.* of 1330) per year, payable at the feast of St. Peter in August. The artist made a recognition of debt in favor of the lessor promising to pay 4 *l.* at the next feast and 4 *l.* at the following feast. Later (f. 264v), he sold the land for 8 *l.* current money and the wood merchant received a *laudimium* of 16 *s* (worth 9.4 per cent of the purchase price).

[109] On these leases, *v* Roger Aubenas, *Cours d'histoire du droit privé*, IV, pp. 70–86. *v* P. Ourliac and J. de Malafosse, *Les biens*, pp. 162–168. On medieval tenure, the collected papers in *Recueils de la société Jean Bodin*, III: *La tenure* (1938), are useful. The long-term lease of *emphyteusis* had origins in Roman law. *v* A. Berger, *Encyclopedic Dictionary*, p. 452. Numerous regional studies exist. *v* the bibliography in *Les biens*, pp. 182–83.

[110] John H. Pryor, *Business Contracts of Medieval Provence. Selected "Notulae" from the Cartulary of Giraud Amalric of Marseilles, 1248.* (Toronto, 1981), p. 91. P.-L. Malausséna, *La vie en Provence orientale*, p. 93, noted that the recovery of Roman law led to the attachment of the Roman term, *emphyteusis*, to that of *accapitum*, the *bail à acapt*, which was the only legal form of tenure including concessions from both *seigneurs* and *roturiers*.

[111] For an example of payment in kind, A.D., II E 95/377, B. Egidii, f. 15v, *usaticum* of 5 *sestarii* of wheat in the measure of Melgueil (i.e. Mauguio).

[112] A.D., II E 95/370, f. 54v. The annual payment in this lease was three *sestarii* of olive oil in the measure of Montpellier at the feast of St. Hilary.

[113] cf. P.-L. Malausséna, *La vie en Provence orientale*, p. 95, who found that the *accapitum* fee of the thirteenth century was much higher than the annual *census* payment, but that in the fourteenth and fifteenth centuries, the opposite was true. Montpellier tenures do not seem to have undergone such an evolution.

[114] Roger Aubenas, *Cours d'histoire du droit privé*, IV, p. 70.

[115] *v* n. 112 sup. In this grant nobles were the lessees, a fact which sets Montpellier practice apart from the general concept of an *emphyteusis*. R. Aubenas, *Cours d'histoire du droit privé*, IV, p. 70, stated "l'emphytéose serait une concession de terre, perpétuelle en principe, faite à un preneur roturier par le propriétaire d'un alleu, noble ou roturier."

[116] P. Ourliac and J. de Malafosse, *Les biens*, pp. 165–166, state of the perpetual leases, "Le type de ces tenures est la censive qui se retrouve dans toute la France, sous des dénominations diverses, et qui devient le type normal des tenures roturières. (l'albergement, le bordelage, le champart, l'emphytéose n'en étant que des variétés)." For another regional case, Hubert Richardot, "Le fief roturier à Toulouse aux XIIe et XIIIe siècles," *Revue historique du droit français et étranger*, 14 (1935), 307–359, 495–569, has examined non-noble property in the region of Toulouse.

[117] *v* Table 12.

[118] On the institution of the *albergue*, *v* Roger Aubenas, *Cours d'histoire du droit privé*, IV, p. 86. *v. Liber instrumentorum memorialium, Cartulaire des Guilhems de Montpellier*, ed. C. Chabaneau and A. Germain (Montpellier, 1884–1886), act C, in which Guilhem V, lord of Montpellier, reserved for himself the command of the *albergos* owed by the town *milites* at the occasion of a grant of the *viguerie* of Montpellier to the Aimoin family.

[119] *v* A.D., II E 95/371, J. Holanie, f. 41v. A *domus* inside the Commune Clôture owed two *albergos militum* to the *dominus* of Montpellier. Another unusual type of tenure can be signaled in a grant to a Jew of a house *in precaria* in 1301. *v* A.M., II 2, J. Grimaudi, ff. 13v–14r.

[120] These acts are found in a fragment of a register of Petrus de Pena, inserted in A.D., II E 95/390, Pierre Bourdon, ff. 1r–24r, for the years 1390–1396. They were discovered by chance in a survey which I made of all remaining registers through the year 1400. They have been included in the figures of Table 13.

[121] On the Conchis, *v* J. Combes, "Une famille de négociants quercynols à Montpellier et à Marseille au XIIIe siècle," *Fédération historique, Actes des XXVIIe et XXVIIIe congrès* (Montpellier, 1956), ibid, off-print and "Quelques remarques sur les bourgeois de Montpellier," ibid., 93–132.

[122] A.D., II E 95/377, B. Egidii, ff. 88v, 113r, 228r and 276v. A Raymundus de Conchis of Assas farmed a fortune in real estate to a mint master of Montpellier with whom he had other dealings as well. *v* Marc Bompaire, "L'Atelier monétaire royal de Montpellier et la circulation monétaire en Bas Languedoc jusqu'au milieu du XVe siècle," Thèse, Ecole des Chartes, 1980, p. 111.

[123] A.D., II E 95/368, J. Holanie, f. 61v, for a sale and further grant in *emphyteusis* of a house. *v* also II E 95/377, B. Egidii, f. 65r, for a transfer of an *accapitum* and a *reaccapitum*. A further example occurred on July 26, 1343 (A.D., II E 95/372, J. Holanie, f. 60r): a Dominican prior, of the house of the Dominican nuns of Prouilhan, and his procurator certified the inheritance and *accapitum* of a house with attachments by the wife of a silk merchant, daughter of a pepperer, from her sister. The approval fee stemming from rights of eminent domain was 100 *s.* current money, the fee for the renewal of *accapitum*, 20 *s.*

124 For a synoptic inventory of this *fonds de la Commune Clôture v* Oudot de Dainville and Marcel Gouron, eds., *Inventaire, Fonds de la Commune Clôture et Affaires militaires* (Montpellier, 1974).

125 A.D., II E 95/373, G. de Podio, ff. 1r, 2v, 4r, 5v, 6v, 9r, 13r, 13v, 16v, 17r, 28r.

126 On the legal aspects of the contracts involved in sharecropping and rentals, *v* P. Bouges, "La pratique contractuelle," I, pp. 77-100. *v* also G. Sicard, *Le métayage dans le Midi toulousain à la fin du Moyen-Age* (Toulouse, 1955). For example of sharecropping in an eight-year contract *v* A.D., II E 95/374, G. Nogareti, f 58r R.

127 P. Bouges, "La pratique contractuelle," I, p. 93. For the nuances of the Montpellier contracts and their originality with regard to other southern French sharecropping arrangements, *v* ibid., I, pp. 94-95.

128 Example of instructions are found in A.D., II E 95/377, B. Egidii, ff. 122v and 254v. *v* also II E 95/371, J. Holanie, f. 41r and the discussion by P. Bouges, "La pratique contractuelle," I, pp. 96-97 and II, p. 42, nn. 150 and 151.

129 P.-L. Malausséna, *La vie en Provence orientale*, pp. 105-116. *v* also Mireille Castaing-Sicard, *Les contrats dans le très ancien droit toulousain (Xe-*XIIIe siècles) (Toulouse, 1959), pp. 182-187. Other forms of agricultural exploitation involving a sharing of financial burden and work between lessor and lessee have left brief trace in the documents of Montpellier.

An unusual use of the contract *causa comande cum custodia* appeared in the agricultural context in Montpellier. In this way a merchant confided ten pigs and two sows to a local cultivator for two years. *v* A.D., II E 95/368, J. Holanie, f. 97v. The latter was instructed to raise the animals, and, after the term had elapsed, the profit from their sale was to be divided evenly between the contractants. The operation herein described resembled the *gasaille* or *bail à cheptel* of the Touloûsain district. In the Toulousain *gasaille*, the division of profit was identical. P. Wolff underscored the credit functions of the Toulousain practices which ran the gamut from a disguised loan guaranteed by the herd of animals to the financing of the raising of livestock. The Montpellier contract, the only extant example of this practice before 1350, may have been applicable to other forms of animal husbandry. In Toulouse the *gasaille* was a common technique of local butchers in the breeding of cattle. *v* P. Wolff, "Les bouchers de Toulouse," pp. 379-380, and *Commerces et marchands*, pp. 193-211. Wolff commented regarding the *gasaille*, "Les bouchers," pp. 379-380: "Il s'agît en fait d'une opération assez souple, qui allait du prêt déguisé, gage sur le troupeau de l'emprunteur—ce qui permettait de tourner la législation sur l'usure—, aux pratiques de l'élevage, comme la remise de bêtes à engraisser. Mais le formulaire des notaires ne permet pas toujours par lui-même de faire la distinction." The most common form of animal husbandry in the region of Montpellier, was sheepraising. For a further brief reference to sheep, pigs and cattle, *v* A.D. II E 95/374, G. Nogareti, f. 58R.

130 *v* the Appendix for examples of *locatio*.

131 *v*. e.g., a two-year rental of land in A.D., II E 95/375, P. de Pena, f. 3r.

132 The dates of payment of rent fell on the most important religious feasts as in the case of the fees of long-term leases and loans. *v* the discussion by P. Bouges, "La pratique contractuelle," I, pp. 82-83.

133 The relative frequency of the house rentals is interesting in light of the nature of the *locatio*. One could only rent a house in good condition. *v* Brigitte Basdevant, "Gestion immobilière dans la censive de Saint-Benoît le Bétourné du XIVe au XVIe siècle," *Revue d'histoire du droit français et étranger*, 57 (1979), 231, who states, p. 223, "Le

louage à court terme n'est pas possible lorsque le propriétaire ne peut assurer au locataire le 'clos et le couvert'."

[134] The notarial evidence of the fourteenth century suggests, thus, that the small independent agricultural proprietor was a common phenomenon in the region of Montpellier. Such an hypothesis would benefit from the confirmation of cartulary evidence. cf. D. Nicholas, *Town and Countryside*, p. 278, who found some artisan owners but many patrician and nouveaux riches among the owners.

[135] E.g., A.D., II E 95/368, J. Holanie, f. 100v *v* the discussion by P. Bouges, "La pratique contractuelle," I, pp. 86-87 and II, p. 36, n. 69. Land exchanges, another form of real estate transaction, are treated below.

[136] *v* A.D. II E 95/368, J. Holanie, f. 62r.

[137] D. Nicholas, *Town and Countryside*, p. 304, found fifteen or more years a common recovery period. In Montpellier, some periods were probably less long.

[138] A.D., II E 95/373, G. de Podio, f. 5r. On the Pisan *fondaco v* A. *Germain, Histoire du commerce*, I, 93-96. The Pisan *fondaco* lay on the via Francigena in the twelfth century.

D. Herlihy, *Pisa in the Early Renaissance*, p. 78, estimated that Pisan rents were being capitalized at 12 per cent of their value. House values and rentals were so variable in Montpellier as to prevent any comparable estimate of recovery costs.

[139] A.D., II E 95/368, J. Holanie, f. 101v.

[140] For a house with a shop and second story, A.D., II E 95/371, J. Holanie, f. 47r.

[141] A.D., II E 95/369, J. Holanie, f. 80v.

[142] A.D., II E 95/369, J. Holanie, f. 7r. See f. 6v for a butcher's table in the new meat market.

[143] A.D., II E 95/375, P. de Pena, f. 33r.

[144] A.D., II E 95/371, J. Holanie, f. 12v.

[145] A. Berger, *Encyclopedic Dictionary*, p. 755.

[146] ibid., p. 670: *reditus*. The Montpellier documents use the spelling *redditus*.

[147] For example, A.D., II E 95/368, J. Holanie, ff. 45v and 71r.

[148] For an example involving rights over shops, *v* A.M., II 1, J. Grimaudi, f. 18v; rights over two shops of *blancaria* were sold by a lady *burgensis* to a Jew.

[149] Occasionally, the term was as long as nine years. *v* A.D., II E 95/368, J. Holanie, f. 33r, for the sale of the *redditus* of a vineyard for nine years.

[150] J. Combes, "Les investissements immobiliers à Montpellier au commencement du XVe siècle, "*Recueil*, fasc. II (1951), p. 22, commented on the various ways of capitalizing on this sort of purchase. *v* A.D., II E 95/377, B. Egidii, ff. 299v and 306v for sales where the buyer intended to cultivate the lands.

[151] A.D., II E 95/368, J. Holanie, f. 100v.

[152] A.D., II E 95/372, J. Holanie, f. 147v.

[153] A.D., II E 95/371, J. Holanie, f. 124v.

[154] A.D., II E 95/374, G. Nogareti, f. 198r. The Cabanis brothers and their mother Martha had numerous real estate holdings. It is probable that Jacobus intended to sublet this shop during the period of his purchase. He had family connections with pepperers through a brother-in-law, Guiraudus Naturalis.

[155] *Le Petit Thalamus*, "La chronique romane," p. 348, provides details of floods, droughts, and famines which began in the late thirteenth century. After a series of disastrous years, in 1333 it was reported that young men were weakened by a poor diet of raw herbs and that people were dying in the streets.

[156] P. Ourliac and J. de Malafosse, *Les obligations*, p. 291, stated that it was difficult in Roman law to distinguish a sales contract (*venditio*) juridically from a rental (*locatio*).

157 A. Berger, op. cit., p. 567.

158 Only two shops were noted in this context.

159 A.D., II E 95/372, J. Holanie, f. 47r.

160 A.D., II E 95/370, J. Holanie, f. 34r. The term *arrendatio* was utilized in this act. It was relatively common in ecclesiastical farms. On *arrendatio v.* P. Bouges, "La pratique contractuelle," I, pp. 100-106. Another example demonstrating the large sums in these farms involved the acquittal granted by another canon of Maguelone for his priory which had been farmed for 400 *l.t.* in 1333 for two years; 300 *l.* of the payment due were acquitted. *v* A.D., II E 95/369, J. Holanie, f. 44r.

161 A.D., II E 95/372, J. Holanie, ff. 35r and 35v.

162 A.D., II E 95/377, B. Egidii, ff. 32r and 34v; A.M. Montpellier, II 1, J. Grimaudi, f. lv.

163 A.M., II 2, J. Grimaudi, ff. 49v-50v.

164 On the *vente à rémeré, v* P. Wolff, *Commerces et marchands,* pp. 359-360 and E. Fournial, *Les villes et l'économie d'échange en Forez,* pp. 698-700. P. Wolff, 360, called the *vente à rémeré* "une forme détournée de prêt à intérêt."

165 J. Combes examined the institution of the annual rent in "La constitution de rente à Montpellier au commencement du XVe siècle," *Annales de l'Université de Montpellier et du Languedoc—Roussillon,* 22 nos. 3-4 (1944), 216-223. He commented, 220 "Nos investigations dans les registres notariaux des XIVe et XVe siècles conservés aux Archives Départementales de l'Hérault et aux Archives Municipales de Montpellier ne nous ont livré, jusqu'ici, qu'une quarantaine de contrats de rente constituée, presque tous concentrés dans un seul registre consacré aux opérations de Bernard Salmon et de Pierre Jourda: c'est dire qu'on ne saurait affirmer qu'à Montpellier cette institution ait été particulièrement pratiquée." On the rent in general in the Middle Ages in France, *v* P. Petot, *La constitution de rente aux XIIe et XIIIe siècles dans les pays coutumiers* (Dijon, 1928).

166 A.D., II E 95/372, J. Holanie, f. 204v. Alamanni acted as *negotiorum gestor.* The phraseology cited by J. Combes, "La constitution de rente," pp. 222-223, in his *pièces justificatives* is similar: *"quinque libras turonensium annuales consuales et perpetuales",* although not identical.

167 Occasionally in sales of allods, the notarial acts carried the mention of a continuing payment. Mention of an annual *pensionem* owed the preceptor of the house of Saint-Jean-de-Jérusalem in Montpellier was made in A.D. II E 95/377, B. Egidii, f. 256r. *v* also II E 95/370, J. Holanie, f. 29v. Elsewhere in Europe records of annuities have survived. In Flanders, D. Nicholas, *Town and Countryside,* p. 309, found common use of life annuities. According to P. Desportes, *Reims et les Rémois,* p. 127, the life annuity (*rente viagère*) was a popular form of local investment. Annual *rentes* were also noted elsewhere in Champagne. (Desportes, 128-129). No process of establishment of life annuities has been detected in Montpellier.

168 J. Combes, op. cit. p. 218 and p. 219, n. 3.

169 *v* n. 99 sup.

170 J. Combes, "Les investissements immobiliers," pp 218-28, isolated three categories of acquisition of property in the transactions of a certain rich pepperer, Bernard Salmon. The first type of investment involved the outright purchase of eminent domain and all rights, that is, allodial ownership. The second category discerned by Combes covered the acquisition of revenues of a variety of kinds for a limited period. The third consisted in the establishment of an annual rent on real estate or revenues from property rights and other prerogatives. This rent was in theory perpetual but could generally be terminated if the holder desired. Combes identified these three practices as profitable

ways of avoiding the stigma of usury in loans. On the issue of usury and the *rente v* Bernard Schnapper, "Les rentes chez les théologiens et les canonistes du XIIIe au XIVe siècle," *Etudes d'histoire du droit canonique dédiées à Gabriel Le Bras,* II (Paris, 1965), pp. 965-995.

171 *v* my forthcoming book, *Business, Banking and Finance,* and my article, "Les opérations de crédit dans la coutume et dans la vie des affaires à Montpellier au moyen âge: le problème de l'usure," in *Diritto comune e diritti locali nella storia dell'Europa* (Milan, 1980), 189-209.

172 *v Business, Banking and Finance.*

173 Marie-Odile Piquet-Marchal, "Doctrines monétaires et conjoncture aux XIVe et XVe siècles," *Revue internationale de l'histoire de la banque,* 4 (1971), 373-374.

174 Benjamin Z. Kedar, *Merchants in Crisis. Genoese and Venetian Men of Affairs and the Fourteenth-Century Depression* (New Haven, London, 1976), p. 63.

175 ibid., pp. 62-65 and 86-90.

176 There were no mortgages in the notarial registers. Some survive in the cartulary evidence, however. *v Business, Banking and Finance.* On the usefulness of the mortgage as a credit instrument, *v* Patricia A. Lewis, "Mortgages in the Bordelais and Bazadais," *Viator,* 10 (1979), 23-38.

177 Anne Marin, "Montpellier à la fin du moyen âge d'après les compoix," p. 129: "L'élément rural n'est pas dominant dans les fortunes montpelliéraines. Seuls les lauradors possèdent une fortune essentiellement rurale, surtout ceux qui vivent dans les faubourgs."

178 ibid., p. 153: "L'essentiel est constitué par les patrimoines à prédominance urbaine et mobilière." David Herlihy and Christiane Klapisch-Zuber, *Les Toscans et leurs familles. Une étude du catasto florentin de 1427* (Paris, 1978), p. 253, graphs, found that Florentines had a smaller percentage of their fortunes in land than did inhabitants of secondary towns. Perhaps, then, the late medieval city shows consistent characteristics in this regard.

179 P. Wolff, *Les "Estimes",* pp. 72-73.

180 ibid., 109.

181 *v* my article, "Changes in Testamentary Practice." Political change also occurred at this time with the purchase of Montpellier from the king of Majorca by Philip of Valois in 1349.

182 "La Chronique romane," in *Le Petit Thalamus,* p. 349: 1352.

183 ibid., p. 391: 1374.

184 Pierre Desportes, *Reims et les Rémois,* pp. 258-261.

185 David Nicholas, *Town and Countryside,* pp. 287-290.

186 P. Desportes, *Reims et les Rémois,* p, 258: "le statut normal du grand domaine en France du Nord est encore d'être tenu en fief et doté de droits seigneuriaux."

187 D. Nicholas, *Town and Countryside,* p. 281.

III

THE ADOLESCENT APPRENTICE/WORKER IN MEDIEVAL MONTPELLIER

ABSTRACT: *This study explores the experiential dimensions of apprenticeship and work as part of the adolescent life phase in fourteenth-century Montpellier on the basis of approximately two hundred surviving notarial contracts. The strong role of family in apprenticeship of young men and women, the acquisition of specific occupational skills, character formation, and the well-being of the apprentice/worker are discussed. Apprenticeship for Montpellier youth represented a lengthy (early teens to late twenties) and elaborate transition between childhood and adulthood.*

Philippe Ariès' controversial work, *Centuries of Childhood,* gave great impetus in the early 1960s to a study of childhood and family (Ariès 1960, 1962). Ariès accorded relatively little space to adolescence because of the early absorption, in his view, of the child into the adult world. Apprenticeship for Ariès was the archtypical example of the medieval mingling of youth with adults in contrast to modern age-structured education (Wilson 1980, pp. 141-143). While aspects of childhood have caught the attention of medievalists, adolescence has not proved a central focus of work to date. (Lyman 1974; Mclaughlin 1974; Ross 1974; Riché 1973; Herlihy 1958, 1969, 1985;

Herlihy and Klapisch-Zuber 1978, 1985; Klapisch-Zuber 1973). However, there is now emerging a scholarly debate about whether the Middle Ages recognized a separate life phase of adolescence. A recent study by James A. Schultz casts doubt on the existence of a separate period of adolescence in the Middle Ages, given the failure of Middle High German texts to mention it (Schultz 1991). Other scholars such as Barbara Hanawalt have recognized and given shape to this life phase (Hanawalt 1986). The present study provides support for the existence of medieval adolescence on the basis of insights derived from apprenticeship and work contracts of the late thirteenth and first half of the fourteenth centuries.

Adolescence is generally defined today as the interval from about twelve to eighteen, after which in most modern societies one is considered an adult. According to James Schultz, "generational conflict and identity formation"—part of the modern popular conception—are used by historians as indicative of adolescence. Schultz noted that psychologists focus on "identity formation" including "role experimentation and vocational choice" in describing adolescent experience (Schultz 1991, p. 521). While his German texts do not supply Schultz with support for a medieval period of adolescence, the apprenticeship and work contracts of this study permit the discussion of character development and the acquisition of occupational skills, demarcating a passage from childhood to adulthood in the Middle Ages. The adolescent apprentice/worker will be examined in a transitional period of training between childhood and adult economic activity which was not limited chronologically to the same years as the modern life phase of adolescence.

Other eras had differing conceptions of life phases of childhood, adolescence, and adulthood. Terminology is, in fact, a significant issue in the study of adolescence.[1] In the Middle Ages one might be considered an adolescent into the mid or late twenties or beyond (Klapisch-Zuber 1973; Shahar 1990, pp. 27-31). Adult responsibilities could, however, be assumed in early adolescence.[2] Literature from the medieval period was ambivalent about adolescence, considering the fifteen-year-old male at times a man, at times a child.[3] Theoretically, according to Roman law, one came of age at twenty-five (Tisset 1951). In practice, the ages of fourteen for boys and twelve for girls seem to be working ages of majority in many parts of medieval Europe.[4]

A number of studies exist on the legal and/or economic aspects of medieval apprenticeship, but surprisingly few of these have exploited apprenticeship data for the experiential dimensions of adolescence. Admittedly, the topic of adolescence can be addressed only indirectly in the Middle Ages, but there is certainly much scattered data about the age between childhood and adulthood in the contracts of apprenticeship. Apprenticeship represents a particularly apt prism through which to view this transitional life phase. Herein one finds information about young people outside their family context, in preparation for future careers of greatly differing complexity. There is insight into their living conditions, the specific arrangements of their engagements, the remuneration or lack thereof for their labor, and their relations with their masters.

Two hundred eight contracts of apprenticeship and work survive in the extant notarial registers of Montpellier from 1293 to 1348. Thirty relate to women.[5] These contracts are a rich source of information on a number of levels. They provide data on training and employment in a wide variety of fields, including skilled artisanal trades and sophisticated financial and mercantile occupations, such as changers and apothecaries. These contracts also furnish considerable information about the activities of young people who would fall most probably in the category of adolescents.

Apprenticeship data from Montpellier paint the picture of a structured existence for the adolescent trainee in some skilled craft useful to the urban economy. The first and most obvious motive in apprenticeship was that of learning an occupation for support and sustenance during adult life. Contingent upon the acquisition of a skill in most cases was the ability to start a family, to prosper and acquire material goods and, at a more basic level, simply to exist above a level of hand-to-mouth misery, vagabondage, and beggary, in short, above a subsistence level leading to disease and early death. The period of training was frequently long and not always cost-free to the apprentice's family. Family members often took a role in the contractual arrangements. The contracts themselves show concern for the apprentice's growth, development, well-being, health, and maintenance. Surviving contracts show many more males than females, both as masters taking apprentices and as apprentices. Girls were usually apprenticed to women, occasionally to men, and the rare exception saw a young male apprenticed to a woman. Young women were trained in specific fields, especially in the textile trades and the food industry, luxury decorations, mercery, and silk work rather than in the most prestigious trades of apothecary, changer, draper, and merchant for which the town was known (Reyerson 1986). A comparison of apprenticeship experiences for young men and young women is, nonetheless, an important aspect of any treatment of adolescence.

In the Montpellier contracts a term referring to learning (*diciplina* or *discipula*) might be combined with language associated with work (*opera*), implying that at least some level of occupational competence had been achieved. *Colloquare* or *collocare* was the usual verb employed in both work and apprenticeship situations; *colloquo in dicipulum, in scolarem, in juvenem* or *colloquo obrerium* or *obrerem et omnes operas meas* or a combination of such phrases would be used.[6] I have generally employed three categories for the Montpellier contracts: *diciplina,* i.e. pure and simple apprenticeship, a mixture of *diciplina* with work, and work alone. For the purposes of this study, the first two categories are the more pertinent though some work contracts involved young people. There is little distinction among contract types possible on the basis of the particular arrangements in regard to living expenses, salary, and piece-work price. I will at times group them together in the following tables. The apprenticeship contracts of Montpellier provide the historian with the same problems of definition that Philippe Wolff discovered in his study of the contracts of Toulouse and Françoise Michaud-Fréjaville in the Orléanais (Wolff 1954; Michaud-Fréjaville 1982). It is difficult if not impossible to distinguish between beginner apprentices, those with some professional experience, and journeymen who had already acquired considerable professional training (Reyerson 1979).

Twenty-one of the surviving Montpellier contracts actually quote the age of apprentices or laborers.[7] In all but one case where the male apprentice was specifically described as under fourteen, contracts give ages of over twelve for

Table 1
Length of Engagement: Apprenticeship and Labor Contracts
$N = 83$

	Numbers of Years									
Occupation	*1*	*2*	*3*	*4*	*5*	*6*	*7*	*8*	*10*	*12*
Changers	2	9	2	1		1				
Apothecaries	1	1	1	1				1		
Wood merchants		1		1		1				
Pepperers		1	1	1	1					
Merchants	2		1	1		1				
Mercers		1	1			1	1	3		
Drapers	1	2		1				1		
Goldsmiths	1	2	4	2		1		1		
Silversmiths	3		1		1	2				1
Shoemakers	1			2		1		1		
Bakers				3	2	2			1	
Furriers	1	4	2							

females and over fourteen for males.[8] In the south of France, following the legacy of Roman law, twelve was the practical age of majority for girls, fourteen for boys (Gouron 1958). When the male apprentice had attained the age of fourteen, his oath was expected in the provisions of the contract.[9] In the absence of age data the length of engagements in contracts may also be seen as an indication of apprentices' youth. Long contracts of six years or more probably involved adolescents under practical majority or even younger children. Exit ages from apprenticeship arrangements could be as young as seventeen and as old as 26 in those contracts where age was mentioned.[10] Presumably by 25, the official age of majority in Roman law, apprentices would have finished training. In those cases without age data, where the apprenticeship was longer than eight years, the apprentice was either younger than adolescence at inception or exited at a mature age.

The length of apprenticeship for boys and young men varied considerably, even within specific professions as Table 1 shows. The professions in Table 1 reflect a range of complexity, but all recorded lengthy apprenticeship periods. The longest surviving contract in Montpellier—twelve years in duration—involved the son of a late mercer training to be a silversmith who was described as over fourteen in his contract (A D II E 95/372, f. 101r). In contrast to the findings of Philippe Didier for Burgundy and Anne-Marie Landes-Mallet for the Rouergue, there seems to be little demonstrable correlation, either in the inverse, as in the Didier findings, or directly as Landes-Mallet suggested, between the sophistication of the trade and the length of training, pepperers being on a par with shoemakers and wood merchants (Didier 1976; Landes-Mallet 1988). But, by the same token, instruction in those professions for which there are multiple surviving apprenticeship contracts was an intensive process for the completely untrained person. Learning to make a shoe was perhaps as difficult a task, depending on innate talent, as acquiring the expertise to craft an intricate silver dish. The absence of precise age data makes it impossible to gage the appropriate point at which the learning process in specific trades began.

No detectable correlation appears between the age of apprentices and the distance over which they were drawn to Montpellier. Nonlocal apprentices had slightly longer apprenticeships. Local girls were apprenticed at a beginning level on average for 4.3 years and nonlocal girls for 5.4 years. Local boys averaged 3.3 years of apprenticeship while nonlocal boys contracted on average for 6 years (Reyerson 1979, p. 272, n. 77). Distance of displacement and type of occupation correlated with the prestige of the occupation. Less prestigious trades drew from the Montpellier hinterland while the highly reputed trades of commerce and finance were a magnet for a broader region (Reyerson 1979, pp. 266-270).

For females the length of apprenticeship went from two years to learn basket making or second hand clothes marketing to six years to learn tailoring and eight years to learn the mercer's trade, to ten years to learn the baking trade (Reyerson 1986, pp. 120-121). The last example concerned a twelve-year-old and clearly inexperienced apprentice.

Of the 208 apprenticeship and work contracts, only eleven are of sons following fathers in the same trade. In two additional instances the correlation was close: the son of a silk merchant was apprenticed to a mercer; and the son of a goldsmith was hired as a servant (not an apprentice) by another goldsmith. It can be argued that sons following their fathers' trade would be kept at home to acquire such skills, but the fact remains that many sons were pursuing other occupations according to this data. Occasionally, a youth might be apprenticed to a relative. In only one case was there close verifiable correlation between a girl's family and her profession (A D II E 95/368, f. 135v). However, fourteen of the 30 surviving female contracts of work and apprenticeship involved in-migrants for whom no family profession was indicated.

Placing a child or adolescent for apprenticeship may well have involved considerable diplomacy and negotiation among families. Strength of ties within family units is revealed in the apprenticeship which was initiated by one or the other parent or by both, by another relative, by a seemingly unattached individual, or by the individual him- or herself (Duxbury 1986). As far as work contracts are concerned, the status of the worker is not at all clear. Work contracts could indeed involve adolescents but might also concern older individuals who were engaging themselves in some project. Table 2 gives the breakdown of apprenticeship initiation for males. The largest category involved males apprenticing themselves; other significant categories included fathers who apprenticed what must have been young sons (in the absence of age data) and fathers who acted with sons who apprenticed themselves. Mothers were somewhat less commonly engaged in apprenticing their male offspring. In four cases the mothers were specifically identified as widows. In only three instances did mothers act alone in apprenticing their sons. Françoise Michaud-Fréjaville remarked on the high percentage in the Orléanais (about 50% for males) of orphans appearing in apprenticeship contracts (Michaud-Fréjaville 1980). The Montpellier data would suggest a high incidence of loss of one or more parents, but in the contracts of individuals apprenticing themselves, the status of

Table 2
Apprenticeship Initiation—Males
N = 126

Abbreviations: P = Parents; S = Self; M = Mother; F = Father; O = Other

Parents	Self	P/S	Mother	M/S	M/ Widow	M/S Widow	M/ Kin	Father	F/ Self	S/O
3	48	1	6	4	2	1	5	16	22	18

Self/Other: *fideiussores*, guardians, kin, certifiers, unidentified parties

parents was not always given. Orphan status could have contributed to the absence of carryover of occupations from one generation to another, noted above. Few cases of parents acting together were present in any of the categories.

Males frequently apprenticed themselves with the advice or certification of other relatives or with males who were unidentified in blood relation to the apprentice. Family friends or business colleagues might have served in this capacity. *Fideiussores* (sureties) could be invoked to guarantee an arrangement. When no curators existed and no family members were in evidence, adults still might be present, perhaps the business colleagues of deceased parents who were looking out for young persons, known to them, by standing as *fideiussores* or vouching for young men in a contractual setting. This additional insurance was present frequently in contracts involving foreign apprentices whose family and background might not have been as well-known as those of local apprentices. Further, legal guardians who were often family members or business associates apprenticed their male wards.[11] Certifications were offered by several of the participants in the self/other category. Boys who had no curator and were noted as over fourteen or over fifteen often received this type of certification though they were theoretically of legal age in a practical sense. No clearly discernable rule in the data indicates that a boy over fourteen had to have references bolstering his apprenticeship, and, in fact, cases remain where a boy over fourteen had none.

One might conjecture whether the humbler classes were as well-provided with curators and tutors and assistance in general in finding employment, but there is evidence to suggest that apprenticeship cut across rather large social and economic chasms. In the case of a fisherman's son apprenticing to a pepperer, the son of the pepperer was the acting representative before the notary on the master's side, suggesting that a factor of childhood acquaintance might have been at work (A D II E 95/371, f. 50v). Were these boyhood friends or street acquaintances? Notarial contracts do not elucidate the sort of networks which adolescents and children enjoyed.

In no instance in the remaining data did young women apprentice themselves without relatives' participation (see Table 3). No sureties were recorded in female contracts, for the young women were not acting alone. In four cases mothers (two of them specifically identified as widows) apprenticed daughters. In another contract a mother and a cousin apprenticed a daughter. In two additional cases daughters apprenticed themselves with their mothers' consent. Finally, in one other

Table 3
Apprenticeship Initiation—Females
N = 24

Parents	Mother	Widowed Mother	Mother/ Kin	Father	Self/ Father	Self/ Mother*	Self/ Other*	Other
2	2	2	1	5	5	2	1	4

Self/Other: Widowed Mother, Maternal Uncles and Friends

Other: Brother 1
Paternal Uncle 1
Unidentified Kin 1
Guardian 1

In three cases * it was the consent and advice, not the actual initiation by the involved individuals, which was mentioned.

instance a widowed mother acted with a maternal uncle's and friends' advice along with the daughter. In two cases parents did the apprenticing, and in four instances fathers did. In five cases daughters apprenticed themselves with their fathers' approval, and in five contracts fathers initiated the process. The intervention of a paternal uncle, a guardian, and a brother in additional contracts reinforces the historian's impression of the role of males in determining the fate of young women. In apprenticeship females passed from paternal authority to the authority of the master.[12]

In the vast majority of work contracts where males contracted on their own behalf, age of practical majority must be presumed (see Table 4). Three females placed themselves alone in work relationships; one of these was identified as over thirteen with no curator. She engaged herself to become a domestic servant or *ancilla* in the household of a silversmith (A D II E 95/371, f. 50r). The absence of any supporting adult suggests that she was an orphan—her dead father was mentioned in the contract—with sufficient grit and savy to use the notary as a means of legal protection. She was a country girl from Posquières in the Gard. The presence of family members in some work arrangements makes it highly likely that young persons were involved. The participation of spouses in the work contract of their marital partners suggests the strength of the marriage bond (Duxbury 1986, p. 18).

Further insights into adolescence relate to the place of apprentices and workers in the medieval artisan family or household (Duxbury 1986). The domestic family unit was also an economic unit which could expand into a household containing family and non-family members. Apprenticeship had many implications for the

Table 4
Work Initiation—Males and Females
N = 58

Self/Female	Self/Male	Male/Wife	Female/Husband	Parents	Kin	Other
3	45	3	2	2	2	1

artisan household. The atelier could gain in productivity and efficiency were the apprentice able to assume some of the unskilled tasks related to the trade, leaving the master and journeymen time to tackle the more complex operations associated with a particular occupation. Skills might be better attuned to the task and overall labor better distributed, resulting in a potentially better-quality product.

The master provided service to his profession in training new personnel. To enable the perpetuation of skilled labor in various trades, it was necessary for the training process to be well organized. Skills were passed on from one generation to the next in this fashion as they were in all societies in an era before technical schools permitted an independent education or training in applied skills. Thus, the traditions of a town in a particular type of artisanal industrial activity could be sustained over time. For Montpellier among the most prestigious products were those of the red or scarlet dyeing industry and the precious metal trades (Germain 1861; Thomas 1936; Reyerson 1974).

Mireille Castaing-Sicard, using information from the trade and consular statutes of the *capitouls* of Toulouse found that with the privilege of trade membership came the obligation for the artisan to teach his trade to apprentices in return for payment, both to reward his work in instruction and to reimburse any inconvenience occasioned by beginners in the trade (Castaing-Sicard 1958; Mulholland 1941). As an apprentice grew in skill, the burden of payment shifted, and the artisan owed the apprentice a minimal monetary compensation.

The same system with much variation of salary amount and timing of payment, according to the particular contract, operated in Montpellier as well. Arrangements have been summarized in Table 5 to illustrate the range and gradations of involvement of both masters and apprentices in trades where multiple contracts survive. The table includes humble and prestigious trades. Arrangements with a master varied as much as other aspects of the apprenticeship process. The contracts take on an individual character as if they were, in essence, tailor-made to the particular apprentice (Gouron 1958). This may have been a common feature of such engagements. Steven Epstein found that Genoese contracts even provided for the return of children to their families at chestnut gathering time (Epstein 1988). The master might furnish anything from no support to a substantial living including food, clothing, shoes, and some salary. As Table 5 demonstrates, many trades offered some sustenance to apprentices. Beyond room and board, methods of remuneration involved loans advanced against future salary, periodic salary, and payment on a piece-work basis. In the case of a credit extension, the artisan in question was generally an advanced apprentice or journeyman—undoubtedly late adolescent or young adult—whom the master could hold legally responsible in a credit engagement (Duxbury 1986, pp. 23-28). Alternatively, the apprentice might provide living expenses and a monetary contribution or some other form of financial inducement to the master. Comparatively speaking, young women were more often offered support and required to make little material contribution to the apprenticeship process. In light of the substantially smaller number of female apprentices in the remaining records, this finding suggests that families of female apprentices may have been hesitant to invest funds in young women for whom they would later have to furnish dowries and that masters were reluctant to support large numbers of females trainees.

Table 5
Arrangements of Artisans with Apprentices*

Occupation	*Contribution*	*Remuneration*	*Both*
Changers	3	7	5
Apothecaries	2	1	2
Wood merchants	2	1	1
Pepperers		2	2
Merchants		4	1
Mercers	1	3	2
Drapers		2	3
Goldsmiths	1	2	8
Silversmiths		3	4
Shoemakers	1	4	2
Bakers (female)		6	
Furriers		3	2
TOTAL	10	38	32

* In almost all cases of apprenticeship, contracts noted either remuneration from the master or a contribution from the apprentice or both.

Table 6 shows the frequency of residence of the apprentice in the master's household on the basis of the notary Johannes Holanie's contracts. The phrase *ad morandum vobiscum* was a common feature of apprenticeship contracts and was occasionally found in work contracts as well (Duxbury 1986, pp. 13, 17, and Table 1, p. 30). Exceptionally, the commitment *ad viatgiandum vobiscum* (to travel with you) might replace simple residence in the master's household (A D II E 95/371, f.16v). Merchants took apprentices on voyages to the Levant. In 1333 Petrus Selant, merchant of Millau, apprenticed himself to the Montpellier merchant Petrus Guersii for a voyage to Cyprus in a Venetian vessel moored at Aigues-Mortes (A D II E 95/369, f. 72v). Guersii passed numerous *comanda* contracts to finance this trip and clearly needed an assistant in his travels (Reyerson 1985, p. 20). There must have been a point beyond which it was no longer practical for the master to acquire additional apprentices, when his facilities or travel resources could no longer easily accommodate more workers, and when the number of mouths to feed was no longer in line with the potential accommodations of the work/living space. Yet, economic gains probably far outstripped losses with the apprentice system.

Contracts placed considerable emphasis on the apprentices' working only at the master's bidding and not at that of some other individual. Disciplinary aspects of apprenticeship are absent in the contracts, but the expectation of the apprentice remaining with the master is specified in numerous contracts, as noted above. For an adolescent apprentice, male or female, the master became, in essence, a surrogate father. Masters in Montpellier were endowed with legal competence to police the apprentices in their households (Gouron 1958, p. 275; Teulet 1863, p. 277, article 65; Smith 1973, p. 151; Epstein 1988, p. 123) (see Table 6).

The cancellation of an apprenticeship agreement before the full term suggests that problems arose on one side or the other. Table 7 records the full-term acquittals and the premature cancellations in contracts of the five surviving Holanie registers

Table 6
Residence of Apprentice with Master*

ad morandum vobiscum—A D Hérault, J. Holanie—*ad operandum vobiscum* (to stay with you)		(to work with you)
36	II E 95/368	19
14	II E 95/369	2
10	II E 95/370	4
28	II E 95/371	4
24	II E 95/372	0
Total 112		Total 29

* Formulae implying residence with a master or work with the master were common in apprenticeship contracts.

Table 7
Cancellations in the Holanie Contracts

Full-term acquittals		*Early cancellations*
6	II E 95/368	2
4	II E 95/369	0
1	II E 95/370	3
5	II E 95/371	5
3	II E 95/372	6
Total 19		16

where such inclusions have been preserved. Cancellation clauses could be added to the initial apprenticeship or work contract, or a separate notarial act might be written and often remains as the only evidence that there once had been an apprenticeship relationship. In the vast majority of contracts, no indication of completion of the engagement was noted. However, sixteen premature cancellations can be identified out of a total of 154 Holanie contracts or approximately ten percent, suggesting that early annulments were not uncommon. All of the premature cancellations concerned males, suggesting that medieval adolescence may have been more turbulent for young men than for young women, as it was in the early modern era (Davis 1975; Smith 1973). Early cancellations could be indicative of conflict between master and apprentice. In all but one instance these early annulations seem to have been mutually agreed upon without penalties. There was thus some escape possible for an apprentice in an intolerable situation or for a master saddled with a rebellious apprentice. In the one exception involving a changer and a tutor, money was withheld for food and damages when the contract was cancelled before the contractual term had ended (A D II E 95/371, f.55v). The apprentice's tutor received a loan from the changer, undoubtedly as a part of his agreement to the cancellation (A D II E 95/371, f.56r). No motives for cancellation appear in the annulation clauses, but in the above case the existence of the loan suggests a complex interlace of involvements.

Occasionally, the apprenticeship relationship was abandoned before it even began, due in all likelihood to a failure of master and apprentice to agree on the specific arrangements. In one such circumstance, Petrus de Molino of Sarlat attempted to engage himself *in dicipulum et juvenem* to the apothecaryAndreas Dalini for three years in return for food, drink, and instruction (A D II E 95/372, f.9v). The contract was almost completed when the phrase *non habuit effectum* was inserted by the notary. The notary then began again, adding a surety this time in the person of a local apothecary (A D II E 95/372, f. 10r). Was this a simple oversight or a last minute precaution on the part of the master? It is impossible to say. However, the additional assurance of performance by the apprentice was not enough to prevent the early cancellation of the contract two months after its inception.

Unabbreviated copies of some contracts were made by the notary, with a notation left in the register to that effect. While most extractions were done on behalf of the master and would have provided him with his own copy of the legalities of the arrangement, occasionally an apprentice requested an extraction. Such was the case with a merchant apprentice in 1333 (A D II E 95/369, f. 88r).

In an unusually cautious contract, a particularly suspicious master had an apprentice spice merchant from Carcassonne swear to the general clauses of residence and obedience and then added further protection against theft or secret wrongdoing by requiring him to reveal any such acts by others that he observed (A D II E 95/372, f. 128v). In turn the apprentice had a long list of material requirements: food, drink, shoes, shirts, etc. After the list the contract broke off with a non-effect clause, both parties having perhaps thought better of an expensive (for the master) arrangement which was based on a lack of trust.

In essence, the apprentice was joining an artisan household as a participant and member. If the apprentices lived in the masters' households, these assumed responsibility for the moral education of the children or adolescents apprenticed in their workshops. Contracts carry formulae that speak to the good mores expected of the apprentice; work habits and living habits would be inculcated in this fashion (A D II E 95/372, f. 159v). By the same token, the apprentice was expected to do only the licit bidding of the master (A D II E 95/370, f. 14r). The Montpellier contracts carry no indications of expected days and hours of work, feast days or other holidays, but one must assume that the apprentice's schedule was coordinated with that of the master and more broadly with that of the trade.[13] Both parties to the contract swore to uphold the provisions, and, when the male apprentice was of practical age of majority, his oath would be recorded as noted above.

Preservation of the apprentice's well-being was a feature of most contracts. That the apprentice should be maintained in health was a recurring formula; at times the wording was more explicit with the phrase "well and not sick" (*sano et non egro*). Occasionally, further precision was noted. In the case of deceased silk merchant's son (over fourteen and without a curator) who was apprenticed for six years to a mercer, the master was obliged to care for the apprentice during one month of sickness as well as to provide food, clothing, and shoes (A D II E 95/371, f. 56v). To sweeten this agreement, the apprentice gave the master mercer a nine-year usufruct and all fruits of a vineyard in the vicinity of Montpellier. The apprentice promised not to flee or leave during the six-year period of apprenticeship and to do the master's bidding. Most contracts do not spell out the length of time for sick care, but there is implicit in them a veritable form of health insurance for apprentices.

For the family of the young person there were positive consequences of the apprenticeship system. The family of origin would have fewer mouths to feed if the apprentice lived with his or her new master. However, in some cases, as noted above, the family furnished necessities to the apprentice while he resided within the master's household (see Table 5). Moreover, apprenticeship was a means of assuring sons or daughters a livelihood and an opportunity to establish households if they perfected the trade into which they had been apprenticed. For the apprentices' families, then, the master performed a considerable service. In an era of high mortality, medieval apprenticeship offered families the means of raising more children successfully than they might have been able to support and train on their own. A final consideration for the apprentice's family might have been the old-age insurance which having well-trained, successful children provided. If one's children were self-sufficient, then one could hope for a means of support and necessary care once productive economic years were at an end. Medieval society through the apprenticeship system arranged for the transfer of power and economic responsibility from one generation to the next. These provisions are not to be undervalued as we contemplate in our own society the difficulties posed for the baby bust generation in supporting the baby boom generation in old age.

A final dimension of apprenticeship experience in Montpellier lies in actual workshop practices which are perhaps best revealed in contracts associated with the silversmiths and the goldsmiths (Reyerson and Powe 1984). The notarial registers contain over twenty contracts related to the apprenticeship and work in precious metals, fifteen of which directly concern men and boys involved in the silversmith and goldsmith tasks; the remainder relate to auxiliary services and industries, the burnishing of silver, the making of gold embroidery, and the spinning of gold thread, often involving women connected to these artisans. Ten of the fifteen contracts involve the *deaurator* or goldsmith, five the *argenterius* or silversmith. Six of the ten goldsmith contracts relate to the Jacobus Augerii workshop whose employment practices can be traced over a period of seventeen years from 1327 to 1344 (A D II E 95/368, f. 75v, 102r, 118r; II E 95/369, f. 5/6r; II E 95/371, f. 96v, sometimes foliated as 105v; II E 95/372, f. 175r).

The Augerii workshop would seem, at least from 1342, to have been a father and son operation; the documents distinguish a Jacobus Augerii *major diebus* or *senior* from a Jacobus Augerii without label. Both *senior* and *junior* were involved in real estate transactions in similar urban locations (A D II E 95/370, ff.16v, 28r-30r, 37r; II E 95/371, ff. 77r, 135r, 152r, 155r; II E 95/372, f. 89v). Both, termed *deaurator,* hired apprentices. The elder Augerii also hired workers in 1327 and 1333.

The Augerii workshop employed several apprentices and workers at a time. There was considerable gradation in training among the personnel. The terminology of these contracts reflects the rather fluid usage in apprenticeship and work in Montpellier. Thus, the Augerii hired in the categories of *dicipulum* and *juvenem,* which traditionally could be assimilated with apprenticeship and journeymen status, respectively, but also in the joint category of *dicipulum et servitorem.* When the engagement was that of apprenticeship, the contractual term was longer than the work term, i.e. six to eight years, and the commitment from the master involved instruction in the goldsmith's craft. Six to eight years of training in apprenticeship, in turn, suggests that the apprentices were in adolescent years. In three instances the elder Augerii hired work outright in *obrerem et omnes operas, famulum* and *juvenem et operas* from already trained individuals who were labeled *deauratores* and undoubtedly formed the group of skilled workers, *operarii,* referred to in another contract (A D II E 95/372, f. 175r). These workers were generally hired for a three-year period (see Table 1). Within their ranks, there were varying degrees of expertise, as the payment arrangements indicate (see Table 5).

The financial conditions offered individuals of the Augerii workshop varied considerably, sustaining the hypothesis that among workers and apprentices, differences of experience, skill, and background entered into calculations. The Augerii recruits were unmarried. Some of the workers may have lived in the Augerii household, but it is more likely that some of the apprentices did. In one instance the son of a butcher, over fourteen years of age, was apprenticed to the Augerii for eight years in return for instruction in the trade and food, clothes, shoes, and other necessities. In another instance the son of a butcher was apprenticed for three years with a salary of eight s.t./year to be paid to his mother. In yet a third apprenticeship the son of a late longshoreman was apprenticed for six years in return for six s. annual salary. He probably lived at home as his mother was to feed and maintain him, and he was to serve the Augerii and their workers while being taught the trade.

Workers were hired by the Augerii at salaries ranging from 43 s. per year to 61 per year. The financial arrangements could be connected to the worker's production (A D II E 95/368, f. 97v). Payment for piece work was accompanied by a loan to the worker in one contract with the expectation that the loan be repaid on demand (A D II E 95/368, f. 118r). In monetary value the loan was the equivalent of eleven pieces. A fifty-piece production in a two-year period would have paid off the loan in another case.[14] The Augerii workshop revealed at least a threefold hierarchy of expertise among workers and some gradation of skill, as well, at the apprentice level.

The silversmith workshops in Montpellier also showed a differentiation of skills among personnel. The hiring of already trained workers and of uninitiated apprentices can be documented. The term of apprenticeship could be as long as twelve years though shorter terms might also be arranged (A D II E 95/372, f. 101r). The only surviving instance of foreign apprenticeship in this trade concerned an individual from Alès in the Cévennes region (A D II E 95/372, f. 159v). The engagement was for five years with the master craftsman supplying teaching and maintenance in return for a ten l.p.t. current money payment to be made within six months. The foreign apprentice's brother acted as surety in this operation. Where trained personnel called *argenterii* were employed, they worked at piece work as did the goldsmiths [A D II E 95/369, f. 98v (or 106v)]. Loans might also be a part of the remuneration of workers.

Work in precious metals in Montpellier spawned what one might term auxiliary industries. The wives of goldsmiths could be engaged in the spinning of gold thread. Two work contracts and one apprenticeship contract survive for this activity (A D II E 95/368, ff. 56v, 131v, 135v). The contracts between goldsmiths and silversmiths are revealed in the one apprenticeship contract in which the daughter of a silversmith was apprenticed to a goldsmith for four years so that she might learn the spinning of gold thread from his wife. When the hiree was experienced, as in the case of an oil merchant's wife employed by the wife of a goldsmith for about one year, a salary was paid, in this instance, per ounce of spun gold. A silversmith's wife might also be involved in activities related to her husband's trade. In one apprenticeship a girl was engaged to learn the burnishing of silver cups from the wife of a silversmith (A D II E 95/369, f. 37v).

The effects of apprenticeship on the medieval adolescent were many. Marriage was delayed until after adolescence for most apprentices (Hughes 1975, p. 23). Late marriage, in turn, had demographic consequences for the artisanal groups of medieval towns as fertility declines with age. The acquisition of skills in an apprenticeship situation became a very human process, not depersonalized as it might be in modern society. Discipline was undoubtedly strict, but the master's control may have provided useful guidance in a city offering multiple temptations to the young and naive.[15] However, premature cancellations of contracts imply some level of conflict between apprentice and master. On the one hand, a turbulent apprentice could disrupt a workshop. On the other, the apprentice was at the mercy of the master, and in the case of a cruel, demanding master without understanding or patience for the still untrained hands and mind of a young adolescent, the experience of apprenticeship in the Middle Ages must have rivaled, if not resembled, all of the unpleasantness of the nineteenth-century Dickinsian world. The industrialization of the late eighteenth and nineteenth centuries produced a society less human in scale if equally, though differentially, harsh in potential for the young and vulnerable of its members who were trying to enter the work force.

Medieval apprenticeship contracts demonstrate close contacts between youths and adults in the work place, as Ariès argued, but they also reveal a program of growing and learning for the apprentice, suited to and consistent with a transitional phase between childhood and adulthood. In the hands of an understanding master, apprentice training for the adolescent must have been very rewarding. If apprenticeship occurred at twelve to fourteen, the age when individual identity was beginning to form, then the experience may have enhanced the individual's self doubt through the departure of the youth from an accustomed family context. He/she embarked on a formative transition which would extend to the end of apprenticeship, perhaps as late as the mid-twenties. Some anxiety was removed by the certainty of future occupation in the Middle Ages, as it was in the early modern period (Smith 1973). Apprenticeship offered hands-on training, learning by example and experimentation, and, in the best of circumstances, careful guidance, not offhand instruction. For some youth, however, apprenticeship must have meant a rude insertion into an adult world, an abrupt severing of family ties, and a rupture with the familiar. Apprenticeship represented for the urban middle classes of the Middle Ages a lengthy and elaborate economic rite of passage from childhood into adult society.

NOTES

1. Georges Duby (1964, p. 835) discussed the terminology associated with adolescence: "puer, adulescentulus, adolescens imberis." "Ces vocables sont employés par eux à propos de jeunes gens qui sont nettement sortis de ce que nous appelons l'enfance, qui ont dépassé quinze, dix-sept et même dix-neuf ans, mais qui n'ont pas terminé leur apprentissage." He contrasted the *juvenis* as an "homme fait, un adulte" and, of course, in his study, a member of the nobility. In the construction of Duby the state of being *juventus* could extend well into midlife if the knight errant did not marry. See also the brief discussion by Shulamith Shahar (1990, pp. 21-31) on stages in childhood. Webster's *New Collegiate Dictionary* (Springfield, MA: G. C. Merriam Company, 1974) defined adolescence as "the period of life between puberty and maturity."

2. Medieval kingship offers perhaps the most poignant examples of this fact in the early succession of rulers such as Philip Augustus, who was just fifteen when Louis VII died.

3. Doris Desclais Berkvam (1981, p. 60) illustrated the responsibilities thrust on youth in the romance hero of the *Chanson de Guillaume,* who was young yet confronted with adult tasks: "Petit est Gui et li cheval est grant."

4. See the discussion of age in apprenticeship below. André Gouron (1958, pp. 268-269) spoke of the ages of fourteen to twenty-five as those of pubescent minority. In the United States age of majority is measured by such standards as the age to vote, age of military service, drinking age.

5. For a breakdown by year and notarial register of the surviving apprenticeship and work contracts of Montpellier before 1350, see Reyerson (1979, p. 267). I have used these contracts previously to study in-migration. I have also looked at women's business activities through them (Reyerson 1986) and at workshop practices in the precious metals trades in an unpublished paper (Reyerson and Powe 1984). Susan Duxbury, a University of Minnesota graduate student, examined the contracts surviving in one notarial register, A D Hérault, II E 95/368, J. Holanie, for a Plan B Master's paper (Duxbury 1986). On the legal support offered by notarial acts, see the useful discussion by David Herlihy (1958, pp. 1-20). On the rarity of female apprentices, see P.J.P. Goldberg (1986) and Davis (1986).

6. For contracts having similar phrases, see Anne-Marie Landes-Mallet, (1988, pp. 91-98). She discussed the legal formulae which derive from the Roman law *locatio-conductio* contract. See also Pryor (1981, pp. 111-113).

7. A D II E 95/371, J. Holanie, f. 103v and others. The age data for Montpellier is much less full than that of Michaud-Fréjaville (1982, pp. 183-208) and 1980, pp. 61-71). Michaud-Fréjaville found contracts involving individuals from three years to twenty-four years, with most in the range of age seven to twenty. For boys, she was certain of their minority at age thirteen and their majority at age sixteen; for girls majority came at twelve. Compare Epstein (1988, p. 128) who suggested that seventeen or eighteen was a more common age for swearing oaths. The youngest apprentices appeared to be between ten and twelve in Genoa. On age in Languedocian contracts, see Gouron (1958, pp. 268-269).

8. A D Hérault, II E 95/371, J. Holaine, f. 103v. Michaud-Fréjaville (1982, pp. 190, 193) for the years 1380-1480 in the Orléanais found that only one-fourth of the contracts were without age mention. She also found evidence that "14 ans n'est pas l'âge normal de l'entrée dans le monde du travail, il n'est même pas l'âge moyen (15 ans et demi)." Wolff (1954, p. 434) found few age indications in the Toulousan contracts of 1350-1450.

9. A D Hérault, II E 95/371, J. Holanie, f. 103v. See also Michaud-Fréjaville (1982, p. 191): "Les contrats cependant précisent pour des mineurs qu'ils s'obligeront quand ils auront 14 ans." Didier (1976, p. 38) found that fourteen was the normal age of majority when the apprentice, male or female, could contract alone.

10. For a female apprentice who would have finished at a later age, see A D Hérault, II E 97/377, B. Egidii, f. 262r, for a girl of Pompignan near Nîmes, over twelve, engaged for ten years to bakers and II E 95/372, J. Holanie et al, f. 101r, for the son of a mercer, over fourteen, engaged for twelve years to a silversmith. For the youngest, see, for example, A M II 1, B. Grimaudi, 36r, for a male of Arles of fifteen who engaged himself to a Montpellier changer for two years.

11. At age fourteen the lack of curator was often mentioned as in the case of a boy and his widowed mother who apprenticed him to a goldsmith. See A D Hérault, II E 95/371, J. Holanie, f. 105v. For the presence of a tutor, see II E 95/371, J. Holanie, f. 55v. For an uncle who was curator of a boy, see II E 95/371, J. Holanie, f. 63r. On guardianship in Montpellier, see Gaillard (1897) and de Charrin (1961); in Marseille, see Bruschi (1985).

12. For a brief discussion of the legal position of women in Montpellier, see Reyerson (1986, pp. 118-119). The apprenticeship data reflect the patriarchal nature of medieval society. On medieval patriarchy, see Howell (1986).

13. On the rhythm of medieval work, see, for example, Thrupp (1972, pp. 221-273).

14. A D Hérault, II E 95/368. J. Holanie, f. 68r. Susan Duxbury first pointed this arrangement out to me as a student in my seminar.

15. On the city as source of temptation, see Appleby (1963), or selections from Dobiache-Rojdestvensky (1931). I am indebted to Mark Vesley, graduate student in Classical Studies at the University of Minnesota, for these suggestions.

REFERENCES

Abbreviations

A D = Archives départementales de l'Hérault
A M = Archives municipales de Montpellier
Annales:ESC = *Annales: Economies, Sociétés, Civilisations*
Recueil = *Recueil de mémories et travaux publiés par la société d'histoire du droit et des institutions des anciens pays de droit écrit.* Montpellier.

Cited Works

Appleby, John T., ed. 1963. *The Chronicle of Richard of Devizes of the Time of King Richard the First.* London: Thomas Nelson and Sons.

Ariès, Philippe. 1960. *L'Enfant et la vie familiale sous l'Ancien régime.* Paris: Librarie Plon.

________. 1962. *Centuries of Childhood.* New York: Vintage Books.

Berkvam, Doris Desclais. 1981. *Enfance et maternité dans la littérature française des XIIe et XIIIe siècles.* Paris: H. Champion.

Bruschi, Christian. 1985. "La tutelle des mineurs à Marseille (seconde moitié du XIIIe siècle-début du XIVe siècle)." *Recueil.* Fasc. XIII: 61-70.

Castaing-Sicard, Mireille. 1958. "Contrat de travail et louage d'ouvrage dans la vie toulousaine des XIIe et XIII siècles." *Recueil.* Fasc. IV: 83-89.

de Charrin, Louis. 1961. *Les testaments dans la région de Montpellier au moyen âge.* Ambilly: Cooperative "Les Presses de Savoie."

Davis, Natalie Zemon. 1975. "The Reasons of Misrule: Youth Groups and Charivaris in Sixteenth-Century France." Pp. 97-123 in *Society and Culture in Early Modern France. Eight Essays.* Stanford: Stanford University Press.

________. 1986. "Women in the Crafts in Sixteenth-Century Lyon." Pp. 167-197 in *Women and Work in Preindustrial Europe,* edited by Barbara Hanawalt. Bloomington: Indiana University Press.

Didier, Philippe. 1976. "Le contrat d'apprentissage en Bourgogne aux XIVe et XVe siècles." *Revue historique de droit français et étranger* 54: 35-57.

Dobiache-Rojdestvensky, Olga. 1931. *Les poésies des Goliards.* Paris: Rieder.

Duby, Georges. 1964. "Au XIIe siècle: les 'jeunes' dans la société aristocratique." *Annales: ESC* 19: 835-846.

Duxbury, Susan. 1986. "The Medieval Artisan Household in Montpellier, An Economic Unit as Viewed Through Apprentice and Work Contracts." University of Minnesota. Plan B Master's paper.

Epstein, Steven. 1988. "Labour in Thirteenth-Century Genoa." *Mediterranean Historical Review* 3: 114-140.

Gaillard, Bernardin. 1897. *La tutelle maternelle.* Montpellier: Imprimérie de Jean Martel.

Germain, Alexandre. 1861. *Histoire du commerce de Montpellier antérieurement à l'ouverture du port de Cette.* 2 vols. Montpellier: Imprimérie de Jean Martel.

Goldberg, P.J.P. 1986. "Female Labour, Service and Marriage in the Late Medieval Urban North." *Northern History* 22: 18-38.

Gouron, André. 1958. *La réglementation des métiers en Languedoc au moyen âge.* Geneva: Librarie E. Droz.

Hanawalt, Barbara A. 1986. *The Ties That Bound, Peasant Families in Medieval England.* New York: Oxford University Press.

Herlihy, David. 1958. *Pisa in the Early Renaissance.* New Haven: Yale University Press.

________. 1969. "Vieillir à Florence au Quattrocento." *Annales: E.S.C.* 24: 1338-1352.

________. 1985. *Medieval Households.* Cambridge, MA: Harvard University Press.

Herlihy, David, and Christiane Klapisch-Zuber. 1978. *Les Toscans et leurs familles. Une étude du Catasto de 1427.* Paris: Editions de l'Ecole des Hautes Etudes en Sciences Sociales.

________. 1985. *Tuscans and Their Families. A Study of the Florentine Catasto of 1427.* New Haven: Yale University Press.

Howell, Martha. 1986. *Women, Production and Patriarchy in Late Medieval Cities.* Chicago: University of Chicago Press.

Hughes, Diane Owen. 1975. "Urban Growth and Family Structure in Medieval Genoa.' *Past and Present* 66:3-28.

Klapisch (Zuber), Christiane. 1973. "L'Enfance en Toscane au début du XVe siècle." Pp. 99-122 in *Annales de démographie historique*.

Landes-Mallet, Anne-Marie. 1988. "Travail et apprentissage en Rouergue médiévale." Pp. 91-98 in *Libertés locales et vie municipale en Rouergue, Languedoc et Roussillon,* Actes du LXIXe Congrès de la Fédération historique du Languedoc méditerranéen et du Roussillon (Millau 19-20 juin 1987). Montpellier.

Lyman, Richard B. Jr. 1974. "Barbarism and Religion: Late Roman and Early Medieval Childhood." Pp. 75-100 in *The History of Childhood,* edited by Lloyd de Mause. New York: Psychohistory Press.

McLaughlin, Mary Martin. 1974. "Survivors and Surrogates: Children and Parents from the Ninth to the Thirteenth Centuries." Pp. 101-181 in *The History of Childhood,* edited by Lloyd de Mause. New York: Psychohistory Press.

Michaud-Fréjaville, Françoise. 1980. "Contrats d'apprentissage en Orléanais, les enfants au travail, (1380-1450)." Pp. 61-71 in *L'Enfant au Moyen-Age: littérature et civilisation.* Aix-en-Provence: Université de Provence.

———. 1982. "Bons et loyaux services: Les contrats d'apprentissage en Orléanais (1380-1480)." Pp. 183-208 in *Les Entrées dans la vie, initiations et apprentissage.* Nancy: Presses Universitaires de Nancy.

Mulholland, M. A. 1941. *Early Gild Records of Toulouse.* New York: Columbia University Press.

Pryor, John. 1981. *Business Contracts of Medieval Provence: Selected Notulae from the Cartulary of Giraud Amalric of Marseilles, 1248.* Toronto: Pontifical Institute.

Reyerson, Kathryn. 1974. "Commerce and Society in Montpellier: 1250-1350." Two vols. Diss. Yale University. New Haven.

———. 1979. "Patterns of Population Attraction and Mobility: The Case of Montpellier, 1293-1348." *Viator* 10:257-281.

———. 1985. *Business, Banking and Finance in Medieval Montpellier.* Toronto: Pontifical Institute.

———. 1986. "Women in Business in Medieval Montpellier." Pp. 117-144 in *Women and Work in Preindustrial Europe,* edited by Barbara A. Hanawalt. Bloomington: Indiana University Press.

Reyerson, Kathryn and Faye Powe. 1984. "Metalwork of Montpellier: Techniques and Workshop Practices in the Fourteenth Century." Paper at the International Congress on Medieval Studies, The Medieval Institute, Western Michigan University, Kalamazoo, Michigan.

Riché, Pierre. 1973. "L'Enfant dans le haut Moyen Age." Pp. 95-98 in *Annales de démographie historique: Enfant et Sociétés.*

Ross, James Bruce. 1974. "The Middle-Class Child in Urban Italy, Fourteenth to Early Sixteenth Century." Pp. 183-228 in *The History of Childhood,* edited by Lloyd de Mause. New York: Psychohistory Press.

Schultz, James A. 1991. "Medieval Adolescence: The Claims of History and the Silence of German Narrative." *Speculum* 66: 519-539.

Shahar, Shulamith. 1990. *Childhood in the Middle Ages.* London and New York: Routledge.

Smith, Stephen R. 1973. "The London Apprentices as Seventeenth-Century Adolescents." *Past and Present* 61: 149-161.

Teulet, Alexandre, ed. 1863. *Layettes du Trésor des Chartes.* Vol. 1. Paris: Librarie Plon.

Thomas, Louis J. 1936. *Montpellier, ville marchande, histoire économique et sociale de Montpellier des origines à 1870.* Montpellier: Librarie Valat, Librarie Coulet.

Thrupp, Sylvia. 1972. "Medieval Industry, 1000-1500." Pp. 221-273 in *The Fontana Economic History of Europe. The Middle Ages,* edited by Carlo M. Cipolla. London: Collins/Fontana.

Tisset, Pierre. 1951. "Placentin et son enseignement à Montpellier. Droit romain et Coutume dans l'ancien pays de Septimanie." *Recueil* Fasc. 2:67-94.

Wilson, Adrian. 1980. "The Infancy of the History of Childhood: An Appraisal of Philippe Ariès." *History and Theory* 19:132-153.

Wolff, Philippe. 1954. *Commerce et marchands de Toulouse* (*vers 1350-vers 1450*). Paris: Librarie Plon.

IV

Changes in Testamentary Practice at Montpellier on the Eve of the Black Death

The Black Death arrived in southern France, at Marseille, in January 1348.[1] It then spread westward, reaching Carcassonne by February and Perpignan by March. There is no exact chronology of the outbreak of the plague in Montpellier. However, the disease probably appeared by March 1348, since it spread along trade routes and the town was considerably closer to Marseille than both Carcassonne and Perpignan.[2] The recorded toll of the Black Death in Montpellier at first seems great enough to account for any changes in the behavior of the population in the plague year. For this commercial and financial capital of Lower Languedoc, 1348 was generally termed "lan de la mortalidat."[3] Ten of the twelve town consuls died that year, and as the late French historian Yves Renouard commented, "At Montpellier whose University was reputed for the science of its medical corps, all the doctors were killed by the plague."[4] The consular and medical *milieux* were among the most powerful and prosperous of the town, and such high mortality at the upper levels of society was probably true for inhabitants of the poorer social groups.

The testamentary practice of a town presents one area in which it is possible to investigate how much the plague really altered the religious attitudes of inhabitants.[5] From the rich series of extant, unpublished

1. Philip Ziegler, *The Black Death* (New York, 1969), provides a useful bibliographical orientation on the plague. Regarding the chronology of its arrival in Europe, see p. 40ff.
2. The dispersion of the disease was somewhat erratic. See William Bowsky, "The Impact of the Black Death upon Sienese Government and Society," *Speculum* 39 (January 1964): 14.
3. "La chronique romane," in *Le Petit Thalamus de Montpellier,* ed. Ferdinand Pégat *et. al.* (Montpellier, 1840), p. 348.
4. See Alexandre Germain, *Histoire de la commune de Montpellier depuis ses origines jusqu'à son incorporation définitive à la monarchie française* (Montpellier, 1851) 1:412–413, for publication of the consular lists and the deaths of that year. See also Yves Renouard, "La Peste Noire de 1348–1350," *Revue de Paris* (March, 1950): 109.
5. The most recent study of the religious history of Montpellier is *Le diocèse de Montpellier,* ed. Gérard Cholvy (Paris, 1976). Still useful are the numerous studies by Alexandre Germain in the *Mémoires de la société archéologique de Montpellier,* 1-8 (Montpellier, 1850–1893). Of interest for the reaction of the town to the Albigensians is Augustin Fliche, "La vie religieuse à Montpellier sous le pontificat d'Innocent III (1198–1216)," *Mélanges Louis Halphen* (Paris, 1951), pp. 217–224.

Reprinted with permission from *Church History* 47: 3 (1978), pp. 253-269.

Table 1

CHRONOLOGICAL DISTRIBUTION OF EXTANT WILLS

1200–1292	1293–1345	1346	1347	1348	Total
22	72	—	38	28	160

wills in Montpellier, summarized in Table 1, it is evident that religious behavior during the plague differed considerably from that of the thirteenth and much of the early fourteenth centuries.[6] After 1348 the number of extant wills diminishes radically due to a lacuna in the notarial evidence from 1348 to 1361.

To show the evolution of testamentary practice, tables of the most frequently appearing traits of the funeral ceremony, the donation patterns of testators and their choices of burial place have been established for three chronological periods: 1200–1345; 1347; and 1348. The evidence of the plague year 1348 will be explored first in relation to the period before 1346, and then the data of 1347 will be discussed. This study shows that significant changes in the testamentary practice at Montpellier began at least one year before the plague, in a period of economic and political difficulties; thus the plague accelerated a change in religious behavior, but was not its catalyst.

In Montpellier, as in most of southern France, wills kept a relatively constant form.[7] In stylized notarial clauses they reflected the piety of the

6. Materials for this study were drawn from the Archives Départementales de l'Hérault (hereafter abbreviated A. D. Hérault), notarial registers II E 95/368–II E 95/377 and from the Archives Municipales de Montpellier (abbreviated A. M. Montp.), registers II 1–3. Also consulted were the Série EE, *fonds de la Commune Clôture* and the *Grand Chartrier* of the municipal archives. For inventories of the last two collections, see Maurice de Dainville and Marcel Gouron, *Inventaire, Fonds de la Commune Clôture et Affaires militaires* (Montpellier, 1974) and Joseph Berthelé, *Archives communales de Montpellier antérieures à 1789, Inventaires et documents: I. Notice sur les anciens inventaires, inventaire du Grand Chartrier* (Montpellier, 1895). *Grand Chartrier* documents will be cited in the Louvet numbering system used in the above inventory. *Le Cartulaire de Maguelone,* ed. Jean Rouquette and Augustin Villemagne, 5 vols. (Montpellier, 1912–1925) yielded four wills for the thirteenth century only; see vol. 2, acts CCXCIII, CCCLXIII, CCCCLXXXVII, DCXXXVII. Although Montpellier cannot boast the wealth of notarial archives of many Italian towns, one extant register written by the notary Bernardus Egidii and several clerks (A. D. Hérault, II E 95/377), spanning the period January 17, 1347 to March 31, 1348, contains forty-eight wills.
7. Many scholars have analyzed French religious behavior by examining wills; e.g. Robert Folz, "L'Esprit religieux du testament bourguignon au moyen âge," *Mémoires de la société pour l'histoire du droit et des institutions des anciens pays bourguignons, comtois et romands* (Dijon, 1955), pp. 7–27; Robert Boutruche, "Aux origines d'une crise nobiliaire: Donations pieuses et pratiques successorales en Bordelais du XIIIe au XVIe siècle," *Annales d'histoire sociale* 1 (April, 1939): 161–177; Marguérite Gonon, *Les institutions et la société en Forez au XIVe siècle d'après les testaments* (Mâcon, 1960); Marie-Simone de Nucé de Lamothe, "Piété et charité publique à Toulouse de la fin du XIIIe siècle au milieu du XVe siècle d'après les testaments," *Annales du Midi* 76 (January, 1964): 5–39; Marie-Thérèse Lorcin, "Les clauses religieuses dans les testaments du plat pays lyon-

testator, a commitment of the soul to God, the choice of a place of burial, the institution of an heir and of testamentary executors to watch over the fulfillment of the last wishes and the stipulation of pious donations.[8] The French historian Louis de Charrin, in a study of the legal form of wills preserved in Montpellier, noted that prior to 1340 the protocol of the will typically included an invocation to the Trinity.[9] In about 1340, he maintained, there were increasingly frequent reflections on the fragility of things human and on the immutability of future destiny. However, he noted that the preambles soon became stereotyped, probably under the influence of notarial formulae, and, except for their translation into French, varied little until the end of the Ancien Régime.

Although the formulae of wills were mostly stylized, the testator usually chose his or her own burial place. While traditional burial took place in the parish cemetery in the tomb of parents or spouse, the choice of burial site remained a personal prerogative, and there were frequent instances in the Middle Ages in which husband and wife chose to be buried in different cemeteries.[10] In keeping with canon law, hallowed ground was the one prerequisite for a burial place.[11]

The right of the parish church to the burial of parishioners was challenged during the thirteenth century by new and old religious orders.[12] In the first half of the century, the Dominicans received permission to bury anyone who requested burial with them, and the Fran-

---

nais aux XIVe et XVe siècles," *Le Moyen Age* 78 no. 2 (4th ser., 27) (1972): 287–323; Noël Coulet, "Jalons pour une histoire religieuse d'Aix au bas moyen âge (1350–1450)," *Provence historique* 22 fasc. 89 (July–September, 1972): 203–260; Michelle Bastard-Fournier, "Mentalités religieuses aux confins du Toulousain et de l'Albigeois à la fin du moyen âge," *Annales du Midi* 85 (July–September, 1973): 267–287; Jacques Chiffoleau, "Pratiques funéraires et images de la mort à Marseille, en Avignon et dans le Comtat Venaissin (vers 1280–vers 1350)," *La religion populaire en Languedoc du XIIIe siècle à la moitié du XIVe siècle. Cahiers de Fanjeaux* 11 (1976): 271–303.

8. Lorcin, "Les clauses religieuses," p. 287, argues that the preambules of the region of Lyon were too formulaic to be relied upon as a faithful transmission of the testator's thoughts. However, the wills of some areas may take exception to this generalization. See the comments of Nucé de Lamothe, "Piété et charité publique," p. 7, regarding pious formulae and p. 10, regarding the problems of testamentary evidence. Roger Aubenas, *Le testament en Provence dans l'ancien régime* (Aix-en-Provence, 1927), pp. 161–162, recounts that in the time of plague, preambules differed from the norm and might mention the plague. According to Aubenas, one notary sat in a tree at Grasse to avoid contagion from his clients. See also Folz, "L'Esprit religieux," p. 9. I have not encountered specific references to the plague in the Montpellier wills.
9. Louis de Charrin, *Les testaments dans la région de Montpellier au moyen âge* (Ambilly, 1961), p. 54, uses the notarial and Commune Clôture records, but does not discuss religious mentality.
10. Ibid., p. 135. Gonon, *Les institutions et la société en Forez,* p. 97, found on the contrary that for the Forez region burial generally took place in the parish cemetery in the tomb of parents, or, if a wife were making the will, with her husband. New tombs were rare.
11. Antoine Bernard, *La sépulture en droit canonique du décret de Gratien au concile de Trente* (Paris, 1933), p. 85 ff.
12. Ibid, pp. 70–76, 169–170, 174–183.

ciscans obtained this privilege in 1250, by which time the Premonstratensians, Augustinians and Benedictines also possessed it. The pope exempted the Franciscans in 1253 from the traditional payment of one-fourth of the burial fee to the church of the parish of the deceased.[13] The actual burial fee was often augmented by pious donations such as anniversary masses and legacies for the illumination of altars in the burial church.[14] Moreover, there was a tendency for a family tradition of burial to be established in a new church, once the initial separation from the parish church had occurred. By the end of the thirteenth century there were usually preferences in burial choices among urban inhabitants.[15]

The churches and religious establishments of Montpellier whose cemeteries and chapels attracted the patronage of Montpelliérains were not numerous, although the town had many churches, hospitals and monasteries. Originally, Montpellier had two parish churches, Saint-Firmin in the seigneurial sector of town and Saint-Denis outside the walls, in the episcopal sector.[16] The cathedral of Saint-Pierre was located about six miles away, at Maguelone near the Mediterranean coast.[17] The church of Notre-Dame-des-Tables in the southeastern corner of the communal fortifications was from the eleventh century an important oratory for pilgrims on their way to Santiago de Compostella.[18] Inside the walls there were also other churches by the end of the thirteenth century, but these appeared infrequently in the extant wills and were never cited as burial choices.

Outside the walls the suburbs held numerous monasteries, convents and hospitals. Franciscan and Dominican houses were founded here in 1220.[19] Here the hospital or asylum of Saint-Barthélémy had a chapel and a cemetery which may have acquired some reputation at the end of

13. Richard Wilder Emery, *Heresy and Inquisition in Narbonne* (New York, 1941), p. 123, n. 53.
14. Technically both Spiritual and Conventual Franciscans probably did not solicit such gifts; not so, perhaps, for the Dominicans. See Bernard, *La sépulture en droit canonique*, p. 75.
15. See Table 2. Coulet, "Jalons pour une histoire religieuse d'Aix," p. 253, argued that burial choice suggested a preference for a specific religious order.
16. On the parishes of Montpellier, see Germain, "La paroisse à Montpellier au moyen âge," *Mémoires de la société archéologique de Montpellier* 5 (Montpellier, 1860–1869): 1–56, and Louise Guirand, *La paroisse Saint-Denis de Montpellier* (Montpellier, 1887).
17. On the cathedral see Jean Rouquette, *Histoire du diocèse de Maguelone*, 2 vols. (Montpellier, 1921–1927). Frédéric Fabrège, *Histoire de Maguelone*, 3 vols. (Paris-Montpellier, 1893–1911) is somewhat dated.
18. See *Le guide du pèlerin de Saint-Jacques de Compostelle*, 3rd ed. Jeanne Vielliard (Mâcon, 1963), p. 2 and Louise Guiraud, "Recherches topographiques sur Montpellier au moyen âge," *Mémoires de la société archéologique de Montpellier*, 2d ser. 1 (Montpellier, 1899), p. 122.
19. Dating of the installation of mendicant convents is often disputed. For details see Richard Wilder Emery, *The Friars in Medieval France* (New York, London, 1961).

the twelfth century, for the town chronicle reports that the famous Italian jurist Placentinus, the founder of the law school of Montpellier, was buried there in 1192.[20] Each year at Easter there was a procession of the town consuls to the chapel.

These religious establishments inside the walls and in the suburbs were the most frequently designated sites of burial in the extant wills. Only the oratory of Notre-Dame was an exception. It was located in a central commercial part of town and probably did not have burial facilities; moreover, it was never mentioned as a burial place.

In the thirteenth century and the first four decades of the fourteenth century the merchants' favorite burial place was the cathedral cemetery at Maguelone. The reason for its popularity may lie in Pope Urban II's grant of indulgences to those who chose to be buried there.[21] As Table 2 shows, fifteen of the twenty-two wills before 1293, in which burial place was given, specified the cathedral cemetery.[22] The remaining burial places were scattered. The parish churches of Saint-Firmin and Saint-Denis were not mentioned as sites of burial in wills before 1293. The cemetery of Saint-Barthélémy was designated two times before 1293. The mendicant cemeteries gained their first burial clients in the 1280s, the Franciscan house in 1286 and the Dominican in 1288.[23] In both cases requests were recorded several decades after permission to bury had been accorded.

From 1293 to 1345 the testamentary behavior of inhabitants of Montpellier in the selection of a burial place changed little.[24] The cathedral of Maguelone remained the most popular site. From 1200 to 1345, fourteen women and twenty-five men sought burial at Maguelone. They requested burial only within the cemetery. There were no requests for a special chapel or cloister burial.[25] The testators' backgrounds were similar in status, since they belonged to the commercial, financial and legal classes of Montpellier. They were merchants, drapers, changers and legal specialists, those holding the title of bourgeois and their wives, daughters and widows. Twelve of the wills cited the testator's wish to be

20. "La chronique romane," in *Le Petit Thalamus de Montpellier,* p. 330. On Saint-Barthélémy, see Jean Baumel, *Histoire d'une seigneurie du Midi de la France, Naissance de Montpellier (985-1213)* (Montpellier, 1969), p. 198, and Germain, *Histoire de la commune de Montpellier* 3:337.
21. De Charrin, *Les testaments dans la région de Montpellier,* p. 135.
22. In addition to the wills tabulated in Table 2, there were eleven requests for burial outside Montpellier, two of which chose the Franciscan cemetery at Sommières. The remaining wills for which no mention of place of burial is given either neglect this stipulation, or are known only in fragmentary or indirect form.
23. A. M. Montp., EE 149, November 23, 1286 and EE 682, October 29, 1288.
24. The first extant notarial register dates from 1293–1294. See A. M. Montp., II 1, Jean Grimaud.
25. The choice of special chapels was common for burial in the Middle Ages. See Bernard, *La sépulture en droit canonique,* pp. 37–38.

Table 2

BURIAL PLACES IN WILLS OF MONTPELLIER FROM 1200 TO 1348

BURIAL PLACE	1200–1345		1347	1348
	1200–1292	1293–1345		
	22 wills	72 wills	38 wills	28 wills
Cathedral of Maguelone (St.-Pierre)	15 (68%)	24 (33⅓%)	3 (8%)	2 (7%)
St.-Barthélémy	2 (9%)	9 (12½%)	11 (29%)	5 (18%)
Franciscans	1 (5%)	6 (8%)	13 (34%)	7 (25%)
Dominicans	1 (5%)	8 (11%)	1 (3%)	6 (21%)
St.-Denis	0	2 (3%)	5 (13%)	2 (7%)
Augustinians	0	0	1 (3%)	1 (4%)
Carmelites	0	1 (1%)	0	1 (4%)
St.-Jean of Jerusalem	0	1 (1%)	0	0
St.-Firmin	0	0	0	1 (4%)
Valmagne	1 (4.5%)	0	0	1 (4%)
St.-Côme and St.-Damien	0	0	0	0

buried in a family tomb.[26] These included two requests from mothers in 1279 and 1299 to be buried in their children's tombs, one for the tomb of an uncle, three for the tomb of a mother, two for that of a father, one for that of a father and brother, one for that of a mother and husband, one for that of a paternal grandfather and one for that of parents.[27] Maguelone was by far the most popular cemetery for prosperous inhabitants during the period of economic expansion in the thirteenth century.

The continued preference for Maguelone suggests that the religious attitudes of those Montpelliérains making wills remained relatively conservative. The close relations which had existed between Montpellier and the papacy since the twelfth century may have sustained traditional loyalties.[28] The prevailing spiritual influence in the area around Montpellier, that of Benedictines and Cluniacs, may also have contributed to the stable religious stance of the Montpelliérains.[29] The venerable Bene-

26. Blood relations are shown to be stronger than relations by marriage in these wills.
27. A. M. Montp., EE 328, August 22, 1279; *Grand Chartrier,* Louvet no. 2315, January 30, 1299 (n. s. 1300); EE 680, April 18, 1259; EE 590, November 28, 1297; II 1, f. 31r; *Grand Chartrier,* Louvet no. 31, January 16, 1313 (n. s.); *Ibid.,* Louvet no. 3007, March 23, 1324; EE 757, August 26, 1325; EE 761, December 13, 1335; EE 383, October 13, 1343; EE 375, April 5, 1345.
28. See Benjamin Gaillard, "Les relations des Guilhem de Montpellier avec le Saint-Siège," *Mémoires de la société archéologique de Montpellier,* 2d ser. 9 (Montpellier, 1924): 41–61, and Bernard Guillemain, *La cour pontificale d'Avignon (1309–1376): étude d'une société* (Paris, 1962) and idem., "Les Français du Midi á la cour pontificale d'Avignon," *Annales du Midi* 74 (January, 1962): 29–38.
29. Studies of the ecclesiastical history of the region can be found in the classic history of Languedoc by Dom Claude Devic and Dom Joseph Vaissète, *Histoire général de Languedoc,* 15 vols. (Toulouse, 1872–1892). See also Cholvy, ed. *Le diocèse de Montpellier* and Rouquette, *Histoire du diocèse de Maguelone.*

dictine monasteries at Aniane and Saint-Guilhem-le-Désert, both about nineteen miles from the town, had been important spiritual centers since the Carolingian period. Closer still was the Cluniac priory of Saint-Pierre-de-Clunéset.

If stability characterized religious practices in Montpellier in the thirteenth and early fourteenth centuries, by 1348 new preoccupations had surfaced. For example, in April and May of 1348 alternative burial sites were provided by testators. In April the merchant Stephanus de Monteolivo wanted to be buried in the tomb of a spice merchant in the Dominican cloister.[30] As an alternative site he chose the chapel of Saint-Georges in the Augustinian convent. In May 1348 the daughter of a draper stated that her first choice of burial would be in her parents' tomb behind the altar of the church of the Dominicans.[31] If refused entrance there, she would choose the cemetery of Saint-Barthélémy. Overcrowding may account for the increased choices of burial sites in the plague year 1348.

Additional details suggest the effects of plague mortality. In 1348 testators were more often concerned to include substitute heirs in the case of the decease of their first heir. Before 1346 there were eighteen cases where alternative arrangements were specified in case of the decease or failure of the first heir to satisfy the testator's expectations. By 1348 testators had become more exacting, and twelve of the twenty-eight wills stipulated substitutions.[32]

Alternative burial choices and more substitutions of heirs in 1348 indicate changes in testamentary practice which are confirmed in an examination of the burial choices of that year. The cathedral of Maguelone registered twenty-four requests for burial in the period 1293–1345. In 1348, however, only two of the wills named Maguelone as the cemetery of choice. In contrast, the most popular burial sites were now the Franciscan and Dominican convents.[33]

This shift in favor of the friars is confirmed by the upsurge of support for the *mensa* of these orders as Table 3 shows. In general, the traditional charities, such as the Wednesday alms, retained their support in 1348, although a decline can be noted in gifts to recluses, local churches and hospitals. Increased numbers of gifts to *confrèries* and the frequent establishment of chantries may reflect an institutionalization of benevolent

30. A. M. Montp., EE 426, April 2, 1348.
31. A. M. Montp., EE 214, May 23, 1348. The possibility of refusal of burial always existed. See Bernard, *La sépulture en droit canonique*, p. 113ff.
32. Philippe Wolff, *Commerces et marchands de Toulouse* (Paris, 1954), p. 74, remarked that there were only a few notarial registers remaining for 1348, "mais les testaments les envahissent, rédigés par des malades, mais aussi par des 'bien portants' qui craignent de mourir. La prévision des morts possibles *pestilencia vigenti* y multiplie les substitutions d'héritiers."
33. See Table 2.

Table 3

CHARACTERISTICS OF TESTAMENTARY PRACTICE

CATEGORY	CHRONOLOGICAL PERIODS					
	1200–1345		1347		1348	
	94 wills	%	38 wills	%	28 wills	%
Substitution of heirs	18	19%	15	39%	12	43%
Mensa of Maguelone	12	13%	3	8%	0	0
Mensa of Dominicans	18	19%	5	13%	8	29%
Mensa of Franciscans	17	18%	12	31.5%	8	29%
Mensa of Augustinians	15	16%	6	16%	8	29%
Mensa of Carmelites	16	17%	6	16%	7	25%
Wednesday alms	25	27%	6	16%	10	36%
Purgatory alms	5	5%	4	11%	3	11%
Recluses	46	54%	5	13%	10	36%
Churches	33	35%	6	16%	8	29%
Hospitals	27	29%	8	21%	7	25%
Confrèries	7	7.5%	8	21%	13	46%
Chantries	20	21%	5	13%	11	39%
Masses and Pious Works	14	15%	18	47%	10	36%
Pallbearers	2	2%	6	16%	7	25%
Funeral Beds	3	3%	5	13%	2	7%

activities in a search for spiritual protection.[34] More frequently in 1348 the testator admonished his survivors to use excess funds from pious donations and funeral arrangements to commission additional masses and pious works. Requests for up to five thousand masses appeared in the 1348 wills and were addressed most frequently to the Franciscans.[35] Other funeral practices, such as the choice of poor inhabitants as pallbearers, became more common in 1348.[36]

34. On confrèries see Paul Adam, *La vie paroissale en France au XIVe siècle* (Paris, 1964), p. 15ff. On the organization of trades which often supported charitable associations, see André Gouron, *La réglementation des métiers en Languedoc au moyen âge* (Geneva, Paris, 1958). The chantry foundations of Montpellier have been described by Achille Montel, "Le catalogue des chapellenies," *Revue de langues romanes* 3 (Montpellier, 1872): 292–310; 4 (Montpellier, 1873): 5–43. Their chronological distribution is the following:

Before 1300	1300–1320	1320–1346	1347–1348	1349–1377
5	7	8	16	57

35. A. D. Hérault, II E 95/377, f. 310v, March 16, 1348; A. M. Montp., EE 426, April 2, 1348; EE 415, May 17, 1348; A. M. Montp., EE 566, April 20, 1348.

36. Generally a gift of clothing, often a shirt, accompanied the provision for poor inhabitants to carry the defunct's body. See, for example, A. D. Hérault, II E 95/377, f. 282v, 312r, 317r, and A. M. Montp., EE 426.

In addition to the donation patterns discussed, there were numerous scattered gifts to specific urban and suburban churches for the fabric, the infirmary, the support of priests, alms or other services. Such donations were recorded for the cathedral of Maguelone in the years before 1346 when burial practice focused on its cemetery. There does not seem to have been a transference of these patterns of giving to the

Table 4

DISTRIBUTION OF WILLS BY MONTH IN THE REGISTER OF BERNARD GILLES, 1347–1348

Figures in parentheses indicate burial choice of the Franciscan convent.

Year	Jan.	Feb.	Mar.	Apr.	May	June	Jul.	Aug.	Sept.	Oct.	Nov.	Dec.
1347		1	2	5	7	8	4	3	5	1		
			(1)	(1)	(2)	(2)	(4)		(2)			
1348	1	1	10									
			(4)									

Total wills: 48
Franciscan choices: 16

DISTRIBUTION OF WILLS BY MONTH FROM THE FONDS DE LA COMMUNE CLOTURE*

Figures in parentheses indicate burial choice of the Franciscan convent.

Year	Jan.	Feb.	Mar.	Apr.	May	June	Jul.	Aug.	Sept.	Oct.	Nov.	Dec.
1347		1				1						
						(1)						
1348			1	3	8	1			1			
			(1)	(1)	(1)							

Total wills: 16
Franciscan choices: 4

*The Commune Clôture was the local name for the municipal defense organization.

DISTRIBUTION OF WILLS FROM GRAND CHARTRIER

Year	Jan.	Feb.	Mar.	Apr.	May	June	Jul.	Aug.	Sept.	Oct.	Nov.	Dec.
1348				1	1							

Total Number of Wills: 66
Franciscan Choices: 20

Because these shifts in testamentary practice seem to coincide with the outbreak of the Black Death, the plague should be investigated as their cause.[37] Table 4 shows the distribution of wills in the years 1347 and 1348. The probability of the outbreak of the disease in March 1348 is supported by the eleven wills recorded in that month. Further wills in April and May suggest that the epidemic may have continued through the spring. The scarcity of wills extant for the summer months indicates

mendicant churches. The findings of Lorcin, "Les clauses religieuses," pp. 301–310, and Nucé de Lamothe, "Piété et charité publique," p. 12, provide useful comparisons with the Montpellier data.

37. Ziegler, *The Black Death*, pp. 188–189, suggested that charitable donations and religious fervor increased manyfold because of the plague.

that the plague may have diminished during hot weather in Montpellier, as it did in Perpignan.[38] No further wills were preserved after September 1348, nor do any survive for 1349. While it is possible that no documents survive for these years, it is also likely that so many people had died that there was no longer time for the establishment of a will, or indeed, for a decent burial.[39]

The Black Death was a catastrophe of such sweeping social, economic and psychological dimensions that some scholars think it explains the crises of the later fourteenth century.[40] However, more recent studies of its effects have demonstrated that the seeds of economic disaster were present well before the mid-century and that the cataclysmic effects of the plague itself have at times been over-dramatized.[41] In her case study of Orvieto during the Black Death, Elisabeth Carpentier was especially sensitive to conditions immediately preceding the arrival of the disease. While she did not dismiss the effects of the plague, she found extensive economic, social and psychological crises in Orvieto before the plague struck, including grain shortages in 1346 and changing municipal funerary legislation of July 1347.[42]

The foregoing examination of religious behavior in Montpellier has compared data for the period 1200–1345 with those for the year 1348. It is useful in the case of Montpellier to look closely at the years immediately preceding the plague. There are no extant wills from 1346. For the year 1347, however, thirty-eight wills are preserved, the largest number in any single year before 1350. In spite of the often random preservation of medieval documents, the concentration of thirty-eight wills in 1347 and twenty-eight in 1348, representing over one-third of all one hundred-sixty extant wills before 1350, may in itself reflect a heightening of crisis before the plague.[43]

38. For differing views of the behavior of the plague in hot weather, see Richard Wilder Emery, "The Black Death of 1348 in Perpignan," *Speculum* 42 (October, 1967): 611–623, David Herlihy, *Medieval and Renaissance Pistoia* (New Haven and London, 1967), p. 107, and Wolff, *Commerces et marchands de Toulouse*, p. 74.
39. On the trauma of the plague, see especially Millard Meiss, *Painting in Florence and Siena after the Black Death* (New York, 1951), p. 64ff, and William Bowsky, *The Black Death, A Turning Point in History?* (New York, 1971), p. 13.
40. James Westfall Thompson, "The Aftermath of the Black Death and the Aftermath of the Great War," *American Journal of Sociology* 26 no. 5 (March, 1921): 565–572; Yves Renouard, "Conséquences et intérêt démographiques de la Peste Noire de 1348," *Population* 3 (July-September, 1948): 458–466.
41. Bowsky, "The Impact of the Black Death," pp. 1–34; Emery, "The Black Death," pp. 611–623; Philippe Wolff, "Trois études de démographie médiévale en France méridionale," *Studi in onore di Armando Sapori* (Milan, 1957), 1: 493–503; Geneviève Prat, "Albi et la Peste Noire," *Annales du Midi* 64 (January, 1952): 15–25.
42. Elisabeth Carpentier, *Une ville devant la peste: Orvieto et la peste noire de 1348* (Paris, 1962), pp. 76–94.
43. Bastard-Fournier, "Mentalités religieuses," p. 268 proposed that a graph of the chronological frequency of wills permits the discernment of years of crisis in the Late Middle Ages.

Pre-plague changes are suggested because major shifts in the testamentary behavior of 1348 can be traced back to 1347.[44] Already fewer testators had selected the cemetery of the cathdral of Maguelone; only three testators wished to be buried there in 1347. The Franciscans were overwhelmingly popular in 1347, receiving thirteen burial choices compared to seven in 1348. Saint-Barthélémy also gained burial choices; it received eleven requests while Saint-Denis received five.

The social background of the testators requesting burial at Saint-Barthélémy changed slightly in 1347. Before that date, requests came from the wealthy merchant classes and important artisans, such as a draper, merchants, a goldsmith, a pepperer, a mercer and notaries, as well as a wax candle maker and the daughter of a fisherman. In 1347 the clientele belonged in large measure to a humbler social station like the widow of a poultry merchant, a belt maker, a wood merchant, four cultivators and a blacksmith. That year's requests included those from a barber and a moneyer. In 1348 the clientele was again more bourgeois; requests came from a moneyer, a hemp merchant, a pepperer, the daughter of a draper, the widow of a parchment maker, as well as from a cultivator and a cultivator's widow. Sixteen of the twenty-seven requests before 1350 mention a family burial tradition at Saint-Barthélémy, and all six testators of cultivator background cite this tradition. There may have been progressive democratization of Saint-Barthélémy's adherents in the 1340s.

The Franciscans profited most from the new orientation of burial choices during 1347 and 1348. The Dominicans also shared in the increased attachment to the mendicant orders, as did the Carmelites and the Augustinians to a lesser degree. There was a remarkable upsurge of interest in the Franciscan house as a burial site in 1347 and 1348.[45] Of a total of twenty-seven burial requests, seven fell before 1346, thirteen in 1347 and seven in 1348.[46] Seventeen requests came from men and ten from women. Nine of these indicated family tradition. In five cases, special chapels such as that of Mary Magdalene or Saint Catherine and the cloister of the Franciscan house attracted testators. Peasants and artisans were clients of the Franciscans, but nine requests came from persons of

44. See Tables 2 and 3.

45. On shifts in spiritual loyalties of individuals in the later Middle Ages, see Decima L. Douie, *The Nature and the Effect of the Heresy of the Fraticelli* (Manchester, 1932); David Saville Muzzey, *The Spiritual Franciscans* (New York, 1907, reprint ed., 1914); Gordon Leff, *Heresy in the Later Middle Ages* (Manchester, 1967). Two recent volumes of collected essays are also useful for background on the religious mentality of this era: *Franciscains d'Oc. Les Spirituels ca. 1280–1324,* ed. Marie-Humbert Vicaire, *Cahiers de Fanjeaux 10* (Toulouse, 1975) and *La religion populaire en Languedoc du XIIIe siècle à la moitié du XIVe siècle,* ed. Marie-Humbert Vicaire, *Cahiers de Fanjeaux* 11 (Toulouse, 1976).

46. For a comparison of burial choices of Mendicant convents in Toulouse, see Nucé de Lamothe, "Piété et charité publique," p. 15 ff.

mercantile background, six of these in 1347–1348. The merchant classes in Montpellier, a town whose fortunes depended upon international trade, were important Franciscan supporters in 1347.

The Dominicans were chosen in burial requests in nine wills before 1346, in one in 1347 and in six in 1348. Thirteen of the testators were men. The Dominicans seem to have attracted testators of the financial, mercantile and legal classes of the town. Family tradition was well established with twelve instances of request for burial in the tomb of a relative. Burials might be in special chapels such as those of Saint Peter the Martyr, Mary Magdalene and Saint Peter and Saint Paul, or in the cloister, or in the cemetery of the Dominican house.

In addition to shifts in burial choice, the changes in testamentary behavior of 1348 appeared for the most part in 1347. For example, alternative burial choices were first recorded in 1347.[47] There were eighteen cases of stipulation of masses and/or pious works as the destination of any excess funds from funeral arrangements. The first three instructions for thousands of masses occurred in 1347. Donations to the Franciscan *mensa* were also numerous by that year; the friars received twelve gifts, while the *mensa* of the cathedral was mentioned only three times. Five wills carried provisions for funeral beds and six had arrangements for poor pallbearers in 1347. Increased interest in donations to *confrèries* appeared in that year. There was also a decline in gifts to recluses, Wednesday alms, churches and hospitals.

The medieval testator placed great importance upon the destiny of his or her soul, and although the patterns of charitable contributions and the establishment of masses for the soul might vary over time, the concern for personal salvation remained strong. While the medieval merchant typically showed some ambivalence regarding material fortune because of traditional Christian teachings in favor of poverty, in a town like Montpellier much effort had usually been expended in the course of a lifetime in the accumulation of worldly goods.[48] In addition to preparations for the salvation of the soul, the testator felt the significance of the designation of heirs to his or her worldly estate. Before 1346 the universal heirs were in all but five cases family members by marriage or blood, and in only two of these exceptions was a charity or a religious establishment selected as heir. In the substitutions of heirs in the same period, charities received two mentions. In two other cases

47. One testator, Guillelma, wife of Johannes Audrigol, raw wool merchant, specified in her will of May 21, 1347, that if the forty shillings which she set aside for a funeral bed were not sufficient for the prior of Saint-Denis where she requested burial, then she would prefer to be buried at the convent of the Augustinians. On May 30, she broke the old will and made a new one with the same stipulation. See A. D. Hérault, II E 95/377, f. 63v and 73r.

48. On the subject of merchant guilt, see, for example, Meiss, *Painting in Florence and Siena*, p. 71ff.

the estate, in the event of a substitution of heir, was to be divided between a family member and a charity; in another instance the sale of the estate was ordered without a specified destination of the proceeds. Finally, bad conduct or remarriage on the part of an heir in two cases resulted in the passage of the estate to a chantry and to the poor.

The picture changed in 1347. There were fifteen substitutions of heirs in 1347 (thirty-nine percent) while in the previous period only nineteen per cent of the wills carried a substitution clause. In the choice of universal heirs, there were eight designations of non-family members in 1347, and two additional designations dividing an estate between a family heir and the poor of Christ. Of the non-family heirs, two were religious establishments, the Franciscan convent and the *opus* and *operarii* of Saint Gilles. Only once were charities mentioned in substitutions of 1347, twice as sharing in the inheritance with family members. Masses were the ultimate destination of an estate in case of the death of substitute heirs in two other instances.

In 1348 charities were universal heirs in four cases and religious orders in two. In seven instances, masses and alms were designated as the substitutions of heirs of an estate. The substitution clause reached a frequency of forty-three per cent inclusion by 1348. The available evidence is not sufficient to permit more than an hypothesis concerning the significance of these developments. It suggests a growing uncertainty about the survival of heirs, and in turn it may imply an increasing mortality rate among the population. Such a demographic trend would have begun before the plague, according to the 1347 evidence, and would have been accentuated in the plague year of 1348.

From this survey of features of testamentary practice, new developments can be traced back at least to 1347, thus preceding the arrival of the plague in Montpellier. The impact of the plague should not be underestimated, but it is best understood when placed in the context of the local situation in Montpellier. The relative absence of wills for 1344–1346 does not permit a precise chronological definition of the period of change in testamentary practice. However, political and economic events of the mid-1340s show that a situation conducive to change existed.

Although in normal years local grain production was adequate for the population of Montpellier, after a poor harvest the town depended upon foreign grain. There were few notarial transactions in grain in the early 1340s, and those recorded actually involved exports of grain from Montpellier, thereby implying an agricultural surplus.[49] However, for

49. See A. D. Hérault, II E 95/372, f. 66v, for an example of exports. On grain exports from southern France, see Wolff, *Commerce et marchands de Toulouse,* pp. 169–187, and Edouard Baratier, "Marseille et Narbonne au XIVe siècle d'après les sources marseillaises," *Fédération historique du Languedoc méditerranéen et du Roussillon, Narbonne au moyen âge* (Montpellier, 1973), p. 88.

late 1346 and early 1347 the Montpellier archives preserve a unique record of five hundred-fifty small sales of grain by a merchant of Savona to some inhabitants of Montpellier. This record suggests that grain was purchased for individual consumption and that the local grain supply was insufficient.[50] The notarial register of 1347–1348 preserves a pattern of sales consistent with shortages.[51] In the acts of this register eighty-eight per cent of the grain sellers were of Montpellier origin, and were thus potential importers, while persons from the countryside, usually the source of local grain, represented sixty-six per cent of the grain clientele. In the same period merchants of Montpellier dealt in the international grain trade and they, along with foreign merchants such as the dealer from Savona, procured imports to feed a needy rural and urban population.[52]

The appearance in April and May of 1347 of a new pattern of credit transactions involving commitments of future harvests of grain in return for ready cash confirmed the increasing poverty of notarial clients.[53] A parallel trend was evident in grape futures.[54] During the years 1347 and 1348 a heavy volume of trade in agricultural products contrasted with the dearth of sales of silks, spices, leather and cloths and with the scarcity of recorded partnerships associated with international trade.[55] The economic conditions of these years were less dynamic than in 1343–1344 when there was ample evidence of the Levant trade upon which the commercial reputation of the town was based.[56]

The distress of the economic situation in the late 1340s was echoed by political conditions. In 1342-1344 the seigneur of Montpellier, Jacme III of Majorca, had lost all his lands with the exception of the seigneury of Montpellier and a few minor holdings in a defeat by the king of Aragon.[57] In 1349 Jacme's severe financial problems and political mistakes forced him to sell his share of Montpellier to Philip VI, thereby

50. Maurice de Dainville, *Inventaires, Archives municipales de Montpellier, XI, Documents comptables* (Montpellier, 1959), *Livre de dépenses de l'Hôpital Saint-Lazare,* f. 27r–50v.
51. A. D. Hérault, II E 95/377.
52. For imports by Montpelliérains, see A. D. Hérault, II E 95/368, f. 19v, 30v, 44r and II E 95/369, f. 52v, 84v.
53. A. D. Hérault, II E 95/377, f. 36v, 41v, 42r, 46v, 51r, 56r, 62v, 71r, 119r.
54. A. D. Hérault, II E 95/377, f. 13v, 62v, 71v, 75r, 75v, 76v, 89v, 301r.
55. See A. D. Hérault, II E 95/371, 372, 374.
56. On the commercial history of Montpellier, see Alexandre Germain, *Histoire du commerce du Montpellier antérieurement à l'ouverture du port de Cette,* 2 vols. (Montpellier, 1861), and Louis J. Thomas, *Montpellier, ville marchande: histoire économique et sociale de Montpellier des origines à 1870* (Montpellier, 1936).
57. On the political history of Montpellier, see Germain, *Histoire de la commune de Montpellier,* See also Charles de Tourtoulon, *Etudes sur la maison de Barcelone, Jacme Ier le conquérant, roi d'Aragon, comte de Barcelone, seigneur de Montpellier, d'après les chroniques et les documents inédits,* 2 vols. (Montpellier, 1863), and Emile Bonnet, "Les séjours à Montpellier de Jacques le conquérant roi d'Aragon," *Mémoires de la société archéologique de Montpellier,* 2nd ser. 9 (Montpellier, 1927): 153–232.

permitting the French crown to complete the acquisition which Philip IV had begun in 1293 by purchasing the episcopal quarter of the town.[58]

Against this background of economic and political difficulties the most easily isolated facet of change in testamentary practice in Montpellier is the increased popularity of the Franciscan order. The activities of the Franciscans had accelerated in Montpellier in the 1330s, and the population in 1347–1348 was strikingly loyal to the order. This attachment to the Franciscans by the inhabitants may have developed because the Spirituals had been suppressed, and along with them the view of their leader Peter John Olivi that Franciscans should not participate in burials, a stance which had been shared by many friars.[59] In the late thirteenth century the town was a center of Spiritual activity. Olivi, an ardent partisan of the Spirituals, was a target of Conventual opposition in the period 1274–1287; finally rehabilitated in 1287, he was promoted to the Montpellier *studium* in 1289 and taught there until his death in 1298.[60]

The growing discontent with the Spirituals in the fourteenth century was reflected in Montpellier. Spirituals were removed from the office of custodian in Montpellier and Narbonne in 1314 and replaced by Conventuals.[61] In the first quarter of the fourteenth century there were recorded, in addition, the first burnings of heretical sympathizers of the Spirituals in Montpellier.[62] General opposition to the Spirituals culminated in Pope John XXII's condemnation of evangelical poverty in 1323 and of Spiritual leadership in 1328.[63]

At the time of greatest Spiritual influence in Montpellier, during Olivi's presence and in the first quarter of the fourteenth century, the scarcity of source material makes it impossible to assess the effect of the Spirituals on the population at large. Montpellier was the birthplace of Spirituals and heretics such as Bernard Délicieux and the Béguine Na-

58. See Albert Lecoy de la Marche, *Les relations politiques de la France avec le royaume de Majorque,* 2 vols. (Paris, 1892), and Louis J. Thomas, "Montpellier entre la France et l'Aragon pendant la première moitié du XIVe siècle," *Monspeliensia, Mémoires et documents relatifs à Montpellier et à la région montpelliéraine,* (Montpellier, 1928–1929) 1, fasc. 1: 1–56.

59. On Olivi see David Burr, *The Persecution of Peter Olivi* (Philadelphia, 1976), especially pp. 65–78 and 91, for his ideas on burial. On Spiritual activity at Montpellier, see Emery, *Heresy and Inquisition,* p. 145, and Henry C. Lea, *A History of the Inquisition of the Middle Ages* (New York, 1922) 3:77.

60. Burr, *The Persecution,* pp. 36–41, 67, 78; see also John Moorman, *A History of the Franciscan Order from Its Origins to the Year 1517* (Oxford, 1968), pp. 193, 197.

61. Malcolm D. Lambert, *Franciscan Poverty. The Doctrine of Absolute Poverty of Christ and the Apostles in the Franciscan Order 1210–1323* (London, 1961), p. 205.

62. Germain, *Histoire de la commune de Montpellier* 3:222ff.

63. On the condemnations, see Malcolm D. Lambert, "The Franciscan Crisis under John XXII," *Franciscan Studies* 32 Annual X (1972): 123–143. See also Charles T. Davis, "Le pape Jean XXII et les Spirituels. Ubertin de Casale," *Franciscains d'Oc. Les Spirituels ca. 1280–1324. Cahiers de Fanjeaux* 10 (Toulouse, 1975): 263–283.

prous Boneta whose home was a refuge for persecuted Spirituals.[64] However, both the long tradition of good papal relations which the town entertained and the importance of the papal court at Avignon for the university and commercial classes of the town suggest that most townspeople supported the papacy against the Spirituals.[65] In particular, Avignon was a market for the luxury products of merchants and a magnet for masters of medicine and professors of Montpellier.[66] Finally, the testamentary evidence of the thirteenth and early fourteenth centuries suggests a stable attachment of the population to the cathedral of Maguelone, to the church of Saint-Barthélémy and to the pilgrimage church of Notre-Dame-des-Tables.

By the 1330s, although Olivi's works were still read within the Franciscan order, the position of the Conventuals was firmly entrenched.[67] In the 1330s and 1340s the wills of Montpellier residents reveal intense activity on the part of individual Franciscans.[68] The skeptic might question whether the growing preference for the Franciscans was a result of their omnipresence at death beds, their cultivation of the sympathies of the sick and their peddling of amulets; yet, with the Spiritual controversy in the past, the merchant classes of Montpellier may now have found new sources of inspiration in the Franciscan order.[69]

Given the absence of documents it is impossible to trace the evolution of testamentary practice during the decade following the plague. The

64. On Bernard Délicieux, see Gordon Leff, *Heresy in the Later Middle Ages* (New York, Manchester, 1967) 1:204; Yves Dossat, "Les origines de la querelle entre Prêcheurs et Mineurs Provencaux. Bernard Délicieux," *Franciscains d'Oc. Les Spirituels ca. 1280–1324. Cahiers de Fanjeaux* 10 (Toulouse, 1975): 315–354. On Naprous Boneta, see Leff, *Heresy* 1:212–215; Lea, *A History of the Inquisition* 3:82–83; William Harold May, "The Confession of Prous Boneta, Heretic and Heresiarch," *Essays in Medieval Life and Thought Presented in Honor of Austin Patterson Evans* (New York, 1955): 3–30.

65. According to Leff, *Heresy* 1:230, the primary towns of heretical outbreak at this time were Narbonne, Béziers, Lodève, Carcassonne and Agde.

66. See Guillemain, *La cour pontificale* pp. 377–379 and Karl Heinrich Schäfer, *Die Ausgaben der apostolischen Kammer unter Johann XXII, nebst der Jahresbilanzen von 1316–1378* (Paderborn, 1911).

67. Burr, *The Persecution,* pp. 90–91.

68. Testators made only ten references to personal confessors in the extant wills, but six of these fall in the 1330s and 1340s and mention Franciscan confessors. They were Guillelmus de Peyrotes; A. M. Montp., II 3, f. 13; A. D. Montp., II E; 95/377, f. 282v; Jacobus de Asperis; A. D. Montp., II E 95/369, f. 106r; II E; 95/377, f. 38r. See also, II E 95/377, f. 58v; f. 83r; 282v and A. M. Montp., EE 149, EE 335, EE 433.

Among the clergy singled out for pious gifts in wills, the Franciscans were cited eighteen times with the next most numerous group, the Dominicans, recorded only five times.

The Franciscan position of influence in Montpellier may have expanded when their educational facilities were elevated to the status of *studium generale* in 1346. See Moorman, *A History,* p. 366.

69. On Franciscan critics, see Wallace K. Ferguson, *Europe in Transition, 1300–1520* (Boston, 1962), pp. 341–342. On courage during the plague, see Ziegler, *The Black Death,* p. 259ff.

wills before 1350 have demonstrated that the Black Death appeared on the heels of the growth of Franciscan popularity and of shifts in testamentary behavior. It may well have hastened and accentuated the observed trends, but they would have come anyway in the crucible of change that was the fourteenth century.[70]

This study is a revised version of a paper delivered at the Eleventh Annual Conference on Medieval Studies at Western Michigan University, Kalamazoo, Michigan in May 1976.

70. Ziegler, *The Black Death,* p., 269.

V

Flight from Prosecution: The Search for Religious Asylum in Medieval Montpellier

Although historical precedents and modern parallels exist, the institution of asylum reached its apogee in the Middle Ages.[1] This study will examine religious asylum in the commercial, financial, and university center of Montpellier in the early fourteenth century through the record of a municipal inquest of 1332 contained in a lengthy manuscript dossier from the Archives municipales de Montpellier.[2] This document preserves testimony by contemporaries about religious asylum and the reaction of lay authorities to it. The inquest itself focused on the question of whether it was Montpellier practice to interrogate persons accused of crimes in religious houses where they sought asylum. Much of the interest of this evidence for historians lies in the incidental, yet otherwise unavailable, information it provides on crimes, criminals, criminal law, the local legal establishment, and the interaction of the local court systems in an era from which judicial court registers have not survived. It is important to note at the outset, however, that the dossier of the present study has a distinctly secular bias. Al-

Kathryn L. Reyerson is professor of history and former director of the Center for Medieval Studies at the University of Minnesota. She is the author of *Business, Banking and Finance in Medieval Montpellier* (Toronto, 1985) and co-editor of *The Medieval Castle, Romance and Reality* (Dubuque, Iowa, 1984) and *The Medieval Mediterranean: Cross-Cultural Contacts* (St. Cloud, Minn., 1989).

[1] General background on the law of asylum can be found in Pierre Timbal Duclaux de Martin, *Le Droit d'asile* (Paris, 1939); and in J. Charles Cox, *The Sanctuaries and Sanctuary Seekers of Mediaeval England* (London, 1911). Barry James in the *International Herald Tribune*, 26 December 1989, recently reviewed the issue, " 'Sanctuary' Principle Tested," in light of the request for asylum by General Manuel Noriega at the Vatican Embassy in Panama. See also L. -R. Misserey, "L'Asile en Occident," *Dictionnaire de droit canonique* (Paris, 1935), 1:1089–1104.

[2] Archives municipales de Montpellier (hereafter designated as AM), *Grand Chartrier*, Louvet 1011.

though religious houses and religious personnel are mentioned throughout the inquest, the position of the local ecclesiastical establishment on the issue of asylum remains unknown. In contrast, differing secular interpretations of the procedures surrounding the institution of religious asylum can be fruitfully explored.

Asylum—construed broadly—was well known in the Middle Ages and could take secular as well as religious forms. Medieval towns offered immunity to fleeing serfs if they managed to reside a year and a day within the town,[3] and new urban foundations often extended such protection to immigrants, with crosses staked at the corners of the urban *sauveterre* or *salvetat*, the site of such immunity.[4] Surviving toponyms in present-day France suggest the degree to which asylum was available in the Middle Ages as a lure for settlement.[5] The Peace of God movement protected the noncombatants of eleventh-century Europe, who were potential victims of violence.[6] According to the medieval law of asylum or refuge, anyone pursued by a public authority could request asylum in a church or monastery from which he or she could not be extracted.[7] The fugitive's goods were also protected from seizure. In the case of debtors fleeing creditors, the bishop could decide about the surrender of the debtor's goods but not about the person of the debtor.[8] The option of religious asylum gave the church a considerable role in the criminal and civil justice systems. Yet, already in twelfth-century England, the special and supposedly sacred immunity of a church building had not saved Thomas Becket, even at the high altar of Canterbury cathedral, from death at the hands of Henry II's

[3] Henri Pirenne, *Medieval Cities* (New York, 1956), 138: "Die Stadtluft macht frei." For an interesting exploration of the "liberty" of Westminster, see Gervase Rosser, *Medieval Westminster, 1200–1540* (Oxford, 1989).

[4] See, for example, Paul Ourliac, "Les Villages de la région toulousaine au XIIe siècle," *Annales: Economies, Sociétés, Civilisations* 4 (1949): 268–77.

[5] Southwestern France offers numerous examples for small agglomerations. See, for example, La Salvetat-sur-Agout north of St. Pons.

[6] On the Peace and Truce of God, see Hartmut Hoffman, *Gottesfriede und Treuga Dei* (Stuttgart, 1964). For the South of France, see Thomas N. Bisson, "The Organized Peace in Southern France and Catalonia, ca. 1140–ca. 1233," *American Historical Review* 82 (1977): 290–311. Further examples of the copious bibliography on these institutions include H. E. J. Cowdrey, "The Peace and the Truce of God in the Eleventh Century," *Past and Present* 46 (1970): 42–67, and the collection of studies, *Essays on the Peace of God: The Church and the People in Eleventh-Century France*, ed. Thomas Head and Richard Landes, vol. 14 of *Historical Reflections/Réflexions historiques* (1987).

[7] Jacques Ellul, *Histoire des institutions*, vol. 3: *Le Moyen Age* (Paris, 1962), 243 and 285. Gratian in the *Decretum* addressed the issue in CXVIII qu. 4 c.8, "Non licet alicui hominem de ecclesia rapere." For this and other canon law texts, see P. Timbal, *Le Droit d'asile*, 459–64. For further background on the right of asylum, see L.-R. Misserey, "L'Asile en Occident."

[8] Ellul, *Histoire des institutions*, 243.

henchmen.[9] In the 1205 accords of Paris, Philip Augustus and his barons won for lay jurisdiction what Henry II of England had not: according to John Baldwin, the accords of Paris, which included some restriction on asylum for anyone pursued for serious crime, were peaceably accepted in Capetian France, becoming the French equivalent of the Constitutions of Clarendon, an 1164 formulation of customs in England that dealt with a variety of issues including royal intervention in ecclesiastical jurisdiction.[10] The French royal assembly of Vincennes in 1329 again called into question ecclesiastical jurisdiction, reinforcing royal prerogatives.[11]

The dossier to be examined in this article assembles testimonies about religious asylum that were given only a few years later, in 1332. A brief description of the economic, political, and legal background in Montpellier is in order before exploration of this dossier. Montpellier in this era was a sophisticated cosmopolitan environment. A population of thirty-five to forty thousand people placed it among the first cities of France after Paris.[12] The university, strong in law and medicine, attracted scholars from all over southern Europe. Numerous merchants handled the luxury trade of the Mediterranean world and were heavily engaged in international finance, drawing immigrants and foreign visitors to the Lower Languedocian town. Specialized tradespeople served its artisanal and industrial needs.

Montpellier was a town of split political allegiance and as such was an unusual judicial arena because of the dual jurisdictions in place through the mid-fourteenth century. In the twelfth century, the Guilhem lords and the bishop of Maguelone governed Montpellier and the episcopal quarter of Montpelliéret, respectively, until 1204, when the Guilhem were replaced by the king of Aragon. The quarter of Montpellier passed to the king of Majorca in 1276, and in 1293 the king of France purchased the episcopal quarter of Montpelliéret. The court of the bailiff, technically the court of the king of Aragon, then from 1276 that of the king of Majorca, was the de facto court of the

[9] See for example, Thomas M. Jones, ed., *The Becket Controversy* (New York, 1970).

[10] John Baldwin, *The Government of Philip Augustus: Foundations of French Royal Power in the Middle Ages* (Berkeley, 1986), 325–28; Baldwin mentions the issue of asylum specifically. On the Constitutions of Clarendon, see W. L. Warren, *Henry II* (Berkeley and Los Angeles, 1973), 474–75; on royal intervention, 437–38. See also Bryce Lyon, *A Constitutional and Legal History of Medieval England* (New York, 1980), for example, 302–3.

[11] See Olivier Martin, *L'Assemblée de Vincennes de 1329 et ses conséquences: Etudes sur les conflits entre la juridiction laïque et la juridiction ecclésiastique au XIVe siècle* (Paris, 1909).

[12] On the population of Montpellier, see my article, "Patterns of Population Attraction and Mobility: The Case of Montpellier, 1293–1348," *Viator* 10 (1979): 257–81.

municipal consuls of Montpellier because they participated in the choice of the bailiff.

The 1204 *Consuetudines* had endowed this court of the king of Aragon with civil, commercial, and criminal jurisdiction. Its territorial focus was the commercially dynamic seigneurial quarter of Montpellier.[13] From 1205 on, a court of appeals existed under the auspices of the lieutenant of the king of Aragon,[14] and beginning in 1206, the bishop of Maguelone also had his own court in the less dominant episcopal quarter of Montpelliéret.[15] Episcopal jurisdiction gradually became subordinate to Aragonese royal justice, and in 1241 or 1242 the bishop renounced his rights to appeals and to jurisdiction of capital crimes in Montpelliéret in favor of Jacme I of Aragon-Majorca.[16]

Beginning in 1205 and reinforced in 1211–12, the consuls of Montpellier wrested the power of legislating, *potestas statuendi*, from royal and then episcopal authorities, enjoying an apogee of municipal authority until Jacme I of Aragon challenged this independence in 1254–58. Thereafter, consular legislative initiative, though still existent, was less expansive. This power, in its heyday, according to André Gouron, was almost unique west of the Alps, that is, outside of Italy.[17]

An era of direct conflict of jurisdiction between the king of Majorca (heir of Jacme I for the kingdom of Majorca in which the seigneury of Montpellier was included) and the king of France opened in 1280.[18] An agreement of 22 July 1282 acknowledged the criminal ju-

[13] On consular jurisdiction, see Jean-Marie Carbasse, "Consulats méridionaux et justice criminelle au Moyen Age," Thèse d'état, Faculté de droit et des sciences économiques de Montpellier, Université de Montpellier 1, 1974. Details on the court system in the seigneurial quarter of Montpellier can be found in C. Chabaneau and A. Germain (eds.), *Liber Instrumentorum Memorialium, Cartulaire des Guilhems de Montpellier* (Montpellier, 1884–1886), acts CCXXXIX –CCXLIV, 400–407. See also the studies of Archibald R. Lewis, "The Development of Town Government in Twelfth-Century Montpellier," *Speculum* 22 (1947): 51–67, and "Seigneurial Administration in Twelfth-Century Montpellier," *Speculum* 22 (1947): 562–77. The best version of the *Consuetudines* of August 1204 is that of A. Teulet (ed.) *Layettes du trésor des chartes* (Paris, 1863), 1:255–66. Other editions were published in *Le Petit Thalamus de Montpellier*, ed. F. Pégat et al., (Montpellier, 1840), 1–59, with Latin and vernacular versions in Charles Giraud, *Essai sur le droit français au moyen âge*, vol. 1 *preuves* (Paris, 1846), 47ff.

[14] See Teulet, *Layettes du trésor des chartes*, 1:289–91, article 9.

[15] This court would become that of the rector after Philip IV's purchase of Montpelliéret in 1293 from the Bishop of Maguelone. See André Gouron, "L'Origine du Tribunal du Petit-Scel de Montpellier," *Fédération historique du Languedoc méditerranéen et du Roussillon* (Mende, 1955) (Montpellier, 1957), 58.

[16] Luc d'Achéry, *Spicilegium* (Paris, 1723), 3:622, for the published text of this act.

[17] André Gouron, "La *Potestas statuendi* dans le droit coutumier montpelliérain du treizième siècle," *Diritto comune e diritti locali nella storia dell'Europa. Atti del Convegno di Varenna, 12–15 guigno 1979* (Milan, 1980), 95–118, especially 100–105.

[18] For general background, see Henri Michel, *L'Administration royale dans la sénéchaussée de Beaucaire au temps de Saint-Louis* (Paris, 1910).

risdiction of the king of France in the *sénéchaussée* of Beaucaire-Nîmes within which Montpellier was an enclave.[19] Further penetration of French justice occurred in 1293, when Philip IV purchased the episcopal quarter of Montpellier.[20] The French king received all temporal jurisdiction over Montpelliéret; the bishop retained the right to judge his clergy and the less important crimes committed by his servants. In 1293 the procurator of the king of France established royal jurisdiction in the name of the seneschal under a rector. The procurator indicated at that time the French king's desire to install a court for the authentification of contracts, the *cour du Petit Scel*, a court of voluntary jurisdiction without territorial limitation under a judge attached to the rector.[21]

The judicial situation in Montpellier was thus complicated in the early fourteenth century by the existence of two lay court systems: that of the bailiff for the town consuls and the king of Majorca and that of the rector for the king of France.[22] Both judicial administrations had numerous lesser personnel including lieutenants, vice-bailiffs, judges, notaries, and sergeants, variously termed *curiales* in the documents. Litigants on both sides of a dispute might be represented in court by *procuratores* drawn from the significant legal population of Montpellier. In such a large urban environment, law and order were important issues. Mediation, arbitration, amicable resolution of differences, and guarantees of protection from bodily harm were used to humanize the otherwise harsh regulations of the Montpellier judicial legislation.[23]

Religious asylum must have seemed an attractive alternative to

[19] Dom Devic and Dom Vaissete *Histoire générale de Languedoc* (Toulouse, 1879), 9:81–83.

[20] A. Lecoy de la Marche, *Les Relations politiques de la France avec le royaume de Majorque (Iles Baléares, Roussillon, Montpellier, etc.)* 2 vols. (Paris, 1892), 1:311ff, discusses incidents leading to the purchase of Montpelliéret. See also Devic and Vaissete, *Histoire générale de Languedoc*, 9:167–70. Alexandre Germain, *Histoire de la commune de Montpellier*, 3 vols. (Montpellier, 1851), 2:354, includes the document of sale, as did Jean Rouquette, ed. *Cartulaire de Maguelone*, 5 vols. (1912–1925), 3:506.

[21] On this court, see André Gouron and Jean Hilaire, "Les 'Sceaux' rigoureux du Midi de la France," *Recueil de mémoires et travaux publié par la société d'histoire des institutions des anciens pays du droit écrit* (cited hereafter as *Recueil*), fasc. IV (1958): 41–77; and André Gouron, "L'Origine du Tribunal du Petit Scel de Montpellier," 57–70.

[22] On the legal personnel of Languedoc, see Joseph Strayer, *Les Gens de justice de Languedoc sous Philippe le Bel* (Toulouse, 1970); and Jan Rogozinski, "Ordinary and Major Judges," *Studia Gratiana* 15 (1972): 589–611; idem., "The Counsellors of the Seneschal of Beaucaire and Nîmes, 1250–1350," *Speculum* 44 (1969): 421–39; idem., *Power, Caste and Law: Social Conflict in Fourteenth-Century Montpellier* (Cambridge, Mass., 1982); and idem., "Lawyers of Lower Languedoc," Ph. D. diss., Princeton University, 1967. On the bailiffs, see Henri Gilles, "Notes sur les bayles de Montpellier," *Bulletin philologique et historique (jusqu'à 1610) du Comité des travaux historiques et scientifiques*, année 1961 (Paris, 1963): 441–55.

[23] For treatment of these issues, see my monograph, *Business, Banking and Finance in Medieval Montpellier* (Toronto, 1985), chap. 4.

physical punishment, but its misuse or overuse had apparently become a problem in Montpellier as early as the mid-thirteenth century. Pope Alexander IV (1254–1261) published a bull prohibiting priests from protecting debtors who fled from Montpellier merchants and took refuge in churches.[24] The inquest that forms the documentary basis for this study pertains to criminal procedure with regard to religious asylum and does not address the matter of debt.[25] A particular case of homicide, which came to the attention of the king of France, provoked the Montpellier inquest into religious asylum. Letters patent of 7 May 1325, from the king of France to the seneschal of Beaucaire, raised the question of the validity of religious asylum from crimes in Montpellier with regard to the murder of Johannes Seguerii by Guillelmus Roca or Roca Maura, resident of the French quarter of Montpellier.[26] The rector of the French royal quarter had refused to permit the interrogation of the accused murderer in a religious house, stating that it was against the customs of the town of Montpellier. The king requested inquiry into local practices in order to be able to determine royal policy regarding the justice of pursuit and interrogation of suspects by royal officials in religious houses.

There is no further surviving trace of this matter until, in October 1332, in a somewhat tardy response to the above order, the consuls of Montpellier, at the instigation of Petrus Mauselli, cleric, French royal *juge mage*, and lieutenant of the seneschal of Beaucaire-Nîmes proceeded to conduct an investigation into the matter of religious asylum in Montpellier. Petrus Garusii, procurator of the consuls, produced

[24] AM, *Grand Chartrier*, Louvet 2866. Pierre Timbal, *Le Droit d'asile*, 257, cited a bull of Pope Alexander IV (5 January 1257) in response to complaints from the town consuls, with confirmations of Pope John XXII (2 November 1318), of Pope Urban V (2 January 1363) and of Pope Gregory XI (17 January 1376), prohibiting the clergy of the diocese of Maguelone from extending sanctuary to debtors. There was attached to the twelfth-century Provençal legal treatise, *Lo Codi*, a Latin gloss on the law of asylum and on violations of ecclesiastical immunities. See Felix Derrer (ed.), *Lo Codi, Eine Summa Codicis in Provenzalischer Sprache aus dem XII. Jahrhundert. Die Provenzalische Fassung der Handschrift A (Sorbonne 632)* (Zurich, 1974), 253–55. For a discussion of this manuscript, see André Gouron, "Le Manuscrit 632 de la Sorbonne: A la convergence des droits savants en Pays d'Oc," *Mélanges de la Bibliothèque de la Sorbonne* 6 (1985): 6–20, especially p. 9. Further study of the issue of asylum by legal historians would be welcome.

[25] There was severe punishment for debt in Montpellier. See Pierre Tisset, "Placentin et son enseignement à Montpellier. Droit romain et coutume dans l'ancien pays de Septimanie," *Recueil*, fasc. 2 (1951): 84–85. By the fourteenth century, the severe debt legislation had been modified in practice by the *cessio bonorum* clause of notarial acts. See Reyerson, *Business, Banking and Finance*, 96–97; and Michel Lacave, "Recherches sur la *cessio bonorum* dans le droit méridional à la fin du moyen âge," *Recueil*, fasc. 9: *Mélanges Roger Aubenas* (1974): 443–460. In 1323 Charles IV allowed debtors to cede their goods to avoid punishment. See AM, *Grand Chartrier*, Louvet 197.

[26] AM Louvet 1011, pp. 3–4.

for Petrus de Banio, *jurisperitus* and substitute procurator of the king of France and the seneschal of Beaucaire, a list of twenty-five persons summoned for questioning about the authorization of interrogation of accused in religious houses. The resulting recorded testimony of nineteen witnesses, representing the collective memory of a mature segment of the Montpellier legal establishment, occupies over one hundred unpaginated folios in the surviving dossier.[27] Individuals who failed to appear as witnesses were involved in a protest filed against the intrusion of the French king into the prerogatives of the bailiff's court of Montpellier.

Eight notaries, five *jurisperiti*, three *advocati*, two *burgenses*, and one *legum doctor* were questioned in the matter of religious asylum and, in particular, about the issue of interrogation of accused criminals in religious houses (table 1).[28] Because Montpellier was a town of split allegiance between France and Majorca, each of the witnesses was asked whose subject he was. Ten responded that they were subjects of the king of Majorca; five more admitted living in the Majorcan quarter of the town. One French royal notary lived in the French quarter and was presumably a French subject.[29] One *burgensis*, Colinus Bertrandi, a former bailiff of the court of Majorca, stated that he lived in the Majorcan quarter but was a French subject.[30] One witness was a subject of the Majorcan king in civil matters and of Maguelone, that is, the bishop's *officialité*, in criminal matters.[31] One final witness was a cleric, though living in the Majorcan quarter, and thus subject to ecclesiastical jurisdiction.[32] Thus, this was an inquest conducted by French authorities among a majority of witnesses of Majorcan allegiance. As the case of Colinus Bertrandi shows, a mix of allegiance was possible. Moreover, one should not assume that the witnesses were totally cooperative and pliant in all cases.

The witnesses commented about the contents and employment of this investigative procedure and about specific instances when they recalled its use. Their testimonies were remarkably convergent regard-

[27] See note 2 above.

[28] AM Louvet 1011, p. 97: Petrus de Manso.

[29] AM Louvet 1011, pp. 205–10.

[30] AM Louvet 1011, pp. 187–95: Petrus de Taurinhano. On ecclesiastical jurisdiction at Montpellier, see Gérard Sautel, "Une Juridiction paroissiale dans le Midi de la France au moyen âge: La Cour de Saint Firmin à Montpellier," *Recueil*, fasc. 2 (1951), 47–65.

[31] AM Louvet 1011, p. 164: Berengarius de Fabrica.

[32] The demographic characteristics of the nineteen witnesses are interesting in and of themselves. Their stated memories stretched back from between twenty-five and seventy-two years. If one assumes that their professional recall would have begun at the earliest about age twenty, one can estimate their ages at approximately forty-five to ninety-two years.

TABLE 1
WITNESSES RECORDING TESTIMONY
(In order of appearance)

Name	Profession	Residence	Allegiance	Memory
Bernardus Garnerii	notarius	Montpellier	Majorca	50 yrs.
Arnaudus Bodonis	notarius	Montpellier	Majorca	50 yrs.
Andreas de Sancto Egidio	advocatus	Montpellier	Majorca	45 yrs.
Petrus Fornerii	advocatus	Montpellier	———	50 yrs.
Bernardus de Caranta	jurisperitus	Montpellier	Majorca	30 yrs.
Guillelmus de Mora	jurisperitus	Montpellier	———	50 yrs.
Johannes Andree	advocatus	Montpellier	Majorca	50 yrs.
Petrus de Manso	notarius regius	Montpellier	France (?)	72 yrs.
Raymundus de Capite Vilario	jurisperitus	Montpellier	Majorca	30 yrs.
Guillelmus de Podio	notarius	Montpellier	Majorca	40 yrs.
Stephanus Vitalis	notarius	Montpellier	Majorca	40 yrs.
Johannes Clareti	jurisperitus (former notarius regius)	Montpellier	France (?)	40 yrs.
Berengarius de Fabrica	legum doctor	Montpellier	clericus	48 yrs.
Jacobus de Milhano	notarius	Montpellier	France	25 yrs.
Franciscus Viaderii	notarius	Montpellier	Majorca	30 yrs.
Petrus de Taurinhano	jurisperitus	Montpellier	Majorca in civil (Maguelone in criminal)	40 yrs.
Nicholaus Ymberti	burgensis (former bailiff)	Montpellier	Majorca	40 yrs.
Colinus Bertrandi	burgensis (former bailiff)	Montpelliéret	France	30 yrs.
Petrus Pagesii	notarius	Montpellier	Majorca (?)	30 yrs.

NOTE: Montpellier = Majorcan quarter; Montpelliéret = French quarter; notarius regius = French royal notary.

ing the routine practice of consular officials in interrogating alleged offenders in religious houses, once their hiding places had been discovered through the revelation of their whereabouts by friends or relatives, and once a series of specific procedural steps had been accomplished.

The investigative procedure referred to in the consular survey derived from the municipal statutes of 29 June 1221, legislation on appeals and procedure that treated the plight of fugitives from justice.[33]

[33] Teulet, *Layettes*, 1:519–20: "Si pro injuria vel delicto aliquis ad ecclesiam vel domum religionis confugerit, vel a Montepessulano se absentaverit, et inventus alicubi et a curia citatus sive amonitus non venerit infra decem dies, vel non inventus, precone publice clamante ut ad curiam veniat, infra triginta dies curie se non presentaverit, ex publica preconizatione, habito ipso pro legitime citato, pro convicto vel conffesso [*sic*] criminis vel injurie habeatur."

This legislation fell in the era of consular legislative apogee referred to above.[34] According to these statutes, if an accused fled on account of wrongdoing or crime to a religious house or left Montpellier and was found and cited before the court and failed to come within ten days, or if the accused was not found and did not appear within thirty days of a public summons by a town crier, then the accused was considered legitimately summoned and held as convicted or confessed of the crime or wrongdoing in question. Sentence was pronounced against the absent accused. Witnesses of the 1332 inquest testified to the basic form of this procedure with two additional provisions: first, that a defender might represent the accused fugitive before the court; and second, that the court might send judicial personnel to interrogate the accused fugitive or his defense attorney in the religious house where the accused was in refuge.

The witnesses were asked whether they were familiar with the statutory legislation, who had authored it, and how long it had been in use. Also, they were questioned about specific cases in which they had been involved, about court personnel handling interrogations—or inquisitions, as they were called in the documents—about defenders of the accused, about the nature of the crimes so pursued, and the type of sentences meted out. Inquiry was made about French royal officials' use of this procedure. Witnesses were asked further whether anyone ever interrupted this practice.

The following pages examine the responses of the witnesses to these inquiries and analyze the results of this survey of collective judicial memory. All witnesses were familiar with the statutory procedures and confirmed the use of defenders and of interrogation in religious houses by personnel of the court of the bailiff of the king of Majorca. Five witnesses quoted the *incipit* of this legislation at the pertinent paragraph: "Si pro injuria vel delicto," while all stated that they had seen it in books of *consuetudines* of Montpellier housed in the court of the king of Majorca.[35] Two stated that they had seen but not read the statute, one because he could not read, surprising in that he was termed an *advocatus* and thus must have enjoyed some measure of legal education.[36] The second witness who had not read the statute was the *burgensis* Colinus Bertrandi of Montpellier, who stated that, as a layman, he did not read Latin.[37] In one further instance, the notary re-

[34] A. Gouron, "La *Potestas statuendi*," 107.
[35] See note 33 above.
[36] AM Louvet 1011, e.g. p. 86: Johannes Andree, advocatus.
[37] AM Louvet 1011, p. 197.

cording the testimonies stated that he had explained his deposition (probably reread) to the witness Arnaudus Bodonis, notary of Montpellier, in *romana linga*.[38] Some witnesses themselves went as interrogators of the accused in religious houses; others said that they read the written record of the interrogations in the books of the inquisition of the court of the bailiff of the king of Majorca. The two former bailiffs admitted authorizing the interrogatory procedure.

Seven of the witnesses responded to the question of authorship of the statute, citing the king of Majorca, sometimes referred to as king of Aragon and Majorca, a political situation that had ceased at the death of Jacme I the Conqueror in 1276, with one including the consuls of Montpellier and two the consuls with the *universitas* of the town.[39] One witness, Guillelmus de Mora, *jurisperitus*, dated the authorship to the time of King Philip or the Blessed Louis (French kings) and leaned toward the time of King Louis (1226–1270), stating that it was written in a book containing the statute, kept in the French *curia regia* in Montpellier, and that the king generally ordered that *consuetudines* or *statuta* of places be preserved and observed without violation during his reign.[40] A further witness, Nicholaus Ymberti, *burgensis* of Montpellier, stated that bailiffs of the king of Majorca swore yearly with the beginning of the new consular regime to preserve the statute.[41]

In answer to the question of how long the statute had been in use, witnesses recalled specific cases more or less vaguely in which they had observed it practiced. The most venerable witness, Petrus de Manso, notary of the French king and inhabitant of the French royal quarter, claimed a memory of seventy-two years but made specific reference to events twenty and thirty-five years ago.[42] Most witnesses, even those claiming fifty-year memories, had specific recall within a shorter memory span.

From the responses it is possible to identify some of the French and Majorcan legal personnel of Montpellier. Many witnesses named the bailiffs, under whose regimes interrogations took place, and also judges, notaries, servants of the court, and defenders of the accused. A

[38] AM Louvet 1011, p. 33.

[39] For example, AM Louvet 1011, pp. 59, 83, 113. On the reign of Jacme I at Montpellier, see Emile Bonnet, "Les Séjours à Montpellier de Jacques le Conquérant, roi d'Aragon," *Mémoires de la société archéologique de Montpellier*, 2nd ser., (1927), 153–232. On the relations between France and Majorca, see A. Lecoy de la Marche, *Les Relations politiques*.

[40] AM Louvet 1011, pp. 83–84.

[41] AM Louvet 1011, p. 203.

[42] AM Louvet 1011, pp. 97–104.

notary and one or two servants of the court, along with an occasional judge, were usually present at interrogations in religious houses. Most of the notaries had served as notaries of inquisition in religious houses or as *scriptores* of the court; others had served as judges, and a few as bailiffs and, in that capacity, had dispatched notaries to take depositions of accused in refuge in religious houses[43] (see the Appendix). Those serving as bailiffs or as judges had handed down sentences to absent accused as if they had confessed or been convicted by the court.[44]

The defenders of the accused are perhaps the most interesting parties to the procedure (see the Appendix for names). They might be present at the interrogations. Their role was significant in the procedure because the accused sending a defender was tried on the basis of the facts of the case and not summarily condemned in absentia. Twenty-two were mentioned by name in the testimonies, some recurring in individual testimonies as many as twelve times. Most, if not all, were *advocati* at the time of their role as defenders. Seven of the witnesses stated that they had served in this capacity.[45]

One town crier, a certain Guillelmus Ferreti, responsible for the public proclamation summoning the accused to court, seemed to be a known quantity to most of the witnesses.[46] A few witnesses stated that they had never seen the proclamation part of the procedure used. However, one witness, the *jurisperitus* Raymundus de Capite Vilario, was most explicit about the spots in town where the proclamation took place: in the *trivium* of the court of the king of Majorca, in the Canabasseria, in the canton of the Pelliperia, in the old court in Montpelliéret, now the French quarter, and in other places.[47]

Testimony was less consistent on the issue of whether the procedure of interrogation of accused in religious houses was practiced at the court of the French king. Most witnesses had not observed the procedure in use at the French court or stated that they did not know whether it was employed there as it was at the court of the bailiff of the king of Majorca. However, several witnesses were quite specific about instances in which they had seen *curiales* of the French court use the procedure. Several other witnesses cited the Ruppemaura or Rippemaura, that is, the Roca Maura, case, which provoked the whole investigation, as an example of use of the procedure by the French court be-

[43] For example, AM Louvet 1011, p. 37.
[44] For example, AM Louvet 1011, pp. 125, 166.
[45] For example, AM Louvet 1011, pp. 65 and 202.
[46] For example, AM Louvet 1011, p. 140.
[47] For example, AM Louvet 1011, p. 109.

cause the *commissarius* of the seneschal interrogated Roca Maura in the Friars Minor house in the French quarter of Montpellier.[48] Roca Maura was said to be an inhabitant, and in one instance a *burgensis*, of the French quarter. Theoretically, the Majorcan court could not procede against him, though one witness stated that *curiales* of Majorca conducted inquests in religious houses in Montpelliéret.[49] Inhabitants of Montpellier were, in principle, subject either to Majorcan or French jurisdiction, but some benefited from clerical exemption. In a few cases, witnesses were able to describe the procedures of both Majorcan and French courts, and those who conducted the inquest certainly presumed that witnesses were acquainted with both court systems. There was considerable fraternization across the whole legal establishment in Montpellier, whether specific members were in French or Majorcan employment.

Personal allegiance was used to determine jurisdiction when it was applicable, but in other cases the location of the crime determined the court jurisdiction. In a homicide involving foreigners, the killing of a Lombard by another Lombard, the criminal was remitted to the court of the bailiff by the judge of the seneschal, Stephanus de Cabanis, because the crime was committed in the Majorcan part of town, according to the testimony of one witness.[50]

A majority of witnesses had heard of a suspension of the procedure of interrogation in religious houses. Several were quite precise in their recall. The prohibition was attributed to the seneschal of Beaucaire, Hugo Quireti, within the last year. Most of those knowledgeable about the prohibition had heard of it in gossip at the court of Majorca. Bernardus de Caranta, *jurisperitus*, was the most precise commentator. He suggested that Hugo Quireti had indeed prohibited the use of the statute in the episcopal audience hall in a public instrument written by Petrus de Montibus, notary to Thomas de Sauteyrargues, *legum doctor*, lieutenant of the king of Majorca, in the presence of Caranta himself.[51] Sauteyrargues was said to have consented to this decree. Out of fear, Caranta as judge did not use the statute after the prohibition. Other witnesses were questioned about the subsequent use of the statute by the court of Majorca after the seneschal's prohibition. Most answered that interrogations in religious houses by *curiales* of the court of Majorca had stopped, though a few of the witnesses were unsure.

[48] AM Louvet 1011, pp. 59, 176, 184.
[49] AM Louvet 1011, p. 184. On Majorcan intrusion, see p. 59.
[50] AM Louvet 1011, p. 199.
[51] AM Louvet 1011, p. 68.

In addition to the content of specific responses to the questions of the survey, this lengthy dossier yields interesting information on the sorts of criminals who took refuge from prosecution in religious houses. Never was a case of debt invoked, though interestingly, the most detailed references to religious asylum in extant notarial registers involved massive debt.[52] Table 2 provides a breakdown of alleged criminals and crimes. Most frequently mentioned in the testimony was homicide, occasionally multiple murders. One witness, Andreas de Sancto Egidio, *advocatus*, ascribed the interrogatory procedure to crimes and delicts, both capital and non-capital.[53] The last witness called, Petrus Pagesii, notary of Montpellier, stated that the procedure was used in crimes and especially in homicide and wounding, but not in simple wrongdoing.[54] The infliction of wounds came second to homicide in mention. One also finds insults, forgery, rape, sodomy, and injurious exactions that one might assimilate with extortion. Though it could be argued that the crimes and the criminals discussed in this dossier are somewhat unusual because of the element of religious asylum, the types of crimes present in the testimonies reflect tendencies of criminality in the fourteenth century that Yvonne Lanhers found from evidence collected by the Parlement de Paris from 1319 to 1350.[55] Violence and insecurity surrounded the fourteenth-century individual, but it is difficult to determine whether more or less so than in other eras.

Criminals ran the social gamut (see table 2). All of the mentioned were men. In the passing reference to specific crimes and criminals in the testimony, many criminals were identified only by name, if that, not by profession or socioeconomic standing. Among those more fully labeled, the greatest preponderance of criminals came from the group of lesser artisans. A blacksmith, wood merchant, button maker, and four stonemasons—the single most violent group—were accused of homicide; a pursemaker was suspected of theft and wounds. Retailers and wholesalers, a silversmith, a furrier, and the son of a grain merchant were accused of homicide; the latter's victim finally died of inflicted wounds.[56] One agricultural worker, hiding in the Friars Minor house in Montpellier, allegedly hurled insults against the church of

[52] See Archives départementales de l'Hérault (hereafter AD), II E 95/375, Petrus de Pena, fols. 124ff, for an example.

[53] AM Louvet 1011, pp. 37–38.

[54] AM Louvet 1011, pp. 211–12.

[55] Yvonne Lanhers, "Crimes et criminels au XIVe siècle," *Revue historique* 240 (1968): 325–38.

[56] AM Louvet 1011, p. 189.

TABLE 2
Accused in Refuge in Religious Houses

Name When Given	Occupation	Interrogation Site	Crime	Victim	Sentence
———	marescallus	Valmagne	homicide	man	exile
Johannes Martini	polerius	Maguelone	homicide	man	absolution
Jacobus Spanieri	argenterius	Friars Minor	homicide	Gallician	dead before sentencing
Berengarius Arnaudi	pelliperius	Maguelone	homicide	son-in-law	absolution
Petrus Garnerii	lapicida	Maguelone	homicide	his barber	hanging but remanded to the *officialité* as a cleric in appeals
———	———	Friars Minor	homicide	man of curia	———
Raymundus de Conchis	burgensis family	Friars Minor	rapes	———	———
Guillelmus de Rippe Maura (Roca Maura)	lapicida of Montpelliéret	Friars Minor	homicide	Johannes Seguerii	———
———	scutifer of Alès	———	homicide	peysonnerius	hanging
Andreas de Mora	tabernarius of Montpelliéret	———	rape	———	absolution in French court
———	borsserius	———	theft and assault	———	composition
Guillelmus Pascalis	———	———	homicide	his brother Johannes, lapicida	absolution in parte regia
Johannes de Aniana	———	Friars Minor	assault	his brother	absolution
Bernardus Marcialis	candalerius cere	Maguelone	homicide	———	———
Petrus de Manso	notarius	Friars Minor	forgery	———	absolution
Canayre	cultor	Friars Minor	insults against St. Eulalie	———	———
Jacobus Vigani	cultor	Friars Preacher	assault	———	———
man	———	Friars Preacher	homicide	woman	———
[illegible]	[illegible]	[illegible]	———	———	death

	[illegible]	Carmelites	———	———	absolution
son of Guillelmus Fabri	lapicida	Carmelites	homicide	———	———
Johannes Martini alias Polerii	———	first at Friars Minor, then at Maguelone	homicide	moneyer	———
Bernardus Grimaudi	notarius (?)	Friars Preacher	———	———	———
Johannes and Guillelmus Avinionis	———	———	homicide	Franciscus Blegerii	condemned
Petrus Massona	fusterius	———	homicide	Guillelmus de Albia	condemned
Raymundus de Conchis	burgensis family	———	injurious exactions	———	———
Jacobus Vilas	———	———	homicide, assault, theft	Hugo Peysonnerii and others	———
Cobrat Tento Nico	familiaris and domesticus of the Master Hospitalier	St. Jean de Jérusalem	sodomy	———	———
Bisbe	———	Maguelone	assault	Causitus son-in-law	———
Guillelmus de Conchis	burgensis family	Friars Preacher	homicide	familius	———
Petrus de Fonte and Massana	fusterii	Maguelone	homicide	Albia	———
Guillelmus ?	burgensis of Montpelliéret	———	homicide	Satgerii lapicida	———
son of ordearius	———	Carmelites	assault, homicide	woman	———
son-in-law of Magister Martinus Bedelli	———	Friars Preacher	homicide	woman	———
Bernardus de Broha Johannes Alamanni	———	Friars Preacher	homicide	Stephanus de Asperis merchant and others	———
a Lombard	———	Friars Minor	homicide	a Lombard	drowning but remitted to court of bailiff
an accused	———	Friars Minor	———	———	———
an accused	———	Friars Minor	———	———	———

St. Eulalie in Montpellier.[57] The witness with the longest stated memory span, Petrus de Manso, French royal notary, had had to defend himself twenty years earlier against an accusation of forgery in the French court, brought, he said, falsely and against truth.[58] He was interrogated in the Friars Minor house and was present in court to hear his sentence of absolution. He had had no defender and did not know by whom he had been denounced. A servant of the Master Hospitalier was accused of sodomy and took refuge in the church of St. Jean de Jérusalem in the Majorcan quarter of the town.[59]

The elite Conchis family, who included among their numbers nobles and *burgenses*, could count two of those remembered by witnesses as criminals in search of asylum from prosecution in religious houses. The problem of homonyms for this family makes it impossible to identify specifically these figures, aside from linking them through the *Leitnamen* Raymundus and Guillelmus to the extended Conchis family in question.[60] One witness recalled that a Raymundus de Conchis was accused of injurious exactions and other enormous crimes; another witness remembered his crime as that of multiple rapes.[61] According to the latter testimony, the accused had taken refuge in the Friars Minor house in the French quarter of Montpellier and was interrogated there by *curiales* of the king of Majorca. A Guillelmus de Conchis, charged with homicide of one of his servants, had been interrogated in the Friars Preacher house some nine years before the current inquiry.[62] One foreigner, a Lombard, purportedly killed a sleeping compatriot. The alleged criminal who was in refuge in the Friars Minor house in the French quarter was turned over to the jurisdiction of the bailiff because the crime had been committed in the Majorcan part of Montpellier.[63] Another foreigner, a *scutifer* of Arles, had also been accused of homicide of a fisherman five years before.[64]

Among the victims of crime, many were unidentified in the testimonies (see table 2). On the other hand, foreigners, a Galician and a Lombard, figure among specifically mentioned victims.[65] Family vio-

[57] AM Louvet 1011, p. 117.

[58] AM Louvet 1011, pp. 100–101.

[59] AM Louvet 1011, p. 168.

[60] On the Conchis, see Jean Combes, "Quelques remarques sur les bourgeois de Montpellier au moyen âge," *Recueil*, fasc. 7: *Mélanges Pierre Tisset* (Montpellier, 1970), 103–5. See also George Beech, "Prosopography," in *Medieval Studies*, ed. James Powell (Syracuse, N.Y., 1976), 151–84.

[61] AM Louvet 1011, pp. 59, 167.

[62] AM Louvet 1011, p. 181.

[63] AM Louvet 1011, p. 199.

[64] AM Louvet 1011, pp. 65–67.

[65] AM Louvet 1011, pp. 43, 199.

lence accounted for three cases of homicide or wounds, two regarding brothers, one a son-in-law. Five women were noted as victims of homicide, death after wounding, and rape, though the witnesses alluded to other instances of crimes against women. A moneyer, a merchant, a barber, a servant, and the above fisherman were victims whose station was recorded.

Punishment was, in the words of some witnesses, in keeping with the severity of the crime. Imprisonment was never cited as a punishment. In this, the evidence of these testimonies is consistent with findings by Roger Grand and Annik Porteau-Bitker that imprisonment was used for detention, not punishment, in the Middle Ages.[66] Banishment and execution were the preferred severe sentences. In the inquest testimony, sentences reported after condemnation were varied: death in one form or another, such as hanging or drowning, mutilation, otherwise termed amputation (*membrorum abcizionem*), whipping, and civil punishment resulting in a money fine (see table 2). One witness, a former bailiff, Nicholaus Ymberti, stated that he condemned many on the advice of his judges. Absolution might be granted. In one accusation of rape, the accused was absolved, and in the other rape cases witnesses mentioned no punishment.[67] Porteau-Bitker found in her study that many rapes went unpunished.[68] Homicide defendants might also be absolved.[69] Some witnesses of the present inquest, such as Jacobus de Milhano, notary of Montpellier, recalled writing many instruments of condemnation to death or mutilation of absent accused.[70] In one case a silversmith of probable Spanish origin died before he could be sentenced, whether of foul play or not is unknown.[71] The blacksmith accused of homicide with a hammer was exiled from the town.[72]

Where did these defendants, rightly and wrongly accused, seek refuge from prosecution? They sought out most of the major religious orders' houses in Montpellier, but among the secular religious estab-

[66] Roger Grand, "La Prison et la notion d'emprisonnement dans l'ancien droit," *Revue historique de droit français et étranger* 19–20 (1940–41): 58–87; and Annick Porteau-Bitker, "L'Emprisonnement dans le droit laïque du moyen âge," *Revue historique de droit français et étranger* 66 (1968): 211–45, 389–428. On penal law in general, see the interesting new study by Jean-Marie Carbasse, *Introduction au droit pénal* (Paris, 1990).

[67] The sentence of absolution for rape was granted in the French royal court. See AM Louvet 1011, p. 82.

[68] A. Porteau-Bitker, "La Justice laïque et le viol au moyen âge," *Revue historique de droit français et étranger* 66 (1988): 491–526.

[69] For absolution for homicide, AM Louvet 1011, pp. 42, 91.

[70] AM Louvet 1011, p. 172.

[71] AM Louvet 1011, p. 43.

[72] AM Louvet 1011, p. 39.

lishments only the cathedral of Maguelone and the church of St. Jacques in the nearby town of Melgueil (see table 3). The Franciscan house in the French royal quarter and the Dominicans in the Majorcan quarter were the most commonly mentioned as choices of asylum seekers, but the Carmelites, the Augustinians, and the cathedral of Maguelone received numerous citations as well.[73] Refugees also sought a safe haven in the hospital of the St. Esprit, the former Templar house, the Montpellier branch of the Cistercian monastery of Valmagne, the house of St. Jean de Jérusalem, and the hospital of the Trinity. It may be that these establishments offered more nooks and cranies for hiding than the average parish church. Then, too, a parish church might have been too vulnerable a hiding place. It may also be that the religious orders were more sympathetic to requests for refuge than was the secular clergy of the local parish churches. Some witnesses were quite precise about the location in which the accused were questioned, reporting that interrogation took place wherever they were hiding: inside the church, in the sacristy, in specific chapels, before specific altars, in the *capitulum*, in outbuildings, in the cemetery, in the cloister, and in the garden. Once the court personnel had been alerted to a fugitive's presence in a religious establishment, they were tenacious in getting to their prey.

TABLE 3
RELIGIOUS HOUSES OF REFUGE

Religious House	Blanket References	Specific Cases
Hospital of St. Esprit	4	
Templar house	6	
Augustinian friary	9	
Friars Preacher friary	15	6
Friars Minor friary	12	11
Carmelite friary	14	3
Cathedral of Maguelone	11	7
Valmagne house	5	1
St. Jacques of Melgueil	1	
St. Jean de Jérusalem house	4	1
Hospital of the Trinity	1	
Total	82	29

[73] On the topography of medieval Montpellier, the best work remains that of Louise Guiraud, "Recherches topographiques sur Montpellier au moyen âge," *Mémoires de la société archéologique de Montpellier*, 2nd ser., 1 (1899): 89–335. For more recent, fruitful archeological research, see Jacques Peyron, "Montpellier médiéval, urbanisme et architecture," *Annales du Midi* 91 (1979): 255–72.

On the basis of the testimony of the witnesses and in spite of a consistent municipal policy detailing procedure for condemnation of the accused in refuge in religious houses, many suspects fled there to avoid prosecution. On a pragmatic level, the prevalence of asylum points to its assumed effectiveness in the minds of the accused, and in fact, such refuge must, with the complicity of the ecclesiastics of the particular religious house in which they were hiding, have been at times successful. For the innocent, the adoption of asylum may imply some real doubt about the ability of the accused to obtain a fair trial in the civil courts. The use of asylum also suggests a belief in the power of the bishop or other religious to protect an alleged wrongdoer. Canons who were present at interrogatory procedures at Maguelone or brothers who were present at the St. Jean de Jérusalem house may have reflected simple curiosity or a more concerted desire to monitor the correctness and fairness of the proceedings, to provide some security for the accused, or to challenge in silent, potentially antagonistic gestures, the invasion of the religious sanctuary by an alien secular power.[74] However, the testimonies never mentioned ecclesiastical resistence to the intrusion of royal judicial personnel of either France or Majorca into the haven of the religious house.[75] The present dossier was not designed to record ecclesiastical protests to secular criminal procedures. The recorded inquest raised no questions regarding the actions of church personnel, who might well have complained about the secular authorities' procedures of interrogation, which represented an affront to the church and to church power, an intrusion into the timeless sanctuary, an invasion of holy space. There is no room for equivocation that this was an invasion of the spiritual by the temporal power. By the same token, from the inquisitors' perspective, the truthfulness of testimony given in the interrogation may have been increased somewhat by the rather dramatic surroundings in which the accused were questioned about their alleged crimes. The blacksmith, for example, was questioned before the altar of the church of Valmagne; others were interrogated before altars such as that of St. Martin at the Friars Minor house. To prevaricate in such circumstances would have required nerves of steel.

Panic, fear of detainment, and a desire to escape detection were

[74] AM Louvet 1011, pp. 41, 168–69.

[75] I have not found any local record of the ecclesiastical position on religious asylum. Liberto Valls, archiviste adjoint of the Archives départementales de l'Hérault, who is currently inventorying the Série H, Clergé régulier, has found no mention either.

among the probable motives of asylum-seekers. Beyond these pragmatic considerations lie possible magical or spiritual powers that were imputed to holy space. Religious were endowed by some believers with the power to conger away evil threats. Viewed objectively, asylum was a shortsighted or temporary respite from prosecution; flight from town would have provided greater assurance of escape. But with flight came the unknown and a total uprooting from one's familiar surroundings and means of support. Whatever the individual refugee's real motives, asylum seems to have offered some protection and relief. Moreover, knowledgeable defendants may have chosen to invoke the procedures occasioned by asylum in order to gain time, to put their affairs in order, to marshall a defense, to develop an alibi, and to negotiate with witnesses in regard to their innocence or their alibi. In fact, the number of instances of absolution in the cases that were reviewed speaks for the efficacity of asylum tactics (see table 2).

Although it is unlikely that only the guilty hid from the authorities, the fact that some accused were absolved of their crimes is no guarantee that they were actually innocent of wrongdoing. The defenders surely had a role in the verdict of the litigation, just as defense attorneys today influence the outcome of particular cases. One must also recognize that denunciation and subsequent pursuit by the agents of either the king of France or the king of Majorca could have frightened the timid, guilty or innocent, into seeking asylum.

The sworn testimony of the legal establishment of Montpellier should have proven conclusive for the French king in determining practice regarding interrogation of accused in religious houses. Some of the witnesses had been present at actual interrogations in religious houses, some had conducted them, some had ordered them, and some had read about the procedures in written court instruments. The constant solicitation by those in charge of the inquest of specific names of participants, of criminals, of crimes, and of punishments reveals the painstaking nature of the inquest.[76] It would seem that the seneschal of Beaucaire had cavalierly overturned past procedure in prohibiting

[76] On the inquest and collective testimony, see Jean-François Poudret, "Réflexions sur la preuve de la coutume devant les juridictions royales françaises aux XIIIe et XIVe siècles, notamment le rôle de l'enquête par turbe," *Revue historique de droit français et étranger* 65 (1987): 71–86. Poudret noted that the inquest procedure was to determine facts and process. The inquest developed considerably during the reign of St. Louis but probably was first effectively used under Philip Augustus. See Baldwin, *The Government of Philip Augustus*, 248–56. In a recent paper at the conference "City and Spectacle in Medieval Europe," Center for Medieval Studies, University of Minnesota, winter 1991, André Gouron noted that southern French judges questioned witnesses according to the Roman law of evidence, *ut singuli*, not collectively, according to the *per turbam* practices.

such interrogations; and though these orders were obeyed out of fear by members of the legal establishment in Montpellier, French royal officials appeared more faint-hearted than the consular personnel in challenging the sanctity of asylum. In fact, the forty to fifty years preceding 1332, the span of witnesses' recall in their testimonies, and the decades immediately following the consular survey may have been a period of transition in juridical procedure. That municipal procedures were evolving toward greater severity against those in refuge in religious houses is suggested in a series of documents surviving from the year 1353.[77] Rapid justice at the hands of officials of the bailiff's court went astray in the case of six foreigners suspected of wounding and leaving for dead a *legum doctor*, Guillelmus Augerii. These foreigners had been lodging in a religious house and took refuge in a church after their misdeed. They were extracted forcibly by municipal officials from the church where they were hiding and then brought before the court of the bailiff where they confessed to the crime. Four of them were condemned to death and executed. On the gallows they revealed several other crimes and homicides which they had committed. One defendant, a priest, was remanded to the church court and condemned to perpetual imprisonment.

However, when the victim Augerii did not die of his wounds, there was popular protest about the death sentences and subsequent executions. The consuls requested that King John order an investigation. Relatives of the executed argued that municipal authorities had seized the personal property of the foreigners and had condemned them to die unjustly, given the fact that the victim of the crime did not expire. This case suggests that municipal procedure in the bailiff's court had evolved from simple interrogation of accused in religious houses and future sentencing or absolution, to a bold and summary seizure of the defendants, their condemnation, and execution. It may be that the chaos of the Black Death, which claimed the majority of Montpellier's population in 1348, encouraged harsher criminal law procedure.[78] By the same token, the restrictions on ecclesiastical prerogatives in justice are in evidence.

By the first third of the fourteenth century, therefore, lay administration was winning out against the authority of the church and against the concept of religious asylum in Montpellier. The practices of Mont-

[77] AM Louvet, documents 377–86.

[78] On the Black Death at Montpellier, see my article, "Changes in Testamentary Practice at Montpellier on the Eve of the Black Death," *Church History* 47 (1978): 253–69.

pellier/Majorcan consular justice seem to have gone beyond the French royal prerogatives of the 1205 accords and the Assembly of Vincennes in challenging the immunity of religious asylum. In contrast to the seneschal of Beaucaire's tactic of suspending the interrogatory procedure, at least one witness said that the Majorcan *curiales* pursued their investigations not only in religious houses of their own quarter but of the French quarter as well.[79] The municipal regime showed little hesitation in asserting the rights of lay justice over religious asylum. Here the influence of the Roman law of Justinian may, in fact, be felt.[80] The late Middle Ages witnessed only the beginning of a mounting challenge to religious asylum that would culminate in future centuries.[81]

APPENDIX

The following lists are reconstructed from the scattered references to legal personnel of Montpellier. It was not always clear from the testimonies whether a particular individual was in the employ of the king of France or of the king of Majorca. Some may have been both during their careers. Some other officials—several rectors, *commissarii,* and so on—were too few in number to list separately.

Defenders of Alleged Criminals

Johannes Andree**
Petrus Bata
Johannes Clareti**
Henricus de Colleyo Gallicus
Bertrandus de Conilheriis
Berengarius de Fabrica*
Petrus Fornerii**
Firminus Francisci
Guinetus
Stephanus de Luenhis
Petrus Massal
Berengarius Mayfredi (Matfredi)
Bernardus Menatoris
Bertrandus Menatoris
Johannes Menatoris
Petrus de Montanhola
Guillelmus de Mora**
Stephanus Rosselli
Andreas de Sancto Egidio**
Petrus de Taurinhano**
Bernardus Tinturerii
Berengarius de Turre

*Called himself *advocatus* and *consiliarius* not *defensor* in his testimony with regard to an accused murderer
**Witnesses of the inquest

[79] AM Louvet 1011, p. 59.

[80] Pierre Timbal, *Le Droit d'asile,* 261, sees Roman law as the starting point for secular opposition to religious asylum. On differences and similarities between the legal systems of northern and southern France, see my collaborative article with John Bell Henneman, "Law, French: In South," *Dictionary of the Middle Ages* 7 (1986): 461–68. The findings in this article suggest that further work is necessary to address the impact of Roman law on the position of medieval lay jurisdictions regarding religious asylum.

[81] Pierre Timbal, *Le Droit d'asile,* 261–454; and L. R. Misserey, "L'Asile en Occident," especially "Cas exceptés."

APPENDIX *continued*

Notarii and Scriptores*	
Petrus Cardinalis	Jacobus de Milhano**
Johannes Clareti**	Petrus de Montibus
Stephanus Fabri	Petrus Pagesii**
Petrus Fornerii**	Guillelmus de Podio**
Raymundus Fornerii	Bernardus Refferre
Antonius Galocherii (Gualuche)	Raymundus Rogeriii
Bernardus Garnerii**	Guillelmus Valserie
Bernardus Holanie	Franciscus Viaderii**
Bonetus Jaca	Johannes de Vineis
Firminus Madroni	Stephanus Vitalis**

*Most had Majorcan authorization, some had French, some few had both (Jacobus de Milhano)
**Witnesses of the inquest

Bailiffs	
Pontius Alamandini, jr.	Nicholaus Imberti
Pontius Alamandini, sr.	Pontius Lamberti
Petrus Aymerici de Paleata	Raymundus Lamberti
Petrus Benedicti	Raymundus de Latis
Colinus Bertrandi**	Johannes Marci
Petrus Boniamici	Johannes de Montearnaudo
Pontius Boniamici	Johannes Mora
Raymundus Boniamici	Johannes Palmerii
Petrus Calvelli	Stephanus Pluerii
Radulphus de Carssilhaco (Cassilhaco)	Guillelmus de Putheo, jr.
Sulplycus de Carssillhaco	Johannes de Ripa Alta
Raymundus de Conchis	Bernardus Roardi
Bertholomeus Don	Stephanus Sabbaterii
Bertrandus Genesii	Petrus Seguini
Guiraudus Genesii	Franciscus Ymberti
Geraudus Givesii	Hugo Ymberti
Salvator Guillelmi	Huguetus Ymberti
Pontius de Homelhacio	Nicholaus Ymberti**
Franciscus Imberti	

**Witnesses of the inquest

Judges	
Guillelmus Aymerici, *judex regius**	Berengarius de Fabrica, *vice judex, judex ordinarius***
Bernardus Baudini, *judex*	Johannes de Montearnaudo, *judex*
Johannes Bernardi, *judex regius**	Johannes Ricardi, *judex*
Stephanus de Cabanis, *judex* of seneschal*	Bernardus Roardi, *judex*
Raymundus de Capite Vilario, *judex***	Stephanus Sabbaterii, *judex*
Bernardus de Caranta, *vice judex, judex, advocatus, procurator* of bailiff's court**	Petrus de Taurinhano, *judex, assessor, vice judex* of bailiff's court**

**Witnesses of the inquest
*Attached to French court

APPENDIX *continued*

Others

Bernardus Arnaudi, vice bailiff
Stephanus de Arssones, jurisperitus of Nîmes, comissarius
Bernardus de Cadellis, legum doctor, comissarius
Johannes Coteli, vicarius
Guillelmus de Curia, domicellus, lieutenant of rector
Thomas de Santaranicis, legum doctor, lieutenant of king of Majorca
Arnaudus de Salivo, miles, lieutenant of rector
Bertrandus Turreta, rector regius

Commercial fraud in the middle ages: the case of the dissembling pepperer

Medieval business ethics is a topic of recent interest among historians. This study examines a case of commercial fraud, the falsification of saffron, in the southern French town of Montpellier in the mid-fourteenth century. Impure saffron was seized by urban inspectors at the workshop of a pepperer, Johannes Andree. Upon the testimony of witnesses, the impurity of the saffron was corroborated, and municipal justice decreed that it be publicly burned. Johannes Andree chose to contest this verdict, claiming exemption from judgment upon the grounds that he was a royal moneyer. A conflict of jurisdiction ensued, with the rector of Montpelliéret supporting Andree against the municipal consuls and the town bailiff.

This study focuses on the documentary evidence of the law suit: the nature of the accusation against Andree, the legitimacy of his defence, the precedents for consular supervision of the pepperers' trade and the importance of quality control over merchandise, and the background of the jurisdictional dispute between the consuls and the rector. Finally, the legal terminology of this case of commercial fraud is considered in the context of legal theory and medieval jurisprudence. From this analysis of municipal justice in practice, standards of business ethics, consumer protection and quality control emerge as important concerns in a trading centre such as Montpellier.

Historians have only recently begun to explore the full range of legal offence in the middle ages. Violent crime has been the most commonly studied aspect of medieval criminality; it was punished habitually by compensation or vendetta, especially in the early middle ages, more rarely with physical retribution or through incarceration.[1] Less frequently scrutinized by historians until lately have been the subtler crime involving a violation of medieval business ethics. The diversity of medieval legal opinion is revealed in such an investigation. Medieval attitudes towards illegality often varied according to the system considered. Provisions of canon law, civil law, customary law and royal legislation failed to coincide on all legal points. Municipal statutes established divergent norms. Business went its own pragmatic way. Merchants would turn pirate in propitious circumstances, mintmasters might embezzle, and respectable businessmen could practice usury (Cheyette 1970; Mate 1969; Lane 1964; Reyerson 1980). Yet, mutual faith and trust underlay business operations in the middle ages. Commenting on medieval leaders of commerce, industry and finance, R. S. Lopez said, "Unlimited liability and commercial honesty were the pillars upon which rested the credit enjoyed by the Italian merchant companies" (Lopez 1948:66–7). Municipal governments and trade organizations took it upon themselves to police weights and measures and to assure the quality of merchandise. They acted to protect consumers from fraud, and when an abuse was detected, there were consequences for the offender.

A law suit over commercial fraud in the Languedocian town of Montpellier in the mid-fourteenth century provides a context in which to examine medieval business ethics. Preserved in the Municipal Archives of Montpellier are extensive records of litigation of the mid-1350s in which a local pepperer, Johannes Andree, was accused of selling adulterated, that is, impure saffron. The first information extant reveals legal proceedings already in progress on 10 June 1355.[2] For the next two and a half years, until the end of March 1358, there remain two notebooks of legal procedures, one of which contains fifty folios of the testimony of witnesses, and further documentation including letters from King John of France to the seneschal of Beaucaire, *vidimi* of the seneschal, *arrêts* of the *Parlement* of Paris, and finally, records of a commission from the *Parlement* of Paris and of an accord between Johannes Andree and the consuls of Montpellier in connection with this case.[3] In spite of the accord, the suit dragged on, leaving one later trace in the local documents: an *arrêt* of the *Parlement* of Paris of 15 February 1364 announced that an appeal by the consuls, guardians of mercery, and the bailiff of Montpellier against the rector of Montpelliéret would be heard at the next *parlement* of the *sénéchaussée* of Beaucaire.[4] The results of this appeal have not been uncovered, but the earlier documents permit the exploration of legal practice regarding commercial fraud.

On the basis of the evidence assembled, the nature of the accusation against Johannes Andree, the procedure of prosecution, the tactics of the defence, and the compromise between Andree and the consuls will be examined in turn. Then, an analysis of the levels of conflict in this case will reveal the complex network of jurisdiction in Montpellier. Finally, Andree's crime will be considered in the context of medieval jurisprudence.

The Andree case was heard in two courts of law in Montpellier, the *curia ordinaria* of the French rector, administrative head of the *pars antiqua* of Montpellier, that is to say Montpelliéret, the quarter of the town belonging originally to the bishop of Maguelone which was purchased by Philip the Fair in 1293, and the *curia ordinaria* of the bailiff of the seigneurial quarter of Montpellier, governed by twelve municipal consuls (Lecoy de la Marche 1892a:311ff; Germain 1851b). The consuls' quarter had been purchased in 1349 from James III of Majorca by Philip of Valois and was technically under the supervision of another royal official, the governor (Thomas 1928–9). The bailiff's court was, officially, first a seigneurial and then a royal court, but, in practice, it operated as the consuls' court (Carbasse 1974; Chabaneau and Germain 1884–6:400–7; Lewis 1947). The organization and personnel of these courts were well developed by the mid-fourteenth century (Rogozinski 1967, 1969, 1972; Strayer 1970). The rector and the bailiff were assisted by a lieutenant and a vice-bailiff, respectively, and by judges, notaries and sergeants. At times, *procuratores* appeared in court to represent plaintiffs, defendants, and the authorities of justice.[5] It was in these courts with this personnel that the Andree case would be heard.

The circumstances surrounding the discovery of adulterated saffron at the workshop of Johannes Andree were related on several occasions during the lengthy proceedings.[6] Two guardians (*custodes*) of the pepperers' trade made inspections in their function as deputized, sworn representatives of the consuls, charged with the responsibility of determining whether any falsification, wrong doing or adulteration was being practised in their trade. In what seems to have been a routine investigation at Andree's shop, the guardians came upon impure saffron which they confiscated and transported to the consular house, according to customary procedure.[7] The consuls, declaring the saffron adulterated, turned it over to the bailiff in order that he might administer justice. Inquiring into the affair, the bailiff received the testimony of numerous witnesses (eight in the first instance, sixteen in the final investigation) that the saffron was indeed adulterated.[8] He then ordered that the saffron be publicly burned, according to custom, as a deterrent to future offenders.

The saffron in question amounted to about twelve pounds. It was found in two linen sacks, one white, one black.[9] The witnesses included pepperers, apothecaries, weighers and merchants from Montpellier and foreigners from Spanish lands such as Tarrega and Majorca. One testimony is printed in the Appendix. With varying terminology but with general agreement, all of the witnesses asserted that the saffron was adulterated to some degree. Some suggested that one sack was more corrupt than the other, although their testimonies were inconsistent on this score.[10] One possible motive for the adulteration was offered: incorporation of foreign elements might make the merchandise weigh more.[11] When asked to identify the foreign substance which had been added to the saffron, most witnesses stated that they were unfamiliar with the material but that it was not saffron. A few suggested that a sweet or honeyed substance had been added, making the end product easily distinguishable from saffron, which was bitter in taste. Other suggestions included a sweet liquor, a powder, and a heavy and sharp matter such as oats.[12]

Andree's offence was public knowledge in Montpellier. The accusations against him were phrased in unambiguous terms.[13] He was described as a son of inequity and evil, spurred on by a diabolical spirit. He was indicted with *fraus* and *dolus*. It was further alleged that, since he had sold adulterated saffron as if it had been good, legal and sufficient, he had committed a crime of falsification which was viewed as a violation of the public good. Andree's acts were termed *maleficia et delicta*. Should they go unpublished, they would encourage bad practices.

Andree's reactions to these accusations can be reconstructed.[14] He admitted that the confiscated saffron contained in the two sacks carrying his seal and mark was indeed his. He stated that he had purchased four of the twelve pounds from a certain Johannes de Sancto Guillermo, and of these, he had retailed about two pounds. The remaining saffron he had bought from other men whose names he did not remember. Andree affirmed that the saffron was good and sufficient when it was taken from his workshop and home. Several times in the course of the inquiry, Andree stated that he sold good saffron, denying any adulteration. He did admit that he had wet down the saffron with water. Although some of Andree's testimony was taken under interrogation during protective custody, there was no indication that he was coerced or tortured.[15]

Andree's defence did not stop at the level of denial of the charges against him. In records of the first appeal by the consuls, the bailiff, and the guardians of the pepperers' trade on 10 June 1355 against a ruling by the rector, it became clear that Andree had asserted that he was a moneyer and had requested the masters of the royal mint to prohibit the bailiff and other royal officials from intervening in any way regarding the said saffron.[16] Andree had alleged that since he was a moneyer, he had no other judges than the aforesaid mint-masters. Although the mint-masters did not welcome Andree's demand, they commissioned a royal lawyer to inform himself about the saffron and, if he found it to be adulterated, to remit it to the bailiff for judgment. Having taken testimony from fifteen trustworthy witnesses that the saffron was false and adulterated, the lawyer returned the saffron to the bailiff so that justice could be executed.

In spite of this finding, the rector intervened in the proceedings at this stage to order that the guardians of the pepperers' trade return the saffron to Andree; the rector ruled that the guardians' responsibilities were terminated. This action on the rector's part provoked protests and then a formal appeal to the king from the consuls.[17] They took issue with Andree's attempt to pass himself off as a royal moneyer, offering a series of arguments to the contrary. The consuls alleged that, if Andree had been received as a moneyer, it was after 1351. They avowed, in fact, that he publicly held the office and workshop of a pepperer. According to the consuls, it was through favour and money that Andree sought to defraud the king and royal justice by withdrawing from the collectivity of the realm and from ordinary jurisdiction. Andree had had himself received as a moneyer, in the consuls' view, only that his fraud go unpunished. They observed that the mint-masters themselves had stated to the court that they were not empowered to defend moneyers received after 1350. The consuls further maintained that it could not be accepted that Andree was a moneyer, endowed with the privileges of moneyers. Moreover, since he kept a workshop as a pepperer, he could not legally decline inspection by the guardians of the trade. The consuls, bailiff and guardians went so far as to assert that Andree was a suspect individual, notorious for similar crimes, as were his father and brother who had been publicly condemned and punished for falsification and adulteration of saffron and other merchandise. No details of these earlier condemnations were provided. The consuls' appeal further related that Montpellier had many workshops of *averum et specierum* (*avoirdu-poids* and spices). Those reprobate individuals who adulterated, falsified and dishonoured the trade of pepperer were thrown out. The court of the bailiff customarily seized and burned false merchandise. To impede this process was to pervert the good mores and customs of the town. Finally, the consuls, bailiff and guardians affirmed that they were in no way subordinate to the rector. They chose to lodge their appeal with the king of France and his court.

The rector answered the complaints of the appellants point by point, recognizing the privileges of moneyers and asserting his position as the lieutenant, commissioner and conservator of those privileges.[18] In the rector's view, Andree had requested an appropriate remedy. The rector argued that the bailiff was not the competent judge in this case. He reiterated his demand for the restoration of the saffron to Andree. He further declared that it was incorrect to state that he, the rector, had failed to uphold the mores of the patria and to punish the guilty. It was not his intention to rule against justice but rather to proceed on account of contumacy and disobedience. The rector viewed his jurisdiction as superior to that of the officials of the newer part of Montpellier, arguing that the bailiff and the governor had no recourse to appeal, unless on the grounds of deficient justice. Since, in his view, this was not the case, he refused to consent to the appeal. He fined the consuls, bailiff and guardians in the event that the saffron were not returned.[19]

The Andree case reached at least an interim resolution in 1357 as a result of a compromise between the defendant and the consuls. Andree submitted himself to the jurisdiction of the consuls, renouncing the privileges of moneyer.[20] What prompted his change of heart is unknown. Again, there was no indication that he was coerced into submission, although he was held in protective custody during the testimony of witnesses.[21] It seems more likely that Andree finally recognized the futility of his strategy of defence and agreed to admit some level of guilt. After the testimonies, he was released upon sufficient guarantees to await his sentence. His wife Mirabelle acted as his *fidejutrix*, principal defendant, debtor and *paccatrix*, making a series of renunciations of legal protection stemming from her status as a woman.[22] Finally, on 22 March 1358 (n.s.) Andree was found guilty and deprived in perpetuity of his trade of pepperer. He was prohibited from selling publicly or secretly in Montpellier, and within its jurisdiction, saffron, ginger, pepper, cloves, sugar or any subtle substance pertaining to the pepperers' trade.[23] Already in July 1357, *arrêts* of the *Parlement* of Paris had ordered the bailiff to carry out the forthcoming sentence.[24] A further order of the *Parlement* of Paris to the seneschal of Beaucaire in August 1357 prohibited the rector from interfering with the above accord.[25]

Such was the sequence of events in the Andree case. A closer examination of the levels of conflict underlying this affair is merited: first, the justification for consular intervention in a matter of fraud; then, the problems of professional designation and privilege; finally, the quarrel over jurisdiction within Montpellier.

Consular governments in the south of France, at Montpellier, Toulouse and other towns, frequently took a direct role in the supervision of urban trades, even when these were organized into professional corporations (Gouron 1958:177ff.). The claim of the consuls of Montpellier to supervise, through guardians, the quality of merchandise in general, and of spices in particular, was well established by 1355. A document of 4 October 1326 described the formal installation by the consuls of three pepperers and an apothecary as *custodes mercerium et averum*.[26] The guardians took an oath in Occitan to guard against fraud and adulteration and to report any violations to the consuls. The oath was termed in the text an accustomed one, suggesting that the procedure was in existence earlier. It may have dated from the mid-thirteenth century when trade organization became common (Gouron 1958:386–8; Pégat and others 1840:98–100).

Not only were there precedents for trade supervision but also for the confiscation of adulterated saffron. On 11 September 1326 inspection by the same guardians, clearly reinstituted in October, had revealed five skins of impure saffron in the possession of several Catalan merchants.[27] Examination by twenty pepperers and merchants of Montpellier and men of Marseille brought another ten skins of adulterated saffron to light.[28] Witnesses were called upon to attest to the falsification. While the punishment meted out to the Catalans was not recorded, consular prerogative and procedure of inspection were demonstrated clearly in these acts.

Consular preoccupation with the quality of merchandise in a town such as Montpellier was amply justified. Located in proximity to the Mediterranean in lower Languedoc, Montpellier served as an entrepôt for imported goods, silks, spices, and pharmaceutical products of Mediterranean origin (Germain 1861a and b; Thomas 1936; Reyerson 1974a and b). International trade was vital to the urban economy. Saffron of Catalonian provenance had become by the late thirteenth century an important item of commerce transshipped through Montpellier to northern markets in Champagne; by the late 1330s and 1340s, Parisian markets were frequent destinations of saffron exports from Montpellier (Reyerson 1974b:261–7). Saffron was a precious and expensive product, the quality of which reflected upon business activities in Montpellier. The town had a reputation to maintain, not only in the marketing of spices, but in their usage in such delicacies as spiced wine (Dion 1959:316ff.). The pepperers of Montpellier were among the most prestigious urban professions, sharing in the lottery for the top position in the consular hierarchy, and participating in the front ranks of municipal parade ceremony (Gouron 1958:56ff., 286). High standards in the pepperers' trade were a necessity for the preservation of urban economic renown.

The issues of professional designation and privilege raised by Andree's defence against consular prerogatives deserve investigation. The mid-fourteenth century was a period when there was still flexibility of professional designation in Montpellier. In the notarial acts of the time, individuals might be termed merchants in one instance, changers, apothecaries or pepperers in another (Gouron 1958:179, 283). The prestigious pepperers (*pebriers sobeirans*) did not form an official corporation; it was only in 1366 that they founded a charitable organization (*confrèrie*) (Gouron 1958:288). Furthermore, it was possible to exercise two professions or to change professions in Montpellier (Gouron 1958:282–3). Andree's defence encountered no difficulties on the grounds of dual professional designation.

The special privileges of jurisdiction which Andree claimed as a moneyer were first instituted by a charter of Philip Augustus, dated 26 November 1211 (Germain 1850–4:164). These privileges involved an exemption from ordinary jurisdiction in all instances except those of homicide, rape and arson. In all other cases, royal moneyers were to be judged by the provosts or masters of the mint and by no one else (Germain 1850–4: 166–72). The privileged status of moneyers persisted into the mid-fourteenth century. However, King John had ruled in 1350 that municipal tax exemptions, were valid only if the moneyers were practising their profession (Henneman 1971:311). The appeal document of 1355 suggested a limitation of juridical exemptions for moneyers received into the profession after 1350.[29] The era was one of some ambiguity over moneyers' privileges, an unpropitious moment for Andree to assert his membership as a means of defence against the accusation of saffron fraud. The evidence of the case provides no proof beyond his allegations and the reception given them by the mint-master and the rector that he had ever enjoyed official acceptance as a moneyer, or that he had ever practised the trade.

Rivalries of jurisdiction within Montpellier further complicated the Andree case. After the French acquisition of the seigneurial quarter of Montpellier in 1349, this section and the episcopal quarter of Montpelliéret, acquired in 1293, remained separate jurisdictions. After 1349, the consuls and the bishop of Maguelone, no longer in charge of the episcopal quarter, complained repeatedly to the king that the rector, the royal representative in Montpelliéret, was protecting deliquents from prosecution and permitting tax exemptions to some bourgeois. Royal decisions went initially in the consuls' favour (Combes 1970:111ff.). Later, in 1360, the regent Charles reaffirmed all the prerogatives of the rector. Before 1349, the rector had been a champion of royal prerogative. However, since that date, the consuls had also become direct French subjects. To reassert his preeminence in the town, the rector had established a pattern of protecting inhabitants from consular jurisdiction. The rector's actions in the Andree case were consistent with his general stance. The king had to intervene on several occasions to prevent the rector from interfering with the appeal process instituted by the consuls, and to maintain the final agreement between the consuls and Andree.[30]

One last issue, the nature of Andree's crime, merits consideration in the context of medieval jurisprudence. It would seem that the consuls of Montpellier had discovered by the fourteenth century the legal principle of *Fraus omnia corrumpit* which would later find its place in the French *Code civil* (Vidal 1957). Andree was accused of all manner of offence: *fraus*, *dolus*, *crimen*, *delicta* and *maleficia*. In the south of France, the use of Roman law terminology of a related nature can be dated to the twelfth century when formulae such as *sine dolo* and *sine ulla fraude* began to appear (Meynial 1929:534). Medieval jurists of the thirteenth and fourteenth centuries refined the classifications of *fraus* and *dolus*, introducing distinctions between them (Ourliac and de Malafosse 1969:131–41). Bartolus termed *dolus* the genus and *fraus* the species (Fransen 1946:59; Coing 1939). It was asserted that *dolus* was committed through acts and words, while *fraus* involved only acts (Fransen 1946:59). Bad faith and deception underlay these crimes (Vidal 1957:2). The theory of fraud, of Romanist not canon law origin, gave rise to various remedies of justice: an action *de dolo*; an exception; and a remedy of restitution (Meynial 1929:545; Berger 1953).

The documents of the Andree case, representative of juridical practice rather than of theory, reveal no attempt to distinguish between *fraus* and *dolus* which were employed synonymously with other terms to characterize the offence.[31] Andree's crime was viewed by the consuls, bailiff and guardians, and their legal personnel as one of deception, of the bad intention of cheating saffron clients through the sale of corrupt merchandise, and of an offence against the public good. The consistency of evaluations by all witnesses concerning the impurity of Andree's saffron leaves little doubt about the factual level of the accusation. The remaining evidence does not permit inquiry into the possibility of falsification of the saffron unbeknown to Andree in his shop or after seizure by the guardians. However, Andree's wily defence and ultimate submission to the consuls imply some admission of guilt. The punishment handed down, that of deprivation of the practice of the pepperer's trade, was commensurate with the offence of fraud.

This example of commercial fraud prosecution illustrates the complexity of medieval justice in a case involving business ethics. Rival authorities vied for jurisdiction. Privileges of legal immunity clouded the issues. The legal terminology of the case was imprecise on a theoretical level but explicit in its reflection of the severity of the crime of commercial fraud for the inhabitants of Montpellier. The time invested in the prosecution of the crime, and the expense of the law suit for the consuls, demonstrate the importance which they assigned to the protection of consumers.[32]

Appendix: Sample testimony against Johannes Andree (Louvet no. 1765, fos. 19v–21r)

Jacobus Pauli piperarius Montispessulani testis receptus, juratus et examinatus super contentis in dictis titulis perventionis predicte contra dictum delatum sive perventum formatis, omnibus et singulis sibi lectis et in linga [*sic*] Romana expositis. Dixit interrogatus se recordari aliquid super aliquibus de contentis in dictis titulis deposuisse et depositionem suam scriptam fuisse per notarium huius cause qui tunc erat; quam depositionem ante omnia peciit sibi legi et in lingua Romana exponi ne variare valeat suo dicto seu depositioni. Cum memoria hominis labilis existat quod quidem dictum seu depositio fuit eidem testi loquenti lecta et in lingua Romana exposita cuius dicti sive depositionis tenor sequitur et est talis.

Jacobus Pauli piperarius Montispessulani testis, receptus per modum secrete informationis, juratus ad Sancta Dei Quatuor Evvangelia per ipsum corporaliter tacta, et diligenter interrogatus super predictis denunciatis dixit se hoc scire et verum esse videlicet quod safranum sive croceum predictum utriusque saculi sibi hostensum et per ipsum loquentem inspectum non est mercabile. Ymo est, ut dixit, falsum et incameratum pro eo, ut dixit, quia dictum saffranum est honeratum seu mixtum cum alia materia que non est de substancia safrani. Ymo est aliena. Cuius materie speciam ipse loquens non potest aliquid cognoscere propter quam mixtionem dictum safranum est incamaratum quia posita est ibi dicta materia, judicio ipsius loquentis, ad finem ut plus dictum croceum cum dicta materia ponderet.

Qua quidem depositione eidem testi loquenti lecta et in lingua Romana exposita. Dixit ipse testis loquens dictam depositionem esse suam et ita aliquid deposuisse prout in ipsa depositione continetur. Qui quidem depositioni tanquam verati et veritatem in se continenti stare et perseverare vult et intendit nichil addito, nichilque remoto.

Deinde fuit ipse testis loquens interrogatus post dictam eius depositionem si amore, timore, gratia, odio vel favore doctus, instructuctus, conductus aut aliquo per aliquem subornatus deposuit, dixit quod non.

Interrogatus si fuit aliquid sibi datum, quitatum, promissum aut remissum ut ita deponeret, dixit quod non.

Interrogatus quam partem mallet obtinere, an partem curie pro qua fuit receptus, an partem contra quam producitur, dixit quod de jure habente in eadem.

Interrogatus si habuit cum aliquo colloquium seu tractatum ut uno et eodem modo deponerent, dixit quod non.

Interrogatus si spectat habere comodum si curia in causa presenti ipsum producentem obtineat aut incomodum si subcumbat, dixit quod non.

Super aliis idem testis loquens interrogatus dixit deposita supra per eundem esse vera prout ea deposuit et aliquid nichil scire nisi prout supra, depositum extitit per eundem.

Notes

1 This study was first presented at the Fifteenth International Congress on Medieval Studies, Western Michigan University, Kalamazoo, Michigan, May 1980. Research was supported by the Graduate School of the University of Minnesota in a Summer Research Fellowship. Thanks are due to the Archives Municipales of Montpellier for assistance in assembling the primary sources, and to the Interlibrary Loan Division of Wilson Library, University of Minnesota, for aid in the consultation of some secondary studies.

2 Louvet no. 1750. The sixteenth-century inventory numbers of Louvet retained by Berthelé in his inventory will be used henceforth in reference to further documents of the *Grand Chartrier* of the Archives Municipales at Montpellier (Berthelé 1895).

Louvet nos. 1751–65 and 2584.

Louvet no. 1766.

For examples, see Louvet nos. 1750 and 1765.

Louvet no. 1750, 10 June 1355, p. 3 and Louvet no. 1765, f.2r, article v. Louvet no. 1765, spanning the period 7 August 1357–22 March 1358, is a fifty-folio dossier which can be cited with recto and verso folio pages. Louvet no. 1750 is a collection of documents of twenty pages without folio designation; specific legal proceedings in the latter will be given by date and page.

7 Louvet no. 1750, 10 June 1355, p. 4: dictus baiulus per suam diffinitivam sentenciam cognovit et finaliter pronunciavit dictum saffranum fore publice conburendum.

8 Witnesses' depositions are recorded in Louvet no. 1765, fos. 13v–39r.

9 See, for example, Louvet no. 1765, fos. 34v–35r: Michael Folqueti, mercator de Terrega se vidisse, palpasse et diligenter inspexisse saffranum existens in duobus saquis lineis quorum unus saqus est aliquantulum albus et alter est aliquantulum niger.

10 Compare the testimony of Folqueti, Louvet no. 1765, fos. 34v–35r, who affirmed that the saffron in the black sack was heavier than that in the other, with the testimony of Guillermus Bedocii, pepperer of Montpellier, Louvet no. 1765, fos. 13v–15r, who did not distinguish between the two sacks.

11 Louvet no. 1765, fos. 18r–19v. Bernardus Vincentii, pepperer of Montpellier, gave this testimony: dixit viso et inspecto dicto safrano seu croceo utriusque saculi; quod in dicto safrano est alia materia a substancia dicti safrani; in dicto safrano mixta que materia est posita seu mixta in dicto safrano ad finem ut plus ponderet propter quam materiam mixtam dictum croceum sive safranum est falsum et incamaratum.

12 Merchant manuals carried descriptions of merchandise to assist in quality decisions. According to a fifteenth-century manual, "Saffron ought to be new, free of small seeds, and dry" (Lopez and Raymond 1955:352).

13 Louvet no. 1765, f. 1v–3r.

14 Louvet no. 1765, f. 4r–4v.

15 R. Grand (1940:59) stated that there were three juridical aspects of imprisonment: as a preventive measure; for coercion; or for punishment. Andree was in protective custody for the purposes of the investigation of 1357. It does not seem that he was in custody in 1355.

16 Louvet no. 1750, 10 June 1355, p. 4: asseret se esse monetarius. . . .

17 The points of this appeal were articulated, in Louvet no. 1750, 15 June 1355, pp. 6ff., before the rector, his lieutenant, Laurentius Sazi, *jurisperitus* and Pontius de Boniaco, royal cleric and judge of the *curia ordinaria* of the *pars antiqua*.

18 Louvet no. 1750, 15 June 1355, pp. 11ff.

[19] The details regarding these fines were recorded in royal letters. See Louvet nos. 1751, 1752, 1753 and 1755. The consuls were fined 2500 marks, the bayle 200 and the guardians 100 marks.

[20] Louvet no. 1761, 3 July 1357.

[21] Louvet no. 1765. See note 8 above. While it cannot be satisfactorily answered, the questions of collusion on the part of the witnesses and of framing of Andree on the part of the guardians or the consuls must be raised. Andree argued that the saffron was not adulterated when it left his home. However, all of the witnesses invoked in the surviving evidence of the case testified to the impurity of the spice.

[22] Louvet no. 1765, fos. 44r–45v.

[23] Louvet no. 1765, f. 49r.

[24] Louvet nos. 1762 and 1763.

[25] Louvet no. 1764.

[26] Louvet no. 272. This document was published by Germain (1861a:422–4, p. j. xcv). The guardians in this instance were designated not by their trade but by the products or merchandise involved in their commerce (Gouron 1958:178–9). Handlers of such merchandise formed part of the mercantile elite of international trade in Montpellier.

[27] Louvet no. 1748, edited by Germain (1861a: 474–7) and translated by Lopez and Raymond (1955: 270–1).

[28] Louvet no. 1749.

[29] Louvet no. 1750, 15 June 1355, p. 9.

[30] Louvet no. 1756, letter of King John of 6 July 1356; Louvet no. 1758, letter of 14 July 1356; and Louvet no. 1764, 31 August 1357, a commission of the *Parlement* of Paris ordering the seneschal to prevent the rector from interfering in the accord.

[31] The general opprobrium attached to Andree's crime reflects the attitude conveyed by the *Digest*. Infamy was closely associated with the *actio de dolo* (Fransen 1946:30). The expressions *infamia publica* (Louvet no. 1765, f. 1r) and *diffamatus*, used to describe Andree (Louvet no. 1750, 15 June 1355, p. 9), suggest some links between theory and practice.

[32] They termed themselves *expensibus et laboribus fatigati* in Louvet no. 1750, 15 June 1355, p. 10.

Literature

Berger, A. 1953. Encyclopedic dictionary of Roman law. Philadelphia.

Berthelé, J. 1895. Archives communales de Montpellier antérieures à 1789, Inventaires et documents: I. Notice sur les anciens inventaires, inventaire du Grand Chartrier. Montpellier.

Carbasse, J.-M. 1974. Consulats méridionaux et justice criminelle au moyen-âge. Thèse d'Etat, Faculté de Droit et des Sciences Economiques de Montpellier. Université de Montpellier I.

Chabaneau, C. and A. Germain. 1884–6. Liber instrumentorum memorialium. Montpellier.

Cheyette, F. L. 1970. The sovereign and the pirates, 1332. Speculum 45:40–68.

Coing, H. 1939. Simulatio und fraus. Festschrift Paul Koschaker 3:403–19. Weimar.

Combes, J. 1970. Quelques remarques sur les bourgeois de Montpellier au moyen âge. Recueil de mémoires et travaux publié par la société d'histoire du droit et des institutions des anciens pays de droit écrit. Mélanges Pierre Tisset fasc. 7:93–132.

Dion, R. 1959. Histoire de la vigne et du vin en France des origines au XIXe siècle. Paris.

Fransen, G. 1946. Le dol dans la conclusion des actes juridiques. Evolution des doctrines et système du code canonique. Gembloux.

Germain, A. 1850–4. Mémoire sur les anciennes monnaies seigneuriales de Melgueil et de Montpellier. Mémoires de la société archéologique de Montpellier 3:133–257.

Germain, A. 1851a, b, and c. Histoire de la commune de Montpellier. 3 vols. Montpellier.

Germain, A. 1861a and b. Histoire du commerce de Montpellier antérieurement à l'ouverture du port de Cette. 2 vols. Montpellier.

Gouron, A. 1958. La réglementation des métiers en Languedoc au moyen âge. Genève, Paris.

Grand, R. 1940. La prison et la notion d'emprisonnement dans l'ancien droit. Revue historique de droit français et étranger 4th ser. 19:58–87.

Henneman, J. B. 1971. Royal taxation in fourteenth-century France. Princeton.

Lane, F. C. 1964. Investment and usury in medieval Venice. Explorations in entrepreneurial history 2nd ser. 2:3–15.

Lecoy de la Marche, A. 1892a and b. Les relations politiques de la France avec le royaume de Majorque (Iles Baléares, Roussillon, Montpellier etc.). 2 vols. Paris.

Lewis, A. R. 1947. The development of town government in twelfth-century Montpellier. Speculum 22:51–67.

Lopez, R. S. 1948. Italian leadership in the medieval business world. Journal of economic history 8 suppl. 63–8.

Lopez, R. S. and I. W. Raymond. 1955. Medieval trade in the Mediterranean world. New York, London.

Mate, M. 1969. A mint of trouble, 1279 to 1307.

Speculum 44:201–12.
Meynial, E. 1929. Note sur l'histoire du dol et de la violence dans les contrats dans notre ancien droit français. Mélanges Paul Fournier. Paris.
Ourliac, P. and J. de Malafosse. 1969. Histoire du droit privé, I: Les obligations. Second edition. Paris.
Pégat, F. and others (eds.) 1840. Le Petit Thalamus de Montpellier. Montpellier.
Reyerson, K. L. 1974a and b. Commerce and Society in Montpellier:1250–1350. 2 vols. Dissertation, Yale University.
Reyerson, K. L. 1980. Les opérations de crédit dans la coutume et dans la vie des affaires à Montpellier au moyen âge: le problème de l'usure. Diritto comune e diritti locali nella storia dell'Europa. Atti del convegno di Varenna (12–15 guigno 1979). Milano.
Rogozinski, J. 1967. The lawyers of lower Languedoc. A study of the social origins, training, career patterns and wealth of the professionally trained lawyers and judges resident in the sénéchaussée of Beaucaire and Nimes and the baronnie of Montpellier between circa 1270 and circa 1345. Dissertation, Princeton University.
Rogozinski, J. 1969. The counsellors of the seneschal of Beaucaire and Nimes, 1250–1350. Speculum 44: 421–39.
Rogozinski, J. 1972. Ordinary and major judges. Studia gratiana 15:589–611.
Strayer, J. R. 1970. Les gens de justice du Languedoc sous Philippe le Bel. Toulouse.
Thomas, L. J. 1928–9. Montpellier entre la France et l'Aragon pendant la première moitié du XIVe siècle. Monspeliensia, mémoires et documents relatifs à Montpellier et à la région montpelliéraine 1, fasc. 1:1–56.
Thomas, L. J. 1936. Montpellier ville marchande: histoire économique et sociale de Montpellier des origines à 1870. Montpellier.
Vidal, J. 1957. Essai d'une théorie générale de la fraude en droit français. Paris.

VII

LES OPERATIONS DE CREDIT DANS LA COUTUME ET DANS LA VIE DES AFFAIRES A MONTPELLIER AU MOYEN AGE: LE PROBLEME DE L'USURE

La pratique et la répression de l'usure au moyen âge soulèvent des problèmes importants pour l'histoire du droit et l'histoire économique. Les effets économiques de la doctrine scolastique à propos de l'usure forment le sujet d'un débat plusieurs fois renouvelé entre la position soutenue par Max Weber et plus récemment par Raymond de Roover, selon laquelle les idées religieuses auraient eu une influence économique, et l'opinion partagée par Henri Pirenne, Gino Luzzatto et Robert S. Lopez, entre autres, selon laquelle la prohibition de l'usure n'aurait eu que peu ou pas d'effets sur l'activité de tous les jours des hommes d'affaires médiévaux (1). Selon le raisonnement de Lopez, les marchands et les banquiers du moyen âge pratiquaient l'usure sans remords sauf peut-être à la fin de leur vie, à l'établissement de leur testament, quand le souci de leur âme immortelle surgissait (2).

En revanche, Raymond de Roover et Frederick C. Lane ont suggéré des effets concrets de la prohibition de l'usure sur l'évolu-

(1) Raymond de Roover s'est le plus occupé de ce problème pour le moyen âge. Parmi ses nombreux travaux il faut citer son oeuvre de synthèse, *La pensée économique des scolastiques: doctrines et méthodes* (Paris et Montréal, 1971). Voir également *The Scholastics Usury and Foreign Exchange*, dans *Business History Review*, 41 (1967), 257-271 et *The Scholastic Attitude toward Trade and Entrepreneurship*, dans *Explorations in Entrepreneurial History*, 2e sér., 1 (1963-1964), 76-87. Voir aussi Max WEBER, *The Protestant Ethic and the Spirit of Capitalism* (version allemande, 1904-1905; 2e éd., 1920; trans. Talcott Parsons, London, 1930, réimp., 1938) et R. H. TAWNEY, *Religion and the Rise of Capitalism* (New York, 1926, réimp., 1938).

Du côté des sceptiques on peut consulter Henri PIRENNE, *Histoire économique de l'Occident médiéval* (Bruges, 1951); Gino LUZZATTO, *Storia economica di Venezia dall'XI al XVI secolo* (Venise, 1961); Robert S. LOPEZ, *La prima crisi della banca di Genova (1250-1259)* (Gênes, 1956) et son compte-rendu de Benjamin N. NELSON, *The Idea of Usury* (Princeton, 1949), dans *Speculum*, 26 (1951), 404. Julius Kirshner appelle ces trois derniers historiens, « la nouvelle vague » (p. 320), dans *Les travaux de Raymond de Roover sur la pensée économique des scolastiques*, dans *Annales: Economies, Sociétés, Civilisations*, 30, 1 (1975), suppl., 318-338.

Sur la question d'influences, voir enfin J. GILCHRIST, *The Church and Economic Activity in the Middle Ages* (London, New York, 1969).

(2) R. S. LOPEZ, *Italian Leadership in the Medieval Business World*, dans *Journal of Economic History*, 8 (1948), suppl., 65.

tion économique médiévale. Tout en laissant au domaine de la conscience, voire au terrain inviolable de la confession, une partie du champ de recherches sur les effets économiques des idées religieuses, Raymond de Roover a précisé sa pensée à propos de l'usure dans ses études de l'histoire de la banque européenne. De Roover croyait notamment que la doctrine prohibitive à propos de l'usure augmentait le coût de l'emprunt et poussait les banquiers à se fier aux opérations de change à la fois plus chères et plus spéculatives. Selon de Roover, les origines de la banque moderne se situent dans ces opérations de change (3). Frederick C. Lane s'est penché sur une solution intermédiaire en ce qui concerne l'influence de la doctrine scolastique à propos de l'usure (4). Envisageant des effets économiques indirects, il a suggéré que la prohibition de l'usure aurait pu décourager les prêts à la consommation. Cet interdit aurait pu, en conséquence, encourager les hommes d'affaires à investir leurs capitaux dans des domaines plus productifs (5). Les progrès dans notre compréhension de l'économie médiévale à l'échelon local et général continuent à fournir des nuances importantes au débat sur l'influence économique des idées scolastiques.

Le problème de l'usure a été abordé d'une façon nouvelle par Bernard Schnapper (6). Il a confronté les changements dans la politique de répression de l'usure avec l'évolution économique européenne en tirant la conclusion que l'usure se pratiquait plus ouvertement et s'attirait des mesures répressives aux époques d'expansion économique (XIIe et XIIIe siècles d'une part et XVIe siècle d'autre part). En revanche, à la fin du moyen âge, lors d'une « régression économique », les investissements fructueux se firent rares, les prêts à la consommation furent essentiels pour une grande partie de la

---

(3) R. DE ROOVER, MONEY, *Banking and Credit in Mediaeval Bruges: Italian Merchant-Bankers, Lombards and Money-Changers* (Cambridge, Mass., 1948), pp. 49, 54, 311. Voir aussi *The Medici Bank* (New York, 1948); *The Rise and Decline of the Medici Bank, 1397-1494* (Cambridge, Mass., 1963); *Early Banking before 1500 and the Development of Capitalism*, dans *Revue internationale d'histoire de la banque*, 4 (1971), 1-16; et *New Interpretations in the History of Banking*, dans *Journal of World History*, 2 (1954), 38-76.

(4) Frederick C. LANE, *Investment and Usury in Medieval Venice*, dans *Explorations in Entrepreneurial History*, 2e sér., 2 (1964), 3-15.

(5) *Ibid.*, p. 12.

(6) Bernard SCHNAPPER, *La répression de l'usure et l'évolution économique (XIIIe-XVIe siècles)*, dans *Tijdschrift voor Rechtsgeschiedenis*, 37, fasc. 1 (1969), 47-75.

population et la répression de l'usure diminua (7). La police de l'usure a été accaparée par le roi de France et par les juges royaux qui s'occupaient plus d'exigences fiscales que de questions morales (8). Ces hypothèses intéressantes méritent considération. Par ailleurs, les interprétations des effets de la pratique et de la répression de l'usure au moyen âge peuvent être servies par la multiplication des études de cas particuliers. La ville languedocienne de Montpellier nous offre un contexte dans lequel il est possible d'examiner le problème de l'usure à travers des périodes de progression et de contraction économiques (9).

Une synthèse à l'échelle européenne sur les conséquences pratiques de la prohibition ecclésiastique de l'usure n'a pas encore vu le jour bien que nous ayons à ce propos des études de la pratique des affaires à Bruges, Venise, Lucques, Florence, San Gimignano et Toulouse, pour ne citer que quelques exemples (10). En tant que centre commercial et financier d'envergure, Montpellier mérite un examen particulier dans l'optique de la synthèse future. L'omniprésence du crédit dans l'économie montpelliéraine au moyen âge soulève, ici comme ailleurs, le problème de contradiction entre la pratique des affaires et la position théorique de l'église concernant la moralité du commerce et de la finance (11). Cette étude se limitera à la période qui s'étend de la fin du XIIe siècle au milieu du XIVe.

---

(7) *Ibid.*, pp. 74-75. Marie-Odile Piquet-Marchal a remarqué que le domaine du crédit s'étendait énormement au XIVe, en entraînant une baisse des taux d'intérêt. Cf. *Doctrines monétaires et conjoncture aux XIVe et XVe siècles*, dans *Revue internationale de l'histoire de la banque*, 4 (1971), 373-374. Ceci aurait pu contribuer à un ralentissement de la répression de l'usure. Voir, cependant, les remarques de B. Schnapper, *La répression de l'usure*, pp. 58-59.

(8) B. Schnapper, *La répression de l'usure*, p. 63.

(9) Je prépare actuellement une étude sur le crédit et l'investissement à Montpellier au moyen âge.

(10) Cf. notes 4 et 5 ci-dessus et Gino Luzzatto, *Tasso d'interesse e usura a Venezia nei secoli XIII-XIV*, dans *Miscellanea in onore di R. Cessi* (Rome, 1958); Reinhold C. Mueller, *The Procuratori di San Marco and the Venetian Credit Market: A Study of the Development of Credit and Banking in the Trecento* (New York, 1977); Thomas W. Blomquist, *Trade and Commerce in Thirteenth-Century Lucca*, Diss. University of Minnesota, 1966; Enrico Fiumi, *Storia economica e sociale di San Gimignano* (Florence, 1961); Marvin C. Becker, *Gualtieri di Brienne e la regolamentazione dell'usura a Firenze*, dans *Archivio storico italiano*, 114 (1956), 734-740; et Philippe Wolff, *Commerces et marchands de Toulouse (vers 1350- vers 1450)* (Paris, 1954).

(11) Sur les opérations de crédit au moyen âge cf. Michael M. Postan, *Credit in Medieval Trade*, dans *Economic History Review*, 1 (1928), 234-261.

Une telle délimitation chronologique permet l'examen de deux époques précises pour lesquelles des données théoriques et pratiques sont préservées à Montpellier: la fin du XIIe et le début du XIIIe, quand les premières indications locales sur l'usure sont trouvables, la fin du XIIIe et la première moitié du XIVe (1293-1348), période favorisée par la préservation de registres notariaux (12). Nous aurons souci de comparer, dans la mesure du possible, la position théorique de l'église, les actes législatifs laïcs et la pratique des affaires à Montpellier.

La doctrine scolastique sur l'usure a été étudiée en profondeur par de nombreux historiens tels Raymond de Roover, Benjamin Nelson, Gabriel Le Bras, John T. Noonan, Terence P. McLaughlin, John W. Baldwin et J. Gilchrist (13). Il n'est pas dans nos intentions de revoir leurs conclusions. Cependant, quelques précisions seront utiles en introduisant le sujet de l'usure à Montpellier. Il faut d'abord distinguer entre une définition étroite de l'usure et une définition large. La définition la plus succincte a été donnée par Raymond de Roover qui s'est inspiré du droit romain: « gain certain en *mutuum* », c'est à dire l'intérêt résultant d'un prêt (14). Les scolastiques appelaient usure tout profit au delà du principal (le sort) dans un prêt, et non pas simplement, comme nous le faisons aujourd'hui, un intérêt exorbitant (15). Cette définition étroite allait s'élargir au cours des interprétations des commentateurs du *Décret*

---

(12) Mes recherches ont été menées aux Archives Municipales de Montpellier et aux Archives Départementales de l'Hérault.

(13) Cf. notes 2 et 4; Benjamin N. Nelson, *The Idea of Usury* (Princeton, 1949); Gabriel Le Bras, *L'Usure* dans *Dictionnaire de Théologie Catholique*, XV, 2e partie (1950), 2336-2372 et *Conceptions of Economy and Society*, dans *Cambridge Economic History*, III (Cambridge, 1963), 554-575; John T. Noonan, *The Scholastic Analysis of Usury* (Cambridge, Mass., 1957); Terrence P. McLaughlin, *The Teaching of the Canonists on Usury (XII, XIII and XIV Centuries)*, dans *Mediaeval Studies*, 1 (1939), 81-147 et 2 (1940), 1-22; et John W. Baldwin, *The Medieval Merchant before the Bar of Canon Law*, dans *Papers of the Michigan Academy of Science, Arts and Letters*, 44 (1959), 287-299.

Par la doctrine scolastique, il faut entendre les interprétations du droit canon et de la théologie faites par les érudits médiévaux. Parmi les intellectuels appelés scolastiques, il n'existait pas un accord général sur tous les aspects de l'usure.

(14) R. de Roover, *Money, Banking and Credit*, p. 54. Pour une définition du *mutuum* en droit romain, cf. Adolf Berger, *Encyclopedic Dictionary of Roman Law, Transactions of the American Philosophical Society*, n. sér., 43, 2e partie (Philadelphia, 1953), p. 591.

(15) R. de Roover, *La pensée économique*, p. 76.

et des *Décrétales*. Hostiensis († 1270) a admis que l'usure se pratiquait normalement dans le contexte du prêt mais il critiquait par contre ceux qui disaient qu'elle n'existait pas dans d'autres contrats (16). Plus tard, Saint Bernardin de Sienne (1380-1444) allait établir une distinction entre l'usure ouverte dans un prêt et l'usure cachée dans des contrats *in fraudem usurarum* (17). L'extension de la définition de l'usure est à l'origine de différences d'opinions parmi les scolastiques à propos des opérations légitimes. Par ailleurs, la position des scolastiques envers l'usure fut compliquée par le fait que le droit civil du *Code* et du *Digest* de Justinien permettait l'usure à un taux modéré (18). Dans un centre important d'études de droit romain tel que Montpellier, ces conflits sont à retenir bien qu'il n'y ait pas d'études modernes qui voient une préoccupation de résoudre les contradictions entre le droit canon et le droit civil à propos de l'usure à l'université de Montpellier au moyen âge (19).

Le résultat de l'élargissement de sa définition fut que, peu à peu, certains contrats d'affaires, étant considérés comme des contrats *in fraudem usurarum*, n'échappaient plus à la condamnation pour usure: des prêts sur gages qui portaient fruits, des ventes fictives, des achats et des ventes à crédit et des changes secs (*cambium siccum*) (20). C'est ainsi qu'une part importante des opérations courantes de crédit a été rendue illégitime. De plus, il est évident que le droit canon des *Décrétales* connaissait la tendance, dans le monde des affaires, à manipuler certains contrats afin d'éviter la condamnation pour cause d'usure (21).

Grâce aux interprétations habiles de certains scolastiques, sensibles aux besoins pratiques des affaires, les contrats d'association, le change classique, les rentes perpétuelles et annuelles et le rende-

---

(16) T. P. McLaughlin, *The Teaching of the Canonistes*, I, 113.

(17) R. de Roover, *La pensée économique*, p. 78.

(18) T. P. McLaughlin, *The Teaching of the Canonists*, I, 87-95, a fait état des interprétations du droit romain et des canons du *Décret* de Gratien concernant l'usure. Cf. pp. 82-83. Nous laisserons de côté la position du droit civil à propos de l'usure.

(19) Sur les juristes de Montpellier, voir André Gouron, *Les iuristes de l'école de Montpellier*, dans *Ius Romanum Medii Aevi*, pars IV, 3, a (Milan, 1971), 1-35. Il est mon intention d'étudier la position de Petrus Jacobi sur l'usure dans son ouvrage, *Subtilissimi et acutissimi legum interpretis Dominis Petri Jacobi ... aurea famosissima practica* (Lyons, 1527), dans un article prochain.

(20) T. P. McLaughlin, *The Teaching of Canonists*, I, 95-124.

(21) *Ibid.*, p. 112.

ment de dettes communales étaient autorisés (22). Certains principes, selon ces commentateurs, justifiaient l'usure: en particulier, celui de *damnum emergens*, c'est à dire la perte financière causée par une opération qui mériterait des dommages et intérêts. L'idée de *lucrum cessans*, introduisant la possibilité de compensation pour le créancier qui aurait écarté d'autres investissements peut-être plus rémunératifs, a été moins rapidement admise. Le concept de *periculum sortis* qui admettait une indemnité pour les risques courus dans le commerce et dans la finance était également appelé à justifier l'usure (23). Parmi les scolastiques, les canonistes étaient en général plus pragmatiques que les théologiens dans leurs théories à propos de l'usure (24).

Avec un petit groupe de contrats d'affaires considérés comme légitimes tandis que beaucoup d'activités restaient suspectes aux yeux de l'église, le marchand médiéval devait jouer au funambule s'il voulait éviter des entreprises de moralité douteuse. Une tension entre la théorie ecclésiastique et la pratique du marché peut s'entrevoir dans la coutume de 1204 à Montpellier (25). Dans l'examen du cas de Montpellier, il convient d'abord d'étudier les données locales sur l'usure à la fin du XIIe et au début du XIIIe siècle.

Trois articles de la coutume de 1204 concernent l'usure. La méfiance vis-à-vis des usuriers apparaît dans l'article 9 où leur témoignage était mis en question:

> Les renoviers ou usuriers qui reçoivent deniers pour deniers ne sont pas entendus en témoignage (26).

Le texte de cet article dans la version de la coutume en langue vulgaire traduit le mot « témoignage » (*testimonio*) par *guerencia*,

---

(22) *Ibid.*, 120-144.

(23) *Ibid.*, 144-147. Cf. aussi R. de Roover, *Joseph A. Schumpeter and Scholastic Economics*, dans *Kyklos*, 10 (1957), 115-146.

(24) J. Gilchrist, *The Church and Economic Activity*, pp. 62-70, surtout, p. 69.

(25) La meilleure édition de la coutume de 1204 se trouve dans *Les Layettes du Trésor des Chartes*, I, éd. A. Teulet (Paris, 1863), 255-266. D'autres versions ont été publiées dans *Le Petit Thalamus de Montpellier*, éd. F. Pégat, E. Thomas et Desmazes (Montpellier, 1840), pp. 1-59 (avec une version dans le vernaculaire) et dans Charles Giraud, *Essai sur le droit français au moyen âge*, I (Paris, 1846), preuves, pp. 47 ss.

(26) *Layettes*, I, 256: « Renovarii seu usurarii, qui denarios pro denarios accomodant, non recipiuntur in testimonio ».

c'est à dire, « guarantie ». En outre, cette version décrit les usuriers comme ceux « que preston deniers ». (27) La coutume de 1204 avait été autorisée par Pierre II d'Aragon lors de l'établissement du consulat montpelliérain, mais une première ébauche de la coutume avait été rédigée vers 1190 sous Guilhem VIII, le dernier seigneur local (28). Les vingt-sept premiers articles, dont l'article 9, faisaient déjà partie de la coutume à cette époque (29). Cette interdiction de témoignage ou de guarantie pouvait avoir des conséquences négatives dans les domaines juridiques et économiques où la parole était nécessaire: devant un tribunal, pour jurer sur les faits ou les personnes, dans une affaire commerciale ou financière comme caution ou sûreté personnelle (30). La liberté d'action d'un usurier était restreinte par l'article 9.

En revanche, l'article 68 de la coutume de 1204 exigeait la prestation d'un serment de la part d'emprunteurs chrétiens et juifs:

> La demande de l'usure des deniers pour deniers est nulle et ne doit pas être écoutée si elle n'est pas promise avec serment ou pleine foi; et ceci est le droit commun entre Chrétiens et Juifs, que le serment et lapleine foi soient utilisée dans l'usure qui doit se donner (31).

---

(27) *Le Petit Thalamus*, pp. 8-9, article 10, le vernaculaire: « Renovier ni uzurier que preston deniers per deniers non son pres en guerentia ».

(28) Sur l'établissement du consulat en 1204-1206, voir Bernardin GAILLARD, *Origines de la commune de Montpellier*, dans *Bulletin de l'Académie des Sciences et Lettres de Montpellier* (Montpellier, 1914), tiré-à-part; Alexandre GERMAIN, *Histoire de la commune de Montpellier*, 3 v. (Montpellier, 1851), I, 22-52; Dom DEVIC et Dom VAISSÈTE, *Histoire générale de Languedoc*, 15 v. (Toulouse, 1872-1904), VI, 213-216. Monsieur le Professeur André GOURON s'est adressé au problème législatif à Montpellier dans sa communication, *La ' potestas statuendi ' dans le droit coutumier montpelliérain*, Milan-Varenna, juin 1979.

(29) Pour la version de 1190 cf. *Liber instrumentorum memorialium*, ed. C. Chabaneau et A. Germain (Montpellier, 1884-1886), p. 405, acte CCXLIV.

(30) Sur la question de guaranties personnelles, cf., par exemple, Mireille CASTAING-SICARD, *Les contrats dans le très ancien droit toulousain, Xe-XIIIe siècles* (Toulouse, 1959), 379-403. Voir aussi *Recueils de la société Jean Bodin*, XVII: *La Preuve* (Bruxelles, 1965).

(31) *Layettes*, I, 261: « Petitio usure de denariis pro denariis nulla est nec audiri debet, nisi cum sacramento vel fide plevita sit promissa; et hoc est jus commune ut in Xpistianis et Judeis sacramentum et fides plevita in danda usura servetur ».

Le Petit Thalamus, pp. 36-37, article 69, le vernaculaire: « Demandamens duzuras de deniers per deniers non val ni non deu esser auzistz, si ab sagramen o fe plenida non era promessa, Et aysso es dregz comunal que en crestians et en juzueus sagramen e fe plenida sia gardada en dar uzuras ».

Comme le texte l'implique, l'utilisation du serment dans les affaires d'usure était nécessaire et, en fait, courante (32). L'usure étant interdite par le droit canon, la possibilité de recouvrer ses revenus n'était pas admise devant les tribunaux ecclésiastiques dont le délit d'usure était toujours justiciable au début du XIIIe siècle (33). Le recours au serment offrait au créancier un moyen de mieux s'assurer le remboursement éventuel du sort et de l'intérêt de la part du débiteur.

Au moyen âge le serment engageait l'âme immortelle de celui qui jurait; et on ne s'en déliait pas facilement (34). En matière d'usure un serment à trois volets pouvait être exigé: d'abord de payer tout simplement l'usure; puis, de ne pas en demander la restitution; et enfin, de ne pas dénoncer l'usurier aux autorités. (35) Dans la discussion engagée par les canonistes à propos du serment en matière d'usure, ces derniers ont réussi à vider de leur importance les deux derniers serments, mais le premier restait toujours en vigueur; en être délié n'était pas admissible. Les débiteurs devaient, selon le droit canon, demander restitution de l'usure et dénoncer l'usurier, mais ils étaient néanmoins tenus par leur serment à payer l'usure. Le dénouement d'une affaire d'usure donnait ainsi au créancier la position de force s'il acceptait, lui, de vivre dans un état d'excommunication (36). L'article 68 de la coutume montpelliéraine favorisait le créancier et ainsi l'usurier dans son exigence de la prestation d'un serment en matière d'usure.

Une réglementation du taux d'intérêt apparaît dans le troisième article de 1204 concernant l'usure. Le taux d'intérêt ne devait pas excéder le niveau du sort, comme le dit l'article 116:

> Lorsque l'usure sera l'équivalent du principal, elle n'augmentera plus avec le temps, et même si elle est promise avec serment ou pleine foi, elle ne sera pas adjugée plus aux Juifs ou aux Chrétiens parce qu'ils sont payés par ce statut (37).

---

(32) T. P. McLaughlin, *The Teaching of the Canonists*, II, 18-20.

(33) B. Schnapper, *La répression de l'usure*, p. 48.

(34) Sur le serment au moyen âge, voir Henry Charles Lea, *The Duel and the Oath*, avec document traduits par Arthur C. Howland, éd. Edward Peters (Philadelphia, 1974).

(35) T. P. McLaughlin, *The Teaching of the Canonists*, II, 15-16.

(36) *Ibid.*

(37) *Layettes*, I, 264: « Postquam usura equiparata sorti fuerit, deinde usura nullatenus accrescat, ulla temporis diuturnitate, et si etiam sacramento vel fide

Ainsi, selon la législation locale, l'intérêt ne devait pas dépasser la somme principale, c'est à dire, 100%. Ce taux, très élevé, même pour le moyen âge, implique, soit un intérêt composé, soit une reconduction de dettes au cours de la période d'endettement (38). Devant un tel statut, il serait difficile de décrire le climat local des affaires et la position officielle de l'administration municipale comme intolérants envers la pratique de l'usure.

Bien que l'endettement soit le sujet de multiples statuts consulaires ultérieurs à la coutume de 1204, l'usure n'y figura plus directement (39). La position législative de l'article 9 de la coutume est peu compatible avec les articles 68 et 116, qui favorisaient la pratique de l'usure. La foi des usuriers eux-mêmes était suspecte même si un serment était exigé des débiteurs. Il est possible qu'un raffinement de la coutume locale ait eu lieu lors de la fondation du consulat en 1204. A cette date les enfants illégitimes de Guilhem VIII furent renvoyés et Pierre II d'Aragon, époux de sa fille légitime, Marie, fut installé comme seigneur de Montpellier (40). Les bourgeois de Montpellier, des marchands pour la plupart, qui avaient manigancé ce changement de régime seigneurial et l'établissement

---

plevita promissa fuerit, non judicetur in plus Judeis vel Xpistianis, quia ista constitutione ita taxantur ».

Le Petit Thalamus, pp. 50-51, article 117, le vernaculaire: « Pueys que la usura sera egaleiada ab lo captal, daqui enant la uzura en ulha guiza non acresca per alcuna longueza de temps. E si ab sagramen o ab fe plenida sera promessa, non sia jutgada emplus a juzueus o a crestians, car en aquest establimen ayson taxas ».

(38) Le taux d'intérêt officiel variait de ville en ville au moyen âge. Un taux de 20% semble avoir été la régle à Gênes, à San Gimignano et, au XIIe siècle, à Venise. Cf. R. S. Lopez, *La prima crisi della banca di Genova*, pp. 34-35; F. C. Lane, *Investment and Usury*, p. 7; E. Fiumi, *Storia economica*, p. 87, note 286. Cf. aussi les remarques de Thomas Blomquist, *De Roover on Business, Banking and Economic Thought*, dans *Journal of Economic History*, 35 (1975), 826. A Venise le taux légitime n'était que 5% au XIIIe siècle. Ailleurs, des taux plus élevés avaient cours. Mireille Castaing-(Sicard), *Le prêt à intérêt à Toulouse au XIIe et XIIIe siècles*, dans *Bulletin philologique et historique*, années 1953 et 1954 (Paris, 1955), p. 275, a cité un taux entre 15% et 38% pour Toulouse. P. Wolff, *Commerces et marchands*, p. 398, a noté un taux de 43⅓% au XIVe siècle pour les prêts juifs. R. de Roover, *Money, Banking and Credit*, p. 127, a signalé un taux de 43⅓% à Bruges dans les prêts du XIVe. A Florence, selon Marvin Becker, *Gualtieri di Brienne e la regolamentazione dell'usura*, p. 735, un taux de 30% était toléré sur les prêts à gages en 1343. Selon Becker, p. 735, note 6, le taux aurait été de 40% au maximum à Lucques et de 33% à Pise en 1316.

(39) *Layettes*, I-III, *passim* et *Le Petit Thalamus*, *passim*.

(40) Cf. note 29 ci-dessus.

du consulat, avaient besoin d'un climat législatif favorable à leurs affaires. L'expansion économique de Montpellier démarrait à fond et les besoins locaux de capitaux auraient encouragé une tolérance laïque envers l'usure pour faciliter les opérations de crédit (41). Mais, même le démarrage économique n'enleva pas tout l'opprobre du statut d'usurier. Les trois articles de la coutume, pris ensemble, reflètent une certaine ambiguité traditionnelle à propos de l'usure qui persistait au début du XIIIe siècle. La necessité économique pèsera en faveur de l'usure par la suite.

En dehors des articles de la coutume, il faut interroger d'autres sources locales de la même époque pour des renseignements sur la pratique des affaires, d'une part, et la position de l'église montpelliéraine à propos de l'usure, de l'autre. Nous sommes assez peu renseignés sur les opérations de crédit utilisées à Montpellier aux XIIe et XIIIe siècles, étant donné l'absence de registres notariaux avant 1293 (42). Cependant, le *Liber instrumentorum memorialium*, cartulaire seigneurial des Guilhem, est un riche dépôt d'actes pour le XIIe siècle. Cette source est semée de *pignorationes* (mortgages ou prêts sur gages immeubles), une opération de crédit très utilisée à l'époque (43). Le créancier bénéficiait des fruits du gage pour la durée de l'extension du crédit. Cette technique de *pignoratio* fut réglementée par la coutume de 1204 dans l'article 40 où il était

---

(41) Sur l'histoire économique de Montpellier, cf. Alexandre Germain, *Histoire du commerce de Montpellier antérieurement à l'ouverture du port de Cette*, 2 v. (Montpellier, 1861); Louis J. Thomas, *Montpellier, ville marchande: histoire économique et sociale des origines à 1870* (Montpellier, 1936); et mes thèses, *Commerce and Society in Montpellier: 1250-1350*, Diss. Yale University, 1974 et *Montpellier de 1250 à 1350: Centre commercial et financier*, Thèse d'Etat, Université de Montpellier, I, 1977.

(42) Le premier registre préservé est celui de Jean Grimaud, 1293-1294, Archives Municipales, II, 1.

(43) *Liber instrumentorum memorialium, passim*. Pour ne citer qu'un exemple, prenons l'acte LIII, pp. 93-94. Cette *carta pignoris* décrit la cession de *totum honorem nostrum* par une veuve et son fils à un créancier pour dix marcs d'argent. Le créancier devait tenir l'*honorem* et toutes ses redevances pendant quatre ans et puis, si la gage n'était pas rachetée, d'année en année jusqu'à ce que cela se fasse. En outre, si quelque chose était enlevée à la gage, les débiteurs devaient rembourser le créancier pour sa parte. Cf. aussi sur les prêts à gages, Mireille Castaing (-Sicard), *Le prêt à intérêt à Toulouse*, pp. 273-278.

Pour la période postérieure au XIIe siècle on trouve quelques exemples de gages immeubles dans le *Cartulaire de Maguelone*, éd. J. Rouquette et A. Villemagne, 5 v. (Montpellier-Vic-la-Gardiole, 1912-1925). Cf. par exemple, v. II, 198: en 1219 l'évêque Bernard de Mèze a mis en gage le château de Melgueil à deux de ses chevaliers.

question de gages meubles et immeubles fournis par le débiteur au créancier (44).

Des conciles ecclésiastiques tenus à Montpellier, depuis la fin du XIIe au début du XIIIe siècle, nous fournissent une autre sorte de donnée en ce qui concerne la question de l'usure. Le concile de 1195 reprit la condammation de l'usure formulée par le concile du Latran de 1179. La communion fut refusée aux usuriers; il y eut interdiction de la réception de dons pieux de leur part; et l'usurier fut privé de sépulture chrétienne s'il mourait dans l'état de péché (45). Or, les articles 40, 68 et 116 de la coutume de 1204 ont dû être rédigés peu après la publication locale de ces canons.

Le concile de 1214 à Montpellier apporta une interdiction supplémentaire en matière d'usure. Son canon 5 interdit les prêts sur gages, spécifiquement aux clercs (46). Comme nous venons de voir, et la pratique des affaires et la coutume de 1204 reconnaissaient cette opération de crédit. Il n'y a point de raison de penser que cette technique se soit effacée devant l'extension de l'interdit aux laïcs par d'autres textes des *Décrétales* (47).

L'examen de la première époque étudiée (fin XIIe-début XIIIe) montre une nette discordance entre la position ecclésiastique montpelliéraine, négative à propos de l'usure, et la tolérance implicite des statuts coutumiers et de la pratique locale. Le clergé montpelliérain et le droit canon semblent avoir eu peu d'influence sur le monde du marché et de la bourse à cette époque.

En l'absence de statuts coutumiers sur l'usure postérieurs à 1204, la législation royale, française et aragonnaise, semble avoir relayé la coutume locale en cette matière. Dans la législation française, nous assistons à une évolution d'attitude à propos de l'usure, partant d'une condamnation totale au XIIIe siècle pour arriver dans la première moitié du XIVe siècle à une alternance entre l'ad-

---

(44) *Layettes*, I, 259, article 40.

(45) J. D. Mansi, *Sacrorum conciliorum, nova et amplissima collectio*, v. 22 (Venise, 1778, reprod., Paris et Leipzig, 1903), colonne 670. Cf. aussi T. P. McLaughlin, *The Teaching of the Canonists*, II, 4.

(46) Mansi, *Sacrorum conciliorum*, v. 22, colonne 941, canon 5.

(47) T. P. McLaughlin, *The Teaching of the Canonists*, I, 114, a noté que cette régle fut étendue aux laïcs dans d'autres textes des *Décrétales*. Il s'agît du canon 5 et non pas 4 comme a dit McLaughlin. Le canon 19 de ce même concile de 1214 interdit aux clercs de recevoir des usuriers excommuniés aux sacraments et à la sépulture.

mission de l'usure à un taux modéré et sa répression intermittente (48). Ces phases différentes seront évoquées aux périodes chronologiques appropriées. D'abord, Saint Louis prit position à plusieurs reprises contre l'usure. L'ordonnance royale de décembre 1230 interdit l'usure, définie par le texte comme tout au delà du sort, aux Chrétiens (49). L'ordonnance de décembre 1254 étendit cette prohibition de l'usure aux Juifs (50). *Le Grand Thalamus* de Montpellier ne manqua pas d'enregistrer cette seconde prohibition de l'usure, témoignant de l'influence morale qu'avait Saint Louis bien avant l'achat par son petit-fils, Philippe IV, du quartier épiscopal de Montpelliéret en 1293 (51). Cependant, le pouvoir législatif de Saint Louis ne toucha qu'indirectement Montpellier. Les effets pratiques de ces deux ordonnances y restent inconnus.

En revanche, la législation aragonnaise de Jacques I le Conquérant, seigneur de Montpellier de 1213 à 1276, a dû avoir un effet direct (52). Pour les Juifs vivants sur ses terres, il a toléré un taux d'intérêt de 20% dans les contrats de moins d'un an et de 16 2/3% pour les opérations à plus long terme (53). En 1262 Jac-

---

(48) Sur la liaison entre la fiscalité des rois de France et l'usure, cf. B. Schnapper, *La répression de l'usure*. Cf. aussi J. R. Strayer et C. H. Taylor, *Studies in Early French Taxation* (Cambridge, Mass., 1939); et J. B. Henneman, *Royal Taxation in Fourteenth Century France. The Development of War Financing. 1322-1356* (Princeton, 1971).

(49) *Ordonnances des rois de France de la troisième race*, éd. Eusèbe de Laurière (Paris, 1723), I, 53-54: décembre 1230. Sur les ordonnances du XIIIe siècle contre l'usure, cf. l'article de Gérard Nahon, *Le crédit et les Juifs dans la France du XIIIe siècle*, dans *Annales: Economies, Sociétés, Civilisations*, 24: 5 (1969), 1121-1148.

(50) *Ordonnances*, I, 75: décembre 1254.

(51) Archives Municipales de Montpellier, *Le Grand Thalamus*, f. 125 v., article 336: septembre, 1254 dans *Archives de la ville de Montpellier: Inventaires et documents*, III, par J. Berthelé (Montpellier, 1920), Joffre no. 846. L'interdit est daté de septembre et non pas de décembre dans *Le Grand Thalamus*.

Sur l'achat de Montpelliéret, cf. A. Lecoy de la Marche, *Les relations politiques de la France avec le royaume de Majorque* (*Iles Baléares, Roussillon, Montpellier etc.*), I (Paris, 1829), 311 ss.

(52) Sur Jacques Ier, voir Charles de Tourtoulon, *Etudes sur la maison de Barcelone, Jacme Ier le Conquérant, roi d'Aragon, comte de Barcelone, seigneur de Montpellier d'après les chroniques et les documents inédits*, 2 v. (Montpellier, 1863).

(53) R. W. Emery, *The Jews of Perpignan in the Thirteenth Century* (New York, 1959), p. 84, a noté qu'un tel taux était en vigueur de 1241 à la fin du règne.

Jacques Ier a dû réagir en 1259 en fonction des prohibitions de l'usure juive dictées par le concile de Montpellier de 1258, par une limitation de l'usure juive. Cf. *Archives de la ville de Montpellier: Inventaires et documents*, I, par J. Berthelé

ques I a permis plus particulièrement aux Juifs de Montpellier de combiner l'intérêt avec le sort d'un prêt dans une seule somme sur laquelle, dans le cas de défaut du débiteur, l'intérêt pouvait être exigé (54). Ainsi, au milieu du XIIe siècle, la position aragonnaise à propos de l'usure juive était en conflit avec la position française. Cette dernière allait se modifier au début du XIVe siècle.

Sous le règne de Philippe le Bel on assista à une politique de répression de l'usure qui céda le pas de temps en temps à la tolérance officielle d'un taux d'intérêt entre 15% et 20% (55). Sous Philippe le Bel et ses successeurs cette alternance était liée aux exigences fiscales. A Montpellier au XIVe siècle, la réglementation de l'usure était laissée à l'initiative du roi de France qui dominait de plus en plus fermement la situation politique de la ville à partir de son achat en 1293. Les ordres du roi de France contre l'usure furent exécutés parfois par les consuls montpelliérains, parfois par les commissaires royaux députés en matière d'usure. Le délit de l'usure est passé de la compétence des tribunaux ecclésiastiques à celle de la justice laïque au cours du XIIIe siècle (56).

L'expulsion des Juifs hors de France en 1306 et la confiscation de leurs biens par Philippe le Bel inaugura une ère de répression contre les créanciers soupçonnés d'être des usuriers notoires (57). En juillet 1311 Philippe le Bel autorisa un taux d'intérêt de 15% par an pour les affaires des foires de Champagne et un taux de 20% ailleurs, mais avant la fin de l'année 1311 il avait décrété l'expulsion des usuriers italiens en exigeant le paiement de leurs dettes au roi avant le départ (58). En 1312 se suivirent deux ordonnances concernant l'usure: la première de janvier 1312, dans laquelle le

---

(Montpellier, 1895), *Le Grand Chartrier*, Louvet no. 1933: 1259. Pour le concile de 1258 voir MANSI, *Sacrorum conciliorum*, v. 23 (Venise 1779, reprod. Paris et Leipzig, 1903), colonne 990, canon 5. Voir aussi Salomon KAHN, *Documents inédits sur les Juifs de Montpellier au moyen âge*, dans *Revue des études juives*, 19 (1889), 262.

(54) J. REGNÉ, *Catalogue des actes de Jaime Ier, Pedro III et Alfonso III, rois d'Aragon, concernant les Juifs, 1213-1291*, dans *Revue des études juives*, 60 (1910), 189.

(55) J. B. HENNEMAN, *Taxation of Italians by the French Crown (1311-1363)*, dans *Mediaeval Studies*, 31 (1969), 17, a cité les taux de 15% à 20%, favorisés à l'occasion par Philippe le Bel et ses successeurs.

(56) T. P. MCLAUGHLIN, *The Teaching of the Canonists*, II, 18-21; et B. SCHNAPPER, *La répression de l'usure*, pp. 52-55.

(57) Jean FAVIER, *Philippe le Bel* (Paris, 1978), pp. 198-202; et J. R. STRAYER, *Studies in Early French Taxation*, p. 18.

(58) J. B. HENNEMAN, *Taxation of Italians*, pp. 17, 26-27.

roi se montra favorable à la résidence de ces mêmes Italiens dans son royaume, la seconde à la fin de la même année contenant une nouvelle prohibition de l'usure (59). Ces deux ordonnances sont à mettre en rapport avec le concile de Vienne de 1311-1312 qui condamna tout usurier comme hérétique et proclama illégaux tous les statuts municipaux qui permettaient l'usure à un taux fixe (60). Bernard Schnapper a signalé que l'ordonnance de janvier 1312 fut le premier acte législatif royal qui se soit distingué, à propose de l'usure, des préceptes du droit canon en admettant « l'usure grave » au delà de 20%, comme seule punissable (61).

Les effets de cette législation royale envers les Juifs et les Italiens ont été ressentis à Montpellier. Les consuls de Montpellier se plaignaient au roi de temps à autre de l'usure notoire contrôlée par les ordonnances. Ils obtinrent une intervention royale contre l'usure juive en 1317 et 1319, peu après le retour à Montpellier des Juifs rentrant de leur exode de 1306 (62). Dans le cas des Italiens, la politique royale concernant l'usure a laissé des traces dans les années 1330 et 1340. En 1330 Philippe de Valois s'est fait payer le principal des dettes dues aux Lombards, quitte à réduire la somme due aux trois quarts de la dette originale pour encourager le remboursement (63). Peu après, en 1332, Philippe de Valois autorisa de nouveau un taux d'intérêt de 21,6% ou 1 denier/livre par semaine (64). En 1334 il y eut une nouvelle décision du roi pour punir l'usure notoire; la saisie des biens des Lombards fut effectuée par les consuls à Montpellier (65). Une nouvelle poursuite de ces usuriers eut lieu en 1345 à Montpellier avec une confiscation de dettes dues aux Lombards en 1347 (66).

---

(59) *Ibid.*, p. 27.

(60) *Corpus Juris Canonici*, Clément., V, 5. 1. C. Ex gravis 2. Cf. aussi R. DE ROOVER, *La pensée économique*, p. 76; et T. P. MCLAUGHLIN, *The Teaching of the Canonists*, I, 84 et II, 10. San Gimignano était une ville où les statuts communaux autorisaient l'usure à 20% en 1228. Cf. E. FIUMI, *Storia economica*, p. 87, note 286.

(61) B. SCHNAPPER, *La répression de l'usure*, p. 52.

(62) *Le Grand Chartrier*, Louvet nos. 1935, 1937, 1938 et 1939.

(63) J. B. HENNEMAN, *Taxation of Italians*, pp. 30-32; et *Le Grand Chartrier*, Louvet nos. 1218 et 1219.

(64) Raymond CAZELLES, *Quelques réflections à propos des mutations de la monnaie royale française (1295-1360)*, dans *Le Moyen Age*, 72 (1966), 92.

(65) *Le Grand Chartrier*, Louvet no. 122.

(66) *Le Grand Chartrier*, Louvet no. 1127. Cf. J. B. HENNEMAN, *Taxation of Italians*, pp. 34-35. Cf. également Arthur LAYTON FUNK, *Confiscation of Lombard*

Quelquefois la décision royale fut appliquée de façon trop zélée par les commissaires royaux, députés en matière d'usure juive et lombarde. En 1325 les consuls de Montpellier se plaignirent de ce que ces commissaires persistaient à se saisir des obligations anciennes dues aux Juifs avant la première expulsion en 1306 (67). Certains Montpelliérains furent molestés de cette manière. A cette occasion le roi interdit la perturbation des gens de Montpellier (68). Mais la même plainte fut de nouveau portée par les consuls en 1338 et provoqua une réaction semblable de la part du roi (69). En 1343 le roi se substitua comme créancier pour les dettes dues aux Juifs, et en 1346 il ordonna une fois de plus la révocation de la commission de poursuite de ces dettes (70). Cette alternance entre tolérance et répression de l'usure juive était dictée, d'une part, par les besoins financiers de la monarchie, et d'autre part, par les réactions des habitants sur place.

Les plaintes locales prenaient parfois une forme légèrement différente. En 1325 les consuls protestèrent que les députés royaux ne se contentaient pas d'exécuter contre les biens des usuriers notoires mais procédaient également contre plus d'une centaine des habitants les plus riches du quartier majorcain (71). En 1337 il y eu d'autres poursuites contre les gens qui pratiquaient, selon la plainte locale, « une négoce légitime » (72). Dans ces deux cas la rivalité politique entre le roi de France et le roi de Majorque entra en jeu aussi bien que des considérations de nécessité fiscale (73). Mais, cette répression, était-elle justifiée par les faits?

Dans les deux cas les personnes touchées appartenaient sans doute à la classe marchande dont les membres utilisaient le prêt et d'autres

---

Debts in France, 1347-1358, dans *Medievalia et Humanistica*, 7 (1952), 51-55. Voir aussi Kurt GRUNWALD, *Lombards, Cahorsins and Jews*, dans *Journal of European Economic History*, 4 : 2 (1975), 393-398.

(67) *Le Grand Chartrier*, Louvet nos. 1941, 1942, et 1943.

(68) *Ibid.*, Louvet nos. 1944, 1945, et 1946.

(69) *Ibid.*, Louvet nos. 1948 et 3353.

(70) *Ibid.*, Louvet nos. 2356, 2357, et 3360.

(71) *Ibid.*, Louvet no. 1217.

(72) *Ibid.*, Louvet no. 3344.

(73) Louis J. THOMAS, *Montpellier entre la France et l'Aragon pendant la première moitié du XIVe siècle*, dans *Monspeliensia, Mémoires et documents relatifs à Montpellier et à la région montpelliéraine*, I, fasc. 1 (Montpellier, 1928-1929), 1-56, a étudié ces rapports.

contrats suspects selon les critères du droit canon, notamment le change sec, la vente à crédit et la reconnaissance de dette (74). Dans la documentation notariale de 1293 à 1348 on trouve un nombre impressionnant de contrats illicites *in fraudem usurarum* (75). Comme à Toulouse, la pratique des affaires à Montpellier rend les prohibitions de l'usure « lettre morte » (76). Les prêts, en nombre de 384, représentant à peu près 8,3% de tous les actes notariaux préservés pour cette période, ne font jamais mention d'intérêt. Seule la somme à rembourser est donnée dans l'acte, mais il est fort probable que l'intérêt se trouvait déjà incorporé à cette somme (77). Certains de ces prêts sont qualifiés de « gratuits » ou d'« amicaux » mais la plupart du temps ils portaient la simple phrase *ex causa mutui* et parfois *ex causa veri et legitimi mutui* (78). Toute une gamme de la société montpelliéraine prêtaient de l'argent: des marchands, des changeurs, des artisans, des travailleurs agricoles aussi bien que des Juifs et des Lombards (79).

En dehors des prêts, certaines opérations de change à Montpellier se présentaient comme des changes secs où la possibilité du détournement de la prohibition de l'usure existait. Sont suspects les changes qui ne précisaient que l'argent à rembourser, où le rem-

---

(74) Voir notes 21 et 22 ci-dessus.

(75) J'ai dépouillé les registres notariaux des Archives Municipales, II 1-3 et des Archives Départementales de l'Hérault, II E 95/368-377, les seuls registres préservés avant 1350. Concernant la pratique notariale à Montpellier, cf. Jean HILAIRE, *Pratique notariale et influence universitaire à Montpellier à la fin du Moyen Age*, dans *Hommage à André Dupont. Etudes médiévales languedociennes. Fédération historique du Languedoc-Méditerranéen et du Roussillon* (Montpellier, 1974), 167-178.

(76) M. CASTAING (-SICARD), *Le prêt à intérêt à Toulouse*, p. 278.

(77) Concernant la pratique contractuelle à Montpellier, il faut consulter Philippe BOUGES, *La pratique contractuelle à Montpellier de la fin du XIIIe siècle à la fin du XVe siècle*, 2 v., Thèse d'Etat, Université de Montpellier, I, 1972. Sur le prêt voir aussi R. S. LOPEZ et I. W. RAYMOND, *Medieval Trade in the Mediterranean World* (New York, Londres, 1955), pp. 156-161.

(78) A titre d'exemple, cf. *Archives Départementales de l'Hérault*, II E 95/375, P. Pena, ff. 2 v, 46 r, 88 v, et 100 v. Cf. aussi II E 95/374, G. Nogaret, f. 30 pour un exemple d'un prêt intitulé *veri et legitimi mutui*.

(79) La plupart des prêts juifs, certains en nature, se trouvent dans *Archives Municipales*, II 1, J. Grimaud, *passim*. Cf. R. W. EMERY, *The Jews of Perpignan*, pp. 131-133, Appendice 3. Voir aussi Salomon KAHN, *Documents inédits sur les Juifs de Montpellier au moyen âge*, dans *Revue des études juives*, 19 (1889), 259-281; 22 (1891), 264-279; 28 (1894), 118-141. La participation de tous ces groupes de prêteurs est examinée en détail dans mon étude sur le crédit et l'investissement à Montpellier.

boursement lui-même était attendu à Montpellier (80). L'incorporation de l'intérêt dans la somme à payer a pu se faire ici. Or, le change classique, défini par les scolastiques comme une *permutatio*, avec remboursement dans une deuxième monnaie sur une deuxième place de change, comportait des risques réels qui, eux, enlevaient au profit l'opprobre de l'usure (81). Les cours de change varaient d'endroit à endroit, fluctuant sans pouvoir garantir une prédiction sûre de la part des marchands et des changeurs (82).

Les reconnaissances de dettes et les ventes à crédit occupent 24% et 10% des actes préservés. Ces contrats étaient de réputation douteuse car ils donnaient la possibilité aux vendeurs de vendre plus cher parce qu'ils acceptaient de retarder le paiement (83). Il est impossible de contrôler si, en réalité, à Montpellier, les prix étaient plus chers à cause de l'extension du crédit. Selon le même raisonnement, les achats anticipés sur des récoltes futures étaient des contrats *in fraudem usurarum*. A Montpellier, cette opération était pratiquée dans les marchés de grains et de raisins, et il est possible que l'acheteur ait pu faire une affaire (84). Dans les achats anticipés comme dans les reconnaissances de dettes et dans les ventes à crédit, la moralité des contrats est à juger au niveau de la conscience. Il est cependant probable que les Montpelliérains aient pratiqué l'usure « à la petite semaine » (85).

---

(80) Cf. *Archives Municipales*, II 1, J. Grimaud, ff. 4 v et 18 r; cf. aussi *Archives Départementales de l'Hérault*, II E 95/370, J. Holanie, f. 74, pour ce qui est probablement un change sec. Voir aussi R. S. Lopez et I. W. Raymond, *Medieval Trade*, pp. 162-167. Egalement à consulter est l'article de Christoph Bergfeld, *Essai d'établissement de la théorie du droit de change à partir du droit romain*, dans *Confluence des droits savants et des pratiques juridiques, Actes du colloque de Montpellier, 12-14 décembre 1977* (Milan, 1979), pp. 263-276.

(81) R. de Roover, *La pensée économique*, pp. 27 et 84. De Roover a attribué à Alexandre d'Alexandrie († 1314) la redéfinition de l'opération de change comme une *permutatio*.

(82) Concernant les cours de change, cf. R. de Roover, *Le marché monétaire au Moyen Age et au début des temps modernes. Problèmes et méthodes*, dans *Revue historique*, 495 (1970), 5-40.

(83) Cf. T. P. McLaughlin, *The Teaching of the Canonists*, I, 117-120. Pour sa part, P. Wolff, *Commerces et marchands de Toulouse*, pp. 366-380, ne croît pas à une augmentation.

(84) A titre d'exemple, voir *Archives Départementales de l'Hérault*, II E 95/368, J. Holanie, ff. 35 r et 36 r.

(85) Il existait une situation comparable à Toulouse selon M. Castaing (-Sicard), *Le prêt à intérêt à Toulouse*, et P. Wolff, *Commerces et marchands de Toulouse*. Cf.

Parmi les contrats commerciaux utilisés couramment à Montpellier se trouvaient de nombreux actes susceptibles de condamnation comme usuriers. La pratique d'une usure modérée était sans doute nécessaire pour faciliter l'extension du crédit et le bon fonctionnement des affaires. Les consuls de Montpellier ont pris une position de défense quand la communauté marchande locale était visée par les officiers royaux à la recherche de revenus. Cependant, les consuls se méfiaient de l'usure excessive ou notoire des usuriers professionnels, les Juifs et les Lombards. Les possibilités d'abus furent mises en évidence de façon nette par un texte sans date du XIVe siècle où les consuls firent état de pratiques usurières (86). Ils décrivirent, notamment, la multiplication foudroyante de l'endettement selon les reconductions de dettes aux Juifs. Ainsi était-il possible de passer par reconduction d'une dette initiale de 200 livres pour laquelle 300 livres étaient dues après une échéance de six mois (ce qui donne un taux d'intérêt de 50% au cours de cette première période ou 100% par an) à un endettement de 1012 l. 10 s. à la fin de deux ans, jusqu'à 64,800 livres à la fin de huit ans. Plusieurs inconvénients, au delà du fardeau de la dette, découlaient de ces reconductions. Selon les consuls, les Juifs amenaient de l'argent, de l'or et des biens meubles hors du royaume. Beaucoup de débiteurs étaient emprisonnés et mouraient en prison parce qu'ils ne pouvaient rembourser leurs dettes. Enfin, des Chrétiens quittaient le royaume pour échapper à leurs dettes. Les consuls déposèrent plainte devant le roi en demandant la punition de cette transgression des ordonnances royales.

Cette méfiance des consuls à l'égard de prêteurs professionnels n'empêchait pas les premiers de s'endetter officiellement en temps de nécessité financière dans les années 1330 et 1340 à la suite d'un conflit à propos de la fiscalité municipale entre les éléments populaires (les Populares) de la ville et les consuls (87). Ainsi, en 1339 ils empruntèrent un total de 1100 livres petits tournois aux Falletti,

---

aussi Michel Lacave, *Crédit à la consommation et conjoncture économique: l'Isle-en-Venaisin (1460-1560)*, dans *Annales: Economies, Sociétés, Civilisations*, 32 (1977), 1128-1153.

(86) *Le Grand Chartrier*, Louvet no. 1931.

(87) Jean Combes, *Finances municipales et oppositions sociales à Montpellier au commencement du XIVe siècle*, dans *Fédération historique du Languedoc-Méditerranéen et du Roussillon, XLIVe congrès. Privas, 1971* (Montpellier, 1972), 99-120.

financiers d'Alba en Italie du Nord (88). Un autre exemple d'un emprunt officiel fut préservé par le seul testament d'un usurier qui subsiste dans les archives montpelliéraines avant 1350. Il s'agît du testament de Galerius Lercarii, membre d'une famille génoise bien connue; il reconnut avoir fait un contrat usurier avec les consuls de Montpellier pour lequel il voulait que satisfaction soit faite (89). Par ailleurs, nous pouvons signaler l'endettement de petites communautés des environs de Montpellier vis-à-vis des Italiens et des Juifs (90). L'ambiguité locale et officielle à l'égard de l'usure, qui se montra dans la coutume de 1204, se retrouve également au XIVe siècle.

En conclusion de cette étude sur la théorie et la pratique de l'usure à Montpellier, plusieurs remarques sont à faire. D'abord, il faut reconnaître que la position de l'église à propos de l'usure était sans influence importante à Montpellier (91). En revanche, la pratique locale et la législation coutumière restaient fidèles à l'esprit, sinon à la lettre, de la position du droit civil qui admettait une usure modérée (92). Dans la mesure où les habitants locaux pratiquaient l'usure, ils bénéficiaient de l'interprétation scolastique de certains contrats commerciaux et financiers comme légitimes, mais il n'y a pas lieu de penser qu'ils auraient abandonné ces contrats si l'interprétation avait été autre. Le développement économique de la ville aux XIIe et XIIIe siècles entraîna l'utilisation dans les marchés et à la bourse de contrats notariaux qui convenaient aux besoins des

---

(88) *Archives Municipales*, II 3, J. Laurens, f. 69 v. Cf. Jean COMBES, *Quelques remarques sur les bourgeois de Montpellier au moyen âge*, dans *Mélanges Pierre Tisset, Recueil de mémoires et travaux publiés par la Société d'Histoire du Droit et des Institutions des Anciens Pays de Droit Ecrit*, fasc. VII (1970), 125.

(89) *Le Grand Chartrier*, Louvet no. 1253: le 31 mai 1347. Ce testament est le seul que nous avons rencontré dans nos dépouillements où il est fait état de contrats usuriers.

(90) Cf. Danièle NEIRINCK, *Répertoire numérique détaillé des parchemins de Cournonterral*, mss. (Montpellier, 1969), AA 14. Voir aussi son inventaire des archives d'Agde.

(91) Parfois la réputation du clergé local a dû avoir un effet négatif sur la moralité locale. Arnaud de Verdale, évêque de Maguelone de 1339 à 1352, s'est plaint d'une déchéance morale chez son clergé. Cf. son *Catalogus episcoporum magalonensium*, éd. Alexandre GERMAIN, *Mémoires de la Société Archéologique de Montpellier*, 1er sér., 7 (1881), 441-852.

(92) Voir note 19 ci-dessus.

affaires (93). L'élaboration des opérations de crédit se fit sans considération pour l'interdiction de l'usure. La bourgeoisie marchande de Montpellier, assez orthodoxe dans ses croyances par ailleurs, poursuivait sa vocation commerciale en pratiquant une usure modérée (94).

L'introduction de la législation française à Montpellier a eu des répercussions sur le monde local des affaires. Le roi de France s'est servi des interdictions de l'usure à l'échelle du royaume, quand cela lui était financièrement utile, comme prétexte pour l'encaissement de dettes et pour la confiscation de biens. Cette politique fiscale du roi coincidait à Montpellier, comme ailleurs en Europe méridionale, avec une période de crise agricole et de contraction commerciale due, depuis la fin du XIIIe siècle, aux remaniements politiques du Moyen Orient: pertes des royaumes des croisés, avènement des Turcs et, depuis les années 1330 en Asie, désintégration du royaume Mongol (95). Quand le roi de France n'avait pas besoin d'augmenter rapidement ses revenus par des méthodes de répression, il admettait une usure modérée qui facilitait aussi le bon fonctionnement de l'économie du royaume, tactique qui pouvait également servir les buts fiscaux de la royauté, bien qu'indirectement (96). Cependant, l'alternance de répression et de tolérance dans le domaine de l'usure interrompait périodiquement le déroulement des affaires à Montpellier. De façon plus générale, la récession économique du XIVe siècle semble avoir eu des conséquences sur la répression de l'usure à une époque où l'initiative royale s'affirmait en matière

---

(93) Les litiges en matière de dettes ne manquent pas pour autant. Cf. surtout *Archives Municipales*, II 2, J. Grimaud et II 3, J. Laurens. La ville de Venise est sans doute unique dans la préservation de litiges médiévaux en matière d'usure. Cf. R. MUELLER, *The Procuratori di San Marco*, *passim*.

(94) R. W. EMERY, *Heresy and Inquisition in Narbonne* (New York, 1941), a accepté les conclusions d'Alexandre GERMAIN, *Histoire de la commune de Montpellier*, III, 122 ss., à cet égard.

(95) Concernant la crise financière du XIVe siècle, cf. Edouard PERROY, *A l'origine d'une économie contractée: les crises du XIVe siècle*, dans *Annales: Economies, Sociétés, Civilisations*, 4 (1949), 167-182. Sur les effets des problèmes politiques au Moyen Orient, cf. E. ASHTOR, *A Social and Economic History of the Near East in the Middle Ages* (Berkeley, 1976), pp. 263 ss. Cf. aussi *A History of the Crusades*, III éd. H. W. Hazard (Madison, 1977).

(96) Les impôts des rois de France sur le commerce des foires de Champagne en fournissent un exemple. Sur les foires, cf. Robert-Henri BAUTIER, *Les foires de Champagne. Recherches sur une évolution historique*, dans *Recueils de la Société Jean Bodin*, V: *La Foire* (Bruxelles, 1953), 97-148.

économique, en fonction des besoins militaires et administratifs de plus en plus lourds.

Pour le cas précis de Montpellier, ce n'était pas l'interdiction de l'usure en elle-même mais l'application de l'interdiction par le roi de France qui a exercé un effet perturbateur sur l'économie montpelliéraine. La répression royale de l'usure rejoint d'autres perturbations économiques d'origine royale de la première moitié du XIVe siècle: interdictions d'exportation des matières premières et des produits manufacturés, mutations monétaires et impositions fiscales (97). La politique royale en matière d'usure allait accentuer la conjoncture économique de plus en plus mauvaise à Montpellier.

---

(97) Les impositions royales sont traitées à fond par J. B. HENNEMAN, *Royal Taxation in Fourteenth Century France*. Cf. aussi notes 64 et 95 ci-dessus; et Georges BIGWOOD, *La politique de la laine en France sous les règnes de Philippe le Bel et de ses fils*, dans *Revue belge de philologie et d'histoire*, 15 (1937), 79-103 et 429-457; 16 (1938), 95-239.

VIII

Women in Business in Medieval Montpellier

The legal history of women in medieval Montpellier has been examined in several valuable theses and articles but the role of women in the economic life of this commercial and financial center of Lower Languedoc has not been the focus of investigation to date.[1] In this study I will treat the economic activities of Montpelliéraines in the aggregate through the earliest extant notarial registers of the period 1293–1348.[2] Beyond the economic operations per se, analysis of the social background and marital status of women in business will help illuminate the nature of their participation, as will consideration of the influence of kinship ties in areas of commerce, finance, and real estate. The extent of sexual division of labor and the degree to which sex roles varied in different urban social and economic groups will provide further perspectives on women's roles. I will set my findings within the broader urban economy so that the activities of Montpellier women can be perceived in proper historical context.

Historians posit a decline in the status of women in Europe from the late eleventh century, with the beginnings of political reorganization and the growth of the bureaucratic state.[3] Although the Crusades offered women new responsibilities, and the halcyon days of courtly love still lay ahead, noble familiies increasingly obeyed patriarchal and patrilineal impulses, resulting in the shrinkage of opportunities—economic and other—for women to wield influence.[4] Further decline in women's status is generally assigned to the late Middle Ages, after the demographic catastrophe of the Black Death.[5] The period of the present inquiry falls between these two poles and coincides with the end of an era of urban expansion in medieval Europe.[6]

The urban environment was far removed from the noble feudal context and from the manorial agricultural setting. Within a town such as Montpellier, various social groups with differing economic status coexisted.[7] Women were confronted with many economic opportunities and numerous life styles. Before exploring the range of economic activities recorded for Montpellier women, and the distinctions among these, I want to sketch briefly the legal framework for women's participation in business. It will then be possible to investigate actual business practice as observed in the notarial registers.

Statutes of Montpellier, drafted in the years 1204–21, deal rather obliquely with the issue of women's economic rights.[8] Considerable space is devoted to the questions of dowry, inheritance, marriage, and the right to make a will. Much less local regulation of women's contractual potential in business can be found. However, it is clear from the existing statutes and from the use of renunciations of Roman law that the local law must be distinguished from that of Justinian in its treatment of women. The current notarial practice of renunciation of the *Senatusconsultum Velleianum,* one of the strongest Roman law protections limiting the legal capacity of women, and the statutory validation of obligations undertaken by a woman with her husband's permission removed barriers to her contractual participation.[9] The most elaborate statement of a woman's contractual rights came in article 38 of the 1204 statutes.[10] This statute concerned a woman's ability to act as an *fideiussor* (guarantor) in a contractual agreement, one of the keystones of business law in the Middle Ages.[11] A woman was effectively obligated if she exercised a trade and intervened by reason of it or if she acted according to the wishes of her husband. If women could bind themselves as surety for someone else, by implication they were able to contract obligations on their own behalf, and, of course, in actual business practice that is what one observes. With regard to real property transactions wives acted generally with their husbands' consent.[12] In other contexts, they often acted alone.[13]

Full contractual potential without a curator came at the official age of majority, which for girls, as for boys, was twenty-five years.[14] However, all pacts, agreements, and acquittals that girls made to their fathers and mothers at the time of their marriage, regardless of age, were valid.[15] In practice, girls reached a working majority at age twelve, boys at age fourteen.[16]

Dowry and inheritance were important sources of a woman's financial resources for participation in business. Dotal goods came under the control of the husband but could be alienated only with the consent of both spouses. Some wives retained control of their personal property, termed *bona paraphernalia.*[17] A dowered daughter could not expect a further inheritance from her father's or from her immediate family's estate if there were sons or unmarried daughters. The latter might hope to inherit. A father could, of course, leave a legacy to his married daughter, thus circumventing the statutory regulation.[18] Married women without children could not dispose of their goods through a will without their father's permission.[19] Women with children were free to frame their wills as they chose. At the dissolution of a marriage or at the death of her husband, a woman could, in principle, expect the restitution of her dowry.[20]

Married women with children who found themselves widowed were frequent participants in notarial contracts. While Roman law did not readily allow a mother to be the guardian of her children, in Montpellier such was often the practice.[21] One of the most prominent capacities in which women appeared in business transactions was as tutors or as curators of their children.[22] In these roles and as executors of their husbands' estates, they were involved in the payment of debts, acquittals and real estate acts, and in the apprenticeship of their children.

By and large women were absent from legal, paralegal, medical, and political roles in Montpellier during the era under study. In contrast, their involvement in a wide spectrum of business activities can be demonstrated in the surviving evidence. I will divide this discussion of women's participation in economic matters into five categories: apprenticeship, commerce, partnership, finance, and real estate. Women's activities will be set in the general context of urban business operations in these areas.[23] The following tables analyze women's roles in business in the context of the social categories of the town and according to their own varied backgrounds. These categories were developed in conjunction with a study of the diversity of the notarial clientele.[24] Underlying the participation of women in business in all five areas were the basic female roles of mother and provider of food and household maintenance for the family.[25] The details of women's work in the familial domestic context defy investigation given the lacuna of surviving records.

In the contracts of the notarial registers, women were usually identified by their husband's name and profession or by their father's name and occupation or by both.[26] Some women, presumably but not demonstrably single, were termed simply *habitatrix* (inhabitant) of Montpellier.[27] With very rare exceptions, women were not identified, as men were, with occupational designations of their own, though their geographic places of origin and residence were generally given.[28]

The medieval town of Montpellier enjoyed a great mixture of artisanal/industrial activities. In his study of guild organizations in southern France, André Gouron noted some evidence, particularly regarding Toulouse, that women were associated with men in trades.[29] In the case of Montpellier Gouron cited only the *caritat des fourniers* (a type of baker), whose regulations of 1365 made mention of women participants.[30] Later guild ordinances of the fifteenth and sixteenth centuries contained brief references to arrangements made for widows supported by the assistance of journeymen.

If the evidence for formal integration of women into guild structures is absent in Montpellier, the extant apprenticeship contracts offer a useful glimpse of women employed in the crafts and artisanal industries. Thirty of the 208 contracts surviving from before 1350 concern women.[31] The food trades, the specialized textile industry, and precious metalwork were the primary concentrations of female apprentices. In contrast to most towns in Languedoc by the year 1300, Montpellier had no substantial wool cloth industry; thus, many of the traditional female trades of the cloth industry such as spinning may have been practiced on a more informal, familial level in Montpellier than elsewhere in the south of France.[32]

Fourteen of the thirty female apprentices noted were in-migrants, drawn to the metropolis for purposes of training and employment. Of these the largest number in any trade—six—were destined to be bakers.[33] Five of them came from a radius of within fifty kilometers of Montpellier, the sixth from the region of Saint-Flour in the Massif Central. Women were not found as apprentices in the more prestigious commercial and financial occupations of Montpellier. The money changers, apothecaries, pepperers, merchants, and drapers recruited male apprentices, often from a distance of more than fifty kilometers from the town.[34]

Girls were apprenticed to both men and women and to couples, where, in most cases, the understanding was that the apprentice was to learn the wife's trade.[35] Fathers, mothers, parents, uncles, and brothers apprenticed their children, nieces, and sisters in trade, and husbands at times engaged their wives.[36] Widows, in keeping with their role as guardian of their children, regularly apprenticed their sons and daughters, alone or in conjunction with male relatives.[37]

Where ages of apprenticeship were given, girls were apprenticed at twelve and older, boys at fourteen and older. Local girls apprenticed at the beginner level had engagements of 4.3 years on the average; nonlocal girls spent 5.3 years in training. For local boys the average was 3.3 years, for nonlocal boys, 6 years.[38]

Trades related to the textile-finishing industry were important occupations for girl apprentices. Several contracts for the spinning of gold thread survive. In a typical apprenticeship contract, the daughter of a silversmith was apprenticed to a gilder for four years to learn the spinning of gold.[39] In a second example, the daughter of a furrier was hired by the widow of a grain merchant to spin gold for four years with a remuneration of 10 *s. t.* per year.[40] Here the hiree was already experienced. In yet another variation of terms, an oil merchant hired his wife out to the wife of a gilder for about a year at the rate of 4 *s. t.* per ounce of spun gold.[41] Part of this arrangement was a loan of 40 *s. t.* granted the oil merchant and his wife, with 12 *d. t.* to be deducted in repayment from the salary for each ounce spun. Gold thread was used in embroidery, in cloth trimming, and in the making of brocade.[42] One apprenticeship contract described the instruction of the daughter of a cultivator by the wife of a wood merchant in embroidery.[43] Girls were taught the making of silk and linen corduroy and the tailoring art.[44] The mercery trade was also a focus of female apprenticeship, although no woman in the notarial documents was termed a mercer, and the mercers' statutes of 1328 made no mention of the participation of women.[45] The mercer's trade was one of the most important retail/wholesale occupations of Montpelliéraines. Montpellier had a silk-finishing industry and a linen industry in which the above arts were used.[46] The involvement of women in silk sales and purchases, an active branch of Montpellier commerce, may have been connected to the silk-finishing industry.[47]

Additional skills taught to girls in formal apprenticeship conditions included basket weaving, painting, the marketing of old clothes, and the polishing of silver cups.[48] Domestic service was another outlet for girls.[49] In many other instances girls undoubtedly learned the skills of their mothers without leaving home. The trades of women providing instruction might differ widely from those of their husbands, as in the case of the changer's wife who taught the art of making linen corduroy.[50] Women might, however, train girls in the same trades that their husbands exercised, as suggested by the apprenticeship of a fisherman's daughter to the wife of a tailor to learn the tailoring art; here husband and wife worked at the same or related trades.[51] By the same token, a daughter's instruction might bear some relationship to her father's occupation. Thus, the daughter of a silversmith apprenticed to a gilder to spin gold was still handling precious metals.[52]

With few exceptions women were apprenticed in crafts that might be classified as women's work. These activities have left no trace of formal guild organization. The prestigious occupations of the mercantile elite were male-oriented. There were thus clear sex distinctions, which appear in the apprenticeship evidence.

The notarial registers preserve scattered records of women's transactions in the luxury trade and on the commodities market in Montpellier.[53] They sold silks (Table 1) and wool cloths (Table 2). The accompanying tables provide a view of these market sectors overall, with women's participation broken down by social category. In the silk trade, the connection of wives and widows with a particular branch of trade was directly related to their husbands' occupations. Thus, the widow of a mercer made four sales and wives of silk industry personnel, two. In the one instance where a woman (the wife of a wood merchant) bought silk, she may have been acquiring goods for her own enterprise, perhaps common to wood merchants' wives, as the earlier apprenticeship example might suggest. Female participants in

TABLE 1

Silk Transactions (Total Acts 57)

Social Category	All Sellers No. of Acts	All Sellers % Total Acts	All Buyers No. of Acts	All Buyers % Total Acts	Women Sellers No. of Acts	Women Buyers No. of Acts
Merchants	17	29.8	3	5.3		
Changers/Moneyers	4	7	2	3.5		
Retail/Wholesale	25	43.9	24	42.1	4	
Nobles/*Burgenses*	1	1.8				
Professions/Education						
Jews			6	10.5		
Royal Administration						
Ecclesiastics						
Women	6	10.5	1	1.8	n/a	n/a
Artisans/Service	2	3.5	4	7	2	1
Food Trades						
Agriculture						
Foreigners	2	3.5	16	28.1		
Unidentified						
Local						
Other			1	1.8		

the luxury trade utilized credit recognizances in the capacity of buyer and seller, as did their male counterparts.[54] They generally employed procurators, as men did, to draft their contracts before the notary and to carry out their business. They might also be present in person in such matters.

Widows were most commonly noted as participants in the luxury trade, as can be seen in Table 3, but wives were also represented in greater numbers than single women. The luxury trade demanded capital and commercial organization, resources that married and widowed women may have more readily enjoyed. Single women without a large inheritance would have lacked the requisite capital for luxury trade investments. Widowed mothers were present with their sons as buyers in further transactions of luxury commerce (Table 4.)[55] Women were notably absent from the spice trade, sector *par excellence* of international trade. They were not mentioned as sellers of mercery of Lucca, the elaborate brocades and damasks of the Lucchese silk-finishing industry, a branch of the silk trade that enjoyed considerable marketing specialization in Montpellier.[56] However, among the clients of the most prominent specialists in mercery of Lucca, the Cabanis brothers, merchants and mercers, was a widow of Toulouse, who purchased this product in person in Montpellier.[57]

TABLE 2

Cloth Transactions (Total Acts 140)

Social Category	All Sellers		All Buyers		Women Sellers	Women Buyers
	No. of Acts	% Total Acts	No. of Acts	% Total Acts	No. of Acts	No. of Acts
Merchants	49	35.0	11	7.9		
Changers/Moneyers						
Retail/Wholesale	65	46.4	14	10.0		
Nobles/*Burgenses*			7	5.0		
Professions/Education	1	1.0	2	1.4		
Jews						
Royal Administration			1	1.0	1	
Ecclesiastics			5	3.6		
Women	3	2.1	3	2.1	n/a	n/a
Artisans/Service	3	2.1	19	13.6		
Food Trades			1	1.0		
Agriculture			4	2.9		
Foreigners	18	12.9	70	50.0	1	2
Unidentified						
Local	1	1.0			1	1
Other			3	2.1		

Note: Linen, cotton, and cloth mixtures such as fustian are not included in these calculations.

The agricultural market in Montpellier also witnessed the participation of women. In fact, they were present in considerable numbers in the commodity trade as buyers of grain and grapes (Tables 5 and 6). Women buying grain were concentrated in the more modest urban social and economic categories. Male buyers were more broadly representative of the population as a whole.[58] The foreign women noted in Table 5 were rural villagers who, like their numerous male counterparts, often purchased grain in Montpellier in years of bad harvest such as 1327 and 1333.[59] While few couples were present selling grain, thirteen were recorded in grain purchases (Table 4). By the same token, grain purchases were made by common action of men and women of different surnames from villages surrounding Montpellier; their relationship remains inscrutable in the documents. The involvement of women in grain purchases reflects the role of provider alluded to earlier. Bread was the staple of the medieval diet.

Women were also actively involved in the grape trade in a region where cultivation of the vine was as important in the Middle Ages as it is today.

TABLE 3

Marital Status of Women in Business

Economic Sector	Single Sellers	Buyers	Widowed Sellers	Buyers	Married Sellers	Buyers	Unknown
Luxury Trade							
Spices	—	—	—	—	—	—	—
Silks	—	—	4	—	2	1	—
Mercery of Lucca	—	—	—	4	—	—	—
Woollen Cloths	1	1	—	1	2	1	—
Skins and Leather	—	—	—	—	—	—	—
Commodities							
Wool	—	—	1	—	—	—	—
Grain	1	—	1	8	—	1	—
Grapes	—	—	4	8	2	5	—
Animals	—	—	5	1	—	1	—
	Investors	Workers	Investors	Workers	Investors	Workers	Unknown
Partnerships							
Maritime *Comanda*	1	—	2	—	—	—	—
Maritime *Societas*	—	—	—	—	—	—	—
Land *Comanda*	—	—	9	2	2	—	—
Land *Societas*	—	—	1	1	—	—	—

	Lenders	Borrowers	Lenders	Borrowers	Lenders	Borrowers	Unknown
Finance							
Money Exchange	—	—	—	—	—	—	—
Loans	11	6	11	17	7	7	—
	Sellers	Buyers	Sellers	Buyers	Sellers	Buyers	Unknown
Real Estate							
Land	4	1	29	9	23	16	2
Houses	5	3	3	7	11	3	—
Land Rights	1	1	7	4	2	2	3
House Rights	—	—	4	1	—	—	1
Shop Rights	—	—	1	—	—	—	—
	Lessors	Lessees	Lessors	Lessees	Lessors	Lessees	Unknown
Shop Rents	—	—	10	—	—	—	—
Land Rents	—	—	6	1	1	1	—
House Rents	4	10	19	8	4	2	1
Accapitum/Emphyteusis							
Houses	—	—	1	—	—	2	—
Lands	—	1	8	8	1	9	—
TOTALS	28	23	118	80	57	51	7

TABLE 4

Kinship in Business

Economic Sector	Total Acts[1]	Father/ Son	Father/ Daughter	Mother/ Son	Mother/ Daughter	Parents/ Child	Aunt Uncle/ Nephew	Uncle/ Niece	Siblings	In-Laws[2]	Inter-family[2]	Same Name	Total Kin No.	Total Kin %	Couples
Partnership															
Maritime *Comanda*	53				1I				2W	1	5	1I	10	18.9	
Maritime *Societas*	2										1		1	50.0	
Land *Comanda*	38	1I/1W				1I				1	4	1I	9	23.7	3W
Land *Societas*	22			1W			1I			1	6		9	40.9	
Luxury Trade															
Spices	33								3S			2B	5	15.2	
Silks	47	1S/1B							1S/2B				5	10.6	2B
Mercery of Lucca	13			1B									1	7.7	2B
Woollen Cloth	132	2S/4B		3B					18S/9B			4S/3B	43	32.6	2B
Skins and Leather	35			2B					1S			1S/2B	6	17.1	3B
Transport	43								4C/1T			1T	6	14.0	
Commodities															
Grain	189	2S/6B		3B		4B	1B		5S/6B			4B	31	16.4	4S/13B
Grapes	107	1S		1S		1S						2B	5	4.7	18S/1B
Animals	123	2S										2S	4	3.3	2S
Finance															
Money Exchange	64	2C							4C/5D			4C/5D	20	31.3	
Loans	375	1C/12D		10D	1D	1D	4D	1D	6C/11D	5D	1I	1C/4D	68	18.1	3C/58D

Real Estate															
House Sales	92	3S/1B		1S		2S			10S	1S	3	2S/1B	24	26.1	14S
Land Sales	249	5S		9S	3S	3S			9S/2B	1B	5	0S/1B	48	19.3	49S/3B
House Rentals	136	4L/4R		4L	3L			1L	6L	1L	1	1R	25	18.4	5L/6R
Land Rentals	36			1L			1L		3L	1L		2L/2R	10	27.8	1R
Rentals/Tables and Shops	26								2L	2L			4	15.4	2R
Accapitum/ Emphyteusis															
Houses	8								1L				1	12.5	1L
Lands	107	12L/1R		1L/1R		3L			2L/2R		1		23	21.5	3L/1R
Land Exchanges	22								1			2	3	13.6	9
Sharecropping	23					1L			2L				3	13.0	
Rights of Use	106		1S	2S		3S	1S		6S	1S	3	3S/3R	23	21.7	12S/2R

[1]Figures do not include data from the Nogareti register for the Cabanis family, as these would have skewed the results.

[2]If there is no key symbol, contracts are between family members. In those cases where family members comprised *one* of the contracting parties in contracts of the economic sectors on the left, the specifics of the famliy relationship were broken down. In those cases where *both* parties to a contract were family, the fact was recorded under the category of "Interfamily" and the relationship not broken down.

KEY:

W = Workers		I = Investors	
L = Landlords		R = Renters	
B = Buyers		C = Clients	
S = Sellers		T = Transporters	
C = Creditors		D = Debtors	

TABLE 5

Transactions in Grain (Total Acts 190)

Social Category	Women Sellers No. of Acts	Women Buyers No. of Acts
Merchants		
Changers/Moneyers		
Retail/Wholesale		
Nobles/*Burgenses*		
Professions/Education		
Jews		
Royal Administration		
Ecclesiastics		
Women		
Artisans/Service		2
Food Trades		2
Agriculture		1
Foreigners	1	4
Unidentified		
Local	1	
Other		
Grain Merchants		
TOTAL	2	9

The distribution of women sellers and buyers varied somewhat from the male population of participants.[60] No women of agricultural background were noted selling grapes, while four instances of agricultural women purchasing grapes have been recorded (Table 6). Among men, sellers in agriculture accounted for 45.5 percent of all sales. Vineyard cultivation was a labor-intensive effort in which women may have been less active than men.[61] Women did, however, own vineyards, as the real estate acts show. Women bought and sold on the futures market in grapes, as did their male counterparts. Numerous couples were recorded selling grapes (Table 4). Widows and their sons were involved jointly in a few additional grape and grain purchases.

In yet another sector of the agricultural market, women were present in sales of animals of transport and burden (Table 7). They were primarily of rural background or from the group of cultivators of urban Montpellier. In this area of trade, as in the grape and grain transactions, widows were by far the most heavily involved buyers and sellers (Table 3). Here, as in the luxury trade, women used the same credit and financial mechanisms as their male counterparts. In general, women were modestly represented in the

TABLE 6

Transactions in Grapes (Total Acts 112)

Social Category	Women Sellers No. of Acts	Women Buyers No. of Acts
Merchants		1
Changers/Moneyers		2
Retail/Wholesale	2	
Nobles/*Burgenses*		
Professions/Education	1	
Jews		
Royal Administration	1	
Ecclesiastics		
Women		
Artisans/Service	2	4
Food Trades		2
Agriculture		4
Foreigners		
Unidentified		
Local		
Other		
TOTAL	6	13

luxury and commodities markets of the town. They were not noted in the extant transport contracts by which luxury goods in particular were shipped to markets at Paris and the Champagne Fairs or to Spain and Italy.[62]

Women participated in international and local commerce on another level through partnership contracts, an important form of investment credit in Montpellier. Four types of commercial partnership contracts have survived: the maritime *comanda,* the maritime *societas,* in which no women were participants, the land *comanda,* and the land *societas.*[63] The majority of female partners concentrated their activities in land trade as opposed to international maritime trade (Table 8). Out of fifty-nine surviving maritime contracts, women were mentioned in only three.[64] In one instance two sisters financed their brother's venture in the export of linen cloths to Cyprus and Armenia through a maritime *comanda* of 260 *l. t.*[65] They acquired 250 *l.* of linen cloth on credit and 50 *l.* in loan from a local merchant. In order to secure their debt to him they turned over a credit obligation that they held against a Jew of Montpellier for a house purchase. In a second act a draper's widow and daughter, who were subordinate investors in the export of French wool cloth and local cloths to the Byzantine Empire, contributed 65.2 *l. t.* to a total capital of 625.4 *l.*[66] It was not

TABLE 7

Animal Transactions (Total Acts 124)

Social Category	All Sellers No. of Acts	All Sellers % Total Acts	All Buyers No. of Acts	All Buyers % Total Acts	Women Sellers No. of Acts	Women Buyers No. of Acts
Merchants	5	4.0	15	12.1		
Changers/Moneyers			2	1.6		
Retail/Wholesale	4	3.2	10	8.1		
Nobles/*Burgenses*			2	1.6		
Professions/Education			2	1.6		
Jews						
Royal Administration	1	0.8	3	2.4		
Ecclesiastics			3	2.4		
Women	5	4.0	2	1.6	n/a	n/a
Artisans/Service	17	13.7	20	16.1	1	1
Food Trades	7	5.6	7	5.6		
Agriculture	40	32.3	45	36.3	2	
Foreigners	42	33.9	13	10.5	2	
Unidentified						
Local	2	1.6				1
Other	1	0.8				

only women of the merchant class who chose maritime investment. An innkeeper's widow invested 50 *l. t.* in the trade of a grain merchant on land or on sea for one year.[67] Women were never involved in these partnerships as traveling partners in international maritime trade.

The main role of women in the surviving partnerships was, in fact, a passive one of sedentary investor. Even in the land-based contracts, women rarely played the working role. In one of the exceptions, a Franciscan friar was the investing partner in a land *comanda* with the widow of a cloth cutter who was the working partner.[68] In another instance, the widow of a silversmith accepted four and one-half marks of silver in *comanda* from a bachelor of canon law, perhaps to carry on the trade of her late husband's atelier.[69] Women and their sons might also be involved jointly as working partners.[70]

Women investing in land partnership contracts came from a broad spectrum of the local population, as shown in Table 8. In land *comande* widows predominated in nine of eleven instances, with wives present in two others.[71] Martha de Cabanis, widow of the mercer Guiraudus, acted as *curatrix* in a large bilateral *comanda* with a linen merchant as working partner.[72] Again, in the role of *curatrix*, Martha financed the largest surviv-

TABLE 8

Women in Partnership Contracts

Social Category	Land *Comanda* Investors	Maritime *Comanda* Investors	Land *Societas* Investors	Land *Societas* Jr. Partners	Land *Comanda* Workers
Merchants	2	2			
Changers/Moneyers	1				
Retail/Wholesale	2		1		
Nobles/*Burgenses*					
Professions/Education					
Jews					
Royal Administration					
Ecclesiastics					
Women					
Artisans/Service	1	1			2
Food Trades					
Agriculture	3				
Foreigners	2				
Unidentified					
Local					
Other				1	

ing land *societas* before 1350, capitalizing her partnership with a merchant through an investment of 1340 *l. t.*[73] Women and men united readily in partnership with one another at all levels of society. Family members joined together, as in the case of the fisherman who termed his mother-in-law, the widow of a shoemaker, *dicta socius mea.*[74]

In acts of partnership women were as versatile in their choice of partners as their male counterparts. Thus, the widow of a merchant financed fishermen in two *comanda* contracts, and the widow of a cultivator supplied capital for a silk merchant of Le Puy.[75] Interestingly, women were present in the only two extant *comanda* contracts that clearly show the conversion of real property into liquid capital for the purposes of partnership investment. In addition to the maritime investment by the two sisters noted above, a second act shows the widow of a man of Clermont-l'Hérault who had since migrated to Montpellier investing 20 *l.* from the profits of a home sale in Clermont in a *comanda* with a man of that town.[76] It may be that women's assets were often immobilized in real property, given the sources of their fortune in dowry and inheritance; record of moneyed dowries has, however, survived.[77] In another rare instance of financial practice, a woman demonstrated the negotiability of *comanda* credits by transferring them to a third party to offset a debt.[78]

The few international maritime investments by women were in the mainstream of the Montpellier export of wool cloths and linen to the Levant. The land *comanda* investments of women resembled investments by men in local trade and artisanal activities. Women were noted in substantial placement of funds. The main distinction to be underlined in partnership was the absence of women from the role of traveling merchant and the infrequency of their participation alone as working partners. Departure from the family home would have been more difficult for women at any stage in life—whether as mothers raising children and running a household or as young unmarried women or older widows—than for men. Factors mitigating against the activity of women as long-distance traders were the dangers inherent in travel—robbery and piracy—and the general hardship entailed by primitive roads and transportation systems.[79] Moreover, if no prescriptive literature regarding women's roles survives in medieval Montpellier, there is no reason to suggest that a woman's place as wife and mother was not the norm in local attitudes. This familial role was incompatible with long-distance travel. The career profile of the international merchant included a lengthy period of apprenticeship abroad, which resulted in late marriage for merchants of Montpellier.[80] In the majority of surviving marriage contracts, the man acted alone, a fact suggesting that he was probably at least twenty-five years of age.[81] This phenomenon was corroborated at all levels of society. Although there is no firm proof, given the absence of age statistics in marriage contracts, women may have married earlier. The fact that all obligations to their parents at the time of marriage, regardless of age, were declared valid by statute lends support to this contention.[82] Women contracted marriage in the majority of cases with the consent of both parents, one parent, other family members, or friends. Particularly in the case of merchant-class women, for whom dowry was no problem, marriage may have been early. Such factors would have weighed against the participation of women as traveling merchants.

Closely related to the urban commercial activities of Montpellier residents were those of banking and finance. The connections of foreign-exchange transactions to international trade can be amply demonstrated in the Montpellier evidence.[83] Women were not involved in extant foreign-exchange contracts, the domain of the merchant bankers and money changers.[84] In contrast, women were well represented in local lending activities.[85] They were recorded in 29 loans as lenders (7.6 percent of the total) and in 30 as borrowers (7.8 percent of the total) out of 384 surviving acts. Among the lenders women were rather evenly distributed across a whole range of social backgrounds; their fathers and husbands were changers, moneyers, members of the retail/wholesale trades, artisans, members of the service and food trades, and foreigners. Some women lenders were simply termed inhabitants of Montpellier by the notary. Women lent money to acquaintances and to their sons; especially in the case of widows, these loans were investments for profit.

The involvement of women in lending shows a somewhat different distribution of social groups than that of men. Merchants (12.2 percent of the total lenders) were the most frequently noted male lenders outside of the Jews. Women of merchant background accounted for only 3.4 percent of women lenders. Agricultural and artisan/service backgrounds were more heavily represented among women lenders than among men. While lending money was a common practice in Montpellier, in spite of ecclesiastical prohibitions of usury, women of the mercantile elite may have been less involved in this activity because of the lingering stigma attached to it and because their participation in business overall was a less necessary component of family survival than at other economic levels within society.[86]

Although female lenders and borrowers were of comparable numbers, borrowers were drawn from different social strata. Few mercantile and financial backgrounds were noted. Instead, artisanal and agricultural milieux provided women borrowers, as did the villages within a radius of fifty kilometers from Montpellier. This distribution was similar to that of male borrowers. Fifteen of the thirty women borrowers were not from Montpellier, though thirteen of those fifteen were from nearby. Most of the nonresident borrowers were clients for small loans—some in kind—from Jewish lenders at the end of the thirteenth century.[87] Women were noted further as borrowers in ten loans in association with their sons and in one case with a daughter (Table 4). The pattern of women's borrowing that emerges from these acts was one of consumption and subsistence, consistent with the traditional female role of family food provider. Much of the medieval population lived on the border of starvation.[88] Especially in the rural hinterland around Montpellier, bad harvests created real hardship, causing inhabitants to go into debt.

Single and widowed women were noted in equal numbers as money lenders (Table 3). Married women appeared less often in this role. In all likelihood, single women, after a certain age, and widows had more control over their resources than married women, whose dowries were assimilated with their husbands' goods.[89] Widows of humble background far outnumbered both single and married women as borrowers, suggesting the difficult financial straits of their status.

The activities associated with medieval banking and finance included foreign exchange, lending, and deposit banking. Women made investment deposits and accepted safekeeping deposits. Thus a changer secured the deposit of 200 *l. melg.* made to him by his widowed sister in 1301.[90] In the same year the daughter of a deceased draper requested the transfer of her deposit of 60 *l.*, instituted by court order initially, from one party to another, with the expectation of receiving up to 6 *l.* (10 percent return) a year for her needs.[91] In 1343 a widow recognized before the notary that she held fifty Florentine florins *in custodia* for a master of medicine.[92] Deposit banking left relatively little trace overall in the Montpellier documents; hence, the participation of women is significant here. The degree of sophistication of operations by Montpellier changers, the traditional medieval deposit bankers, remains obscure, but there is no evidence to indicate that women were other than clients in the financial practices of changers.[93] In the related area of recovery and payment of debts, women were heavily involved, often as a reflection of their roles as administrators of the husbands' estates and as guardians of their children.[94]

Women were well represented in the complex real estate market of Montpellier, due undoubtedly to factors of dowry and inheritance.[95] They formed 21.8 percent of the sellers of land, a percentage higher than that of any one category of male sellers, and 10.7 percent of the land buyers; in these transactions women utilized credit infrequently and cash with regularity at rates that fall in the mid-range of male behavior. Less than one-tenth of women's sales of land were on credit while just under one-fifth of their purchases were with credit, an indication that women were perhaps cash poor. The male artisanal and service trades of Montpellier showed an even greater preference, relatively speaking, for credit purchases, with over one-third of their transactions so designed. In general, credit was less commonly employed in real estate than in the luxury trade of Montpellier. Over half of the sales and purchases of women were in vineyards, making them among the most active agents in this type of land sale. The climate of Montpellier and the pride of urban inhabitants in having their own *caves* made vineyards a common real estate investment.

House sales also drew women in impressive numbers, at 20.7 percent of the total participants, again a rate higher than that of any one male social group. Women bought houses with frequency, representing 14.1 percent of the total buyers. They recorded credit transactions in houses in numbers comparable to men. For no one group were credit sales an important feature of house transactions. Women's presence as proprietors of housing may reflect the composition of dowries and inheritance. Urban housing could be a profitable investment if rented out or exploited through one of the several methods described below. Housing management was less complex and less speculative than the administration of rural agricultural lands, whose yields might fluctuate enormously from year to year. Such facility may have been an attractive feature for urban women investors.

The social distribution of women sellers of land spanned a large cross-section of the population, with representation in all groups except nobles, *burgenses*, Jews, and royal administration. However, women of agricultural background were by far the most numerous sellers, accounting for 32.1 percent of female sales. In the general pool of the male population agricultural workers represented only 15.6 percent of the land sellers. Given the rigors and uncertainties of agriculture in the fourteenth century, it may be that many widows of local cultivators found themselves in need of converting land into cash.[96] Such an interpretation is consistent with their infrequent use of credit sales. Widows comprised the largest group of land sellers (Table 3). Married women were also present in important numbers; generally they stated that they had their husband's permission to act.[97]

Women selling and buying houses were more evenly distributed across the local social groups with the retail/wholesale and artisanal/service trades the sources of the largest numbers of women sellers. Buyers were uniformly representative of social groups with the exception of Jews and royal administration, groups absent from the pool of male sellers as well. Women were the only representatives of the category of nobles and *burgenses* to buy houses. For the reasons described above, housing could be a profitable and less burdensome investment than agricultural holdings. Women of the urban nobility were not active in commerce; their behavior may resemble that of a rentier class, for which nonspeculative, conservative investments were preferred.

In the exploitation of real property, women were again active. Many methods of deriving income from real estate were employed in this era: house and land rents, sharecropping, *accapitum* and *emphiteusis* tenurial arrangements.[98] Women were present in smaller numbers as lessees in these engagements. They were particularly dominant in the renting out of tables and shops in the markets of Montpellier, accounting for about one-third of the total transactions; they were never recorded as shop tenants. They were familiar with the means of generating real estate revenues from methods such as sales of rights in lands, houses, and shops for specific periods of time. One can also note their activity in land exchanges. Women as a group showed a preference for short- over long-term contracts in exploiting real estate holdings. This trend was especially marked among women from the artisanal/service trades and from agriculture. Women investors could be more responsive to market evolution and to adjustments for inflation and currency manipulation as a result. In sum, women had important interests in urban and rural property, demonstrating the full gamut of real estate techniques.[99]

As shown in Table 4, women acted with their children in land transactions. Couples were frequently sellers of land. Real estate sales were often accompanied by formal approvals of family members. In southern France, as elsewhere in medieval Europe, there was a strong predilection for families to guard jealously the kin's right of oversight in matters of property.[100]

After this rapid survey of women's participation in business in Montpellier, it is useful to highlight features of the urban environment that may account in part for women's economic roles observed in this study. In the sixty years preceding the Black Death of 1348, Montpellier had between thirty and forty thousand inhabitants, a significant population by medieval standards.[101] The population had reached a plateau by the end of the thirteenth century, and the economy was no longer in an expansive phase.[102] It did, however, demonstrate some resilience. In the uncertain economic conditions of the early fourteenth century, there may have been population pressure creating a tight job market, but the continued influx of foreign apprentices casts doubt on the magnitude of this pressure.[103] What, if any, competition for jobs existed remains unknown. No wage data permit comparison of male and female wages. That inhabitants were discontented is demonstrated by the unrest and factionalism of fiscal revolts in the 1320s and 1330s.[104]

The participation of women in an impressive variety of economic sectors is worth underscoring in light of these social and economic conditions. A cross-section of the urban population of women appeared in the notarial contracts. Distinctions of a social and economic nature among women's activities were more a matter of scale than of type. It comes as no surprise that women of Montpellier were not in the vanguard of international trade and finance, nor is it unexpected that they were not mentioned as traveling merchants on land or on sea. The long training in distant lands of the international merchant was irreconcilable with the demands of home, marriage, and family. Women were occasionally the recipients of local investment partnerships, but in most cases their role was one of sedentary investor. The remaining business contracts portray women as fully cognizant of the standard credit and investment mechanisms of the day. These business techniques were far from obscure; they were utilized by all social groups within the town. Women may have become familiar with these practices through observation of male family members or friends at work or through the advice of such individuals or even from the professional counsel of specialists such as the notary.

Women's work in industry and crafts was concentrated in areas typical of women's involvement throughout western Europe: the food trades, textiles, and precious metals. However, the absence of a significant wool cloth industry in Montpellier reduced the range of traditional textile roles for women. In Montpellier and elsewhere in Europe these women's trades were related to traditional female roles of provider of food, clothing, and ornament for the family. These occupations reflect a sharp sexual division of labor.

Real estate may well have been the sector in which women were most active. In this they shared some of the characteristics of a rentier class. Property was a conservative form of investment, in contrast to trade, where the risks multiplied with distance and difficulty of travel. Women did not specialize in speculative forms of capital investment such as foreign exchange. They lacked experience as changers and merchant bankers. While they were noted in international commercial investment, they seem to have favored economic stability over high profits. Widows often had responsibility for the welfare and support of children, preoccupations that could deter aggressive speculation. The widowed mother's role as guardian of her children was at the root of the frequent cooperation of mothers and sons noted in Table 4.

Widows emerge as the most active group among Montpellier women.[105] Because of their independence and potential means—they were free from their husbands' constraints and probably from their fathers' as well—widows were better equipped to participate in more diverse economic areas. Widows had an incentive not to remarry because the usufruct of their husbands' property was often dependent upon widowhood. The incidence of remarriage appears relatively low in Montpellier. Of the 132 marriage contracts surviving, only 7 instances of remarriage were recorded.[106]

Married women registered sufficient economic activity to vindicate the statutory posture that they might act with their husbands' consent or on their own responsibility if they exercised trades themselves. Their activities have almost the same breadth, if not the frequency, of widows' business operations. The demands of home and family could be reconciled with local economic ventures.

Single women were present in fewer numbers than either widows or wives. They had narrower investment options because without in-laws or children they had more limited contacts. They seem to have preferred reliable sources of revenues to preserve their livelihood. Single women appeared most often in real estate transactions and in loans, suggesting a conservative approach to business on their part. There is no way of knowing what proportion of the urban female population within Montpellier was single. However, the town can be characterized as one of merchants, jurists, doctors, university professors, students, and clerics, men who remained bachelors or married late in life.[107] Montpellier may not have been the most auspicious marriage market.

The notarial contracts of Montpellier portray women in active economic roles in the first half of the fourteenth century. Further work should test whether this relatively positive situation survived the era of the Black Death and the dramatic demographic changes that Montpellier experienced.[108] Before 1348 one possible explanation for women's participation in business could lie, somewhat ironically, in the weaker and less traditional configuration of the family in the urban setting. Urban families were more fragile than rural families because of the difficult living conditions in towns. Immigration itself caused disruption of family ties. Crowding in towns led to poor hygiene and rapid spread of disease. If much of women's influence in the rural setting, which characterized the early Middle Ages, had been through family channels, in some towns family structure, rather than evolving along patriarchal lines, tended to fragment.[109] Women were forced to assume more independence. The low incidence of kinship ties observed in business operations in Montpellier may have favored female activities.[110] There were times when women acted without a base in family enterprise, perhaps on behalf of their own trades. Women's economic involvement was not a direct parallel of men's roles, but the activities of Montpelliéraines were well integrated into the local business community and conspicuous within the urban economy of the pre-plague era.

Notes

1. Thanks go to my colleague Sara Evans for her comments on this paper. Montpellier Law School doctoral theses that treat topics involving the legal status of women include Jean Hilaire, *Le régime des biens entre époux dans la région de Montpellier du début du XIIIe siècle à la fin du XVIe siècle* (Montpellier: Causse, Graille & Castelnau, 1957) and Louis de Charrin, *Les testaments dans la région de Montpellier au moyen âge* (Ambilly, 1961). Useful articles on the subject are by Edmond Meynial, "Des renunciations au moyen âge et dans notre ancien droit," *Revue historique de droit français et étranger,* ser. 3:25 (1901): 241–77, and Pierre Tisset, "Placentin et son enseignement à Montpellier. Droit romain et Coutume dans l'ancien pays de Septimanie," *Recueil de mémoires et travaux publiés par la société d'histoire du droit et des institutions des anciens pays de droit écrit,* fasc. 2 (1951): 67–94. By way of general background on the topic of this study, a somewhat anecdotal treatment of the urban woman in the Middle Ages is to be found in several chapters of Frances and Joseph Gies, *Women in the Middle Ages* (New York: Barnes & Noble, 1978).

2. Future studies will address the role of women through an investigation of the charter and cartulary evidence and in portraits of individual women's activities, which will flesh out the skeletal nature of this initial analysis. Data for this study were drawn from the notarial registers II 1–3 of the Archives Municipales de Montpellier (hereafter abbreviated A. M.) and II E 95/368–377 of the Archives Départementales de l'Hérault (hereafter abbreviated A. D.).

The notarial registers of Montpellier are collections of legally valid instruments written by notaries who had been licensed by public authority as recorders of public and private law transactions within medieval society. The notarial instrument might be a will, a contract, an act of litigation, an emancipation, an appointment to office, an acquittal, a statement or letter of one kind or another, solemnly registered by the notary in the presence of witnesses. The notary's register or cartulary served the purpose of a much expanded registry of deeds, preserving notations of engagements for which written proof might be needed in the future. These records provide a texture, depth, and range of evidence unequaled in the terse entries of the town chronicle of Montpellier and in the municipal statutes, and a consistency missing from the thousands of individual charters housed in the Archives Municipales de Montpellier. Notarial records furnish a practical laboratory for the study of business operations. On the use of this sort of evidence, see David Herlihy, *Pisa in the Early Renaissance: A Study of Urban Growth* (New Haven: Yale University Press, 1958), pp. 1–20.

3. Jo Ann McNamara and Suzanne Wemple, "The Power of Women through the Family in Medieval Europe: 500–1100," *Feminist Studies* 1 (1972): 136–38. One might note that queens such as Blanche of Castile were still able to exert tremendous influence in a later period. Another study suggesting decline is that of Marion F. Facinger, "A Study of Medieval Queenship: Capetian France, 987–1237," *Studies in Medieval and Renaissance History* 5 (1968): 1–48.

4. On strategies of family preservation, see Georges Duby, *La société aux XIe et XIIe siècles dans la région mâconnaise* (Paris: A. Colin, 1953).

5. Régine Pernoud, *La femme au temps des cathédrales* (Paris: Editions Stock, 1980), recently advanced the hypothesis that the position of women in France declined with the rise of the bourgeoisie at the end of the Middle Ages. A revisionist view of the fate of urban women in early modern Europe is provided by Judith C. Brown and Jordan Goodman, "Women and Industry in Florence," *Journal of Economic History* 40 (1980): 73–80.

6. On the downtrends in urban population in the later Middle Ages, see Harry A. Miskimin, *The Economy of Early Renaissance Europe, 1300–1460* (1969; reprint, Cambridge: Cambridge University Press, 1975), pp. 73–77.

7. On the diversity of the urban population, see my dissertation, "Commerce and Society in Montpellier: 1250–1350," 2 vols. (Ph. D. diss., Yale University, 1974), pp. 1–56. See also Louis J. Thomas, *Montpellier, ville marchande: histoire économique et sociale des origines à 1870* (Montpellier: Librairie Valat, Librairie Coulet, 1936).

8. Alexandre Teulet, ed., *Layettes du Trésor des chartes*, I (Paris: Plon, 1863), provides the most reliable editions of these statutes. For the tenth through the twelfth centuries, David Herlihy has argued for the high status of women in southern France. See "Land, Family, and Women in Continental Europe, 701–1200," *Traditio* 18 (1962): 89–120; reprinted in *Women in Medieval Society*, ed. Susan Stuard (Philadelphia: University of Pennsylvania Press, 1976), pp. 13–45. To date there exist few studies of women in contractual law and business. One work of interest, however, is Susan Stuard, "Women in Charter and Statute Law: Medieval Ragusa/Dubrovnik," in *Women in Medieval Europe*, pp. 199–208.

9. Meynial, pp. 264–67. On the *Senatusconsultum Velleianum*, see Adolf Berger, *Encyclopedic Dictionary of Roman Law* (Philadelphia: The American Philosophical Society, 1953), p. 700. By the *Senatusconsultum Velleianum* women were forbidden to assume liability for others. On marital authorization see Hilaire, pp. 118–32.

10. Teulet, p. 259: "Si mulier fidejusserit pro aliquo vel pro aliqua, tenetur in illis casibus in quibus leges permittunt. Nam secundum leges viget intercessio femine: creditoris ignorancia, obligantis se scientia, largitione, rei proprie racione, renunciatione, pignoris [vel] yppotece remissione, secundo post biennium cautione, coram tribus testibus in instrumento preemissa confessione, libertate, dote, et si

exerceat officium et gratia illius intercedat, vel voluntate mariti, efficaciter obligatur." See also Tisset, p. 87.

11. For a discussion of the institution of *fideiussor,* see Mireille Castaing-Sicard, *Les contrats dans le très ancien droit toulousain* (Toulouse: Imprimerie M. Espic, 1959), pp. 379–403. For an important example of a woman acting as *fidejutrix,* see the case of Mirabelle, wife of Johannes Andree, in my article "Commercial Fraud in the Middle Ages: The Case of the Dissembling Pepperer," *Journal of Medieval History* 8 (1982): 63–73.

12. Hilaire, pp. 112–13.

13. E.g., A. D. II E 95/370, J. Holanie, f. 69r, for a woman acting without her husband's consent.

14. Tisset, p. 80.

15. Article 90 of the 1204 statutes; see Teulet, p. 262.

16. See the discussion of apprenticeship contracts below.

17. Meynial, pp. 266–67, and Tisset, p. 86. See also Hilaire, pp. 102–17. It should also be noted that the husband often made a marital gift to the wife in the form of the *augment.* See Hilaire, pp. 192–201.

18. Tisset, p. 88, and article 12 of the 1204 statutes; Teulet, p. 256.

19. Tisset, p. 98, and article 54 of the 1204 statutes; Teulet, p. 260.

20. Hilaire, pp. 136–91. The issue of restitution was a complex one, often governed by the specific clauses of the marriage contract.

21. De Charrin, pp. 118–22, studied the institution of the guardian in the Montpellier evidence. I plan a future study of the mother's role as guardian of her children in the writings of the early fourteenth-century jurist Petrus Jacobi.

22. Agnes de Bossones, widow of Petrus, money changer, figures frequently in A. M. II 1, J. Grimaudi, in these roles.

23. I will draw the general context for this study from two works, a book, *Business, Banking and Finance in Medieval Montpellier* (Toronto: Pontifical Institute of Mediaeval Studies, 1985), and a long article, "Land, Houses and Real Estate Investment in Montpellier: A Study of the Notarial Property Transactions, 1293–1348," in *Studies in Medieval and Renaissance History* 6 (Old Series, vol. 16) (1983): 37–112.

24. See "Land, Houses and Real Estate Investment," note 27, for a detailed discussion of the selection of these social categories.

25. These roles are sometimes subsumed under the label "breeder-feeder." See Elise Boulding, "The Historical Roots of Occupational Segregation. Familial Constraints on Women's Work Roles," *Signs* 1 (1976) supplement: 95–117.

26. As an example, consider A. D. II E 95/371, J. Holanie, f. 109r: "Johanna, uxor quondam Bernardi Senareti ortolani Montispessulani."

27. Consider "Alazacia, filia Bertrandi de Alamanha, habitatrix Montispessulani" in A. D. II E 95/369, J. Holanie, f. 81v. The name occurs in the dative in the act itself as Alazacia was owed money in a loan.

28. An exception can be found in A. D. II E 95/369, J. Holanie, f. 4r, "Rixenda Ganterius, pistrix" (baker), with the name again in the dative in the act as she was owed money in a loan. On the notarial naming practices in general, see my article "Patterns of Population Attraction and Mobility: The Case of Montpellier, 1293–1348," *Viator* 10 (1979): 266.

29. André Gouron, *La réglementation des métiers en Languedoc au moyen âge* (Geneva: Librairie E. Droz, 1958), pp. 245–46.

30. Ibid. One can contrast the Montpellier situation with that of northern Eu-

rope. See E. Dixon, "Craftswomen in the *Livre des Metiers*," *Economic Journal* 5 (1895): 209–28, and Annie Abram, "Women Traders in Medieval London," *Economic Journal* 26 (1916): 276–85. On women in medieval London, see also Sylvia L. Thrupp, *The Merchant Class of Medieval London* (1948; reprint, Ann Arbor: The University of Michigan Press, 1962, 1968), pp. 169–74.

31. See my article "Patterns of Population," p. 267, for a breakdown of all apprenticeship contracts by year and geographic origin of apprentices.

32. On the absence of a cloth industry, see my article "Le rôle de Montpellier dans le commerce des draps de laine avant 1350," *Annales du Midi* 94 (1982): 17–40.

33. "Patterns of Population," pp. 271–72. Recall the baker's trade of the *fournier* ordinances. The term here is *pistor, pistrix.*

34. Ibid., pp. 272–74.

35. Compare Eileen Power, *Medieval Women,* ed. M. M. Postan (Cambridge: Cambridge University Press, 1975), p. 58.

36. E.g., a brother apprenticing his sister: A. D. II E 95/368, J. Holanie, f. 32v.

37. E.g., the apprenticeship of a son of a first marriage by a wife of a merchant and a cousin: A. D. II E 95/368, J. Holanie, f. 127v.

38. "Patterns of Population," p. 272, note 77.

39. A. D. II E 95/368, J. Holanie, f. 135v. The term for gilder is *deaurator;* an alternative translation might be goldsmith. I am currently collaborating on an article with Faye Powe on medieval metalwork, in which she hopes to determine a better rendition of *deaurator.*

40. A. D. II E 95/368, J. Holanie, f. 56v. See *Business, Banking and Finance,* Appendix II, "Monetary Problems," for a discussion of currencies in the Montpellier notarial registers. *D.t.* = *deniers tournois, s.t.* = *sous tournois, l.t.* = *livres tournois.* All sums have been converted to the good silver standard of April 1330.

41. A. D. II E 95/368, J. Holanie, f. 131v.

42. Women of the Mediterranean world were often involved in such activities. See William N. Bonds, "Genoese Noblewomen and Gold Thread Manufacturing," *Medievalia et Humanistica,* fasc. 19 (1966): 79–81. On the importance of women in the silk industry elsewhere in Europe, see Marian K. Dale, "The London Silkwomen of the Fifteenth Century," *Economic History Review* 4 (1933): 324–35, and Dixon, pp. 218–21.

43. A. D. II E 95/377, B. Egidii, f. 227 r.

44. A. D. II E 95/368, J. Holanie, f. 37r: tailoring; II E 95/371, J. Holanie, f. 38v: tailoring; II E 95/368, J. Holanie, f. 136r: linen corduroy; A. M. II 1, J. Grimaudi, f. 80v: silk corduroy.

45. A. D. II E 95/369, J. Holanie, f. 13v: mercery. The statutes of the mercers are found in A. M., *fonds du Grand Chartrier,* Arm. C, Cass. 1, Louvet no. 1117. Mercery as a trade encompasses a broad range of activities in Montpellier, from silk-cloth sales to what we would today term "notions": ribbons, thread, decorative accessories.

46. On the involvement of Montpellier with silks, see my article "Medieval Silks in Montpellier: The Silk Market ca. 1250–ca. 1350," *The Journal of European Economic History* 11 (1982): 117–40.

47. Ibid. See below.

48. A. D. II E 95/368, J. Holanie, f. 50r: basket weaving; II E 95/377, B. Egidii, f. 28r: painting; II E 95/368, J. Holanie, f. 30r: old clothes; II E 95/369, J. Holanie, f. 38r.

49. A. D. II E 95/371, J. Holanie, f. 50r: *ancilla,* or servant.
50. A. D. II E 95/368, J. Holanie, f. 136r.
51. Ibid., f. 37r.
52. Ibid., f. 135v. It should be noted that sons followed their fathers' trade infrequently according to the extant apprenticeship evidence.
53. Chapter 2, "Credit in the Market Place," in *Business, Banking and Finance,* deals in general with the luxury trade and the commodities market.
54. Ibid., for a discussion of credit mechanisms in Montpellier trade.
55. An earlier version of the table "Kinship in Business" was first presented in a paper entitled "Kinship in Business: The Case of Medieval Montpellier," given at the Eighteenth International Congress of Medieval Studies, Western Michigan University, Kalamazoo, Michigan, May 1983.
56. See "Medieval Silks," p. 128.
57. A. D. II E 95/374, G. Nogareti, f. 38r. Another widow of Toulouse dealt through a procurator in Montpellier to purchase mercery of Lucca. See ff. 30r and 38r.
58. The tables of total participants in the grape and grain trades are published in Chapter 2, "Credit in the Market Place," in *Business, Banking and Finance.*
59. On agricultural problems of the south of France, see Marie-Josèphe Larenaudie, "Les famines en Languedoc au XIVe siècle," *Annales du Midi* 64 (1952): 27–39. See also "Commerce and Society in Montpellier," 1: 212–24.
60. See note 58 above.
61. On grape cultivation in the region of Montpellier, see Gaston Galtier, "Le vignoble et le vin dans le Languedoc oriental de la fin du XIe siècle à la Guerre de Cent Ans," in *Etudes médiévales offertes à M. le Doyen Fliche de l'Institut* (Montpellier: Faculté des Lettres et Sciences Humaines, 1952), p. 9.
62. For a synopsis of transport contracts, see "Commerce and Society in Montpellier," 2: 261–67.
63. For a detailed discussion of partnership in Montpellier, see Chapter 1, "Investment in Business Partnerships," in *Business, Banking and Finance.* Tables of total participants are found in this chapter. It should be noted that *comanda* is the local spelling of *commenda.*
64. Table 3 of "Investment in Business Partnerships" lists two women since only the major investing partners were tallied.
65. A. M. II 2, J. Grimaudi, f. 14r.
66. A. D. II E 95/372, J. Holanie et al., f. 13r.
67. A. D. II E 95/369, J. Holanie, f. 45v. On modest investors in maritime *commenda* contracts in other Mediterranean towns, see Hilmar Krueger, "Genoese Merchants, Their Partnerships and Investments, 1155–1164," in *Studi in Onore di Armando Sapori* (Milan, 1957) 1:259–71, and Rosalind Berlow, "The Sailing of the 'Saint-Esprit'," *The Journal of Economic History* 39 (1979): 345–62.
68. A. D. II E 95/368, J. Holanie, f. 36v.
69. A. D. II E 95/372, J. Holanie et al., f. 48v.
70. See Table 4 and A. D. II E 95/376, J. Laurentii, f. 5r.
71. See Table 3.
72. A. D. II E 95/374, G. Nogareti, f. 18rR.
73. Ibid., f. 12vR.
74. A. D. II E 95/372, J. Holanie et al., f. 38r.
75. A. D. II E 95/369, J. Holanie, f. 52r and 95v; II E 95/371, J. Holanie, f. 22r.
76. See note 65 above, and A. D. II E 95/368, J. Holanie, f. 59r.

77. On moneyed dowries, see Hilaire, pp. 98–100. They became increasingly common after the mid-fourteenth century.

78. A. D. II E 95/369, J. Holanie, f. 43r.

79. There were, of course, female vagabonds who coped with such dangers as best they could. See the comments of Boulding, p. 109.

80. Claude Carrère, *Barcelone: centre économique, 1380–1462,* 2 vols. (Paris: Mouton, 1967), found this to be true for merchants of Barcelona. Diane Hughes, "Urban Growth and Family Structure in Medieval Genoa," *Past and Present* 66 (1975): 25, suggested the opposite to be characteristic of Genoese merchants, who married while still in their teens.

81. The notarial registers, the *Grand Chartrier,* and the *fonds de la Commune Clôture* of the Archives Municipales all contain marriage contracts.

82. See note 15 above.

83. See Chapter 5, "Foreign Exchange," in *Business, Banking and Finance* for general background.

84. For a synopsis of foreign-exchange contracts, see "Commerce and Society in Montpellier," 2:269–78.

85. See Chapter 3, "Loans," in *Business, Banking and Finance* for the tables involving total participants and women participants mentioned below.

86. On usury in Montpellier, see my article "Les opérations de crédit dans la coutume et dans la vie des affaires à Montpellier au moyen âge: le problème de l'usure," in *Diritto comune et diritti locali nella storia dell'Europe* (Milan: Guiffrè, 1980), pp. 189–209.

87. On loans by Jews of Montpellier, see R. W. Emery, *The Jews of Perpignan in the Thirteenth Century* (New York: Columbia University Press, 1959), pp. 131–33, Appendix 3.

88. The muncipal chronicle of Montpellier stated in the year 1333 that famine raged, young men were weakened by a diet of raw herbs, and people were dying in the streets. See "La chronique romane," in *Le Petit Thalamus de Montpellier,* ed. F. Pégat, E. Thomas, and Desmazes (Montpellier, 1840), p. 347.

89. See note 17 above.

90. A. M. II 1, J. Grimaudi, f. 37r.

91. A. M. II 2, J. Grimaudi, f. 53v. For a further example, see A. D. II E 95/375, P. de Pena, f. 119r.

92. A. D. II E 95/372, J. Holanie et al., f. 36r.

93. See the comments in Chapter 5, "Deposit Banking and the Recovery of Debts," in *Business, Banking and Finance.* Robert Favreaux, "Les changeurs du royaume de France sous le règne de Louis XI," *Bibliothèque de l'Ecole des Chartres* 122 (1964): 216–51, found evidence of women changers in a slightly later period. Raymond de Roover, *Money, Banking and Credit in Medieval Bruges; Italian Merchant-Bankers, Lombards and Money-Changers* (Cambridge, Mass.: Mediaeval Academy of America, 1948), pp. 173–74, stated that money changing was open to women.

94. See note 22 above. Women may have enjoyed a more generous fate as debtors than did men, thus benefiting from somewhat greater protection under the law. There is a suggestion in the statutes of 29 June 1221 (Teulet, pp. 519–20) that male debtors were subject to a harsher regime of punishment than females. Debtors specifically identified as male could be turned over to the mercy of their creditors, who, if the debtors did not have the means of nourishing themselves, would feed them according to the decisions of the court of Montpellier.

95. My article "Land, Houses and Real Estate Investment" provides tables of

overall real estate participation and women's participation in property transactions. The comments below regarding real estate are drawn from this study.

96. On general fourteenth-century problems, see Elisabeth Carpentier, "Autour de la peste noire: famines et épidémies dans l'histoire du XIVe siècle," *Annales: Economies, Sociétés, Civilisations* 18 (1962): 1062–92. See also Edouard Perroy, "A l'origine d'une économie contractée: les crises du XIVe siècle," *Annales: E. S. C.* 4(1949): 167–82.

97. E.g., A. D. II E 95/369, J. Holanie, f. 75r. Women at times named their husbands procurator to sell their property. See II E 95/369, J. Holanie, f. 68v.

98. See "Land, Houses and Real Estate Investment" for a discussion of these operations.

99. Herlihy, "Land, Family, and Women," pp. 27–30, found a high incidence of land ownership by women in southern France in the early Middle Ages. In urban Montpellier, such a tradition appears to have been perpetuated.

100. There was, however, no *retrait lignager,* in principle, in Montpellier. On the general problem, see P. Ourliac and J. de Malafosse, *Histoire du droit privé,* 2; *Les biens,* 2d ed. (Paris: Presses Universitaires de France, 1971), p. 167.

101. On the demography of Montpellier, see Josiah Cox Russell, "L'Evolution démographique de Montpellier au moyen âge," *Annales du Midi* 74 (1962): 345–60, and my suggested modifications of this view in "Patterns of Population," p. 257, note 2.

102. On economic trends in southern France, see Archibald R. Lewis, "Patterns of Economic Development in Southern France, 1050–1271 A.D.," *Studies in Medieval and Renaissance History* n.s. 3(1980): 57–83. Lewis (pp. 79–80) maintained that Montpellier continued active after the era of expansion was over. My own work suggests that there was indeed resilience interspersed with crises.

103. See "Patterns of Population."

104. On these problems, see Jean Combes, "Finances municipales et oppositions sociales à Montpellier au commencement du XIVe siècle," *Fédération historique du Languedoc méditerranéen et du Roussillon* 44 (1972): 99–120. See also the study by Jan Rogozinski, *Power, Caste, and Law. Social Conflict in Fourteenth-Century Montpellier* (Cambridge, Mass.: The Medieval Academy of America, 1982).

105. A prominent role for widows was noted by Jean Verdon, "Notes sur la femme en Limousin vers 1300." in *Etudes d'histoire médiévale. Hommage à Philippe Wolff* (Toulouse: Edouard Privat, 1978), pp. 320–29.

106. See note 81 above.

107. For a discussion of Montpellier's population composition, see "Patterns of Population."

108. On the Black Death in Montpellier, see my article "Changes in Testamentary Practice at Montpellier on the Eve of the Black Death," *Church History* 47 (1978): 253–69.

109. David Herlihy, "Mapping Households in Medieval Italy," *The Catholic Historical Review* 58 (1972): 13, speaks of a "proliferation within the city of small, truncated, and incomplete households," in the case of Florence.

110. The influence of kinship may have been subtly active in Montpellier, as it was in Genoa. See Hughes, p. 16.

IX

LUCCHESE IN MONTPELLIER IN THE ERA OF CASTRUCCIO CASTRACANI: THE MINTMASTERS' PENETRATION OF LANGUEDOCIAN COMMERCE AND FINANCE

The international reputation of the Lucchese in medieval France was established long ago thanks to the works of scholars such as Camille Piton, Léon Mirot and Florence Edler de Roover [1]. Of all the Italians whose presence was felt in the Languedocian town of Montpellier in the late thirteenth and

(1) Camille Piton, *Les Lombards en France et à Paris,* 2 vol. (Paris, 1892, 1893); Léon Mirot, *Etudes lucquoises,* in *Bibliothèque de l'Ecole des Chartes,* vol. LXXXVIII (1927), pp. 50-86; *La colonie lucquoise à Paris du XIIIe au XVe siècle,* vol. LXXXVIII (1927), pp. 275-314; *Les Isbarre, monnayeurs royaux, Augustin Isbarre,* vol. LXXXIX (1928), pp. 299-389; *La société des Raponde. Dine Raponde,* vol. XCI (1930), pp. 100-168; *Les Cename,* vol. XCVI (1935), pp. 301-337; *Forteguerra Forteguerra et sa succession,* vol. XCIX (1938), pp. 67-81; *L'Origine des Spifame. Barthelémi Spifame,* vol. CI (1940), pp. 116-156; *Galvano Trenta et les joyaux de la couronne.* Henceforth, the studies of Mirot will be cited by year. See also Florence Edler de Roover, *The Silk Trade of Lucca during the Thirteenth and Fourteenth Centuries,* in *Diss. University of Chicago,* 1930; and *Lucchese Silks,* in *Ciba Review,* 80 (1950), pp. 2902-2931.

fourteenth centuries, the Lucchese stand out as the most active immigrant community. In this commercial, financial and intellectual capital of Languedoc, the Lucchese were merchants, bankers, mintmasters, royal treasurers, proprietors, real estate managers, legal and paralegal specialists and titled bourgeois, often assuming several persone simultaneously and fully exploiting the economic environment of the town ([2]). The means by which the Lucchese penetrated the local business community merit further investigation. It is my purpose in this paper to explore the activities of Lucchese businessmen and the reasons for their success through examination of unpublished notarial and charter material before 1350 ([3]). I will consider the history of Lucchese contacts with Montpellier, the dimensions of Lucchese immigrant identity in the Languedocian center and, finally, the reasons for Lucchese achievement.

The diffusion of Lucchese emigrants throughout Europe may have begun as early as the eleventh century ([4]). The initial impetus for emigration was trade, resulting in the foundation of Lucchese commercial and industrial colonies in western Europe ([5]). Recorded contacts of the Lucchese with Montpellier survive from the mid-

---

(2) I first studied the Lucchese presence in Montpellier in my dissertation, *Commerce and Society in Montpellier, 1250-1350,* 2 vols., Diss. Yale University, 1974.

(3) The present study is based on the notarial registers of the Archives Municipales de Montpellier, II, 1-3 and of the Archives Départementales de l'Hérault, II E 95/368-377. I also consulted *Le Grand Chartrier* of the Archives Municipales as well as the manuscript inventory of the Archives Communales of Cournonterral. See the inventories: *Archives communales de Montpellier antérieures à 1789, Inventaires et documents*: I. *Notice sur les anciens inventaires, inventaire du Grand Chartrier of* JOSEPH BERTHELÉ (Montpellier, 1895); II. *Documents omis dans l'inventaire du Grand Chartrier of* MAURICE OUDOT DE DAINVILLE (Montpellier, 1955); and *Répertoire numérique détaillé des parchemins de Cournonterral of* DANIÈLE NEIRINCK (Montpellier, 1969), manuscript. Archives Municipales de Montpellier will be abbreviated A. M. Montp. and Archives Départementales de l'Hérault, A. D. Hérault.

(4) L. MIROT (1927), p. 54.

(5) L. MIROT, *passim* and F. E. DE ROOVER, *The Silk Trade of Lucca...,* pp. 112-200.

thirteenth century ([6]). In 1266 Pope Clement IV commended the merchants of Lucca residing in the territory of Montpellier to the protection of the town consuls ([7]). In 1266 the Guinigi Company had an agent in Montpellier; other companies would also be represented in the following decade ([8]). A Genoese document of 1272 mentioned the presence of a Lucchese consul in Montpellier, evidence that an organized colony existed in the Languedocian town by that date ([9]). Civil and political strife of the late thirteenth and early fourteenth centuries supplemented commercial motives for expatriation and fed waves of emigration from Lucca ([10]).

Montpellier was a receptive environment for foreign immigrants and for foreign merchants in temporary residence ([11]). Located near the Mediterranean, Montpellier was a commercial entrepot where Mediterranean and Levantine products were collected for northern and western European clients and from which western products were exported south and east ([12]). From 1293 to 1349 when the king of France purchased the town, Montpellier enjoyed dual political allegiance with both French and Majorcan

---

(6) See note 16 above.

(7) ALEXANDRE GERMAIN, *Histoire de la commune de Montpellier,* II (Montpellier, 1851), pp. 42-43, note 6. The Lucchese were in Montpellier at times on papal business. See *Archives communales de Montpellier,* I: *Inventaire du Grand Chartrier,* Louvet no. 2873: 27 January 1293, collection of papal revenues.

(8) F. E. DE ROOVER, *The Silk Trade of Lucca...,* p. 163. The Guinigi were primarily silk merchants. See p. 117.

(9) *Ibidem.*

(10) F. E. DE ROOVER, *Lucchese Silks...,* pp. 2903-2905.

(11) On immigration to Montpellier, see my article, *Patterns of Population Attraction and Mobility: The Case of Montpellier,* 1293-1348, in *Viator, Medieval and Renaissance Studies* 10 (1979), pp. 257-281.

(12) On the commerce of Montpellier, see ALEXANDRE GERMAIN, *Histoire du commerce de Montpellier antérieurement à l'ouverture du port de Cette,* 2 vol. (Montpellier, 1861); LOUIS J. THOMAS, *Montpellier, ville marchande: histoire économique et sociale de Montpellier des origines à 1870* (Montpellier, 1936) and my dissertation.

quarters furthering an already cosmopolitan atmosphere ([13]). The extant notarial evidence of Montpellier over the period 1293-1348 preserved the mention of about thirty Lucchese, seven of whom were specifically described as inhabitants of Montpellier; the others hailed from Lucca itself and from Lucchese colonies in Nîmes, Paris and Avignon ([14]). Many of the Lucchese described in this paper had arrived in Montpellier or in France before the death of Castruccio in 1328. What were the activities of these Lucchese?

The Lucchese were fortunate in having in their home town a silk finishing industry without rival in medieval Europe ([15]). As towns in Europe grew and bourgeois taste became more sophisticated, the opulent damasks and brocades of Lucca were popular items of trade. The Lucchese shipped silks and spun gold to Montpellier from Marseille as early as 1248 ([16]). Trace of Lucchese silk trade in Montpellier was noted in 1293 and in 1336, the latter act a sale by a Lucchese immigrant, Choquin dei Avoccati, who possessed the honorific title of bourgeois of Montpellier ([17]).

---

(13) On the political history of Montpellier, see A. GERMAIN, *Histoire de la commune de Montpellier,* 3 vols. (Montpellier, 1851); A. LECOY DE LA MARCHE, *Les relations de la France avec les royaumes de Majorque (Iles Baléares, Roussillon, Montpellier, etc.*I, 2 vols. (Paris, 1892); CHARLES DE TOURTOULON, *Études sur la maison de Barcelone, Jacme Ier, le Conquérant, roi d'Aragon, comte de Barcelone, seigneur de Montpellier, d'après les chroniques et les documents inédits,* 2 vols. (Montpellier, 1863); LOUIS J. THOMAS, *Montpellier entre la France et l'Aragon pendant la première moitié du XIVe siècle,* in *Monspeliensia, Mémoires et documents relatifs à Montpellier et à la région montpelliéraine,* I, fasc. 1 (Montpellier, 1928-1929), pp. 1-56.

(14) The Lucchese inhabitants of Montpellier were: Giovanni Ysbarre, Barca Ysbarre, Raynunchio Arnulphini, Guido Malagallie, Pelegrino Bossa, Bonacruce Bossi, Choquin dei Avoccati.

(15) On the silk industry, see F. E. DE ROOVER, note 1, and E. LAZZARESCHI AND F. PARDI, *Lucca nella storia, nell'arte e nell'industria,* (Lucca, 1941).

(16) LOUIS BLANCARD, ed. *Documents inédits sur le commerce de Marseille au Moyen-Age,* II (Marseille, 1885), document no. 871.

(17) A.M. Montp., II, 1, f. 5r and A.D. Hérault, II E 95/370, f. 59r. On Choquin dei Avoccati, see JEAN COMBES, *Quelques remarques sur les bourgeois de Montpellier au moyen âge,* in *Mélanges Pierre Tisset, Recueil de mémoires et travaux publié par la société d'histoire du droit et des*

Even more revealing of the importance of Lucchese silks was the active market in Montpellier for « mercery of Lucca ». Fortuitous survival of evidence has revealed the specialization of two merchants of Montpellier, the de Cabanis brothers, in the sale of « mercery of Lucca » to local clients and to foreigners from Toulouse, Valencia, Burgos, Castile and Cahors ([18]). Although only one debt of the de Cabanis to a Lucchese merchant has survived, the likelihood of their having Lucchese suppliers cannot be ruled out ([19]). At the end of the thirteenth century Lucchese merchants were shipping silk from Genoa to Provence and Languedoc, in particular, to Nîmes about fifty kilometers northeast of Montpellier, and of easy access from Montpellier ([20]). Close connections between the Lucchese communities of Montpellier and Nîmes undoubtedly facilitated supply of the Montpellier market ([21]). A further attraction of the Montpellier market in silk was the growth of indigenous silk finishing industries in Montpellier and in other Languedocian towns ([22]).

Other traces of Lucchese commercial activities have survived. Wool cloth was marketed in 1336 by Vanno del Drago and by Raynunchio Arnulphini ([23]). Bruneto and Bartolomeo Scatisse sold wood in 1333 ([24]). Giovanni di Sancto Germano bought

---

institutions des anciens pays de droit écrit, fasc. VII (1970), p. 122. See also L. Mirot (1927), pp. 58 and 73. Mirot mentioned a Cheique « dictus Avogadi » or Checo Avoccati, draper. The spelling of surnames was not uniform in the documents and the identification of individuals was thereby complicated.

(18) On the silk trade in Montpellier, see my article, *Medieval Silks in Montpellier: The Silk Market ca. 1250-ca. 1350,* in *The Journal of European Economic History* II (1982), pp. 117-140. In the documents, « mercery of Lucca »was termed in the Latin *merces de Luca.*

(19) A. D. Hérault, II E 95/374, f. 34r.

(20) Pierre Racine, *Le marché génois de la soie en 1288,* in *Revue des études sud-est- européenes* 8 (1970), p. 410.

(21) See notes 58 and 60 below.

(22) See note 18 above.

(23) A. D. Hérault, II E 95/370, ff. 75v and 108r.

(24) A. D. Hérault, II E 95/369, ff. 105r and 105v.

ginger and sugar in 1336 ([25]). These Lucchese are witness to the involvement of the community in both the luxury market and the trade in necessities.

Beyond the commercial realm, another area of Lucchese prominence lay in monetary expertise ([26]). Numerous Lucchese were masters of the French royal mints in Montpellier and at Sommières, some twenty-five kilometers distant, in the late thirteenth and fourteenth centuries ([27]). Betin and Sornaco Cassinelli were the first mintmasters at the Sommières-Montpellier mint in the 1280's and 1290's ([28]). Toro di Podio participated with two other men as mintmasters in 1310-1312 and served again in the 1320's and 1330's ([29]). Barca Ysbarre was associated with the mint in 1336 and served as a mintmaster for silver coinage in 1341 ([30]). Lucchese mintmasters of the Ysbarre family were also present in the second half of the fourteenth century ([31]).

Association with a mint had advantages throughout the Middle Ages. Cash was in short supply, and seignoriage due

---

(25) A. D. Hérault, II E 95/370, f. 22r.

(26) On the long Lucchese minting experience, see ROBERT S. LOPEZ, *An Aristocracy of Money in the Early Middle Ages* in *Speculum,* XXVIII (1953), p. 9. THOMAS W. BLOMQUIST has studied the financial expertise of the Lucchese in the late Middle Ages. See, for example, *Administration of a Thirteenth-Century Mercantile Banking Partnership*: *An Episode in the History of the Ricciardi of Lucca,* in *Revue internationale d'histoire de la banque* 7 (1973), pp. 1-9. See also RICHARD W. KAEUPER, *Bankers to the Crown*: *The Riccardi of Lucca and Edward I* (Princeton, 1973).

(27) The recent thesis of MARC BOMPAIRE, *L'Atelier monétaire royale de Montpellier et la circulation monétaire en Bas-Languedoc jusqu'au milieu du XVe siècle,* Thesis, Ecole des Chartes, Paris, 1980, has expanded greatly our knowledge of the mint of Montpellier-Sommières.

(28) M. BOMPAIRE, *L'Atelier monétaire...,* p. 99 and Annexe no. 1. C. PITON, *Les Lombards...,* p. vii (lowercase) described Bettin as a « ministre des finances ». Bompaire, p. 99, identified him as « général maître et maître de la monnaie de Paris » at the same time that he was at Montpellier.

(29) M. BOMPAIRE, *L'Atelier monétaire...,* p. 100 and Annexe no. 1. The spelling of the name was Thore dal Poggio.

(30) *Ibidem,* pp. 99-101 and Annexe no. 1.

(31) See also regarding the Ysbarre, L. MIROT (1927), pp. 275-314.

the moneyers and mintmasters represented a valuable source of liquid capital ([32]). While control over exchange functions was no longer a monopoly of moneyers in Lucca and elsewhere, mint personnel and, especially mintmasters, still occupied important positions ([33]). Mintmasters in Montpellier were royal officials who had purchased the farm of the mint from the king of France ([34]).

Furthermore, there was an interesting correlation between the position of mintmaster and the honorific status of bourgeois in Montpellier. A number of Lucchese possessed this pedegree as an award from the king of France: Sornaco Cassinelli held it before 1322 ([35]). Toro di Podio received the bourgeoisie in 1323. Conversely, two members of the Ysbarre family, Giacomo and Puccino were bourgeois from 1317 while Barca Ysbarre and later descendents were associated with the mint ([36]). Other Lucchese to enjoy the distinction of bourgeois of Montpellier included Bartolo Spifame from 1342 and Choquin dei Avoccati from at least 1336 ([37]).

The Lucchese specialized in royal finance. Particularly active in this regard was the Scatisse family, established in Nîmes with the functions of treasurer of the *sénéchaussée* of Beaucaire-Nîmes. In documents concerning financial contributions from Montpellier for the wars in Flanders and wirth England, one finds many mentions of Pietro Scatisse and references, as well, to Bartolomeo,

---

(32) R. S. Lopez, *An Aristocracy of Money...*, pp. 16ff.

(33) *Ibidem*, p. 43. The money changers dominated foreign exchange in the thirteenth century.

(34) M. Bompaire, *L'Atelier monétaire...*, pp. 90ff.

(35) J. Combes, *Quelques remarques...*, pp. 121-122 and also M. Bompaire, *L'Atelier monétaire...*, p. 104 and his note 81.

(36) L. Mirot (1927), pp. 275-314, and M. Bompaire, *L'Atelier monétaire...*, Annexe no. 1: Charles and Richardin Ysbarre after 1350.

(37) J. Combes, *Quelques remarques...*, p. 122: Choquin after 19 August 1332. L. Mirot (1938), p. 71, described Bartolomeo as « changeur, c'est à dire, prêteur sur gages, manieur d'argent et banquier ».

Antonio, Philippo and Marquisio, before and after 1350 ([38]). Toro di Podio also exercized the functions of royal valet and treasurer of the *sénéchaussée* of Beaucaire-Nîmes in the 1330's and 1340's. He received funds from the town of Montpellier for the war with England and for repairs of the French royal port of Aigues-Mortes ([39]). Francisco Ysbarre, brother and associate of Puccino Ysbarre, accepted 1000 l. in *tournois* from the consuls of Montpellier regarding aid for the war in Gascony in 1326 ([40]).

Monetary activities and treasurers' business were not the only financial operations of the Lucchese. Montpellier served as a clearinghouse for Lucchese foreign exchange transactions involving Catalonia, Valencia and Paris ([41]). In 1336 Choquin dei Avoccati, merchant of Lucca and bourgeois and inhabitant of Montpellier, mentioned earlier in the silk trade, borrowed the equivalent of 270 l. of Barcelonese money in Montpellier from a merchant of Vich, agreeing to reimburse the latter in Valencia within twelve days ([42]). Evidence from Valencia reveals the other side of this financial circuit ([43]). In contracts of foreign exchange passed in Valencia over the years 1327-1336, Niccolò Jacobi and

(38) *Archives communales de Montpellier,* I: *Inventaire du Grand Chartrier,* contains many references to the Scatisse. See Louvet nos. 1026, 1042, 1621, 1796, 1797, 1818, 2366, 2436, 2643, 3316, 3871, 3892, 3923, 3983, 3985, 3986, 3989, 3991, 3994, 3995, 3998, 3999, 4003, 4004, 4005, 4006, 4007, 4008, 4009. See also *Archives communales de Montpellier,* II: *Documents omis du Grand Chartrier,* nos. XVI, XVII, LIII, DLXV, DLXVIIII, DCXXVII, DCLIII, DCCCCXVI, DCCCCXVII, DCCCCXIX, DCCCCXX, DCCCCXXI, DCCCCXXII.

(39) *Archives communales de Montpellier,* I: *Inventaire du Grand Chartrier,* Louvet nos. 3756, 3764, 3886. See also *Archives communales de Montpellier,* II: *Documents omis du Grand Chartrier,* nos. DCCCLXXXX, DCCCLXXXVI, DCCCLXXXVIII.

(40) *Archives communales de Montpellier,* I: *Inventaire du Grand Chartrier,* Louvet no. 3868.

(41) See my thesis, Chapter IV.

(42) A. D. HÉRAULT, II E 95/370, f. 27r: 27 March 1336. Choquin received acquittal on 15 May 1336 (f. 49r).

(43) I wish to think Monsieur Guy Romestan of the Université Paul Valéry de Montpellier for the following references from Valencian archives.

associates extended credit in exchange transactions ranging from 96.5 l. in *reales* of Valencia to over 400 l. in *reales* for recovery in Montpellier in amounts of 100 to 450 *agneaux* ([44]). Debtors in these transactions included Montpelliérains, Valencians and Catalonians. The presence in Montpellier of a Valencian clientele for silks suggests that the silk trade was the commercial foundation of Lucchese foreign exchange ([45]).

The Lucchese were also involved in foreign exchange between Montpellier and Paris where they traditionally marketed silks ([46]). On 3 July 1336 Pelegrino Bossa, merchant of Lucca and inhabitant of Montpellier, acted as procurator of Toro di Podio and his brothers Niccolò and Parsivallo in borrowing 480 l. in *petits tournois* from drapers of Montpellier for repayment in Paris in September ([47]). In April 1336 the di Podio brothers had obtained an acquittal from the same drapers for an identical sum ([48]). Again on 3 July 1336 these Montpellier drapers borrowed 200 l. in *petits tournois* by exchange from the di Podio brothers promising reimbursement in Montpellier on 15 January 1337 ([49]). The intricacies of exchange operations as well as the Paris connection emerge from these acts.

Another face of Lucchese financial operations involved loans. Parsivallo di Podio loaned two gold *réaux* to a local notary of Montpellier in 1327 ([50]). Barca Ysbarre granted a loan of 64 s. in *petits tournois* to a man from Beaucaire in 1336 ([51]). In addition to loans to private individuals, the Lucchese also made loans to consulates within Languedoc. Puccino Ysbarre, established

(44) Archivio del Reino de Valencia, Protocolos nos. 2855, 2873.

(45) See my article on the silk trade in Montpellier, note 18 above.

(46) L. Mirot (1927), pp. 51-53 and F.E. de Roover, *The Silk Trade of Lucca...*, pp. 112-141.

(47) A.D. Hérault, II E 95/370, f. 73v.

(48) A.D. Hérault, II E 95/370, f. 33r: 4 April 1336.

(49) A.D. Hérault, II E 95/370, f. 74r.

(50) A.D. Hérault, II E 95/368, f. 94v.

(51) A.D. Hérault, II E 95/370, f. 125r.

in Nîmes by 1335, was prepared to loan the consuls of Montpellier upwards of 1000 l. to enable them to pay off a military fine ([52]). In 1345 Raynunchio Arnulphini, merchant of Lucca and inhabitant of Montpellier, in conjunction with Philippo Scatisse of Nîmes, lent 600 l. in *tournois* to the inhabitants of Cournonterral, a small town just west of Montpellier, for the purchase of a consultate from the king of France ([53]). The Lucchese Theocolino Scatisse of Nîmes and Bonacruce Bossi of Montpellier were in Paris negotiating with the king of France on behalf of Cournonterral at the same date ([54]). In 1349 the consuls of Montpellier had a debt of 2000 gold *écus* outstanding to Pietro Malaprese of Lucca ([55]).

An anecdote will serve to illustrate the clout which Lucchese creditors could exercise in the recovery of their debts. By 1339 Puccino Ysbarre was dead, but his affairs were by no means settled. His children were being represented by their uncle and guardian, Giovanni Ysbarre, *legum doctor,* of Nîmes and of Montpellier, in a claim of the Ysbarre estate against Pierre de Bordellis, merchant of an influential Montpellier family, for debts contracted in Champagne ([56]). Joining them in their suit against de Bordellis were other Lucchese creditors including Vanno del Drago, Docconino di Podio and Toro di Podio. The said de Bordellis had taken refuge in the Friars Minor monastery in Montpellier in fear of his creditors. In Montpellier debt legislation permitted the bodily seizure of the debtor and his retention

---

(52) *Archives communales de Montpellier,* II: *Documents omis du Grand Chartrier,* nos. V and VI.

(53) A. D. Hérault, Archives communales de Cournonterral, AA 14.

(54) *Ibidem,* AA 13.

(55) *Archives communales de Montpellier,* I: *Inventaire du Grand Chartrier,* Louvet no. 4074.

(56) A. D. Hérault, II E 95/375, ff. 124r-137v. On the de Bordellis see A. Germain, *Histoire de la commune de Montpellier,* III, P. J. XIX, pp. 367ff. See also Renée Doehaerd, *Les relations commerciales entre Gênes, la Belgique et l'Outremont d'après les archives notariales génoises aux XIIIe et XIVe siècles,* II (Brussels, Rome, 1941), documents 1658, 1669 and 1670.

on a bread and water diet ([57]). De Bordellis was taking no chances with the Lucchese. As a result of negotiation between creditors and debtor, de Bordellis agreed to hand over his business records in order to enable reimbursement in return for his assured safety and freedom.

The network of Lucchese communities throughout France facilitated their operations in commerce and finance. In 1342 the Lucchese immigrant to Nîmes, Vanno del Drago, appointed the Tadolini, Lucchese merchants who were bourgeois and inhabitants of Paris, to represent him in the purchase of a mint farm in Montpellier or elsewhere ([58]). In 1347 the Lucchese Niccolò Chelondi, a painter and inhabitant of Avignon, joined in an association with a Sienese of Avignon and two Sienese of Montpellier to further their mutual artistic endeavors ([59]). Members of the Ysbarre and di Podio families were mentioned as inhabitants of Nîmes and of Montpellier ([60]). Links between the Lucchese communities in these latter towns were particularly strong.

Beyond the silk trade, mint and treasury expertise, foreign exchange and money lending, Lucchese immigrants were property owners and real estate managers in Montpellier and the surrounding region. Already in the reign of Philip the Fair, the Cassinelli had been given near Montpellier the mill of Lunel and the seigneury of Gallargues ([61]). In 1333 a notary of Lucca and inhabitant of Montpellier, Guido Malagallie, named several

---

(57) Pierre Tisset, *Placentin et l'enseignement du droit à Montpellier. Droit romain et Coutume dans l'ancien pays de Septimanie,* in *Recueil de mémoires etravaux publié par la société d'histoire du droit et des institutions des anciens pays de droit écrit,* fasc. II (Montpellier, 1951), p. 83. See also A. Teulet, ed. *Layettes du Trésor des Chartes,* I (Paris, 1863), pp. 258-259.

(58) A. D. Hérault, II E 95/371, f. 59r. M. Bompaire, *L'Atelier monétaire...,* p. 101, called him Barthélemy. The spelling is not easy to decipher. For other contacts between the Lucchese of Montpellier and of Paris, see A. D. Hérault, II E 95/372, f. 154v.

(59) A. D. Hérault, II E 95/377, f. 12r.

(60) See note 56 above and A. D. Hérault, II E 95/377, f. 74r.

(61) M. Bompaire, *L'Atelier monétaire...,* p. 104. L. Mirot (1927), pp. 71-72, lsted other property holdings of the Cassinelli in France.

procurators, among them Bruneto Scatisse and Theo Arnulfini of Lucca, to rent out some of his property (62). In 1339 Pelegrino Bossa acted on five occasions in the management of the land holdings of the chevalier Raymond alias Guilhem de Conques, member of an important Montpellier family (63). Through the agency of Pelegrino Bossa, in 1397, the di Podio brothers (64) then established in Nîmes, rented out a house and an orchard to a moneyer of Montpellier. Finally, Toro di Podio had a *hòtel* in the central Cannau district of Montpellier (65).

Toro di Podio is a good example of the success achieved by Lucchese immigrants in Montpellier. Mintmaster in 1310-1312 and again in the 1320's and 1330's, Toro di Podio attained bourgeois status in Montpellier in 1323 (66). His involvements in commerce and finance with his brothers and business associates were extensive. Their foreign exchange with Paris has already been mentioned (67). Toro appeared as a creditor of Pierre de Bordellis for debts incurred in Champagne (68). He invested in international maritime trade as the co-owner of a boat, the « Santa Maria », which was captured by agents of the king of Sicily on a voyage to Cyprus in 1331 (69). By the late 1340's Toro was established in Nîmes (70). In the 1330's and 1340's Toro served as French royal valet and treasurer of the *sénéchaussée*

---

(62) A. D. Hérault, II E 95/369, f. 107r.

(63) A. D. Hérault, II E 95/375, ff. 6v, 22v, 81r, 98r and 108r. On the Conques, see J. COMBES, *Quelques remarques...*, pp. 103-105. Toro was the brother-in-law of Raymond alias Guilhem de Conques. See J. Combes, p. 121, note 169.

(64) A. D. Hérault, II E 95/377, f. 74r.

(65) J. COMBES, *Quelques remarques...*, p. 121, note 169. M. BOMPAIRE, *L'Atelier monétaire...*, p. 41, reported that Toro installed the mint in his own house.

(66) J. COMBES, *Quelques remarques...*, p. 121.

(67) See notes 47-49 above.

(68) See note 56 above.

(69) A. D. Hérault, II E 95/371, f. 71r.

(70) See note 60 above.

of Beaucaire-Nîmes ([71]). His career reflects the importance of family ties, geographic mobility and diversity of investment which characterized the Lucchese economic interests in Languedoc.

Individuals such as the Lucchese Toro di Podio exemplified the versatility of a medieval businessman. Within Languedoc the Lucchese combined commerce, monetary and treasury expertise, foreign exchange and real estate holdings, using familial and community ties to exploit effectively a whole range of economic opportunities. The Lucchese had an obvious knack for expatriation and demonstrated an impressive adaptiveness in their adoptive homes. Much has been written of the exploits of the great Italian ports of Genoa, Pisa and Venice and their far-flung foreign colonies ([72]). A balanced view of the Italian economic achievement in the Middle Ages must highlight in counterpoint to the Levantine, Asian and North African expansion of the ports, the early and truly impressive internal European penetration of inland towns such as Lucca. The Lucchese communities in France were striking in their vitality, the degree of their acclimatization, their intense intercommunication and their permanence ([73]). The Lucchese experience in Montpellier is but one chapter in that success story.

---

(71) See note 39 above.

(72) With the exception of Florence, cities of the interior, in contrast to the ports, are not often highlighted. See, for example, Yves Renouard, *Les hommes d'affaires italiens du moyen âge* (Paris, 1949, r. e. 1968).

(73) The studies of L. Mirot have illustrated this permanence effectively.

X

Medieval Silks in Montpellier: The Silk Market ca. 1250 - ca. 1350

One of the most renowned items of the medieval luxury trade was silk. In the High Middle Ages silk was imported to European markets and finishing industries from the Near and Far East.[1] The Tuscan town of Lucca led the way in developing a silk finishing industry in the West which began in the twelfth century to furnish elaborate damasks and brocades to a clientele of churchmen and lay nobles and, with the growth of towns, to bourgeois markets.[2] The reconstruction of many aspects of the silk trade

---

An earlier version of this paper was presented at the Twelfth Conference on Medieval Studies, May 5-8, 1977, Western Michigan University, Kalamazoo, Michigan.

1 Among the still useful older studies of the history of silk, see Francisque Xavier Michel, *Recherches sur le commerce, la fabrication et l'usage des étoffes de soie, d'or et d'argent, et autres tissus précieux en Occident, principalement en France pendant le moyen âge*, 2 vols, (Paris, 1852); Ernest Pariset, *Histoire de la soie* (Paris, 1862); and William F. Leggett, *The Story of Silk* (New York, 1949).

2 The most comprehensive study of the Lucchese silk industry remains that of Florence Edler de Roover, " The Silk Trade of Lucca during the Thirteenth and Fourteenth Centuries," Diss. University of Chicago, 1930. See also her article, " Lucchese Silks," *Ciba Review*, 80 (1950), pp. 2902-2930. Also of interest is E. Lazzareschi and F. Pardi, *Lucca nella storia, nell'arte et nell'industria* (Lucca, 1941).

By the thirteenth century the taste for silks was so widely diffused among the European bourgeoisie that sumptuary legislation was introduced in some towns to limit

has been possible.[3] However, the absence of adequate statistics has prohibited even an approximate assessment of the volume of the medieval silk trade. By the same token, the quality and design of silks have eluded historians because of the limited survival of medieval fabrics and the lack of detailed description of garments in most documents.[4] Recent investigations have been more successful in focusing on case studies of local market activity. P. Racine examined the Genoese silk market of 1288 from the evidence of notarial archives which shed new light on silk operations.[5] As in Genoa, the market activity of silks in Montpellier is also susceptible of exploration through the remaining notarial registers. The participation of merchants of Montpellier along with the commercial elite of towns such as Genoa and Venice in the Levant trade of the thirteenth and fourteenth centuries

---

personal display. Characteristic of this trend was a 1273 consular regulation in Montpellier which prohibited the use of silk and a variety of gems by ladies of the town; only *cendal*, a sort of taffeta, was permitted as a lining. See *Le Petit Thalamus de Montpellier*, ed. F. Pégat, E. Thomas and Desmazes (Montpellier, 1840), p. 146: " Que non porton vestidura de ceda ni daur ni dargen mais cendat. Item establem que non porton vestidura deguna de ceda, ni daur ni dargen, mais cendat puescon portar en folraduras de lurs vestirs, et estiers non ". De Roover, " The Silk Trade of Lucca," p. 178, identified *sendal*, spelled *zendadi* in her sources, as a light-weight silk. F. Michel, *Recherches*, I, pp. 212-213, remarked that by 1350 in the neighboring town of Nîmes such a lining for garments would be denied even the local prostitutes.

[3] Recent specialized studies of the silk trade include Muriel J. Hughes, " Marco Polo and Medieval Silk," *Textile History*, 6 (1975), pp. 119-131; Herbert Gleisberg, " Akten und Literatur zur Geschichte des Seidenhandels und der Seidenindustrie bis zum Beginn des zwanzigsten Jahrhunderts," *Scripta Mercaturae*, Parts 1-2 (1974), pp. 61-76; Andre Guillou, " La soie sicilienne au Xe-XIe siècle," *Byzantino-Sicula II, Miscellanea di scritti in memoria di Giuseppe Rossi Taibbi* (Palermo, 1975), pp. 285-288; Amedeo Miceli, " Agricultural Silk Production in Calabria in the XV and XVI Century," *Rivista di storia dell'agricoltura*, 15: 2(1975), pp. 125-130; Florence Edler de Roover, " Andrea Banchi. Florentine Silk Manufacturer and Merchant in the Fifteenth Century," *Studies in Medieval and Renaissance History*, 3 (1966), pp. 223-285.

[4] On surviving fabrics and silk designs, see Otto von Falke, *Decorative Silks*, 3rd ed. (New York, 1936). Some recent studies of surviving fabrics can be found in *Artes Minores. Dank an Werner Abegg*, ed. Michael Stettler and Mechthild Lemberg (Bern, 1973).

[5] P. Racine, " Le marché génois de la soie en 1288," *Revue des études sud-est-européennes*, 8, no. 3 (1970), pp. 403-417.

has long been established, but the silk trade of Montpelliérains and the operations of the local market have never been the focus of a detailed study.[6] Given the role of Montpellier as a commercial entrepot for Mediterranean imports into Western Europe, such a study can contribute to an understanding of the place of silk in the medieval economy.

There are extant in the notarial registers of Montpellier one hundred and thirty-five recognitions of debt for the purchase of silks and mercery in Montpellier.[7] Market activity can be examined fruitfully at two stages: in 1293-1294 and in 1327-1343. Analysis of these contracts, the distribution of which is given in Table 1, reveals a growing concentration of transactions in silk products

TABLE 1

DISTRIBUTION OF COMMODITY TRANSACTIONS

Notarial register	Year	Silk	Mercery of Lucca	Mercery	Taffeta	Lucchese spun gold	Lucchese brocade
A. M. II, 1	1293-94	31		1		2	2
A. D. II E 95/368	1327-28	1					2
A. D. II E 95/369	1333	4	1	2	1		
A. D. II E 95/370	1336	5	2				
A. D. II E 95/374	1337-42	10	61	2	1		
A. D. II E 95/371	1342	1		1			
A. D. II E 95/372	1343-1344	1	2	2			
Totals		53	66	8	2	2	4

[6] Still valuable as background to the commercial history of Montpellier is ALEXANDRE GERMAIN, *Histoire du commerce de Montpellier antérieurement à l'ouverture du port de Cette*, 2 vols. (Montpellier, 1861). For a short survey, see LOUIS J. THOMAS, *Montpellier, ville marchande: histoire économique et sociale de Montpellier des origines à 1870* (Montpellier, 1936). See also my dissertation, "Commerce and Society in Montpellier, 1250-1350," Diss. Yale University, 1974.

[7] The extant registers are drawn from the Archives Municipales de Montpellier (abbreviated A. M. in Table 1 and A. M. Montp. in specific citations), II, 1-3 and the Archives Départementales de l'Hérault (abbreviated A. D. in Table 1 and A. D. Hérault in citations), II E 95/368-377.

of Lucchese manufacture in the early 1340s and the emergence of Montpellier as a market center for these goods. A brief consideration of the background of the Montpellier silk trade will be useful as an introduction to this examination of market activity.

Precise chronological beginnings cannot be established for the silk trade of Montpellier. Already in 1160 a man of Avignon made a shipment of silk from Genoa to Montpellier.[8] This commercial route persisted a century later when in 1267 a Genoese merchant arranged with merchants of Piacenza to receive payment at the fairs of Troyes for silk worth 392 *livres provinois* which they had received from him in Montpellier.[9] Genoa was the major western European source of raw silk in this period. It was here that the Lucchese purchased most of the supplies for their finishing industry.[10]

By 1248 the Lucchese were engaged in shipping refined silk and spun gold from Marseille to Montpellier.[11] In the same same year Montpellérains were actively exporting finished silks from Marseille to Ceuta.[12] The promise of this silk export trade in the western Mediterranean basin went largely unfulfilled for Montpellier in later decades. It may have been compromised by the political disputes between the houses of Aragon and Anjou.[13]

Direct importation of silks from the Levant to Montpellier was suggested as early as 1221 when the consuls of Montpellier offered their lord, Jacme I of Aragon, a magnificent cloth of

---

[8] MARIO CHIAUDANÒ and MATTIA MORESCO, ed. *Il cartolare di Giovanni Scriba* (Turin, 1935), II, act. XVI, pp. 308-309.

[9] RENEE DOEHAERD, *Les relations commerciales entre Gênes, la Belgique et l'Outremont d'aprés les archives notariales génoises aux XIIIe et XIVe siècles* (Brussels, Rome, 1941), III, act 1259, p. 697.

[10] F. de ROOVER, "Lucchese Silks," p. 2909.

[11] LOUIS BLANCARD, ed. *Documents inédits sur le commerce de Marseille au moyen âge* (Marseille, 1885), II, act 871 of the notary Amalric.

[12] L. BLANCARD, *Documents inédits* (Marseille, 1884), I, acts 6 and 13 of Amalric.

[13] EDOUARD BARATIER and FELIX REYNAUD, *Histoire du commerce de Marseille* (Paris, 1951), II, p. 103ff. Montpellier, it should be noted, was under the aegis of the house of Majorca, cadet branch of Aragon, in this period.

gold on the occasion of his marriage with Eleanor of Castile.[14] Future southern French marketing patterns were foreshadowed in a 1232 request by the King of England in his Bordeaux household for twenty silk cloths and four scarlet cloths from Montpellier.[15] In the early thirteenth century Montpellier was in the process of becoming a distribution center for silks, some of which were probably imported directly from the Levant, others from intermediate markets such as Genoa and Marseille, others still from the silk finishing center of Lucca.

It is only for the end of the thirteenth century that a study of the local market in Montpellier becomes feasible. In the earliest preserved notarial register of 1293-1294 the notary Jean Grimaud drafted thirty-six transactions regarding silks and mercery.[16] In the majority of these acts the purchaser stated that he owed the seller a specified sum of money *pro cerico* (or *serico*) *tantum valenti quod a te ex causa emptionis habui.*[17] Occasionally, greater description of the merchandise was inserted. The provenance of the silk might be noted: *pro cerico de Romania*, that is, silk from the Byzantine Empire; or, *pro cerico de guala giyane* or *de guela*, both of which designations suggest the southern Caspian region of Ghilan as the place of origin.[18] The artistry of a finishing industry might be signaled in these notarial contracts: *argento de Lucha cerico*, a cloth of silver silk of Lucca, possibly silver brocade; or *cerico et auro de Lucha*, which may have been gold brocade.[19]

---

[14] F. MICHEL, *Recherches*, II, pp. 139-140. Michel stated that the cloth was recently brought from the Levant; he suggested that it was perhaps *samite*, *siglaton* or *baudequin*.

[15] Ibid., p. 309.

[16] A. M. Montp., II 1, *passim*.

[17] See, for example, A. M. Montp. II, 1, f. 91r.

[18] *Romania*: A. M. Montp., II 1, f. 11r; Ghilan: A. M. Montp., II 1, ff. 11r and 88v. Ghilan was a common source of medieval silk according to F. de ROOVER, "Lucchese Silks," pp. 2908-2909. On the origin of medieval silks, see also P. RACINE, "Le marché génois", p. 405ff and Wilhelm Heyd, *Histoire du commerce du Levant au moyen âge* (Leipzig, 1886; Amsterdam, 1967), II, pp. 670-674.

[19] A. M. Montp., II 1, ff. 36r and 90v.

In two contracts the silk was termed *cerico refracto* and once *cerico crudo refracto*, the latter clearly raw silk.[20] The term *refracto*, derived from the verb *refringo*, may refer to silk which had been damaged or mutilated.[21] As R. S. Lopez has pointed out, Francesco Balducci Pegolotti cautioned that it was necessary to exercise care when buying China silk because of the problem of damage from rubbing on the long caravan journey from the Orient.[22] Lopez has suggested that the transport wear of China silk could account for the lower prices which it often brought in western markets when compared with Near Eastern silk. While the silk in question in 1293 was not identified as China silk, rubbing damage could have occurred on silk merchandise in general. Without the notation of quantity in these acts, it is impossible to judge whether the highest price quoted for *cerico refracto*, 108 *livres* 19 *sous melgoriens*, reflected a modest price for this type of merchandise.[23]

Evidence of a silk dyeing industry can be documented in Montpellier at the end of the thirteenth century. One contract of 1293 specifically mentioned the dyeing of silk: a local dyer recognized his debt of 14 *livres* 2 *sous melgoriens* to a mercer for the purchase of silk which was to be repaid in the execution of dyeing in green, black and red hues.[24] The participation of the Jews in silk dyeing is suggested by the Montpellier evidence.[25]

---

[20] A. M. Montp., II 1, ff. 29v, 83v and 88r.

[21] See C. T. LEWIS and C. SHORT, *A Latin Dictionary* (Oxford, 1966), p. 1548, for *refringo, refregi, refractum*.

[22] R. S. LOPEZ, " China Silk in Europe in the Yuan Period," *Journal of the American Oriental Society*, 72 (1952), p. 75, and FRANCESCO BALDUCCI PEGOLOTTI, *La pratica della mercatura*, ed. Allan Evans (Cambridge, 1936), p. 382. " Fregata " is the term used by Pegolotti to describe rubbed silk.

[23] A. M. Montp., II 1, f. 83v. The exchange rate between *livres melgoriens* and *livres tournois*, the two currencies most commonly appearing in the Montpellier documents, was about 13 *deniers melgoriens* for 12 *deniers tournois*. See ETIENNE FOURNIAL, *Histoire monétaire de l'occident médiéval* (Paris, 1970), pp. 151-155.

[24] A. M. Montp., II 1, f. 21r.

[25] Six purchases of silk by Jews have been recorded. See A. M. Montp., II 1, ff. 7r, 21r, 27r, 28v, 47v and 50v.

The dyeing trade was a common vocation of medieval Jews in Provence and in Italy.[26] Although the six purchases of silk by Jews in 1293 did not identify the buyers as dyers, in the same year the presence of Jewish dyers in Montpellier was signaled.[27] An important dyeing industry with a specialty in scarlet dyeing had existed in Montpellier since the twelfth century. The 1181 monopoly in the practice of dyeing, accorded by Guilhem VIII, lord of Montpellier, to his men, had been relaxed in 1226 and in 1251.[28] By the end of the thirteenth century participation in the dyeing trade by Jews and by newcomers was undoubtedly possible.[29]

In addition to silk dyeing, further testimony to the presence of a silk finishing industry is preserved in the late thirteenth-century acts. In 1294 a local merchant acknowledged his debt of 17 *livres* 12 *sous melgoriens* in favour of a local mercer for silk which he arranged to pay off by supplying two silk cloths per week until the debt was liquidated: *in solutione et exterminatione dicti debiti duos pannos cericos quorum unus erit senhay ratus cum barraturis aureis pretio xxiiii solidos melgoriensium et alius erit parvus operis montispessulani pretio xvii solidos melgoriensium...*[30] The first cloth worth 24 *sous* was decorated with gold stripes; the second worth 17 *sous* was characterized by Montpellier workmanship. Requisite local trades existed to support the finishing industry alluded to in the description of the second cloth. The making of silk corduroy (*corduraric de serico*) was taught in Montpellier in this period, and the manufacture of gold thread was practised in Montpellier

---

26 Armand O. Citarella, " A Puzzling Question Concerning the Relations between the Jewish Communities of Christian Europe and Those Represented in the Geniza Documents," *Journal of the American Oriental Society*, 91 (1971), p. 305.

27 A. M. Montp., II 1, ff. 47r and 48r.

28 See *Petit Thalamus*, pp. 137-139.

29 Jewish activity must escape detailed analysis since there were no further contracts preserved in the notarial registers of 1327-1343.

30 A. M. Montp., II 1, f. 63r.

as it was in many Mediterranean towns.[31] Spun gold of Montpellier had been shipped from Marseille to Acre in 1248, and, in the fourteenth century, three apprenticeship contracts detailed the instruction of young girls in the spinning of gold.[32]

Other towns of southern France enjoyed individualized designations of workmanship as Montpellier did. In 1294 a man from Alès in the Cévennes, north of Montpellier, agreed to repay a debt of 66 *livres* 13 *sous* 10 *deniers melgoriens* to a Montpellier mercer at the weekly rate of one *pannum cericum operis de Alesto* worth 30 *sous melgoriens*.[33] Whether regional finishing industries had connections with the important silk finishing center of Lucca cannot be answered from the remaining sources. The local industries may, in fact, have existed separately on a small scale. The culture of the silk worm can be documented in the Cévennes in the late thirteenth century and may have acted as a stimulus to the industries of Montpellier, Alès and other towns.[34] By the same token, the existence of finishing industries in Montpellier and elsewhere created a local market demand for imported silk.

At the end of the thirteenth century the role of silk supplier was shared among mercers, silk merchants (*sederii*) and money changers of Montpellier, and merchants of Narbonne.[35] The local documents have left no trace of Montpelliérains travelling to Italy to obtain silks. However, P. Racine noted that the Lucchese drew up many transport contracts in Genoa to ship silk to Provence and Languedoc, especially to Nîmes, at the end of

---

31 A. M. Montp., II 1, f. 80v. WILLIAM A. BONDS, "Genoese Noblewomen and Gold Thread Manufacturing," *Medievalia et Humanistica*, fasc. 19 (1966), p. 79, cites Montpellier with Genoa, Lucca and Milan as centers of manufacture of gold thread in the thirteenth century.

32 L. BLANCARD, *Documents inédits*, II, acts 288, 308, 311, 522 and 630 of Amalric regarding spun gold. For the apprenticeship evidence, see A. D. Hérault, II E 95/368, ff. 57r, 131v and 136r.

33 A. M. Montp., II 1, f. 64r.

34 EMMANUEL LE ROY LADURIE, *The Peasants of Languedoc*, trans. John Day (Urbana, Chicago, London, 1974), p. 71.

35 A. M. Montp., II 1, ff. 16v, 19v, 83v, 88r and 88v.

the thirteenth century.[36] The existence of a Lucchese colony in Montpellier from as early as 1272 supports the possibility of shipments to Montpellier as well, but the Lucchesi immigrants in Montpellier have left only occasional witness to their involvement in sales of Lucchese merchandise.[37] Merchants of Lucca sold a coat and a cape with spun gold of Lucca to a merchant of Montpellier and his wife in 1293 for 6 *livres* 2 *sous melgoriens*, and in 1336 a Lucchese immigrant made a sale of one fardel of partially processed silk, *cirici torchie* (*sic*), to a Montpellier silk merchant for 206 *livres* 9 *sous petits tournois*.[38]

Merchants and mercers of Montpellier predominated in the local market transactions in silks at the end of the thirteenth century. Their clients included local silk merchants and foreigners from Figeac, Limoges, Uzès, Alès and Avignon, for whom Montpellier was a point of entry for Mediterranean silk products.[39] The activities of Jacobus Domigol, mercer, will illustrate the typical retail process. On October 20, 1293, Domigol made a purchase of silk worth 101 *livres* 6 *sous melgoriens* from a common supplier, merchants of Narbonne.[40] From October 20, 1293 to March 13, 1294, Domigol made a series of small sales of silk averaging 30 *livres melgoriens* to mercers of Figeac, to an inhabitant of Avignon

---

36 P. Racine, " Le marché génois ", p. 410.

37 F. de Roover, " The Silk Trade," p. 163, and Thomas W. Blomquist, " Trade and Commerce in Thirteenth-Century Lucca," Diss. University of Minnesota, 1966, p. 63, on the Lucchese settlement in Montpellier. These immigrants were active in local and international finance, engaging in money exchanges, cloth sales, loans of money to local village consulates and property management. See A. D. Hérault, II E 95/370, ff. 49r, 27r, 75v, 79v, 108r and 125r; II E 95/377, f. 74r; II E 95/375, ff. 6v, 22r, 81r, 98r and 108r; II E 95/369, f. 107r. See also Danièle Neirinck, " Répertoire des Archives Communales de Cournonterral ", manuscript inventory (A. D. Hérault, 1969), entry AA 13, 14.

38 A. M. Montp., II 1, f. 5r and A. D. Hérault, II E 95/370, f. 59r. On the throwing process of silk finishing, see F. de Roover, " Lucchese Silks ", p. 2917.

39 A. M. Montp., II 1, ff. 12r, 12v, 15v, 36r, 48v, 50v, 51v, 56r, 64r, 90r, 90v, 91r, 93r.

40 A. M. Montp., II 1, f. 16v.

and to one Bertrandus de Toloso, mercer.[41] He was undoubtedly selling stock acquired from the merchants of Narbonne and from other suppliers. Domigol's sales were slightly smaller than the average silk sales of 1293-1294 as Table 2 shows.[42] The largest and smallest sales of these years are given in Table 3.

A final aspect of market activity to be explored at the end of the thirteenth century is the export of silks. Mercers of Montpellier cooperated occasionally in the export of silks within southern France. Thus, in 1293 Toulouse was the destination of coloured silks worth 150 *livres melgoriens* to be sold by a mercer on behalf of a colleague.[43] Curiously lacking in 1293-1294 and, in fact, in 1327-1343 is evidence of silk exports from Montpellier to Paris and to the Champagne fairs which were frequent destinations of spices and leather recorded in extant transport contracts.[44] Italian competition, expecially Lucchese activity, may account for this lacuna.[45]

Comparison of market activity of 1293-1294 with that of

---

41 A. M. Montp., II 1, ff. 12v, 35v, 48v, 56r, 90v and 91r.

42 For the purposes of comparison the data of Tables 2, 3, and 5 have been converted to probable approximate values in the good *tournois* currency of 1330. Over the years of this study, 1293 to 1343, currency fluctuations make the comparison of prices in any two years hazardous. The computations for these tables were based upon *pied de monnaie* quotations from French mints for specific years. The fact that notaries quoted sums at times in money of account and at times in real money introduces one potential source of error; a second lies in the fact that one cannot be certain how rapidly a reformed currency was substituted for a decadent currency, especially in Montpellier which was until 1349 partially under Majorcan political allegiance. In spite of these difficulties, it has seemed desirable to establish these tables to permit comparative observations on the evolution of the silk market. On the problems inherent in medieval currency, see JOHN BELL HENNEMAN, *Royal Taxation in Fourteenth-Century France. The Development of War Financing 1322-1356* (Princeton, N. J., 1971), especially Appendix I, pp. 331-353, HARRY A. MISKIMIN, *Money, Prices and Foreign Exchange in Fourteenth-Century France* (New Haven and London, 1963), especially Appendix D., pp. 158-169, and E. FOURNIAL, *Histoire monétaire*, p. 78ff.

43 A. M. Montp., II 1, f. 63r.

44 See the list of extant transport contracts in my dissertation, " Commerce and Society, " II, Appendix V, pp. 261-267.

45 On Lucchese activities in Champagne, see F. de ROOVER, " The Silk Trade, " pp. 93-95. On Lucchese colonies in France, see L. MIROT, *Etudes lucquoises* (Paris, 1930).

AVERAGE VALUES OF TOTAL TRANSACTIONS

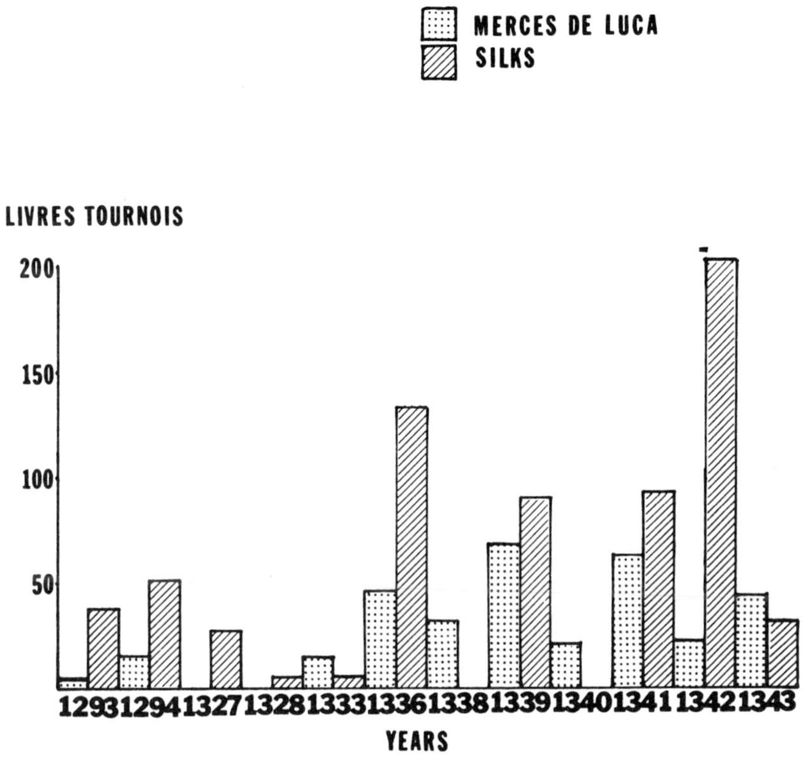

TABLE 2

1327-1343 reveals several changes. An emphasis on Lucchese merchandise is reflected in the appearance of a new notarial formula, *merces de Luca*, in 1333.[46] Tables 2 and 3 show that larger sums of money were involved in the trade in silks and in *merces de Luca* in the later period. The years 1336 to 1343 reflected the peak of this activity. Over the period 1337-1342 the notary Guillaume Nogaret recorded sixty-one transactions in *merces de Luca* for two Montpellier merchants, the Cabanis brothers.[47] While the existing evidence does not permit a precise definition of this term, it is probable that a variety of silk fabrics, such as the damasks and brocades for which Lucca was famous, were implied.[48]

Silks reaching the Montpellier market in the later period attest to geographic origins not mentioned in 1293-1294. In the years 1333-1339 China silk appeared. In 1336 a merchant of Montpellier sold China silk on two occasions to silk merchants in the quantity of one fardel (*fardellum cirici cataie*) and in an unspecified amount.[49] In 1339 the Cabanis brothers made four sales of China silk to silk merchants for sums ranging from 79

---

46 The notary Jean Holanie, A. D. Hérault, II E 95/369, f. 9v, spelled it *merseria de Luca*. In most later acts, it will be *merces de Luca*.

47 A. D. Hérault, II E 95/374, *passim*. The terminology of 1293-1294 was more explicit (note 19 above) and similar to that used by the notary Amalric of Marseille in 1248. See L. BLANCARD, *Documents inédits*, I, acts 6, 13 and 38; II, acts 203 and 871. In act 203, for example, Amalric used the phrase *scarpis auri filato in filo de Lucca*.

48 PHILIPPE WOLFF, *Commerces et marchands de Toulouse* (vers 1350-vers 1450) (Paris, 1954), pp. 232-233, suggested from his consultation of an inventory *post mortem* of a silk merchant of Toulouse that a variety of fabrics, silk velvet, satin, damasks and brocades, were among those referred to by the term *merces de Luca*.

49 A. D. Hérault, II E 95/370, f 31r and 66r. The word *cataya* or *cataie* in various approximate spellings was used to signify Cathay. According to F. de ROOVER, "Lucchese Silks," p. 2909, raw silk imported from abroad usually arrived in "long, narrow bales, called fardels. These varied in weight from seventy to two hundred pounds, most frequently weighing about one hundred pounds. It was a convenient size and shape for transportation by pack animal to and from seaports or for long distances overland."

For a recent discussion of the procurement of China silk, see R. S. LOPEZ, "Nouveaux documents sur les marchands italiens en China à l'époque mongole," *Académie des Inscriptions et Belles Lettres, Comptes rendus* (1977), pp. 445-458.

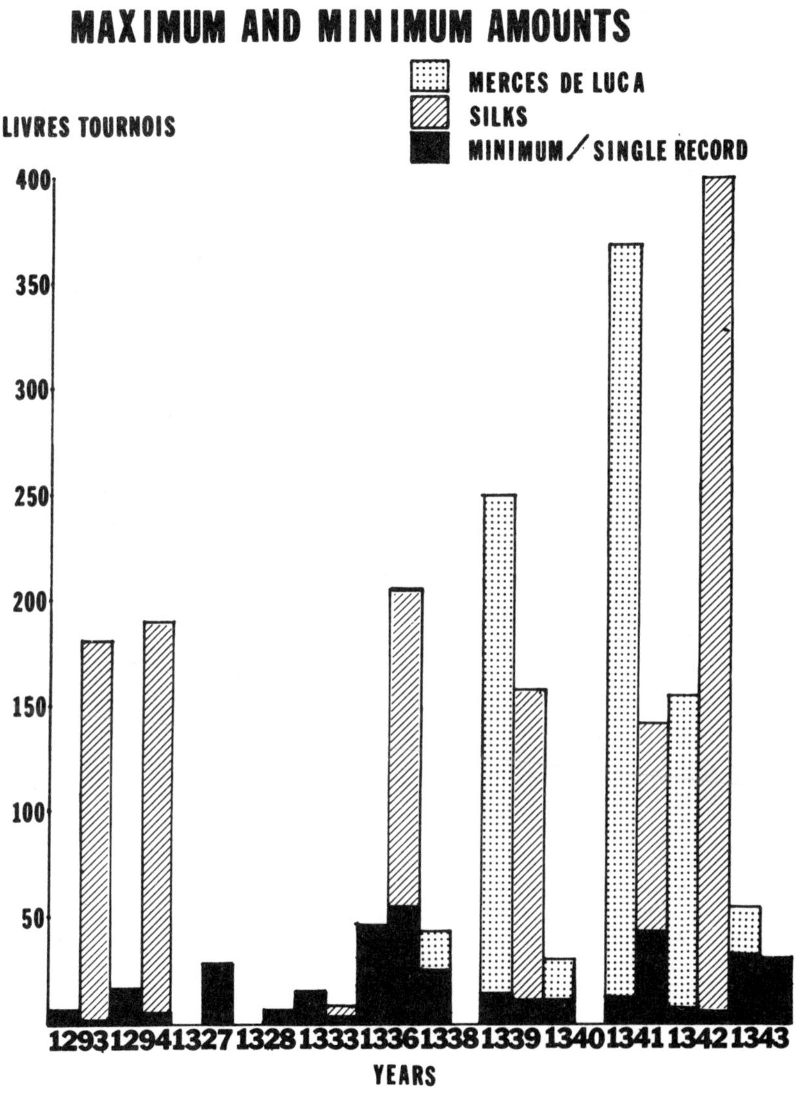
MAXIMUM AND MINIMUM AMOUNTS
MERCES DE LUCA
SILKS
MINIMUM / SINGLE RECORD
LIVRES TOURNOIS
400
350
300
250
200
150
100
50
1293
1294
1327
1328
1333
1336
1338
1339
1340
1341
1342
1343
YEARS

TABLE 3

livres tournois for one half fardel (*pro medio fardello cirici crudi cataya*) to 106.5 *livres* and 147 *livres for a fardel* on other occasions.[50] The fardel of partially processed silk, sold by the Lucchese immigrant in 1336, was more expensive (206 *livres*).[51]

Another silk origin was that of Talich on the eastern shore of the Caspian Sea, noted in 1342.[52] While in most transactions, in Montpellier as in Genoa, the silks were of unspecified provenance, the varieties of geographic origin noted by P. Racine for the Genoese market of 1288 surpass in number those found in Montpellier in either 1293-1294 or 1327-1343.[53] Similarly, the quantity of silk which appeared in Montpellier was undoubtedly small when compared with the Italian markets such as Lucca where a merchant of Genoa was recorded selling thousands of pounds of China silk in the 1330s.[54]

Although the agents and routes of arrival of silk imports in fourteenth-century Montpellier can be only partially reconstructed, silk exports by Montpelliérains prove a more fruitful field of inquiry. During the 1310s and 1320s accounts for the papal court reveal the activity of merchants of Montpellier supplying silks to Avignon. Noteworthy in this respect was Phillipus de Crusolis who furnished silks and silk threads as well as spices and other goods to the papal court.[55]

In the fourteenth century the English court continued to be

---

50 A. D. Hérault, II E 95/374, ff. 22R, 30R and 32R.

51 A. D. Hérault, II E 95/370, f. 59r.

52 A. D. Hérault, II E 95/374, f. 34v. My reading here is *pro cirico... talami*; the latter word was identified by RACINE, "Le marché génois," p. 406 as Talish in the region of Azerbaidzhan, U.S.S.R.

53 P. RACINE, "Le marché génois," *passim*.

54 F. de ROOVER, "Lucchese Silks," p. 2909. R. S. LOPEZ, "European Merchants in the Medieval Indies: The Evidence of Commercial Documents," *Journal of Economic History*, 3 (1943), p. 166, suggested that the Frescobaldi Company imported China silk as far as London. The terminology used was similar to that of Montpellier: "*serico nominato Catewy*."

55 K. H. SCHÄFER, *Die Ausgaben der Apostolischen Kammer unter Johann XXII* (Paderborn, 1911), *passim*.

the recipient of silks exported from Montpellier. Under Edward II several Montpelliérains served as purveyors of the royal wardrobe supplying silks from Montpellier and Languedoc.[56] Records of this activity cease about 1330 at a time when hostilities were multiplying between the English and the French. The outbreak of the Hundred Years War disrupted the silk trade from the south of France to England.[57]

Contemporaneous with the activity of merchants of Montpellier in England and Avignon were silk sales by compatriots in Perpignan, Barcelona and Valencia. In the 1320s and 1330s Montpelliérains were specializing in the sale of French wool cloths in Roussillon and in Spain, but, on occasion, they sold silks.[58] In Barcelona they had a Jewish clientele for their silks.[59] This secondary activity in silks lapsed in the late 1330s when merchants of Montpellier were faced with the increasing monopoly of wool cloth sales on the Spanish market by merchants of Narbonne.[60] This competition forced a general decline in the trade of Montpelliérains in Spain. Perhaps as a result of trade shifts, there was an influx of Spaniards of Burgos, Valencia and Castile to Montpellier as silk clients of the Cabanis brothers in the years 1338-1343. Their activity will be discussed shortly.

The notarial evidence of the period 1327-1343 documents

---

56 See, for example, *Calendar of Patent Rolls, Edward II* (*1307-1313*) (London, 1894), I, p. 45, and F. Michel, *Recherches*, II, p. 308.

57 On the buildup of the Hundred Years War, see Edouard Perroy, *The Hundred Years War*, trans. W. B. Wells (New York, 1965), pp. 34-59.

58 Archives Départementales des Pyrénées Orientales, Series E, reg. 37, f. 32v. The product sold was termed *velorum cirici*. See also A. D. Pyrénées Orientales, Series E, reg. 30, f. 2v; reg. 38, f. 9r; reg. 46, f. 18r. I am indebted to Monsieur Guy Romestan of the Faculté des Lettres et des Sciences Humaines de Montpellier for the Spanish and Roussillonnais references in this study.

59 Archivo de la Corona de Aragon, manuel of Lor. Canals, entries 1336 and 1337.

60 Guy Romestan, " A propose du commerce des draps dans la péninsule ibérique au moyen âge. Les marchands languedociens dans le royaume de Valence pendant la première moitié du XIVe siècle, " *Bulletin philologique et historique*, année 1969 (Paris, 1972), I, pp. 128 and 177-187. Romestan found that some ninety percent of recorded sales of cloth were in the hands of merchants of Narbonne.

the presence on the Montpellier market of a variety of finished silks: red silks of Novara, garments of silk and gold, shirts of silk and gold, black silk cloths, dyed silk of Lucca, silks of various colours, and in profusion, the *merces de Luca*.[61] Local silk merchants assumed a role in local commerce which rivaled that of the mercers, and both trades bought silks from importers and sold them to a foreign and local clientele.[62]

The most sustained market activity is visible in the recognitions of debt recorded by the notary Nogaret for the Cabanis brothers. The latter, investors in the Levant trade of Montpellier, exported wool cloths to Cyprus and the Byzantine Empire.[63] To northern Europe they shipped saffron.[64] They trafficked in raw silk, China silk and dyed silk of Lucca, but their specialization lay in *merces de Luca*.[65] Table 4 describes their clientele for Lucchese merchandise.

Table 4

CABANIS' CLIENTS FOR MERCES DE LUCA
GEOGRAPHIC ORIGIN

	Toulouse	Burgos	Cahors	Montpellier	Valencia	Castile	Unidentified	Total
Number of acts	41	7	5	5	1	1	1	61

Sixty-seven percent of the Cabanis' clients for *merces de Luca* were merchants of Toulouse, whose purchases ranged in value from about 25 *livres* to 200 *livres tournois*. On one occasion in March 1341, Petrus Cotelli of Toulouse, whose purchases through agents can be documented in the years 1339-1343, paid eleven

61 A. D. Hérault, II E 95/368, ff. 74r, 114v, 142*v*, II E 95/369, ff. 100r, 112v, 113v; II E 95/374, ff. 22R, 22vr; II E 95/371, f. 105v.

62 See A. D. Hérault, II E 95/370, f. 31r and II E 95/372, f. 42v for examples.

63 A. D. Hérault, II E 95/374, ff. 27r, 37vR, 43vR, and 45vR.

64 A. D. Hérault, II E 95/374, ff. 36v, 37v, 17vR, 59vR.

65 A. D. Hérault, II E 95/374, *passim*. See sample acts in Appendix.

marks of gold or about 379 *livres tournois* for *merces de Luca.*[66] The Toulousain purchases of these years were the harbingers of expanding commercial relations between Montpellier and Toulouse at the mid-fourteenth century.[67]

Spaniards also began to frequent Montpellier in search of silks in the late 1330s, as suggested earlier. Merchants of Burgos, Castile and Valencia represented almost fifteen percent of the Cabanis' clientele. Typical was Johannes Ferrandes, merchant of Burgos, who bought *merces de Luca* with two associates in 1341.[68] Petrus de Calvo, merchant of Montpellier inhabiting Valencia, bought about 155 *livres* of this merchandise in 1342.[69] Calvo seems to have specialized in the export of silks to Valencia and the import of saffron to Montpellier.[70] The Spanish interest in silks was only part of a broad spectrum of commercial and financial interaction with Montpellier.[71] The Languedocian town acted as a clearing house for Spanish financial obligations.[72] Spaniards frequently borrowed funds in towns such as Valencia and Barcelona through exchange contracts and repaid their debts in Montpellier. The latter was a gateway for Spanish trade in leather and saffron with the Champagne fairs and with Paris.[73] Transportation links, both overland and by sea through short-haul navigation along the Mediterranean coast, were numerous, and the ties between southern France and Spain had been close for

---

66 See A. D. Hérault, II E 95/374, ff. 7v, 31r, 35r, 17vR, 35vR, 37vR and 41vR. See also II E 95/371, f. 67v for a purchase by Cotelli. Re: currency conversions, see note 42 above.

67 P. Wolff, *Commerces et marchands de Toulouse, passim.*

68 A. D. Hérault, II E 95/374, ff. 44vr, 48vr and 57r.

69 A. D. Hérault, II E 95/374, f. 55vR.

70 A. D. Hérault, II E 95/370, f. 48r and Archivo del Reino de Valencia, Protocolos, nos. 2801 and 2880 for examples of the Calvo trade.

71 I have explored this interaction in some detail in my dissertation, "Commerce and Society," *passim.*

72 Ibid., II, Appendix VI, pp. 269-278.

73 Ibid., II, Appendix V, pp. 261-267.

centuries. Silk purchases by Spaniards must be seen in the context of this broad network of contacts.

Equally endowed with close ties, the region of Cahors was the origin of Cabanis' clients as well. Vitalis and Bartholomeus Cavalerii of Cahors bought somewhat smaller amounts of *merces de Luca*, ranging from about 20 to 80 *livres* in price, than did Toulousains and Spaniards.[74] The Lot region of which Cahors was an important center had long entertained relations with Montpellier as a Mediterranean entrepot and a collaborative center of finance.[75]

Completing the Cabanis' clientele were Montpelliérains who in turn engaged in silk sales.[76] Over the five-year period for which data exist on Cabanis' transactions in *merces de Luca*, their sales averaged 48.4 *livres tournois*. Table 5 summarises the total volume of their activity.

Table 5

CABANIS' TRADE IN MERCES DE LUCA

Year	Total amount	Average per sale	Number of *merces* acts	Total acts in year
1338	94.5 livres ⋆	31.5	3	28
1339	743.5	67.6	11	89
1340	64	21.3	3	39
1341	1320.9	57.4	23	80
1342	728.9	34.7	21	58

⋆ Prices have been quoted in *livres tournois* of 1330.

[74] A. D. Hérault, II E 95/374, ff. 6v, 17v, 27v and 29vR.

[75] On links with the Lot region, see Jean Combes, "Une famille de négociants quercynols à Montpellier et à Marseille au XIIIe siècle", *Bulletin de la Fédération historique du Languedoc-Méditerranéen et du Roussillon* (Perpignan, 1953, Saint-Gilles, 1954), offprint and Jean Lartigaut, "Témoignages sur la dépopulation du Quercy au XIVe siècle", *Annales du Midi*, 84 (1972), pp. 5-15.

[76] See, for example, A. D. Hérault, II E 95/374, ff. 36v and 37r. Purchases by a local *velerius* are also worthy of note. See ff. 17R and 22R.

These data suggest that 1341 was the most productive year for the Cabanis, while 1339 showed the largest average sales. The Cabanis' commercial activity can be set in the general context of trade in silk and mercery over the period 1293-1343 by a comparison of the data in Table 5 with those in Tables 2 and 3. Since the Cabanis' sales in *merces de Luca* account for most of the recorded activity in this merchandise, the curve of average sales basically reflects the Cabanis' sales. Average sales of silk were higher in the years of peak trade — 1293-1294 and 1336-1343 — than were sales of *merces de Luca.* The average silk sale made by the Cabanis was 113 *livres*, considerably higher than the average sale of *merces de Luca.* However, Table 3 of maximum and minimum sales, reveals that the largest transactions in both silks and *merces de Luca* — in 1340 and 1341 — fell in the same range of upwards of 400 *livres tournois* in the sound money of 1330. While such a sum may seem modest in comparison with some medieval commodity values, a pittance alongside the thousands of pounds in some Genoese sales of 1288, it still represents a solid investment of capital, greater than the price of a substantial house in Montpellier.[77]

The share of the Cabanis in the silk and *merces de Luca* trade in Montpellier may be due in part to a random survival of evidence, felicitous in their regard, but their specialization in one product is characteristic of the behaviour of Montpelliérains whose activity can be observed in other phases of commerce at the mid-fourteenth century. Specialization was one response to the shrinking commercial possibilities in this period.

The importance of the silk trade in the economy of Montpellier can be best illustrated by the comparative numbers of com-

---

[77] For example, a local pepperer sold a house in the vicinity of Notre-Dame-des-Tables in the financial district of town to another pepperer for 250 *livres petits tournois* in 1336. See II E 95/370, f. 118v.

modity transactions given in Table 6.[78] After agricultural products which were vital to the survival of every medieval town, silks and mercery were the most common objects of commerce in the two periods examined above. Silks and *merces de Luca* were the most frequently sold of Mediterranean imports which included spices and pharmaceutical products. The complements of these imports, wool cloths, were the most common exports of merchants of Montpellier in the Mediterranean world and active commodities of exchange on the local market. The activity of the silk trade in the years 1293-1294 and 1336-1343 reflects two periods of overall economic prosperity when other commodities of the luxury trade were also heavily traded. In contrast, the years 1327-1333 represent a time of agricultural crisis when grain had to be imported to sustain the urban population.[79] Hence the intense activity in grain recorded in Table 6. The years 1347-1348 fall again in a period of agricultural shortages when luxury products were rarely recorded in the remaining documents.[80] The silk transactions of 1336-1343 depict a height of market activity not to be realized again in later years due to the onset first of agricultural crisis and then of the Black Death of 1348.

The silk trade of western Europe was by no means centered in the Languedocian town of Montpellier. Genoa and Venice far surpassed Montpellier in the Asiatic quest for silks and as European silk markets. The silk finishing industry of Montpellier was no rival for that of Lucca. The foregoing examination of market activity has revealed that the preeminent role of Montpellier in the silk trade was that of assembly point for a silk clientele from Spain, and from central and southwestern France. In

---

[78] I am indebted to Marie-Madeleine Compère Julia, archivist-paleographer, for this table based on the extant notarial acts of 1293-1348.

[79] See "Commerce and Society," I, pp. 212-224. On the trade in grapes, see pp. 232-240.

[80] A. D. Hérault, II E 95/377, the register of Bernardus Egidii, remains for the years 1347-1348.

16

CHRONOLOGY OF MARKET TRANSACTIONS

PERCENTAGES

TABLE 6

the absence of an important silk export activity in the western Mediterranean, merchants of Montpellier perfected the role of middlemen in the redistribution of Lucchese silk fabrics. The number of remaining silk transactions in Montpellier suggests a considerable volume of trade. These transactions illuminate the function of Montpellier as an outlet for the Lucchese industry before the Pisan conquest of Lucca in 1342 caused a sharp if temporary decline in production.[81]

---

[81] R. S. Lopez, "China Silk," p. 75, noted that Lucchese exports of silk products declined from an average of 125,000 pounds in 1335-1341 to 50,000 pounds in weight between 1342 and 1369.

APPENDIX OF SAMPLE ACTS

1. Recognition of debt by Toulousains
A. D. Hérault, II E 95/374, f. 34v

June 4, 1342.

Item, die quarta mensis junii.

Ego, Johannes Fabri, procurator et negotiorum gestor Bernardi de Podio, cederii, qui moratur in carreria Deaurate Tholoze, prout de procuratione mea constat fidemque facio publico instrumento inde facto, scripto et signato per magistrum Martinum Mutonis, publicum Tholoze notarium, sub anno predicto et XXVI die mensis madii, nomine procuratorio predicto, et meo proprio nomine, et utroque nomine insolidum confiteor me debere vobis, Guiraudo de Cabanis, mercatori Montispessulani presenti, stipulanti et recipienti una cum notario infrascripto, stipulanti et recipienti pro vobis, et vestris, et Jacobo de Cabanis, fratre et socio vestro absenti, et suis, quadraginta septem libras septem solidos et duos denarios turonensium, pro mercibus de Luca, bonis et recipientibus quas a vobis habui, predictis nominibus, causa emptionis, tam bene valentibus.

Renuncians etc., solvam, predictis nominibus, vobis stipulanti ut supra et dicto fratri vestro, vel vestrum alteri, aut vestris, de die in diem, ad primam et simplicem requisitionem vestram et dicti fratris vestri, vel vestrum alterius, una cum omnibus expensis etc.

Obligo, predictis nominibus, vobis stipulanti et recipienti ut supra, me in personam et omnia bona mea et dicti Bernardi, cujus sum procurator, et cujuslibet nostrum insolidum, presentia et futura, sub sigillo et carcere etc., excepta tamen et excepto remota persona dicti Bernardi cujus sum procurator, ab obligatione virum et districtu sigilli et carceris predictorum. Ita etc. Renuncians etc. Fidem etc.

Hec acta fuerunt in Montepessulano, in hoperatorio habitationis mei notarii infrascripti, in testimonio Guillelmo Amblardi, hostalerii, domini Jacobi Guindonis, presbyteri Montispessulani.

Postquam, anno predicto, dicto domino Philippo etc. et die XVII septembris, de voluntate Firmini Salamonis, procuratoris dictorum fratrum cum instrumento inde facto per Guillelmum Salayrani, notarium suprascriptum sub anno domini M CCC XLI et die XXVII marcii, confitentis nomine procuratorio predicto, sibi per dictos debitores, vel alium per eos solventes, esse de toto predicto debito plenario satisfacti, quitantis, nomine predicto, predictos debitores absentes etc. de predictis, fuit dicta nota cancellata.

Testes: magistri Guillelmus Nogareti, Guillelmus Majorini, notarii regis.

2. RECOGNITION OF DEBT BY SPANIARDS
A. D. Hérault, II E 95/374, f. 38v

November 11, 1342.

Item, eadem die.

Ego, Petrus, filius Johannis PETRI condam mercatoris de Burgos, factor Gonsalo GONSALES, dicti loci, nomine meo proprio, et pro me et meis, ac nomine dicti Gonsalo, et utroque nomine in solidum, confiteor me debere Jacobo et Guiraudo de CABANIS, fratribus, mercatoribus et sociis Montispessulani, absentibus, et tibi notario etc. quadraginta et quatuor libras et sexdecim solidos turonensium pro mercibus de Luca bonis et mercabilibus, quas, a dictis fratribus habui, causa emptionis, tam bene valentibus. Renuncians etc.

Solvam, predictis nominibus, dictis fratribus, vel alteri eorum, aut suis, seu eorum, vel alterius ipsorum certo procuratori, de die in diem, ad primam et simplicem requisitionem dictorum fratrum, vel suorum, seu alterius ipsorum, una cum omnibus expensis etc. Obligo, predictis nominibus, tibi notario infrascripto stipulanti et recipienti ut supra, me et dictum Gonsalao, et quemlibet nostrum insolidum, in personas etc. sub sigillo et carcere etc. Ita etc. Renuncians etc. Fidem etc.

Testes: predicti et mei G. Salayrani.

Grossatum est- Berengarius Duranti, vice magistri Mathei Jennini notarii auctoritate judicis.

LE ROLE DE MONTPELLIER DANS LE COMMERCE DES DRAPS DE LAINE AVANT 1350*

La « Seconda Settimana di Studio » de l'année 1970 à Prato eut comme thème la production, le commerce et la consommation des draps de laine du XIIe au XVIIe siècle[1]. Rappelant l'état des recherches sur l'histoire de la draperie médiévale, plusieurs participants au congrès indiquèrent que des études sur les marchés et la distribution des draps de laine dans les circuits commerciaux seraient à souhaiter[2]. Dans une communication sur la draperie en Languedoc, Philippe Wolff evoqua directement le cas montpelliérain : « il resterait encore à analyser l'organisation de ce commerce des étoffes. L'effort a été accompli pour Toulouse et le pendant en est attendu avec impatience pour Montpellier »[3]. Actuellement, il n'existe toujours pas d'examen du marché montpelliérain des draps de laine[4]. Il est temps de combler

* Cet article est la révision d'une communication, « The Medieval Cloth Market of Montpellier : Mediterranean Exports », présentée au 13e Congrès sur les Etudes Médiévales, Western Michigan University, Kalamazoo, Michigan, en mai 1978. Je voudrais remercier de son aide l'Interlibrary Loan Division de la Wilson Library à l'Université du Minnesota.

1. Les communications du congrès de Prato furent publiées dans *Produzione, commercio e consumo dei panni di lana (nei secoli XII-XVIII)*, a cura di Marco SPALLANZANI (Florence, 1976).

2. Ainsi le commentaire de Jacques HEERS, « Les "analyses de marchés" manquent cruellement ! » dans sa communication, « La mode et les marchés des draps de laine : Gênes et la montagne à la fin du Moyen âge », dans *Produzione*, p. 200 ; et les remarques de Charles VERLINDEN, « Aspects de la production, du commerce et de la consommation des draps flamands au Moyen âge », dans *Produzione*, p. 112 : « Mais, pour le Moyen âge et surtout pour le bas Moyen âge, rien, à mon avis, n'importe autant que de multiplier les études sur la répartition des produits textiles des différents pays dans les autres pays. »

3. Philippe WOLFF, « Esquisse d'une histoire de la draperie en Languedoc du XIIe au début du XVIIe siècle », dans *Produzione*, p. 458.

4. L'œuvre d'Alexandre GERMAIN, *Histoire du commerce de Montpellier antérieurement à l'ouverture du port de Cette*, 2 t. (Montpellier, 1861), n'a pas été remplacée au niveau de la synthèse. Aussi utile est l'étude générale de Louis J. THOMAS, *Montpellier, ville marchande : histoire économique et sociale de Montpellier des origines à 1870* (Montpellier, 1936). L'étude la plus approfondie d'un secteur de l'histoire des textiles à Montpellier est celle de Jean COMBES, « L'indus-

cette lacune pour la période antérieure à 1350 par une étude du marché montpelliérain et des activités commerciales des Montpelliérains dans ce secteur important de l'économie médiévale. Avant 1293, on ne dispose que de sources dispersées, montpelliéraines et autres. De 1293 à 1348, la survie à Montpellier d'une douzaine de registres notariaux permet un examen plus approfondi du commerce des draps[5].

Le rôle de Montpellier et des Montpelliérains dans la draperie médiévale sera envisagé à plusieurs niveaux[6]. D'abord, la production locale de draps et la teinture en graine mériteront notre attention en raison de la renommée de Montpellier pour les draps écarlates si recherchés par les gens fortunés en Europe et dans le monde méditerranéen. Ensuite, le commerce international des draps de laine sera considéré sous deux aspects : les exportations à partir de Montpellier et d'autres places fréquentées par les Montpelliérains, et les ventes à une clientèle étrangère sur le marché local[7]. On soulèvera dans ce cadre la question de l'approvisionnement montpelliérain et celle de la variété des produits. On examinera dans la troisième partie de cette étude le marché de détail à Montpellier. On étudiera enfin la participation de différentes couches sociales au commerce de draps et le problème des prix.

trie et le commerce des toiles à Montpellier de la fin du XIIIe siècle au milieu du XVe », dans *Recueil de mémoires et travaux publié par la société d'histoire du droit et des institutions des anciens pays de droit écrit*, fasc. IX : *Mélanges Roger Aubenas* (Montpellier, 1974), pp. 181-212.

5. J'ai consulté les registres II, 1-3 du fonds des notaires, acquis par le Consulat aux Archives municipales (abrégées désormais A. M. Montp.), et les registres II E 95/368-377 de notaires, acquis par le clergé de Montpellier aux Archives départementales de l'Hérault (abrégées désormais A. D. Hérault). Des lacunes dans la série de registres des A. M. Montp. de 1343 à 1363 et dans celle des A. D. Hérault de 1348 à 1361 expliquent que cette étude doive s'arrêter au milieu du XIVe siècle, à la fin de l'époque majorquine de Montpellier.

6. Je limiterai mon enquête aux draps de laine, laissant de côté tous les autres textiles, mélanges de tissus, cuirs, soieries, etc. Seront aussi exclus les vêtements dont la rareté de mentions dans les registres notariaux suggère que la plupart d'entre eux étaient vendus sur des étals et dans des boutiques de confection de tailleurs, sans établissement de reconnaissance de dette devant notaire. P. WOLFF, « Esquisse », p. 436, pense que les ventes avec paiement en espèces étaient les plus courantes. Pour quelques inventaires après décès, où des vêtements sont énumérés, voir A. M. Montp., fonds de la Commune Clôture, EE 559 : 23 janvier 1309 et EE 459 : 10 juin 1361. Voir aussi A. D. Hérault, II E 95/377, ff. 105 r° et 295 v°.

7. L'utilisation du crédit dans les ventes de draps a fait que des reconnaissances de dette, conservées dans les registres notariaux, permettent une étude plus approfondie du marché montpelliérain de 1293 à 1348. L'exportation de draps de Montpellier, vue à travers les contrats de commande, d'association et de transport, complète ce portrait

Activités de teinture et production locale de draps

Les draps de Montpellier font leur apparition dans les documents lorsque Guilhem V en distribue, ainsi que des draps d'Aumelas, dans son testament de 1121[8]. Dès la fin du XIIe siècle, Montpellier est connue pour sa teinture en graine : teinture fabriquée à partir des corps séchés d'insectes femelles qui se nourrissent des chênes kermès, nombreux dans la région montpelliéraine[9]. En 1181, Guilhem VIII octroie un monopole sur la teinture aux Montpelliérains[10]. La charte des coutumes de 1204 réaffirme ce monopole et interdit la vente de tout drap à Montpellier par des étrangers, exception faite des colporteurs[11]. Dans la même charte, l'utilisation de la graine du chêne kermès est déclarée obligatoire dans la teinture écarlate[12]. Dès 1226, le monopole local en teinture rouge est modifié pour en admettre l'exercice par des étrangers ayant vécu à Montpellier pendant cinq ans, ou pendant deux ans s'ils sont mariés avec des Montpelliéraines[13]. En 1251, la condition de résidence est réduite à deux ans pour tous les étrangers[14]. L'importance de la teinture en graine à Montpellier se reflète dans le troisième rang qu'occupe la draperie rouge dans la hiérarchie des douze consuls de l'administration municipale[15].

A partir du XIIIe siècle, le commerce international en draps écarlates de Montpellier peut être suivi à travers les documents de Gênes et de Marseille. En 1203, trois draps de stamfort teints en graine à Montpellier sont vendus par un marchand d'Arras à un drapier local à Gênes[16]. Du drap flamand teint en rouge à Montpellier est envoyé de Marseille au Levant en 1248[17]. Ces données confirment ce que

8. *Liber instrumentorum memorialium*, éd. A. GERMAIN et C. CHABANEAU, 1 fascicule (Montpellier, 1884), acte XCIV.
9. Ph. WOLFF, « Esquisse », p. 440.
10. *Le Petit Thalamus de Montpellier*, éd. E. THOMAS et al. (Montpellier, 1840), p. 137.
11. *Layettes du Trésor des Chartes*, éd. A. TEULET, t. I (Paris, 1863), p. 263, article 109.
12. *Ibid.*, p. 264, article 110.
13. *Le Petit Thalamus*, p. 138.
14. *Ibid.*, pp. 138-139.
15. *Le Petit Thalamus*, pp. 95-101 et André GOURON, *La réglementation des métiers en Languedoc au Moyen âge* (Paris, 1958), pp. 56 et suiv., sur l'élection au consulat à Montpellier. En fait, la quatrième place revenait aussi aux drapiers, pour la draperie sobeyrane ; voir les remarques de Louis J. THOMAS, *Montpellier, ville marchande* (1936), p. 33.
16. M.W. HALL-COLE, H.G. KRUEGER, R.G. REINEST et R.L. REYNOLDS, éd. *Giovanni di Guiberto (1200-1211)*, t. I (Turin, 1939), acte 881, pp. 408-409.
17. Louis BLANCARD, éd. *Documents inédits sur le commerce de Marseille au Moyen âge*, t. II (Marseille, 1885), acte 522 d'Amalric. Il s'agit ici d'un prêt maritime pour lequel l'arrivée à Acre de quatre draps d'Ypres teints en graine était nécessaire pour que le remboursement fût effectué.

pensait Ph. Wolff, à savoir que Montpellier importait des pièces de draps à teindre[18].

Dans la deuxième moitié du XIIIe siècle, les draps écarlates de Montpellier semblent avoir rencontré de la concurrence sur le marché international. En 1265, Jacques Ier, roi d'Aragon et de Majorque et seigneur de Montpellier, autorise les teinturiers de Montpellier à ajouter de la graine supplémentaire à leurs bains pour maintenir la qualité de la teinture à un niveau compétitif par rapport aux draps de Marseille, de Gênes et de Lucques[19]. Cependant, une deuxième utilisation des bains de teinture est également admise pour traiter « des biffes blanches, faudat, estamfort d'Angleterre ou Arras »[20]. En 1297, Jacques II de Majorque stipule qu'il faut préserver les draps teints en graine de mélanges quelconques de teinture[21]. En dehors des industries de teinture des villes citées en 1265, on constate, dès la fin du XIIIe siècle, une diffusion des pratiques de la teinture en rouge à Alès et en Provence[22]. A cette époque aussi, l'Arte di Calimala de Florence excelle dans la production de draps écarlates[23].

Par ailleurs, à la fin du XIIIe siècle, le marché européen et surtout méditerranéen évolue vers une demande de draps de qualité moyenne et de prix modéré créant des difficultés pour l'industrie des draps de luxe, surtout en Flandre, d'où provient une partie des draps teints en graine à Montpellier[24]. L'essor de nouvelles industries drapières, telle l'industrie languedocienne, répond à la nouvelle demande[25]. En dépit de l'accroissement du nombre des documents grâce à la préservation de registres notariaux montpelliérains à partir de 1293, les mentions de draps teints en graine deviennent rares et éparpillées[26]. En 1301, des

18. Ph. WOLFF, « Esquisse », p. 440.
19. *Ibid.* Voir A. M. Montp., *Grand Chartrier*, Louvet n° 4239.
20. Ph. WOLFF, « Esquisse », pp. 440.
21. *Ibid.*
22. Cette diffusion se voit dans les documents montpelliérains en ce qui concerne la teinture de la soie. Voir A. M. Montp., II 1, f. 21 r° et f. 64 r°. Sur le rôle des Juifs dans la teinturerie, voir E. MARTIN-CHABOT, *Les archives de la cour des comptes, aides et finances de Montpellier* (Paris, 1907), acte 401, p. 78.
23. Yves Renouard, *Les hommes d'affaires italiens du Moyen âge* (Paris, 1948 ; éd. rév. 1968), p. 166.
24. Sur la draperie flamande, l'œuvre d'Henri LAURENT, *Un grand commerce d'exportation au Moyen âge. La draperie des Pays-Bas en France et dans les pays méditerranéens (XIIe-XVe siècles)* (Paris, 1935), est toujours utile. Voir aussi G. de POERCK, *La draperie médiévale en Flandre et en Artois, Technique et terminologie*, 3 t. (Bruges, 1951). Ch. VERLINDEN, « Aspects de la production », p. 109, cite l'avenir des draps flamands, plus légers et moins chers. Une autre perspective sur la production des Pays-Bas est donnée par Raymond VAN UYTVEN, « La draperie brabançonne et malinoise du XIIe au XVIIe siècle : Grandeur éphémère et décadence », dans *Produzione*, pp. 85-97.
25. Ph. WOLFF, « Esquisse », pp. 454-459.
26. La survie, même sous une forme atténuée, de la teinturerie rouge s'explique probablement par l'évolution du goût de la bourgeoisie pour laquelle la couleur rouge représentait une marque de grand luxe. Voir J. HEERS, « La mode », p. 214.

drapiers de Montpellier vendent des draps teints en graine à des clients de Valence[27]. Pour 1341, on conserve la trace d'un envoi de draps rouges à Chypre et à Byzance par des marchands montpelliérains[28]. En 1340, quand les teinturiers de Montpellier établissent des statuts pour régler l'exercice de leur métier, ils incluent une renonciation de leur part à tout monopole de la teinture en graine, ce qui pourrait refléter un déclin dans ce secteur autrefois si célèbre de leur draperie[29].

Si la teinturerie montpelliéraine ralentit ses activités, que devient la production montpelliéraine de draps ? Selon une hypothèse de Ph. Wolff, la teinturerie montpelliéraine travaillait des draps de qualité fabriqués ailleurs pour les exporter au Levant, ceci au moins jusqu'au XIVe siècle[30]. Il se peut que la production locale de draps ait toujours été assez peu importante et que la fonction montpelliéraine ait surtout été une activité d'apprêt. Une telle situation expliquerait l'absence d'une initiative montpelliéraine dans le développement de l'industrie languedocienne de draps. Cette interprétation peut être soutenue par un examen du personnel drapier cité dans les actes notariaux.

A l'exception des drapiers, qui apparaissent comme revendeurs au détail et comme grossistes et des teinturiers, les registres notariaux ne contiennent guère de traces de producteurs de draps. Ainsi les tisserands, les foulons, les tondeurs de draps et les pareurs de l'industrie drapière médiévale sont absents des registres, bien que les tisserands et les tondeurs apparaissent parmi les métiers de la Commune Clôture[31]. En outre, les contrats d'apprentissage préservés dans les registres notariaux ne font état que de l'instruction dans la draperie et dans

27. A. M. Montp., II 1, f. 38 r°.

28. A. D. Hérault, II E 95/374, ff. 27 r° et 43 v°.

29. *Archives de la ville de Montpellier, Inventaires et documents*, t. I, éd. Joseph Berthelé (Montpellier, 1895), armoire C, cassette 1, Louvet n° 1118.

30. Ph. Wolff, « Esquisse », p. 440. Dans une conversation récente, Jean Combes m'affirma sa conviction que l'expansion de la draperie languedocienne n'a pas dépassé le fleuve Hérault dans la direction de l'est. Aucun des documents notariaux que j'ai consultés n'apportent de preuves du contraire.

31. Pour des tableaux de participants dans les actes notariaux de Montpellier de 1293 à 1348 voir ma thèse, « Commerce and Society in Montpellier : 1250-1350 », *Diss. Yale University*, t. II, pp. 136-143. Dans les listes des échelles de la Commune Clôture on trouve mention de « teysseires » ou « teychadors » (tisserands), de « tozoyriers » (tondeurs de draps), de « candoradors » et de « penhadors » mais ni de pareurs ni de foulons. Voir *Le Petit Thalamus*, pp. 95-100 et L. J. Thomas, *Montpellier, ville marchande* (1932), p. 59 et *Montpellier, ville marchande* (1936), p. 56, où Thomas décrit une production drapière à Montpellier. L. J. Thomas, *Montpellier, ville marchande, Conférences faites à la Chambre de Commerce de Montpellier en 1932* (Montpellier, 1932), pp. 57 et suiv., a vu les drapiers comme des dirigeants d'industrie : « Les drapiers de Montpellier ne sont point des artisans, mais de grands industriels, des chefs d'entreprise, des donneurs d'ouvrage, qui ont dans leur dépendance de nombreux métiers subordonnés ». Les preuves de telles activités ne se trouvent pas, malheureusement, dans les documents.

le travail des fils d'or et d'argent[32]. L'effectif réduit des métiers normalement associés à l'industrie drapière distingue Montpellier d'une ville comme Toulouse qui compte quatre-vingt-trois tisserands et quarante-quatre paraires en 1398, ou bien comme Carcassonne, où l'on relève quarante-trois tisserands et cinquante-deux paraires en 1396[33]. En revanche l'implantation de la teinturerie à Montpellier apparaît clairement avec trente-sept teinturiers témoins des statuts de leur métier en 1340, en contraste avec les vingt-et-un teinturiers de Toulouse en 1398 et l'unique teinturier signalé à Carcassonne en 1336[34]. Pour une ville aussi importante que Montpellier, l'existence d'une industrie drapière limitée aux propres besoins des habitants mérite davantage l'investigation.

En fait, sur le marché local et à l'exportation, on trouve des mentions de draps sans désignation d'origine, et, plus significatif, avec comme marque d'identification l'expression « de cette terre »[35]. Quel rapport existe-t-il entre cette désignation notariale et une production locale de draps ? Plusieurs hypothèses peuvent être introduites pour expliquer ce terme de draps locaux. Ph. Wolff a divisé la draperie languedocienne en cinq régions géographiques, dont le Bas-Languedoc[36]. Dans cette dernière sont incluses les villes de Gignac, Narbonne, Saint-Pons, Montpellier et d'autres. Il se peut donc que la désignation « de cette terre » se réfère à la production de petites villes du Bas-Languedoc que le notaire ne jugeait pas bon de nommer de façon spécifique[37]. En outre, on ne rencontre pas de draps dits « de Montpellier » dans les documents notariaux, ce qui permet d'avancer l'hypothèse selon laquelle les draps « de cette terre » seraient de production montpelliéraine ou bien fabriqués dans la région immédiatement voisine. Des conditions propices à une industrie drapière existaient-elles dans le voisinage de Montpellier ?

Au nord et à l'ouest de la ville, l'élevage des moutons était courant. Les marécages salins à l'ouest de Montpellier, près de la Montagne de

32. Par exemple, A. D. Hérault, II E 95/368, ff. 77 v° et 135 v°.

33. André Gouron, *La réglementation*, pp. 96-98, a étudié l'importance numérique relative des effectifs des métiers montpelliérains d'après le nombre de portes de la Commune Clôture qu'ils devaient garder. Les tondeurs de draps se situaient parmi les effectifs les moins nombreux. En revanche, les tailleurs, les blanquiers, et les drapiers fournissaient des effectifs plus importants. Pour les statistiques sur les villes de Toulouse et de Carcassonne, voir P. Wolff, « Esquisse », pp. 447-448.

34. *Ibid.* Voir note 29 ci-dessus. A. Gouron, *La réglementation*, p. 99, a note que quarante-trois sartres, maîtres et compagnons, participèrent à l'établissement des statuts de leur métier en 1352.

35. Par exemple, A. D. Hérault, II E 95/369, f. 75 v° : *huius terre* ; II E 95/374, f. 6 v° : *istius terre*.

36. Ph. Wolff, « Esquisse », p. 452.

37. Cependant, les notaires de Montpellier savent indiquer l'origine des draps. Voir plus loin la note 103 et les tableaux 1, 4 et 9.

Sète servaient au pâturage de moutons locaux et de moutons de la Montagne Noire en transhumance sur la côte. Au nord de Montpellier, dans la garrigue, il y avait des chèvres et des moutons qui pâturaient pendant l'été dans les Cévennes[38]. L'approvisionnement en laine locale n'aurait pas manqué à une industrie drapière : on voit, par exemple un agent de la famille marchande des Cabannes revendre à plusieurs reprises des droits de pâture pour des moutons ; il achète et vend également, de la laine locale[39]. En outre, Montpellier servait de plaque tournante pour la laine bourguignonne. Des marchands locaux allaient en Bourgogne chercher de la laine et d'autres, comme la famille de Cabannes, avaient des représentants en Bourgogne pour l'expédier à Montpellier[40].

Des ressources en eau sont essentielles pour le traitement de la laine. La région de Montpellier ne possède pas de rivières à courant fort, à l'exception de l'Hérault qui se situe à environ trente kilomètres à l'ouest de la ville[41]. Or, plus près, le Lez passait un peu à l'est du centre ville et deux affluents du Lez traversaient la ville médiévale, permettant le fonctionnement des industries de blanchissage de toiles et de traitement de la laine brute situées dans deux quartiers dont les noms, la Blancaria et la Flocaria, existaient depuis le XIIe siècle[42].

Dès la fin du XIIe siècle et au cours du XIIIe siècle, l'introduction de moulins à fouler peut être notée à travers l'Europe[43]. Or on trouve plusieurs mentions de moulins dans l'arrière-pays montpelliérain. Les frères Cabannes possèdent des moulins appelés *mollendinum. bladeria* et *paratoria* sur le Lez près de Saint-Clément-la-Rivière[44]. Jean Combes

38. Emmanuel LE ROY LADURIE, *Les paysans de Languedoc*, t. 1 (Paris, 1966), pp. 17-19. Les drailles existent toujours. Voir J.-B. GÈZE, « Les drailles du Département de l'Hérault », tiré à part (Montpellier, 1926). Voir aussi A. D. Hérault, 2 S 39 pour un rapport du Service Vicinal sur les drailles.

39. A. D. Hérault, II E 95/374, ff. 26 v°, 27 r°, 27 v° et 32 v°.

40. En 1328, des Montpelliérains revenant sans permis sur la Saône avec des toiles et de la laine furent arrêtés à Mâcon. Ils furent libérés par le roi de France qui déclara de plus qu'il ne voulait pas que les Montpelliérains paient d'impôts extraordinaires dans cette région, ce qui fait penser qu'ils fréquentaient l'endroit. Voir A. M. Montp., *Inventaires et documents*, t. I, armoire A, Cassette 17, Louvet n°s 332-333. Sur les Cabannes, voir A. D. Hérault, II E 95/374, ff. 8 v°, 15 r°, 22 r° et 48 r°.

41. Gaston GALTIER, « Les conditions géographiques de Montpellier », dans *Mélanges Philippe Arbos* (Clermont-Ferrand, 1953), pp. 237-246.

42. Louise GUIRAUD, « Recherches topographiques sur Montpellier au Moyen âge », dans *Mémoires de la société archéologique de Montpellier*, 2e série, t. I (1899), pp. 89-355.

43. Eleanor M. CARUS-WILSON, « An Industrial Revolution of the Thirteenth Century », dans *Economic History Review*, t. XI (1941), pp. 39-60, a essayé de voir les effets de cette évolution sur l'industrie drapière en Angleterre. Son interprétation a été discutée par Edward MILLER, « The Fortunes of the Textile Industry during the Thirteenth Century », dans *Economic History Review*, 2e série, t. 18 (1965), pp. 64-82.

44. A. D. Hérault, II E 95/374, ff. 26 v°, 18 r°, 23 r°, 24 r°, 50 r°.

a identifié les *paratoria* comme des moulins pour la préparation de toiles de lin et de chanvre pour l'industrie montpelliéraine[45]. Selon Anne-Marie Bautier, les moulins appelés *paratoria* sont plus fréquemment utilisés dans la préparation de toiles, mais elle signale également que le terme *molendinum parator* indique un moulin à fouler[46]. Dans l'arrière-pays, l'existence de *candoraria*, établissements de blanchissage de lin, confirme la présence de la préparation du lin[47]. Mais le fait que Jean de Sueuilles, agent des Cabannes et lui-même canabassier, s'occupe de la revente de pâtures pour les moutons et de l'achat et de la vente de laine brute, permet de supposer que deux types d'industries rurales voisinaient au nord de Montpellier, la canabasserie et l'industrie drapière[48]. Il est donc possible que l'industrie rurale ait évolué dans le sens d'une réduction des frais de production et de réduction du nombre de foulons, en raison de la diffusion de la technologie des moulins à fouler[49]. Le réseau fluvial limité n'autorisait de toutes façons qu'une industrie drapière modeste.

Une industrie drapière de portée locale pouvait se dispenser du travail des pareurs. Les tisserands et les tondeurs, mentionnés dans les règlements de la Commune Clôture, mais absents des registres de notaires, pouvaient suffire en nombre réduit aux besoins locaux. Il se peut enfin que d'autres couches de la population urbaine aient eu aussi un rôle dans la production de draps aux environs de Montpellier, notamment les cultivateurs dont le nombre important est signalé à Montpellier depuis le milieu du XIIIe siècle[50]. La possibilité de la participation de la population des petites villes voisines de Montpellier

45. Jean COMBES, « L'industrie et le commerce des toiles », pp. 195-196.

46. Anne-Marie BAUTIER, « Les plus anciennes mentions de moulins hydrauliques industriels et de moulins à vent », dans *Bulletin philologique et historique (jusqu'à 1610) du Comité des travaux historiques et scientifiques, année 1960*, t. II (1961), pp. 567-626, surtout pp. 576-579.

47. A. D. Hérault, II E 95/374, f. 32 v°. L. Thomas identifia les candoradors comme des blanchisseurs de laines. Voir *Montpellier, ville marchande* (1936), p. 56.

48. Voir la note 39 ci-dessus et A. D. Hérault, II E 95/374, ff. 27 v°, 28 r° et 36 r°. Pour des ventes de laine par des représentants des Cabannes voir ff. 22 r°, 32 v° et 48 r°.

49. Pour l'industrie anglaise, Paul HARVEY, « The English Trade in Wool and Cloth, 1150-1250 : Some Problems and Suggestions », dans *Produzione*, p. 375, a suggéré que l'industrie s'est retirée du contexte urbain après le XIIe siècle en raison de la concurrence internationale. Il se peut que le même processus se manifeste dans la région montpelliéraine.

50. En 1239 le chiffre, peut-être exagéré de 6 000 à 7 000 cultivateurs est cité dans une chronique de Jacques Ier. Voir Emile BONNET, « Les séjours à Montpellier de Jacques Ier le Conquérant, roi d'Aragon », dans *Mémoires de la société archéologique de Montpellier*, 2e série, t. IX (1927), pp. 176-177. Je dois à Josiah Cox Russell l'hypothèse de l'engagement de cette population dans l'industrie drapière. La représentation des travailleurs reste élevée parmi la clientèle notariale. Voir la note 31 ci-dessus.

n'est pas, non plus, à exclure[51]. Il faut espérer que des recherches futures sur l'histoire de la campagne montpelliéraine permettront d'éclairer ce problème de la production locale des draps de laine. Il est peu probable, cependant, qu'elles révèlent l'existence d'une industrie drapière montpelliéraine d'envergure. Ainsi, la terminologie notariale « de cette terre » se réfère vraisemblablement à la draperie languedocienne, et non pas à la production proprement montpelliéraine.

L'activité des Montpelliérains dans le commerce international des draps

Réexportations et exportations

L'activité des Montpelliérains dans le commerce international des draps ne peut être suivie sporadiquement qu'à partir du début du XIIIe siècle. C'est à cette époque seulement qu'on en trouve des traces indiscutables dans les registres génois, ceci bien que des Montpelliérains aient fréquenté le marché gênois depuis au moins le milieu du XIIe siècle[52]. Plusieurs décennies donc après leur entrée probable dans le commerce des draps, des Montpelliérains enregistrent des ventes de draps septentrionaux à Gênes : des draps anglais (1205, 1263) ; du drap d'Ypres (1210) ; du stamfort d'Arras (1244) et du stamfort sans provenance (1236)[53].

En 1248, les notules d'Amalric de Marseille permettent d'entrevoir ce qui a dû être un réseau commercial montpelliérain liant le bassin occidental de la Méditerranée avec le Levant. Comment expliquer autrement les vingt-deux contrats de commande préservés de mars à

51. Sur le faible taux de l'immigration à Montpellier d'habitants de l'arrière-pays, voir mon article, « Patterns of Population Attraction and Mobility : The Case of Montpellier, 1293-1348 », dans *Viator, Medieval and Renaissance Studies*, t. 10 (1979), pp. 257-281.

52. *Il cartolare di Giovanni Scriba*, éd. de Mario CHIAUDANO et Mattia MORESCO, t. I (Turin, 1935), actes XLVII et CDXXXVIII où apparaissent des témoins portant le nom de famille *Monte Pesulano*, qui pourraient être originaires de la ville. Dans les actes de Jean Scribe, Montpellier est mentionnée comme destination d'envois de Gênes et comme place de repaiement.

53. Draps anglais : *Giovanni di Guiberto*, t. I, acte 1062, p. 493 : 1205 ; Renée DOEHAERD, *Les relations commerciales entre Gênes, la Belgique et l'Outremont d'après les archives notariales génoises aux XIIIe et XIVe siècles* (Bruxelles, Rome, 1941), t. III, acte 1212, p. 667 : 1263. Stamfort : R. DOEHAERD, Les relations, t. II, acte 466, p. 243 : 1236 ; draps d'Ypres : *ibid.*, t. II, acte 268, pp. 130-131 : 1210 ; stamfort d'Arras : *ibid.*, t. II, acte 150, p. 267 : 1244.

juillet 1248 dans lesquels des marchands de Montpellier expédient des draps d'Ypres, d'Arras, de Reims et de Chalons à Saint-Jean-d'Acre ?[54] A ajouter à ce bilan sont les neuf contrats de change maritime dont le remboursement est lié à l'arrivée saine et sauve à Acre d'autres draps septentrionaux[55]. Certains de ces draps ont été teints en graine à Montpellier[56]. Même dans une année exceptionnelle de croisade, 1248, ces contrats passés à Marseille ne peuvent qu'être basés sur des liens préexistants (en dépit du fait que ce sont les premières traces enregistrées de ventes de draps par les Montpelliérains au Levant). La spécialisation des Montpelliérains dans la vente des draps septentrionaux se dénote donc à Marseille comme à Gênes, mais la gamme qu'ils en proposent s'est étendue : outre des draps anglais et flamands, ils offrent également des draps du nord de la France et de la Champagne.

L'approvisionnement des Montpelliérains en draps du Nord était certainement facilité par des intermédiaires flamands et français. Des ventes de draps par des marchands flamands ont laissé des traces à Gênes à partir de la fin du XIIe siècle et on trouvait de tels marchands à Perpignan et à Montpellier dans la deuxième moitié du XIIIe[57]. Au XIIIe siècle, le rôle des marchands du Quercy, notamment de Saint-Antonin, dans le commerce des draps septentrionaux prend de l'envergure[58]. Or des familles montpelliéraines, telles les Crusols et les Conques, dont certains membres participent à l'exportation de draps de Marseille au Levant en 1248, ont des parents et à Marseille et en Quercy[59]. Les foires de Champagne, auxquelles assistent les Montpelliérains depuis les années 1220, augmentent ces possibilités directe et indirecte d'approvisionnement en draps septentrionaux[60]. Le fragment des comptes de la « foire chaude » de Troyes de 1296, découvert par

54. L. BLANCARD, *Documents inédits*, t. II, actes 212 et 561 pour des exemples de cette activité.

55. *Ibid.*, acte 522.

56. *Ibid.* A Marseille, les Montpelliérains passaient des contrats d'association entre eux et voyagaient également pour le compte de marchands de Marseille, Rodez, Le Puy et Sarlat, acceptant des investissements en contrats de commande qui allaient de 50 à 100 l. melgoriennes.

57. Voir Robert L. REYNOLDS, « Merchants of Arras and the Overland Trade with Genoa, Twelfth Century «, dans *Revue belge de philologie et d'histoire*, t. IX (1930), pp. 495-533 et Richard W. EMERY, « Flemish Cloth and Flemish Merchants in Perpignan in the Thirteenth Century », dans *Essays in Medieval Life and Thought in Honor of A. P. Evans* (New York, 1955), pp. 153-166.

58. R. W. EMERY, « Flemish Cloth », p. 157.

59. Jean COMBES, « Une famille de négociants quercynols à Montpellier et à Marseille au XIIIe siècle, dans *XXVIIe congrès de la fédération historique du Languedoc-Roussillon* (Perpignan, 1953, Saint-Gilles, 1954), tiré à part, pp. 1-8.

60. Félix BOURQUELOT, *Etudes sur les foires de Champagne*, t. II (Paris, 1861), p. 155. Voir aussi Jean COMBES, « Montpellier et les foires de Champagne », dans *Actes du 96e congrès national des sociétés savantes (Toulouse, 1971)*, t. I (Paris, 1978), pp. 381-428.

Robert-Henri Bautier, contient des contrats de transport de draps français à Montpellier pour le compte des marchands de Montpellier et de Narbonne[61].

Plusieurs événements affectent ces voies d'approvisionnement à la fin du XIIIe siècle : les hostilités anglo-françaises, le déclin de l'industrie flamande et la rétraction graduelle des foires drapières en Champagne[62]. La législation française envers les territoires ennemis devient plus restrictive concernant l'industrie drapière et les exportations à partir de 1277[63]. Des prohibitions de commerce avec la Flandre et le Brabant sont promulguées en 1315 et 1316[64]. Il n'y a plus de mentions de draps flamands dans les documents montpelliérains après 1293[65]. Il semble que l'approvisionnement du sud de la France — et de Montpellier en particulier — en draps flamands diminue à partir de la fin du XIIIe siècle.

En ce qui concerne la demande, les pertes de territoires subies par les croisés sur la côte syrienne ont dû perturber les débouchés des draps[66]. Plus près de Montpellier, les ambitions angevines et la rivalité entre Montpellier et Marseille dans le Levant contribuent à détourner

61. Robert-Henri BAUTIER, « Les registres des foires de Champagne à propos d'un feuillet récemment découvert », dans *Bulletin philologique et historique (1942-1943)* (Paris, 1945), pp. 157-185. Des contacts fréquents entre Montpellier et la Champagne, d'une part, et entre Montpellier et Paris d'autre part, laissent leur trace dans le premier registre notarial survivant. Voir, par exemple, A. M. Montp. II 1, ff. 24 v° et 87 v°.

62. R.-H. BAUTIER, « Les foires de Champagne. Recherches sur une évolution historique », dans *Recueils de la société Jean Bodin*, t. V, *La foire* (Bruxelles, 1953), pp. 97-148, sur le début du déclin des foires drapières qu'il date des années 1260.

63. Le poids fiscal en Champagne devient plus lourd et le roi ordonne des interdictions d'exportations. Voir *Ordonnances des roys de France de la troisième race*, t. I (Paris, 1723), pp. 326-327 pour la ferme des impôts en Champagne confiée à Biche et Mouche en 1295. Voir *Ordonnances*, t. I, pp. 351-352 pour une prohibition générale d'exportation de draps vers les territoires ennemis du 1er novembre 1302. Le 1er février 1305 (n. s.) une prohibition de toutes les exportations fut proclamée (*Ordonnances*, t. I, pp. 422-426). Sur les problèmes d'exportations, voir Georges BIGWOOD, « La politique de la laine en France sous les règnes de Philippe le Bel et de ses fils », dans *Revue belge de philologie et d'histoire*, t. 15 (1937), pp. 79-102, 429-457 ; t. 16 (1938), pp. 95-239.

64. *Ordonnances*, t. I, p. 605 : le 7 août 1315 ; pp. 619-620 : le 28 février 1316 (n. s).

65. En 1293-1294 des marchands de Saint-Antonin et de Cajarc vendent des draps à Montpellier. (A. M. Montp., II 1, ff. 9 r° et 17 r°). La présence d'un marchand d'Ypres à Montpellier en 1293 suggère également la participation continue des Flamands dans ce commerce. (A. M. Montp., II, 1, f. 49 v°). Après 1294, il y a une trace de ce trafic à l'étranger : Guy ROMESTAN, « Les relations commerciales entre Montpellier et Valence dans la première moitié du XIVe siècle », dans *Actas del VIII° Congreso de historia de la Corona de Aragón* (1967), t. II, n° 3 (Valence, 1973), pp. 243-253, note la vente de cubertes et biffes d'Ypres par un Montpelliérain, Gérard de la Porte, à Valence en 1317.

66. Voir en général, Steven RUNCIMAN, *History of the Crusades*, t. III (Cambridge, 1954) et Kenneth M. SETTON, ed. *History of the Crusades*, t. II (Philadelphia, 1962).

les Montpelliérains de Marseille comme port d'exportation au Levant[67]. Du reste, l'hégémonie génoise sur le commerce montpelliérain est rompue progressivement au cours du XIIIe siècle[68]. Malheureusement, des lacunes documentaires ne permettent pas une analyse approfondie des effets de ces changements sur le commerce montpelliérain des draps.

Les documents notariaux (1293-1348) reflètent une réorientation du commerce international des draps du point de vue montpelliérain. Il n'y a pas de trace d'exportation de draps de laine au Levant en 1293-1294. Cependant, l'importation de soieries et d'épices et l'exportation de toiles à Chypre en 1301 démontrent la continuité de liens commerciaux avec le bassin oriental de la Méditerranée[69]. A partir de 1327 les exportations de draps de Montpellier via le port d'Aigues-Mortes sont destinés à l'Empire Byzantin (la Romanie) et à Chypre, sites d'activités plus assidues après la chute de Saint-Jean-d'Acre en 1291[70].

CONTRATS DE COMMANDE ET DE SOCIÉTÉ A DESTINATION DE LA ROMANIE

Draps

Années	Non identifiés	Français	Locaux	Teints en graine (Montpellier)
1327	3			
1336		1		
1339		2		
1341				1 *
1342	1	2	1	
1343		1	1	
TOTAUX	4	6	2	1

* Draps de laine français, teints à Montpellier.

TABLEAU 1

67. J. COMBES, « Une famille de négociants quercynols », p. 45.
68. Cette hégémonie génoise a été étudiée par André DUPONT, *Les relations commerciales entre les cités maritimes de Languedoc et les cités méditerranéennes d'Espagne et d'Italie du Xe au XIIIe siècle* (Nîmes, 1942).
69. A. M. Montp., II 2, f. 14 r°, pour l'envoi de toiles. Pour des tableaux de vente de soieries et d'épices, voir « Commerce and Society in Montpellier », t. II, pp. 145-168.
70. Sur les rapports entre Montpellier et Byzance, voir mon article, « Montpellier and the Byzantine Empire : Commercial Interaction in the Mediterranean World before 1350 », dans *Byzantion, Revue internationale des études byzantines*, t. XLVIII (1978), pp. 456-476.

CONTRATS DE COMMANDE ET DE SOCIÉTÉ A DESTINATION DE CHYPRE

Draps

Années	Non identifiés	Français	Serge de Chalons	Serge	Narbonne	Toulouse	Limoux	Locaux	Teints en graine
1327	1								
1333	1 *	1					1	2	
1339		3							
1341									1
1342	2		1	1	1			1	
1343		2				1			
TOTAUX	4	6	1	1	1	1	1	3	1

* A double destination de Chypre et d'Alexandrie.

TABLEAU 2

Les contrats de commande et de société qui décrivent ces envois ne fournissent que le prix et, à l'occasion, le type des draps exportés, jamais la quantité[71]. Le tableau n° 1 donne l'esquisse de ces envois à la Romanie ; le tableau n° 2 en donne le complément pour Chypre. Dans les deux cas, des draps français sont l'objet le plus fréquent des frets et la présence de draps languedociens et de draps « locaux » est à signaler.

En 1327, les exportations notées ont été effectuées de Montpellier par des marchands de Narbonne[72]. Mais, dès 1333, les Montpelliérains dominent les contrats qui subsistent[73]. Le commerce levantin de Montpellier et de Narbonne est facilité par l'acquisition commune en 1323 d'une flotte construite auparavant pour une croisade de Charles IV, croisade qui ne se matérialisa pas[74]. De jeunes Montpelliérains ainsi que des marchands de Narbonne, du Quercy et du Massif Central voyagent pour des capitalistes de Montpellier dans ce commerce. L'investissement dans ces envois peut atteindre 2 000 réaux, mais

71. Une analyse de tous les contrats de commande et de société passés à Montpellier est donnée dans « Commerce and Society in Montpellier », t. II, pp. 236-260.
72. A. D. Hérault, II E 95/368, ff. 12 r°, 15 v°, 35 v° et 35 r°.
73. Par exemple, A. D. Hérault, II E 95/369, ff. 72 r°-75 v°.
74. Edouard BARATIER, *Histoire du commerce de Marseille*, t. II (Paris, 1951), pp. 217-218.

dans la plupart des cas n'atteint que 100 livres de monnaie courante[75]. Parfois, des draps ne forment qu'une partie de la marchandise expédiée[76].

L'exportation de draps dans le bassin occidental de la Méditerranée est aussi un élément important du commerce international de Montpellier. Les tableaux nos 3 et 4 en font état. En Italie et en Espagne les produits de l'industrie languedocienne et, surtout, les draps locaux remplissent les cargaisons[77].

CONTRATS DE COMMANDE, DE SOCIÉTÉ ET DE TRANSPORT
A DESTINATION DE LA PROVENCE, DE L'ITALIE DU NORD, DE L'ITALIE DU SUD ET DE LA SICILE

Draps

Années	Non identifiés	Français	Toulouse	Locaux
1327	1			3
1333	2			1
1336	1			
1339	1			
1342		1	1	2
1343		1		1
TOTAUX	5	2	1	7

TABLEAU 3

CONTRATS DE COMMANDE, DE SOCIÉTÉ ET DE TRANSPORT
A DESTINATION DES ILES BALÉARES ET DE LA PÉNINSULE IBÉRIQUE

Draps

Années	Non identifiés	Paris	Limoux (biffes)	Locaux
1293			1	
1294	1			
1328		1		1
TOTAUX	1	1	1	1

TABLEAU 4

75. Par exemple, A. D. Hérault, II E 95/375, f. 2 v°. Le 29 juillet 1327, 2 005 réaux furent investis dans des draps de laine non-identifiés. Voir A. D. Hérault, II E 95/368, f. 15 v°.

76. Ainsi, dans A. D. Hérault, II E 95/370, f. 12 r° : le 13 avril 1336, du safran et des draps de France, du montant de 1141 l. 16 s. 8 d. tournois, furent envoyés en Romanie par des changeurs de Montpellier par l'intermédiaire d'un commerçant de Figeac.

77. A. M. Montp. II 1, ff. 25 bis v° et 83 r° ; A. D. Hérault, II E 95/368, f. 130 v°.

Le commerce des draps entre Montpellier et l'Espagne remonte au XIIIe siècle. Des marchands de Montpellier vendent du drap français à Perpignan en 1283[78]. Ils continuent à vendre ces draps en Roussillon dans les années 1320 et 1330[79]. La présence montpelliéraine à Perpignan ouvre le marché espagnol. Les ventes de draps septentrionaux à Valence sont nombreuses dans les années 1295, 1296 et 1299[80]. Les Montpelliérains participent à ce commerce jusqu'aux années 1317-1320, mais à partir du XIVe siècle, le rôle des Narbonnais s'accentue[81]. Quatre-vingt-dix pour cent des ventes de draps notées à Valence de 1317 à 1340 sont faites par des marchands de Narbonne[82]. En raison de cette pénétration narbonnaise d'une part et de l'expansion des industries locales de draps en Catalogne et à Valence d'autre part, le rôle montpelliérain connaît une éclipse en Espagne.

Par ailleurs, l'industrie roussillonnaise se développe à cette époque[83]. Les échanges entre le Languedoc et le Roussillon sont perturbés par les efforts que réalisent les rois de France pour protéger l'industrie languedocienne de la concurrence roussillonnaise de 1305 à 1333[84]. Bien que les Montpelliérains vendent des draps français à Perpignan jusqu'aux années 1330-40, ce commerce diminue au-delà de cette décennie.

En Italie, les marchands de Montpellier ont une position prééminente dans les envois de draps à Naples et en Sicile tandis que les Italiens du Nord exportent des draps à Coni[85]. Les registres douaniers d'Aix-en-Provence et de Pertuis confirment la participation continue de Montpelliérains et d'autres dans ce commerce au milieu du XIVe siècle[86]. En outre, des marchands d'Italie du Nord utilisent Montpellier comme centre d'exportation de draps parisiens et de draps locaux à Barcelone dans le deuxième quart du XIVe siècle[87]. Montpellier sert

78. R. W. EMERY, « *Flemish Cloth* », p. 161.

79. A. D. Pyrénées-Orientales, Série E, reg. 27, f. 5 r° ; reg. 38, f. 39 r° ; reg. 40, f. 25 r° ; reg. 68, f. 10 v°. Je dois ces références à la générosité de M. Guy Romestan, qui m'a fait part de ces recherches à Perpignan.

80. G. ROMESTAN, « Les relations commerciales entre Montpellier et Valence ».

81. G. ROMESTAN, « A propos du commerce des draps dans la péninsule ibérique au Moyen âge, les marchands languedociens dans le royaume de Valence pendant la première moitié du XIVe siècle », *Bulletin philologique et historique (1969)*, t. I (Paris, 1972), p. 125.

82. *Ibid.*, p. 126.

83. G. ROMESTAN, « Draperie roussillonnaise et draperie languedocienne dans la première moitié du XIVe siècle », dans *Bulletin de la Fédération historique du Languedoc Roussillon* (Perpignan, 1969), pp. 31-60.

84. *Ibid.* Voir aussi Ph. WOLFF, « Esquisse », pp. 441-442.

85. A. D. Hérault, II E 95/368, ff. 29 v°, 42 v°, 74 v° ; II E 95/369, ff. 19 v°, 50 v°, 102 r° ; II E 95/370, f. 94 v° ; II E 95/374 ; ff. 7 r°, 9 v°, 30 v°.

86. O. TAVIANI, « Le commerce dans la région aixoise au milieu du XIVe siècle (1348-49) à travers un fragment de compte du péage d'Aix-en-Provence », *Annales du Midi*, t. 74 (1962), pp. 255-285.

87. A. D. Hérault, II E 95/368, f. 130 v°

ainsi d'intermédiaire dans le commerce entre l'Italie du Nord et la Catalogne.

Ventes à des étrangers sur le marché montpelliérain

Les ventes sur le marché montpelliérain à une clientèle étrangère fournissent une autre perspective du commerce international des draps. La survivance de documents montpelliérains favorise l'examen du marché international et local de draps à trois époques : 1293-1294 ; 1327-1336 et 1338-1343. Les tableaux 5 et 6 détaillent la participation de différents groupes sociaux à la vente et à l'achat. Les tableaux 7 et 8 permettent une comparaison relative de l'activité de ces groupes. Les deux premières périodes enregistrent la clientèle étrangère la plus nombreuse et la plus variée. Des marchands de Narbonne, de Majorque, de Cajarc et de Figeac viennent en nombre considérable à Montpellier, en 1293-1294, à la recherche de draps de Narbonne[88]. Des ventes allant de 79 livres à 150 livres melgoriennes sont ainsi conservées, sans spécification dans la plupart des cas de la dimension ni de la quantité de draps vendus. Les draps blancs de Narbonne sont les premiers produits de l'industrie languedocienne à faire leur apparition sur le marché montpelliérain[89]. A la même époque, des biffes de Limoux apparaissent à l'exportation en Espagne dans un contrat de commande[90]. A la fin du XIIIe siècle, des marchands de Perpignan, Saint-Pons-de-Tomières, Montagnac et Avignon fréquentent Montpellier à la recherche de draps apprêtés dont la provenance n'est pas notée[91]. Des marchands d'Avignon achètent également des draps français et des draps flamands en 1293[92]. La même année des marchands de Limoux se procurent des draps non apprêtés, peut-être pour une finition chez eux[93].

Dans les années 1327 à 1336, la clientèle étrangère sur le marché montpelliérain continue à être nombreuse, mais les clients lointains disparaissent au profit des gens de la région[94]. De nouveau de 1338 à 1343, des acheteurs de draps viennent de tout le sud de la France, de la Péninsule Ibérique et du royaume de Sicile[95]. Ils cherchent des draps français et languedociens et négocient parfois entre eux sans

88. A. M. Montp., II, 1, ff. 38 r°, 50 v°, 57 v°, 63 v°.
89. A. M. Montp., II, 1, ff. 7 r°, 38 r°.
90. A. M. Montp., II, 1, f. 25 bis v°.
91. A. M. Montp., II, 1, ff. 28 v°, 52 v°, 54 r°, 64 r°, 87 r°.
92. A. M. Montp., II, 1, f. 54 r°.
93. A. M. Montp., II, 1, f. 24 v°.
94. Voir pour des exemples A. D. Hérault, II E 95/368, ff. 60 r°, 70 r° : II E 95/369, f. 79 v°.
95. Pour des exemples. A. D. Hérault II E 95/374, f. 15 v° ; II E 95/371, f. 106 v°.

VENDEURS DE DRAPS

Registres	Années	Total	Marchands	Grossistes	Nobles Bourgeois	Droit Education	Juifs	Administr. royale	Ecclésiastiques	Femmes	Artisans Service	Alimentation	Agriculture	Etrangers	Non identifiés	
															Local	Autre
A.M. II 1	1293-94	32	19	3										10		
A.M. II 2	1301-02	1		1												
A.D.E. 95/368	1327-28	46	12	32		1					1					
A.D.E. 95/369	1333	25	2	18						1	1			2		1
A.D.E. 95/373	1333															
A.D.E. 95/370	1336	8	1	4						1	1			1		
A.D.E. 95/374	1337-42	8	8													
A.D.E. 95/375	1339-40	8	6	2												
A.D.E. 95/371	1342	5		3						1				1		
A.M. II 3	1342-43															
A.D.E. 95/372	1343-44	5	1	1										3		
A.D.E. 95/376	1346															
A.D.E. 95/377	1347-48	2		1										1		
TOTAUX		140	49	65		1				3	3			18		1

TABLEAU 5

ACHETEURS DE DRAPS

Registres	Années	Total	Marchands	Grossistes	Nobles Bourgeois	Droit Education	Juifs	Administr. royale	Ecclésias-tiques	Femmes	Artisans Service	Alimentation	Agriculture	Etrangers	Non identifiés	
															Autre	Local
A.M. II 1	1293-94	32	9	3										19		1
A.M. II 2	1301-02	1												1		
A.D.E. 95/368	1327-28	46		2	6				2	1	8	1	1	25		
A.D.E. 95/369	1333	25		1	1					4	5		3	10		1
A.D.E. 95/373	1333															
A.D.E. 95/370	1336	8		1					1		3			3		
A.D.E. 95/374	1337-42	8	2	2		1								3		
A.D.E. 95/375	1339-40	8		4										3		1
A.D.E. 95/371	1342	5							2		2			1		
A.M. II 3	1342-43															
A.D.E. 95/372	1343-44	5		1				1			1			2		
A.D.E. 95/376	1346															
A.D.E. 95/377	1347-48	2								1				1		
TOTAUX		140	11	14	7	1		1	5	6	19	1	4	68		3

TABLEAU 6

l'intervention d'intermédiaires montpelliérains[96]. Durant cette période, les vendeurs viennent de Montpellier et de Narbonne, Limoux, Clermont-l'Hérault, Lodève, Toulouse, Lyon et Lucques[97].

Pour toute la période étudiée à travers les actes notariaux, les grossistes, surtout les drapiers de Montpellier, dominent les ventes sur le marché montpelliérain (tableaux 7 et 8). Les marchands y jouent également un rôle très important[98]. La part des étrangers dans ces ventes n'est pas non plus négligeable. Parmi les acheteurs de draps,

VENDEURS DE DRAPS (140)[1]

	Actes	% total
Marchands	49	35
Grossistes	65	46,4
Nobles / Bourgeois	0	0
Droit / Education	1	0,7
Administration royale	0	0
Ecclésiastiques	0	0
Femmes	3	2,1
Artisans / Service	3	2,1
Métiers alimentaires	0	0
Agriculture	0	0
Etrangers	18	12,9
Non identifiés Locaux Autres	1	0,7

1. Des mentions de draps de lin, de coton et de mélanges de tissus ne sont pas inclus dans ces chiffres.

TABLEAU 7

ACHETEURS DE DRAPS (140)[1]

	Actes	% total
Marchands	11	7,9
Grossistes	14	10
Nobles / Bourgeois	7	5
Droit / Education	1	0,7
Administration royale	1	0,7
Ecclésiastiques	5	3,6
Femmes	6	4,3
Artisans / Service	19	13,6
Métiers alimentaires	1	0,7
Agriculture	4	2,9
Etrangers	68	48,6
Non identifiés Locaux Autres	3	2,1

1. Voir le tableau « Vendeurs de draps ».

TABLEAU 8

96. A. D. Hérault, II E 95/369, ff. 79 v, 110 r.
97. A. D. Hérault, II E 95/369, ff. 64 v°, 65 r°, 110 r° ; II E 95/370, f. 108 r° ; II E 95/372, ff. 26 v°, 120 °, 161 r°.
98. Ces catégories ont été développées pour faire ressortir la variété de métiers et de professions faisant partie de la clientèle notariale.

les participants appartiennent à des groupes sociaux plus variés. La demande locale peut être décelée dans les achats faits par les artisans. Enfin l'importance de Montpellier comme marché international se voit bien dans la forte participation d'étrangers dans la clientèle drapière.

Le marché de détail et le problème des prix

Les documents des années 1327-1328 permettent un aperçu du marché local de draps qui ne trouve d'équivalent ni avant ni après[99]. Ce sont des années troublées où Montpellier connaît des problèmes économiques et sociaux[100]. Outre des difficultés agricoles et une révolte des éléments populaires dans la ville, on note une instabilité monétaire qui se reflète dans le commerce des draps[101]. Le prix de ceux-ci sur le marché local est coté en pièces réelles, et non en monnaie de compte : en réaux, agneaux et petits tournois. La plupart des ventes n'impliquent que de petites sommes : ce sont des achats destinés très probablement à une consommation individuelle ou familiale. La clientèle vient essentiellement des petites villes ou villages voisins de Montpellier. Dans environ cinquante pour cent des ventes, les vendeurs sont des drapiers montpelliérains[102]. Des produits de l'industrie languedocienne sont souvent vendus[103].

Les ventes de 1327-1328 démontrent l'importance de cette industrie régionale. Les foires de Pézenas, Montagnac et Villevayrac fournissent aux grossistes des débouchés pour les draps languedociens destinés au marché de détail et à l'exportation[104]. Des Montpelliérains sont mentionnés comme clients de draps à la foire de la Pentecôte à Pézenas en 1346 ; ils sont d'ailleurs des habitués des foires car des échéances payables aux foires parsèment les documents notariaux de 1293 à 1348[105].

99. A. D. Hérault, II E 95/368.

100. Jean Combes, « Finances municipales et oppositions sociales à Montpellier au commencement du XIVe siècle », dans *Bulletin de la Fédération historique du Languedoc-Roussillon (Vivarais et Languedoc)* (1971), pp. 99-120. Voir aussi « Commerce and Society in Montpellier », t. I, pp. 212-240.

101. Etienne Fournial, *Histoire monétaire de l'Occident médiéval* (Paris, 1970), pp. 91-95. Ces années précèdent la réforme de la monnaie instituée le 8 avril 1330.

102. Parfois des drapiers de petites villes, telle Frontignan, achètent certainement pour remplir leurs propres inventaires de draps. Voir A. D. Hérault, II E 95/368, ff. 50 v°, 58 v°.

103. Un immigré de Novara, Boninus de Meldeo, était spécialisé dans la vente de draps languedociens. A. D. Hérault, II E 95/368, ff. 19 r°, 23 v°, 30 r°, 32 r°, 34 r°, 36 v°, 46 r°, 46 v°, 48 v°.

104. Jean Combes, « Les foires en Languedoc au Moyen âge », *Annales : Economies, Sociétés, Civilisations*, t. 13 (1958), 231-259.

105. *Ibid.*, p. 246. Cette foire fut fondée en 1273 ou 1274 tandis que la plus ancienne foire de Pézenas datait de 1262 (J. Combes, p. 237). L'absence de registres

PRIX DES DRAPS VENDUS

Années	Type de drap	Prix/canne	Prix/pièce
	Carcassonne		
1327	mesclat		2 l. p. t.
1327	impérial		6,5
1327			2,8
1327			2,8
1327			2,35
1327			2,35
1327			2,8
1327			2,3
1328		0,54	
1333	mesclat	0,85	
	Toulouse		
1327			0,94
1327			2,8
1327			2,14
1327			1,9
	Limoux		
1336	blanc		6
1336			0,63
1336			6,5
	Narbonne		
1294	blanc paré		3,04
	Istius ou huius terre		
1333			3-4
1339			5

TABLEAU 9

C'est sur le prix des draps que les ventes de 1327-1328 laissent le plus d'informations. Ph. Wolff a déjà signalé les difficultés d'une étude sur ce sujet[106]. A Montpellier, dans les actes notariaux, les marchands parlent parfois de pièces, parfois de dimensions de draps, mais dans la plupart des cas, seul le type de drap est cité. Ph. Wolff a suggéré que la variation dans les dimensions des pièces de draps dans la même ville rendait une comparaison de pièce à pièce « illusoire ». Une comparaison fondée sur le prix à la canne ne donne que des résultats approximatifs. Les prix relevés dans les actes notariaux de Montpellier ont été transcrits pour différents types de draps dans le tableau 9[107]. La récolte est assez maigre, et ne permet guère d'analyse chronologique.

Mais le problème du mouvement des prix a été abordé d'une autre façon dans le tableau 10. Bien que construit sur des données dispersées, celui-ci montre que l'investissement de capitaux en draps, tel qu'il se reflète dans les ventes sur le marché montpelliérain, va en diminuant de 1293 à 1347, et ceci aussi bien si l'on examine le montant total que la moyenne annuelle des ventes. Le commerce des draps de Montpellier, vu du point de vue montpelliérain, témoigne d'un déclin de vitalité progressif que la pauvreté des données concernant l'exportation ne permet pas de confirmer[108]. Cependant, les effets des changements nombreux intervenus dans l'économie européenne et méditerranéenne à partir du XIIIe siècle se laissent entrevoir sur le marché de Montpellier.

***

La fonction de Montpellier comme marché international de draps se marque à travers toute cette étude. La fréquentation de Montpellier par des étrangers à la recherche d'abord de draps septentrionaux, puis de draps languedociens est une constante. Le rôle de Montpellier comme centre d'exportation de draps, du fait de ses propres marchands ou de marchands étrangers, se retrouve aussi bien dans les années 1340 qu'à la fin du XIIIe siècle. L'évolution dans les types de

notariaux de cette époque à Pézenas et à Montagnac rend impossible une étude des transactions en draps (*Ibid.*, pp. 244-245), mais les échéances montpelliéraines sont abondantes. Par exemple, Villeveyrac : A. D. Hérault, II E 95/372, f. 153 v° ; II E 95/374, f. 5 R ; Pézenas : II E 95/374, ff. 2 v°, 22 R ; Montagnac : II E 95/374, f. 8 v° R.

106. Ph. WOLFF, « Esquisse », pp. 437-438.
107. Tous les prix sont convertis à la bonne monnaie d'avril 1330.
108. Voir les tableaux 1 à 4 ci-dessus.

PRIX DES DRAPS SUR LE MARCHÉ MONTPELLIÉRAIN[1]

Années	Nombre de transactions[2]	Montant total des ventes	Moyenne annuelle
1293	18	1 786,3	99,2
1294	14	814,5	58,2
1301	1	187,6	187,6
1327	35	503,8	14,4
1328	9	70,6	7,8
1333	25	633,7	25,3
1336	8	72,2	9,0
1338	1	55,9	55,9
1339	13	569,0	43,8
1341	1	13,8	13,8
1342	5	93,3	18,7
1343	4	286,5	71,6
1344	1	4,8	4,8
1347	1[3]	10,4	10,4

1. Tous les prix sont convertis en livres tournois d'avril 1330.
2. Seulement une partie des transactions en draps contient des mentions de prix. Ainsi, les chiffres de ce tableau et des tableaux 5 et 6 ne s'accordent pas en nombre total de transactions.
3. Indication d'un paiement partiel.

TABLEAU 10

draps exportés retrace celle du marché montpelliérain : des draps flamands et anglais, on passe aux draps français, champenois, languedociens et locaux. Concentrés d'abord sur l'expédition de draps de luxe destinés au Levant, les efforts des Montpelliérains et des étrangers exportant de Montpellier visent de plus en plus le bassin occidental de la Méditerranée et portent sur des draps de prix modérés.

Les activités drapières de Montpellier évoluent sensiblement du XIIe au XIVe siècle. L'industrie de la teinture en graine qui avait fait la réputation internationale de la ville dans le commerce des draps décline progressivement mais ne disparaît pas complètement. L'industrie languedocienne, en expansion, ne s'installe cependant pas à Montpellier. Les traces d'une industrie drapière — draps locaux — présentent des difficultés d'interprétation. Une modeste industrie domestique, rurale ou semi-rurale, a sans doute existé. Mais les draps de Montpellier se font rares dans les documents du XIVe siècle et le personnel drapier ne compte que des spécialistes, drapiers et teinturiers. Au milieu du XIVe siècle, le commerce des draps à Montpellier connaît une activité ralentie par rapport au passé mais se soutient toujours en dépit des difficultés du temps.

XII

MONTPELLIER ET LE TRAFIC DES GRAINS EN MEDITERRANEE AVANT 1350

Les problèmes de subsistance étaient fondamentaux au moyen âge. Une année sur cinq connaissait une mauvaise récolte.[1] Avec le quatorzième siècle, les mauvaises années pouvaient se succéder.[2] En raison des difficultés de transport par terre, il était presque impossible dans une période de crise pour un pays de subvenir aux besoins d'une autre région avec des envois de grains.[3] Etant donné l'ignorance des méthodes de préservation de la nourriture, le surplus d'une bonne récolte ne pouvait être stocké longtemps.

Aux treizième et quatorzième siècles des régions comme le Languedoc exportaient des céréales dans les bonnes années et en importaient d'importantes quantités en temps de mauvaise récolte.[4]Les registres de notaires de Montpellier, avec certains documents supplémentaires, fournissent des renseignements sur le trafic des grains en Méditerranée du perspectif d'une grande ville du Midi ayant entre 35.000 et 40.000 habitants dans la première moitié du quatorzième siècle.[5] Au moment d'une carence de blé, de grandes importations de céréales sont à noter. L'origine de ces denrées, leurs moyens de transport et les marchands engagés dans ce commerce seront des sujets d'exploration ici. Seront aussi à voir les mécanismes du marché local et le réseau de distribution des blés importés.

Une étude du commerce des céréales soulève, également un autre ensemble de considérations. Il a été soutenu par un historien du moyen âge au moins, le Professeur David Nicholas pour le cas de la Flandre, que les plus grandes fortunes urbaines étaient bâties sur l'approvisionnement d'une population urbaine, c'est-à-dire, sur l'importation des blés, soit de l'arrière-pays, soit des sources plus lointaines.[6] Le rôle du trafic des grains dans la formation des fortunes montpelliéraines reste une question significative, étant donné la vue largement acceptée que le commerce de luxe et la finance servaient de base aux fortunes des marchands de Montpellier tout comme le commerce des draps était supposé être à l'origine de la richesse de la classe marchande en Flandre.

Dans les années de bonne récolte, la population de Montpellier comme celle de Toulouse, de Narbonne et de la plupart des villes du Languedoc pouvait subvenir à ses propres besoins alimentaires grâce à la production agricole locale.[7] La marge d'erreur n'a dû être très grande cependant. En dehors des blés produits sur les terres des habitants de Montpellier, le surplus des établissements ecclésiastiques de la région – tel qu'il était dans des années propices – débouchait sur le marché montpelliérain.[8] Située entre la garrigue et les marécages de la côte méditerranéenne, Montpellier ne bénéficiait pas d'un plat pays fertile. Les étés secs étaient peu propices à la culture du blé. Plus favorisé par le climat était le raisin. Ceci dit, la ville de Montpellier était néanmoins une mosaïque de jardins avant 1350, même à l'intérieur de la Commune Clôture.[9] La plupart des habitants cultivaient les fruits et les légumes dont ils avaient besoin. La Méditerranée fournissait du poisson en abondance. En tout, l'environnement et la géographie locale faisaient de Montpellier un site urbain gâté par la nature. Mais le quatorzième siècle apportait des changements ici comme ailleurs en Europe.[10] Un climat de plus en plus instable occasionnait de mauvaises moissons.

*

* *

Un bref survol de la chronologie des crises servira d'encadrement pour mon analyse du trafic des grains. Les ventes et importations de grains qui survivent reflètent par leur distribution les années où le trafic des céréales occupait une place importante dans les activités économiques des habitants de Montpellier. Il ne reste pas de trace dans les registres de notaires d'importations de grains avant 1327 bien qu'ailleurs, dans des chartes montpelliéraines et dans les archives étrangères, des envois antérieurs de céréales à Montpellier et en Languedoc soient à noter.[11] De grandes importations sont à signaler en 1311 à la suite d'une mauvaise année 1310.[12] La crise s'installerait à la fin des années 1320 et au début des années 1330 quand la famine sévissait en Languedoc avec régularité par suite du mauvais climat et de récoltes désastreuses.[13] Dans le registre du notaire Jean Holanie pour la période 1327-1328 se situent 27,7 % de toutes les transactions en grains dans les registres préservés.[14] La fin des années 1320 fut une époque mouvementée de conflit social et municipal.[15] Une hausse des taxes consulaires sur le moulage des grains occasionna une protestation des populaires en 1327.[16] En 1328 la demande de revenus par le roi de France pour la guerre en Flandres obtint une réponse des consuls qui fit état de multiples problèmes dont l'infertilité du sol.[17] En 1329 une carence de blé est à noter dans les plaintes des consuls au sujet d'exportations secrètes de blé en dépit des ordonnances du sénéchal.[18]

La crise des année 1320 s'aggrave dans les années 1330. Le registre notarial de Jean Holanie pour 1333 évoque particulièrement la crise.[19] 53,8 % des transactions en céréales préservées dans les notaires de Montpellier avant 1350 eurent lieu en 1333. Ces transactions de 1333 représentent 16 % du total des actes dans ce registre, un pourcentage élevé quand on considère la grande variété d'actes écrits par Holanie. L'année 1333 subissait une crise dont « La chronique romane » du *Petit Thalamus* dit que la famine faisait rage, les jeunes étaient affaiblis par un régime d'herbes crues et des gens mouraient en pleine rue.[20] Les consuls se plaignirent au roi Philippe VI des enlèvements de blé des marchands importateurs par les sujets des rois d'Aragon et de Majorque et des villes de Gênes et de Savone.[21] Une marque fut déclarée en janvier 1335.[22] Le Bas-Languedoc manquait de blé en 1334, 1335 et 1336.[23] En 1338 les consuls de nouveau citèrent la stérilité des moissons en réplique à une demande royale de subsides.[24]

Bien que la disette ne disparaisse pas, les registres de notaires écrits après 1333 et avant la fin des années 1340 contiennent un nombre réduit de transactions en blé, pas plus de quatre par registre, ce qui est un chiffre modeste qui témoigne de la fréquence extraordinaire d'actes occasionnés par les années néfastes de 1327-1328 et de 1333. Sauf après le milieu des années 1340 quand les conditions agricoles empirèrent de nouveau, il n'y eut pas la même quantité d'achat de blé. Il faut attendre les années 1346-1348 pour voir une fois de plus un marché actif en grains, et dans les transactions notariales et dans des comptes subsistants de l'Hôpital Saint-Lazare de Montpellier.[25] Les trois périodes – 1327-1328, 1333 et 1346-1348 – offrent une image unique et nette du trafic des grains à Montpellier, en raison de la crise accentuée.

Les quelques statistiques sur les prix qui subsistent – loin de permettre l'établissement d'une série continue – révèlent une inflation accélérée des prix des grains en temps de crise sévère. Des grains d'origine non spécifiée et sans qualification autre que *bladum* dans les documents, et le froment (*fromentum*) prédominaient dans les ventes au détail de céréales. Tenant compte des variations de la monnaie à travers la période étudiée, le prix d'un setier de blé importé de l'empire byzantin en 1327-1328 se situait autour de 4,25 s. tandis qu'un setier de froment atteignait 5,1 s.[26]

En 1333 les prix fluctuaient mais s'élevaient plus haut. Le setier de blé variait de 2 s. à 7. 5 tandis que le setier de froment allait de 4 s. à 9 s. 8 d.[27] Le mélange de froment et d'orge, appelé *mitadenc* dans les documents, se vendait à 7 s. 8 d. le setier.[28]

A la fin des années 1340 du blé importé était vendu à 11 s. le setier, ce qui signifie une nouvelle inflation des prix.[29] Bien que les prix des grains connaissent une tendance à la baisse le long du quatorzième siècle, de mauvaises récoltes ponctuaient l'évolution générale avec des hausses notables et croissantes avec chaque crise.[30]

*

* *

Les sources traditionnelles de grains pour l'antiquité romaine – la Sicile, la Lombardie, la Sardaigne et les terres de Byzance – aussi bien que la Catalogne et l'Aragon fournissaient des céréales à l'Europe médiévale ; elles laissèrent leurs traces dans les importations montpelliéraines, surtout en période de famine.[31] Ces régions produisaient les céréales du monde méditerranéen. En 1327-1328 du blé de l'Empire byzantin fut acheté à Montpellier.[32] La région d'Arles fournissait du blé au marché montpelliérain en 1327.[33] En 1333 « La chronique romane » cite des provisions venant de la Bourgogne et du Comtat Venaissin,ce qui suggère l'idée que ces régions au nord de Montpellier pourvoyaient aux besoins du Midi en période de crise.[34] « La chronique » se lamente sur les hostilités génoises qui empêchaient l'arrivée de ressources de Lombardie et de Sicile tandis que la Catalogne ne fournissait rien cette année. Cependant, des marchands de Narbonne et de Montpellier réussirent à importer des blés en 1333 de Sicile, de Chypre, de Romanie et du Levant.[35] Le Languedoc lui-même subvenait à une partie des besoins frumentaires de Montpellier. Surtout en temps de crise les Montpelliérains demandaient des exemptions de prohibitions d'exportation établies pour les sénéchaussées du Midi par lesquelles la ville en tant qu'enclave majorcaine en terre française aurait, semblerait-il, été contrainte.[36]

Les importateurs de blé à Montpellier étaient surtout des Italiens – les Gênois et les Florentins en particulier. De récentes études des archives méditerranéennes démontrent que les approvisionnements en grains venant de la Sicile et de la Sardaigne au quatorzième siècle étaient dominés par les

Génois avec quelque concurrence des Catalans et des Toscans.[37] Par exemple, un notaire de Marseille nota qu'en 1311, un marchand de Gênes loua son navire à un marchand de Narbonne pour l'achat de blé en Sardaigne destiné au port d'Aigues-Mortes.[38] Une partie, au moins, des envois de blé à Aigues-Mortes débouchait certainement à Montpellier ; d'autres allaient probablement à Nîmes.[39] Aussi en 1311 des Génois habitant Nîmes vendirent au procureur de seize Montpelliérains, dont six consuls, 25.000 setiers de froment de Sicile à la mesure d'Aigues-Mortes pour 8 s. 6 d.p. t. le setier avec la promesse de 40.000 setiers supplémentaires. Les métiers de ces acheteurs démontrent la versatilité économique de l'époque. Ils comptaient parmi eux six marchands, quatre drapiers, plus le procureur lui aussi drapier, un bourgeois, deux blanquiers, un canabassier, un boucher et un seul orgier.[40] La persistance des importations génoises tout le long de notre période se voit dans un autre exemple de 1347 : un Génois voyagea avec une cargaison de blé de Sicile à Aigues-Mortes.[41] En revanche, dans les années de prospérité agricole, le Languedoc n'était pas client de la Sicile pour des céréales.[42]

Dans les documents montpelliérains les italiens apparaissent aussi comme des vendeurs actifs sur la marché local. Un immigré italien, *Boninus de Meldeo* de Novare, écoula 188 setiers de froment en huit fois en 1327-1328 pour un total de 65 anneaux.[43] Meldeo était un marchand aux talents variés qui faisait le trafic du drap languedocien, carcassonnais et toulousain, et prêtait de l'argent. Il servait, également, comme fonctionnaire de la douane française.[44]

En août et de nouveau en octobre 1333 des membres de la Société Bardi de Florence donnèrent quittance à des orgiers de Montpellier pour deux achats de 10.000 setiers chacun de froment.[45] Selon des études modernes sur les besoins alimentaires, le travail dur necessite en calories deux kilos de froment non moulu quotidiennement.[46] Des calculs à base de ce chiffre indiquent que 20.000 setiers auraient pu nourrir 1.210 travailleurs pour une année entière.

Une bonne partie des mêmes orgiers participèrent à ces deux transactions.[47] L'acte d'août fut une quittance partielle de 55 l. dûes sur une dette de 3.000 l. p. t. En octobre une quittance pour la somme totale de 3000 l. p. t dans l'autre achat de 10.000 setiers fut donnée par des représentants des Bardi. Le froment en question a ainsi été acquis à 3 s. le setier.[48] Les orgiers de Montpellier, qui faisaient partie de l'élite marchande, vendaient au détail les céréales achetées.[49] Ces orgiers aux-mêmes ne figuraient pas dans l'approvisionnement des grains à l'étranger. Mais d'autres de leurs concitoyens y participaient, comme nous le verrons bientôt.

Un autre exemple d'importation importante italienne eut lieu en décembre 1346 et en janvier 1347 ; un marchand de Savone débitait 2.200 setiers de blé qu'il avait acquis à 9 s. le setier et qu'il vendait à 11 s., faisant ainsi un profit de 220 l.[50] Si une hausse pareille, c'est-à-dire environ vingt pour cent, est calculée pour le froment acheté par les orgiers de 1333, leur profit aurait été de l'ordre de 1200 l. Mais, au détail, le prix du froment allait de 4 s. à 9 s. le setier en 1333. Ainsi, 20.000 setiers achetés à 3 s. et vendus à 4 s. produiraient 80.000 l., une fortune énorme pour les orgiers.

En dehors des Italiens, les Languedociens et les Provençaux participaient au trafic des grains. Des montpelliérains collaboraient parfois en Sicile et en Sardaigne avec des marchands de Narbonne et de Marseille. Le 24 mai 1309, un document sicilien enregistra l'embarquement du froment sur un navire majorcain en route pour Cagliari et Aigues-Mortes au nom d'un narbonnais et de son associé, le montpelliérain, Raymond Ricard. En juin 1309 Ricard expédia du froment sur un navire valencien dont le capitaine attendait paiement à Montpellier.[51]

En 1333 les archives de Valencia conservent la trace des activités d'un montpelliérain, Etienne Rogier, qui voyageait sur une taride chargée de froment de Sciacca en Sicile à destination de Collioure et d'Aigues-Mortes quand il fut saisi par des corsaires aragonais et obligé d'atterrir à Valencia.[52] Les montpelliérains importaient du blé à Marseille aussi. En 1332 Guilhem Consta de Montpellier s'engagea à deux reprises dans le transport de froment de la Sardaigne à Marseille, une fois en collaboration avec un narbonnais, une autre fois avec un marseillais.[53]

Des montpelliérains voyageant au Levant faisaient également des acquisitions de blé. En 1325 le cog Saint-Nicolas revenant de Famagouste à Aigues-Mortes avec la moitié de sa cargaison en froment fut pris lors d'une escale en Sardaigne ; parmi les Languedociens à bord étaient huit marchands de Montpellier.[54] En 1333 des marchands de Montpellier, Narbonne et Béziers furent victimes de la prise d'un chargement de froment d'une valeur de 1003 l. avec d'autres marchandises pendant un voyage de retour de Constantinople.[55]

De jeunes montpelliérains étaient actifs dans ce trafic à longue distance, étant donné qu'ils fréquentaient l'Italie et le Moyen Orient au cours de leur apprentissage en affaires. En 1333 le marchand Jacques de Magalassio agît pour le compte d'un autre montpelliérain dans la vente à des orgiers locaux de 4.000 setiers de froment à 9 s. 8 d. le setier.[56] Les contacts qu'eut Magalassio avec le Levant plus tard rendent possible le fait qu'en tant que jeune marchand il débutait dans le commerce des blés avec le Moyen Orient pendant une crise de subsistance. Plus tard au début des années 1340, il participait dans le commerce de luxe comme capitaliste sédentaire exportant des draps au Levant par le moyen de contrats de commande[57] On le voyait sur le marché montpelliérain dans d'importantes ventes d'épices.[58] Il est bien possible que les marchands de Montpellier aient bâti leurs fortunes sur l'approvisionnement de la ville en temps de crise, dans les années 1327-1328 et 1333.

*

* *

Dans les années 1327-1328 et 1333 le froment prédominait dans les ventes de blé. Comme céréale de qualité sa fréquence doit être signalée. Le pain blanc confectionné à partir du froment représentait un luxe au moyen âge. De nouveau en 1333, des quantités de froment importé atteignait d'énormes proportions : plus de 24.000 setiers en trois transactions reflètent l'ampleur de la crise à Montpellier et dans l'arrière-pays : ce froment pouvait nourrir au minimum 1.435 personnes pour toute une année.[59]

En 1327-1328 les actes subsistants permettent une analyse du marché local ; le marketing eut lieu en trois phases. D'abord, l'importation du blé, dont les détails nous échappent souvent, et son acquisition par des Montpelliérains. Puis des marchands internationaux de Montpellier débitaient leurs stocks de blé importé en grandes quantités aux orgiers qui à leur tour le vendaient au détail. Ainsi le marchand montpelliérain Pierre Amellier vendit 50 à 300 setiers du blé byzantin pour des prix allant de 10,5 1. à 63, 8 1. cinq fois dans une période de cinq semaines du 3 août au 12 septembre 1327 à des orgiers locaux tel Raymond Macipi.[60] Malheureusement, les méthodes d'approvisionnement d'Amellier ne laissèrent pas de trace.[61] L'orgier Macipi à son tour vendit le 30 juillet 1327 30 s.p.t. de froment aux maçons de Montpellier, peut-être pour l'approvisionnement de leur atelier.[62] Le 5 août il vendit 6,8 s. de blé à un fustier.[63] Puis, manquant probablement de marchandise, il dut se réapprovisionner auprès de Pierre Amellier le 14 août par l'achat de 300 setiers de blé byzantin pour 63,8 l. p. t.[64] En dehors de ces transactions par des professionnels d'origine locale et étrangère, une grande variété de gens des métiers locaux et de l'agriculture (allant des cultivateurs aux merciers et aux poivriers) détaillèrent leurs surplus en 1327-1328.[65]

Parmi les acheteurs de blé sur le marché local à Montpellier à cette époque se trouvaient des habitants de la ville en 65 % des cas, tandis que 35 % venaient de la région environnante. Boninus de Meldeo, qui fit huit ventes en 1327-1328, comptait parmi ses clients des gens de Lattes, Pignan, Loupian, Aimargues et Lunel, et, venant de Montpellier, un orgier, un fustier et un cultivateur. Dans plusieurs cas les achats auraient suffi à nourrir une famille. Ainsi 44 setiers de froment furent vendus par Meldeo à une veuve d'Aimargues et 45 setiers de froment à des hommes de Lattes.[66] Ces quantités auraient pu subvenir aux besoins de 2 ou 3 personnes pour toute une année. Bien que le métier principal dans ces petites villes ait dû être l'agriculture, elles ne pouvaient pas s'approvisionner en blé lors d'une mauvaise récolte.

En tout, des cultivateurs de Montpellier firent 20 % des achats de céréales en 1327-1328. Ceux-ci, d'origine urbaine, s'étaient probablement engagés dans la culture intensive de raisins et achetaient ainsi une partie de leur nourriture, surtout en temps de moison désastreuse, sur le marché montpellierain.

La deuxième période de crise agricole que nous pouvons suivre – celle de l'année 1333 – présente à l'observateur un changement fondamental dans les mécanismes du marché local. En 1333 les petits détaillants de blé disparurent. Ils cédèrent la place aux associations d'orgiers qui achetèrent des quantités importantes de blé importé des italiens et le vendirent au détail à Montpellier.

Trois paires d'associés occupent la plupart de l'évidence.[67] 38 % des ventes en 1333 furent faites par les orgiers, André Roquete et Guiraud de Cortile. Ils débitèrent du blé non spécifié (*bladum*) quarante fois et du froment une fois. Derrière eux dans la compétition venaient les orgiers associés Raymond Babelier et Louis Vidal avec 25 % des ventes en 1333. Ces derniers trafiquèrent uniquement en blé d'origine ignorée (*bladum*). Enfin, 5,7 % des ventes de 1333 concernent les associés Raymond Duranti et Pierre Coste.

Tandis que Roquete et Cortile avec leur rivaux Vidal et Babelier, remplissaient le rôle de revendeurs entre les marchés urbains et la demande de l'arrière-pays, la troisième paire d'associés, Durant et Coste, agissaient comme intermédiaires pour d'autres orgiers de Montpellier qui représentaient 66 % de leur clientèle. Tous ces marchands associés, avec d'autres montpelliérains, étaient les clients de la Société des Bardi dans l'acquisition de 20.000 setiers de blé en 1333, se situant entre les sources étrangères d'importation et les petits revendeurs de Montpellier et de la région environnante.[68]

Les habitants de l'arrière-pays s'attroupaient au marché urbain pour acheter du blé en 1333. Roquete et Cortilis avaient une clientèle composée d'acheteurs des villages autour de Montpellier. Dans cette année de mauvaise moisson, Montpellier servait comme marché de blé pour les besoins de toute la région. Le blé acquis sur le marché urbain aurait pu être revendu dans les villages avoisinants. La plus grande vente notée pour les associés Roquete et Cortile était de 30 l. t. a un homme et une femme de Saussan, à environ dix kilomètres de Montpellier.[69] Bien que le prix du setier n'ait pas été donné dans cet acte, si le prix le plus élevé qui a été noté en 1333 est utilisé (c'est-à-dire, 7,5 s. le setier), l'achat aurait englobé 78,4 setiers de blé, ce qui aurait suffi à nourrir à peu près cinq personnes pour une année. De nombreux couples furent notés dans l'acquisition du blé dans cette période ainsi que des villageois – hommes et femmes de surnom différent – participant ensemble à la même transaction.[70] Le monopole du marché par les orgiers ne passait pas sans plaintes. Des ordonnances du sénéchal de Beaucaire de 1334 citèrent la carence de blé dans les pays occasionnée par les astuces des spécialistes (*dardaniers* ou *bladiers*) qui accaparaient tous les grains de la sénéchaussée.[71].

*

* *

Au début des années 1340 des surplus de blé permettaient parfois des exportations de Montpellier et d'autres régions telle celle de Narbonne.[72] En 1343 un orgier et un verrier crèèrent une association pour vendre du blé d'une valeur de 195 l.[73] Selon le contrat, le commerce pourrait avoir lieu sur la terre ou sur l'eau sauf sur mer. Les exportations et les importations du blé étaient, en effet, réglées d'en haut par des ordonnances du roi de France à partir du milieu du treizième siècle ; ce n'était pas ainsi une activité nouvelle. Dès 1254, une ordonnance de Saint Louis, adressée aux sénéchaux de Beaucaire et de Cahors, permettait l'exportation du blé et du vin ; cette législation suggère que les exportations languedociennes étaient fréquentes à cette époque.[74] En 1283, 1288, 1289, 1297 et 1298 des lettres du roi au sénéchal de Beaucaire permirent des importations de la sénéchaussée à Montpellier.[75] Il en était de même pour la sénéchaussée de Carcassonne en 1304 et 1307 et pour les deux sénéchaussées en 1310.[76] La ville s'assurait ainsi des ressources de la région environnante. En 1302 Philippe le Bel annonça une prohibition générale d'exportation du blé, du vin et de la nourriture du royaume ; le sénéchal de Carcassonne reçut un rappel de cette mesure en 1303.[77] La même prohibition a été renouvellée en 1304 et une prohibition générale déclarée en 1305.[78] L'enclave de Montpellier ne se voyait pas viser par ces ordonnances grâce aux permissions d'importations citées juste ci-dessus, mais l'exportation de la ville à l'étranger aurait dû être contrôlée ainsi. En 1315 Louis X permit le transport de produits alimentaires à l'étranger dans les bonnes années à l'exception des exportations en Flandre.[79] Charles IV s'opposa de nouveau à l'exportation du blé et du froment en 1322.[80] Du règne de Philippe de Valois datent d'autres prohibitions d'exportations de 1340 et 1341 aussi bien que certaines impositions sur les exportations ; ces dernières devaient être plutôt rares dans la première décennie de son règne, c'est-à-dire à la fin des années 1320 et au début des années 1330, où nous avons remarqué, au contraire, de grandes importations.[81]

Dès le milieu des années 1340 la disette devint plus grave. En mai 1344 les consuls de Montpellier réussirent à bloquer 14.000 setiers de blé de Sicile dans le port d'Aigues-Mortes à cause de la carence à Montpellier. Les importateurs de ce blé – marchands de Narbonne et de Toulouse – argumentèrent devant le sénéchal que la disette était pire chez eux et que le blé s'y vendait à 20 s. le setier tandis que dans la sénéchaussée de Beaucaire il n'était qu'à 8 s. le setier. Le lieutenant du sénéchal de Beaucaire laissa partir 6.000 setiers pour Narbonne à condition qu'ils ne quittent pas le royaume.[82] En 1346-1348 des importations de blé réapparaissaient localement. En 1346 à la demande des consuls de Montpellier, le roi Philippe ordonna aux sénéchaux de Toulouse, Carcassonne, Beaucaire et de Rouergue de laisser passer des grains et d'autres aliments venant du comté d'Armagnac à Montpellier.[83] Un marchand italien de Savone, mentionné plus haut, fit cinq cent cinquante ventes modestes sur le marché local en décembre 1346 et en janvier 1347.[84] Beaucoup de clients achetèrent environ un setier chacun, ce qui semblerait être pour leur consommation personnelle. Parmi ces acheteurs on compte six communautés religieuses – les Frères mineurs, les Carmes, les Prêcheurs, les Frères de Saint-Augustin, les Minorites et les Sœurs de Proulhan –, de nombreux cultivateurs, des marchands, un argentier, des changeurs, un notaire, un drapier, un fourreur, et des officiers royaux. L'italien vendit directement aux clients montpelliérains sans l'intermédiaire d'orgiers locaux.

Quand ces ventes directes de la part de l'italien sont prises en considération avec les données du registre du notaire Bernard Gilles, les dimensions des besoins alimentaires s'imposent.[85] La clientèle du notaire dans 66 % des cas était, de nouveau, originaire de l'arrière-pays. En revanche, 88 % des vendeurs dans ce registre venaient de Montpellier.[86]

La pauvreté de l'arrière-pays se confirma par la présence dans les actes du notaire Gilles d'une formule d'endettement – des dettes en froment, une cession de dette en avoine, des dettes pour des mélanges de blé et de froment et pour du blé seul (neuf actes) – en fait, des ventes anticipées.[87] Les promesses de paiement, établies en avril et en mai 1347, avaient comme échéance la fête de la Saint-Jean, le 24 juin, la Saint-Pierre en août ou la fête de la Saint Michel le 29 septembre. Les besoins frumentaires nécessitaient ces ventes anticipées.

*

* *

En conclusion, il est utile de rappeler l'année de crise par excellence à Montpellier : 1333. Le marché au détail en céréales a été dominé par un nombre limité d'orgiers locaux tandis que des marchands internationaux d'origine montpelliéraine et étrangère se partageaient les responsabilités de l'importation du blé. Jouant un rôle dominant parmi les clients en temps de crise, étaient des habitants de l'arrière-pays qui subissaient un rapport économique asymétrique avec les gens de la ville. En période de bonne récolte, s'il produisaient suffisamment de blé pour leur consommation personnelle, ils ne bénéficiaient pas de grand surplus qui auraient pu être vendus en ville. Les habitants urbains par ailleurs possédaient des terres qui, avec la production des établissements religieux environnants, fournissaient probablement une grande partie des besoins de la ville dans de bonnes années.[88] En temps de carence – bien trop fréquents aux XIVe siècle –, ces deux groupes-urbains et ruraux – dépendaient des importations de céréales. Avec la faculté d'adaptation qui caractérise le marchand médiéval, les investissements montpelliérains allaient vers les plus grands profits. Bien qu'il soit difficile de déchiffrer le rôle précis du trafic des grains dans la formation du capital montpelliérain, pendant les années de mauvaise moisson, le placement de fonds et l'engagement d'énergies marchandes dans le commerce des céréales sembleraient être importants. En période agricole propice, ces mêmes talents et leurs capitaux se seraient dirigés vers le commerce de luxe. Certains marchands de Montpellier possédaient des navires ; d'autres utilisaient des vaisseaux d'autres ports d'attaches.[89] Les ressources de l'économie entière ne laissent pas supposer que la flotte pourrait être dédoublée en temps de demande poussée de blé. De même, l'économie urbaine connaissait des limites à l'emploi du crédit en dépit de son omniprésence.[90] Ainsi, surgit un scénario où les marchands changeaient de spécialité commerciale selon les conditions économiques. Les actes préservés dans les registres de notaires révèlent un pourcentage plus élevé de transactions en blé et en produits agricole en général en 1327-1328, en 1333 et de nouveau en 1346-1348 – des années pointes – en contraste avec d'autres années des décennies 1330 et 1340 pour les quelles une documentation survit.[91] Avec l'ironie dont l'histoire s'habille souvent, les profits des investissements en céréales de la fin des années 1320 et du début des années 1330 permettaient le redressement du commerce de luxe à Montpellier à la fin des années 1330 et au début des annèes 1340. Malheureusement, cette remise en vigueur économique serait stoppée par les crises du milieu du siècle.[92]

NOTES

1) Cf., par exemple, Robert Vernet, « La production céréalière dans le Maghreb du XIIIe siècle, » dans *Jaime I y su epoca*, 3, 4, 5 : *Economia y sociedad, Mundo cultural, Historiografia y fuentes*, X Congreso de Historia de la Corona de Aragon (Zaragoza, 1979), 267.

2) Sur les crises du quatorzième siècle, voir Edouard Perroy, « A l'origine d'une économie contractée : les crises du XIVe siècle, » dans *Annales : Economies, Sociétés, Civilisations* 3 (1949), 167-182. Sur les problèmes agricoles en particulier, voir Elisabeth Carpentier, « Autour de la peste noire : famines et épidémies dans l'histoire du XIVe siècle, » dans *Annales : ESC* 18 (1962), 1062-1092, et Marie-Josèphe Larenaudie, « Les famines en Languedoc au XIVe siècle, » dans *Annales du Midi* 64 (1952), 27-39.

3) Sur le transport médiéval, on peut consulter Robert S. Lopez, « The Evolution of Land Transport in the Middle Ages, » dans *Past and Present* 9 (1956), 17-19 ; Jean Combes, « Transports terrestres à travers la France centrale à la fin du XIVe siècle et au commencement du XVe siècle, » dans *Fédération Historique du Languedoc-Roussillon* XXIXe congrès (Mende, 1955), 3-7 ; Robert-Henri Bautier, « Recherches sur les routes de l'Europe médiévale, » dans *Bulletin philologique et historique* (1960) (Paris, 1961), 99-143 ; et Yves Renouard, « Les voies de communication entre pays de la Méditerranée et pays de l'Atlantique au Moyen Age, problèmes et hypothèses, » dans *Mélanges Louis Halphen* (Paris, 1951), 587-594.

4) Très utiles pour une étude des mouvements de céréales en Languedoc sont les articles d'Edouard Baratier, « Marseille et Narbonne au XIVe siècle d'après les sources marseillaises, » dans *Fédération Historique : Narbonne, Archéologie et histoire*, XLVe congrès *II : Narbonne au moyen âge* (Montpellier, 1973), 85-92 et Henri Bresc, « Marchands de Narbonne et du Midi en Sicile (1300-1460), » *idem*, 93-99.

5) J'ai consulté pour cette étude les registres de notaires des Archives Départementales de l'Hérault (cités dorénavant A. D. Hérault), II E 95/368-377 et des Archives Municipales de Montpellier (cités dorénavant A. M. Montpellier) BB 1-3. Pour une discussion de la démographie de Montpellier, cf. mon article, « Patterns of Population Attraction and Mobility : The Case of Montpellier, 1293-1348, » dans *Viator* 10 (1979), 257-281.

6) David Nicholas « Structures du peuplement, fonctions urbaines et formation du capital dans la Flandre médiévale, » dans *Annales :* ESC 33 (1978), 501-527.

7) Pour une discussion de la géographie de Montpellier, voir les études de Gaston Galtier, « Les conditions géographiques de Montpellier, » dans *Mélanges Philippe Arbos* (Clermont-Ferrand, 1953), 237-246 et « Le vignoble et le vin dans le Languedoc oriental de la fin du XIe siècle à la Guerre de Cent ans, » tiré-à-part des *Etudes médiévales offertes à M. le Doyen Fliche de l'Institut* (Montpellier, 1951). Cf. également, Emmanuel LeRoy Ladurie, *Les paysans de Languedoc* (Paris, 1966), I : 17-19. E. Baratier, « Marseille et Narbonne, » p. 88, a dit, « L'exportation des céréales est une constante du commerce languedocien ; lorsque la récolte a été bonne, on vient en acheter de divers ports de la Méditerranée. » Sur les provisions de Toulouse, voir Philippe Wolff, *Commerces et marchands de Toulouse* (Paris, 1954), 169-187.

8) Par exemple, en 1327 un clerc de Lodève fit deux ventes de blé à des habitants de l'arrière-pays montpelliérain (A. D. Hérault, II E 95/368, J. Holanie, f. 18 r et 28 v). En 1346-1347 les consuls de Montpellier vendaient du blé aux habitants de Montpellier dans leur fonction d'administrateurs de l'Hôpital Saint-Lazare de Montpellier (M. Oudot de Dainville, *Archives de la ville de Montpellier, Inventaires et documents, XI : Documents comptables* (Montpellier, 1959), p. 96, *Livre de dépenses de l'Hôpital Saint-Lazare*, ff. 54 ff.).

9) Cf. l'inventaire synoptique par M. Oudot de Dainville et Marcel Gouron, *Archives de la ville de Montpellier, Inventaire, XII : Fonds de la Commune Clôture et Affaires militaires* (Montpellier, 1974).

10) Sur les crises du quatorzième siècle, voir E. Perroy, « A l'origine d'une économie contractée ».

11) Cf. ci-dessous la note 51. On peut noter une exportation en 1293 : voir A. M. Montpellier, BB1, J. Grimaud, f. 5 v.

12) Voir plus loin les notes 38, 39 et 40. Voir aussi Marie Josèphe Larenaudie, « Les famines en Languedoc, » p. 28, qui signale une disette à Montpellier en 1313 et en 1323. Des lettres de Guillaume de Nogaret du 10 juillet 1310 aux sénéchaux de Beaucaire et Carcassonne et au viguier de Béziers permirent aux Montpelliérains l'achat de blé dans ces sénéchaussées en dépit des prohibitions d'exportation à cause de la disette. Voir Ferdinand Castets et Josèph Berthelé, *Archives de la ville de Montpellier, Inventaires et documents, I : Inventaire du « Grand Chartrier »* (Montpellier, 1895), Louvet 1041. Dorénavant, les citations au « Grand Chartrier » seront faites dans la numérotation de l'inventaire Louvet.

13) Sur les problèmes agricoles voir Elisabeth Carpentier, « Autour de la peste noire, » et Marie-Josèphe Larenaudie, » Les famines en Languedoc. »

14) A. D. Hérault, II E 95/368, J. Holanie : 1327-1328.

15) Voir Jean Combes, « Finances municipales et oppositions sociales à Montpellier au commencement du XIVe siècle, » *Fédération historique du Languedoc méditerranéen, et du Roussillon*, XLIVe congrès (Montpellier 1972), 99-120 et Jan Rogozinski, *Power, Caste, and Law. Social Conflict in Fourteenth-Century Montpellier* (Cambridge, Mass., 1928).

16) Louvet 1966, 1968 et 2570. Voir aussi Jan Rogozinski, *Power, Caste, and Law*, pp. 17-18 et 24.

17) Louvet 3869.

18) Louvet 1044. Les consuls demandèrent le blocage au port d'Aigues-Mortes de trois galères coupables remplies de blé.

19) A. D. Hérault, II E 95/369, J. Holanie : 1333.

20) *Le Petit Thalamus*, « La chronique romane, » p. 347.

21) Louvet 1558-1560. Voir aussi 1561-1566.

22) Louvet 1565-1566.

23) Louvet 1045 et 1046. Voir aussi Marie-Josèphe Larenaudie, « Les famines en Languedoc, » p. 29.

24) Louvet 3070.

25) 5,6 % de toutes les transactions des registres en céréales se trouvent dans le registre de Bernard Gilles, II E 95/377 : 1347-1348, ce qui représente 2 % de tous les

actes de ce même registre. Voir aussi la note 8 au-dessus. Les N[os] de Louvet 1052 et 1053 font état d'une carence de blé à Montpellier. Le registre A 4 des Archives Départementale, ff. 248-249, cite de mauvaise conditions en 1347 à Anduze où on vendait du blé au double et au triple du prix ordinaire.

26) Voir le tableau synoptique de transactions en céréales dans ma thèse, « Commerce and Society in Montpellier : 1250-1350, » Ph. D. Yale University, 1974, II : 169-194. Pour une description détaillée des problèmes monétaires dans les documents montpelliérains, voir l'appendice 2 dans mon livre *Business, Banking and Finance in Medieval Montpellier* (Toronto, 1985), pp. 139-146.

27) Voir le tableau synoptique ci-dessus.

28) A. D. Hérault, II E 95/369, J. Holanie, f.49v.

29) *Livre de dépenses de l'Hôpital Saint-Lazare,* ff. 27 r.-50 v.

30) Sur le prix du blé, voir Harry A. Miskimin, *The Economy of Early Renaissance Europe, 1300-1460* (New York, 1969, rep. Cambridge, 1975), par exemple, p. 53.

31) Voir la note 4 au-dessus. Cf. aussi Marie-Josèphe Larenaudie, « Les famines en Languedoc, pp. 35-39 et les citations d'importations ci-dessous.

32) A. D. Hérault, II E 95/368, J. Holanie, ff. 30 v. 34 v. et 44 r. Voir aussi mon artcile, « Montpellier and the Byzantine Empire : Commercial Interaction in the Mediterranean World before 1350, » dans *Byzantion* 48, fasc. 2 (1978), 456-476.

33) En 1327 un prêtre d'Arles débita du blé trois fois aux habitants de Pignan, Grémian et à la veuve d'un cultivateur de Montpellier (A. D. Hérault, II E 95/368, J. Holanie, ff. 30r, 33 r. et 41 r.).

34) Cf. la note 20 ci-dessus.

35) Marie-Josèphe Larenaudie, « Les famines en Languedoc » p. 36.

36) Voir les notes 75 et 76 ci-dessous.

37) Voir la note 4 ci-dessus. Cf. aussi Michel de Boüard, « Problèmes de subsistance dans un état médiéval : Le marché et les prix des céréales au royaume angevin de Sicile (1266-1282), » dans *Annales d'histoire économique et sociale* 10 (1983), 483-501.

38) E. Baratier, « Marseille et Narbonne, » p. 86 : 1.600 émines dans la mesure de Gênes.

39) Sur Aigues-Mortes, voir Jean Combes, « Origine et passé d'Aigues-Mortes, » dans *Revue d'histoire économique et sociale* 50 (1972), 304-326.

40) Louvet 4048 et 4049. Pour la liste des consuls de 1311 publiée par Alexandre Germain, voir son *Histoire de la commune de Montpellier* (Montpellier, 1851). I : 400.

41) H. Bresc, « Marchands de Narbonne, » p. 94.

42) *Ibid.,* p. 95.

43) A. D. Hérault, II E 95/68, J. Holanie, ff. 39 r. 41 r. 41 v. 44 v. 70 v.and 145 v.

44) See « Commerce and Society, » I : 118.

45) A. D. Hérault, II E 95/369, J. Holanie, ff. 52 v. and 84.

46) Cf. Bernard, S. Bachrach, « The Cost of Castle Building. The Case of the Tower at Langeais, 992-994, » dans Kathryn Reyerson and Faye Powe, éd. *The Medieval Castle : Romance and Reality* (Dubuque, Iowa, 1984), p. 52. Voir aussi Colin Clark et Margaret Haswell, *The Economics of Subsistence Agriculture* (London, 1970).

47) Voir le tableau synoptique des transactions en céréales dans « Commerce and Society, » II :p. 169-194.

48) L'émine montpelliéraine était l'équivalent d'à peu près douze litres, le setier montpelliérain de 48,92 litres.

49) Sur les métiers montpelliérains, voir « Commerce and Society, » I : Chapter I.

50) Voir la note 29 ci-dessus.

51) H. Bresc, « Marchands de Narbonne, » p. 93. Dans le premier cas il s'agit de 600 salmes de froment.

52) Guy Romestan, « A propos du commerce des draps dans la péninsule ibérique au moyen âge, les marchands lanaguedociens dans le royaume de Valence pendant la première moitié du XIVe siècle, » dans *Bulletin philologique et historique,* 1969, I (Paris, 1972), 126.

53) E. Baratier et Felix Reynaud, *Histoire du commerce de Marseille,* II (Paris, 1951), p. 140, la note 2 et p. 146 la note 1.

54) *Ibid.,* p. 125-126.

55) Alexandre Germain, *Histoire du commerce de Montpellier antérieurement à l'ouverture du port de Cette,* II (Montpellier, 1861), 150-152, et pièce justificative CIX : p. 506-513 : 1336.

56) A. D. Hérault, II E 95/369, J. Holanie, f. 80 v. Il semble que la vente aie été annulée et des quittances mutuelles échangées.

57) Voir *Business, Banking and Finance,* p. 19-20.

58) Cf. le tableau synoptique des transactions en épices dans « Commerce and Society, » II : 145-150.

59) Bien que la vente mentionnée dans la note 46 ci-dessus ait été annulée, on n'a pas raison de douter que les céréales ne fussent pas disponibles.

60) Voir la note 32 au-dessus.

61) Plusieurs possibilités se présentent. Il aurait pu acheter son blé d'importateurs italiens, le procurer par le moyen de contrats de sociétés et de comandes avec des Montpelliérains ou d'autres ou bien le chercher lui-même en pays étranger.

62) A. D. Hérault, II E 95/368, J. Holanie, f. 18 v.

63) A. D. Hérault, II E 95/368, J. Holanie, f. 23 r.

64) A. D. Hérault, II E 95/368, J. Holanie, f. 30 v.

65) Voir le tableau synoptique de transactions en céréales dans ma thèse, « Commerce and Society in Montpellier : 1250-1350, » II : 169-194.

66) A. D. Hérault, II E 95/368, J. Holanie, ff. 44v. et 70 v.

67) Cf. la note 65 ci-dessus.

68) A. D. Hérault, II E 95/369, J. Holanie, ff. 52 v. et 84 v.

69) A. D. Hérault, II E 95/369, J. Holanie, f. 21 r.

70) Voir la discussion dans mon article, « Women in Business in Medieval Montpellier, » dans Barbara Hanawalt, éd. *Women and Work in Preindustrial Europe* (à paraître de l'Indiana University Press, 1986).

71) Louvet 1045 et 1046

72) Baratier, « Marseille et Narbonne », p. 88.

73) A. D. Hérault, II E 95/372, J. Holanie et al, f. 66 v.

74) *Ordonnances des Roys de France de la troisième race.* 23 volumes (Paris, 1723-1849), I : décembre 1254, article n° 27, M. Guy Romestan a cité des céréales importées à Perpignan de la plaine languedocienne en juin 1276 ; voir « Les relations

commerciales entre Perpignan et la Ligurie aux XIVe et XVe siècles, « dans *Atti del lo congresso storico Liguria-Catalogna* (Bordighera, 1974), p. 370.

75) Louvet 1075, 1076, 1077, 1078, et 1079.

76) Louvet 1041, 1082, 1082, et 1083. Le document Louvet 1040 mentionne la permission d'importer à Montpellier des grains de Catalogne et du royaume d'Aragon à travers les terres de la sénéchaussée de Carcassone/Béziers en 1275.

77) *Ordonnances,* I : le 1 novembre 1320 et août 1303.

78) *Ordonnances,* I : novembre 1304 et le 1re et 6 février 1305 (n. s.).

79) *Ordonnances,* I : avril 1315.

80) *Ordonnances,* I : le 11 mai 1322.

81) Pour les prohibitions voir Louvet 1070, 1071, et 1072. Pour des impositions cf., par exemple, *Ordonnances,* I : le 16 octobre 1340. Des importations des sénéchaussées de Beaucaire et de Carcassone à Montpellier furent permises en 1341, mais le viguier de Béziers protesta contre l'abus de cette permission par des catalans et des génois qui exportaient des grains aux ennemis du roi de France et de la foi. Voir Louvet 1047 et 1048.

82) Louvet 1050 ,et 1052. Voir aussi Marie-Josèphe Larenaudie, « Les famines en Languedoc, » p. 36.

83) Louvet 1052 et 1053. De même, les marchands apportant du blé ne devaient pas être soumis aux impôts. Voir Louvet 1054 et 1066.

84) *Livre de dépenses de l'Hôpital Saint-Lazare,* ff. 27 r.-50 v.

85) A. D. Hérault, II E 95/377, B. Egidii.

86) Voir la note 65 ci-dessus.

87) Cf. ma discussion de ces mécanismes de crédit dans *Business, Banking and Finance* p. 58.

88) Sur le régime des terres à Montpellier, voir mon article, « Land, Houses and Real Estate Investment in Montpellier : A study of the Notarial Property Transactions, 1293-1348, » *Studies in Medieval and Renaissance History* VI (1983), 37-112.

89) Voir « Commerce and Society, » II : 236-248 pour la mention des navires utilisés dans les contrats maritimes à Montpellier.

90) Cf. *Business, Banking and Finance,* sur l'emploi du crédit à Montpellier.

91) Pour un tableau de la distribution des types de transactions des registres de notaires, voir mon article, « Medieval Silks in Montpellier : The Silk Market ca. 1250 –ca. 1350, » dans *Journal of European Economic History* II (1982), 137.

92) *Ibid.* Voir aussi mon article, « Le rôle de Montpellier dans le commerce des draps de laine avant 1350, » dans *Annales du Midi* 94 (1982), 17-40. J'ai étudié le commerce des épices dans une communication, » The Medieval Spice Trade before 1350 : One Index of Mediterranean Commerce from the Perspective of Montpellier, » donnée au Northern great Plains History Conference, University of Wisconsin, La Crosse, Wisconsin, 1976.

Je voudrais remercier les participants du séminaire d'histoire sociale à l'université de Minnesota pour leur commentaire sur la présente étude qui m'a aidé dans la formulation de mes conclusions.

INDEX